MONUMENTA
SERBOCROATICA

THE AMERICAN COUNCIL OF LEARNED SOCIETIES · THE SOCIAL SCIENCE RESEARCH COUNCIL

the Joint Committee on Eastern Europe Publication Series

Number 6

MONUMENTA SERBOCROATICA

A BILINGUAL ANTHOLOGY
OF SERBIAN AND CROATIAN TEXTS
FROM THE 12th TO THE 19th CENTURY

Thomas Butler

MICHIGAN SLAVIC PUBLICATIONS

Michigan Slavic Publications
Modern Language Building
Ann Arbor, Michigan 48109

Sixth in a series of publications
sponsored by the Joint Committee on Eastern Europe
of the American Council of Learned Societies
and the Social Research Council

Library of Congress Cataloging in Publication Data

Monumenta Serbocroatica.
(Publication series - Joint Committee on Eastern Europe; no. 6)
1. Serbian literature.
2. Croatian literature.
3. Serbian literature–Translations into English.
4. Croatian literature–Translations into English.
5. English literature–Translations from Serbo-Croatian.
6. Church Slavic literature–Yugoslavia.
I. Butler, Thomas, 1929–
II. Series: Joint Committee on Eastern Europe.
Publication series - Joint Committee on Eastern Europe; no. 6.
PG1595.E3M6 891.8'2'08 80-10409
ISBN 0-930042-32-8

To my mother Sheila O'Donovan
and my father Cornelius Butler
who brought with them from Ireland
a love of poetry and song

Illustration from a Carolingian MS in Zagreb

CONTENTS

ILLUSTRATIONS

PREFACE

It has been common in the West, even among some students and specialists on the Balkans, to regard Yugoslavia as a country which had been culturally backward until relatively recent times. The responsibility for this "backwardness" has been attributed to the Ottoman Empire, which dominated Serbia and parts of Croatia from the fifteenth to the nineteenth century. Not enough is known, in the West at least, about the five or more centuries between the conversion of the Serbs and Croats to Christianity and the Ottoman conquest, and about the Serbian (and for a time Croatian) tie with the magnificent Graeco-Roman culture of Byzantium, which far outshone Western culture during the early Middle Ages. Also insufficiently appreciated in the West have been the achievements of the Dalmatian Renaissance and Baroque, and particularly the role of Dubrovnik as a vibrant cultural center from the fifteenth through the seventeenth century.

Serious discussion of Serbian and Croatian culture, therefore, often begins with the writers of the eighteenth-century Enlightenment, only cursory attention being given to their predecessors, whose works are regarded as either imitative and non-native, or as reflecting the stagnation associated with "the Turkish yoke." It was partly to counteract such erroneous impressions, as well as to provide some idea of the sweep and vitality of Croatian and Serbian culture through the ages, that I taught a survey course on Serbo-Croatian literature at the University of Wisconsin in Madison for several years. This course, based on the reading and discussion of representative texts, began with the earliest Serbian and Croatian church writings, proceeded through medieval belles-lettres, the works of the Dalmatian Renaissance and Baroque, the Serbian and Croatian Enlightenment, and finished with the "Romantic" Period—the latter term a misnomer, perhaps, but useful nonetheless, in that it ties Croatian and Serbian writing of the first half of the nineteenth century with the European movement which provided some of its impetus. Also studied were examples of the oral literature or folklore that flourished in the Balkans until recent times, parallel to written culture, and often broader than it in scope and influence.

It was my belief (and still is) that the study of representative texts from the early Middle Ages to the middle of the nineteenth century can provide the student and young specialist with a grasp of the main themes of Serbian and Croatian culture, some of which—the language question, for

example—have persisted until the present day. It was to help fill the need for an introductory text of such readings from Croatian and Serbian culture that this Bilingual Anthology was prepared. This book is intended for the use of several categories of readers, including students and specialists on Yugoslavia who do not know the Serbo-Croatian language, students and specialists who know Serbo-Croatian but do not know its dialects or the older forms of the language, and those of Serbian or Croatian origin who would like to know more about their cultural heritage. Just as I have used the oldest available examples of each text, for reasons of authenticity, so have I tried to keep my translations as literal as possible. Sometimes I have sacrificed smoothness of style, in order to imitate the syntax and language of the original, so that the reader might feel the presence of the real author. It seemed preferable, for example, that in reading Sava's touching account of his father's last days the reader be conscious that he is reading the narration of a thirteenth-century Serbian priest, and not the facile product of a late twentieth-century translator.

Meaning has taken precedence over style because these translations are also meant to serve as an aid to specialists and young scholars who want to learn to read medieval čakavian legal documents and belles-lettres, for example, or Dalmatian Renaissance and Baroque poetry. With a basic knowledge of Serbo-Croatian, and with the aid of the translations and a few comments on dialect, such as those contained in the notes, the student can begin to read texts in these idioms. Those who want to improve their reading knowledge of contemporary Serbo-Croatian, on the other hand, will find it useful to read the folklore selections and the selections from the nineteenth-century authors, even though most of these pieces differ in some degree from today's standard language.

This anthology does not claim to include excerpts from all the significant works of a given period, although specialists will generally agree that the majority of the pieces included here belong to this category. The selection has been subjective and eclectic, dependent on my own predilections and not on what others have considered the best of a particular school. For this reason, Lucić's Robinja *is included, but not Pelegrinović's* Jedjupka, *even though most experts on Dalmatian literature consider* Jedjupka *an outstanding work of its time. Because the pieces in this Anthology can only suggest the cultural orientation of a period, the introductory notes that precede each work are often lengthy. They provide some background about the author, the significance of his work, possible connections with social or political currents of the time, and other relevant information. The introductory notes also lend an opportunity for the discussion of such essential topics as the communality of Church Slavonic literature, the medieval heresy called "Bogomilism," the role of the Orthodox Church in the medieval Serbian kingdom, and the economic and*

political importance of the Republic of Dubrovnik–information which could not be derived from the reading of one or even several of these pieces.

The notes were also designed with the hope of exciting the interest of young scholars in particular problems, while providing them with the titles of a few background works to help them on their way. Individual Serbian and Croatian scholars and their works have been cited repeatedly, not only for bibliographical purposes, but also to point up the importance of their contribution to the cultural revival of both nations in the nineteenth and twentieth centuries. In Croatia and Serbia scholars have played a vital role in explaining the past to their people and in stripping away the misconceptions about their history and culture that have arisen as a result of centuries of foreign domination. The works of Rački, Jagić, Šišić, Karadžić, Daničić, Stojanović and others are monuments of great cultural value that deserve to be mentioned along with the writings of Sveti Sava, Marko Marulić, Marin Držić, Kačić-Miošić, and Dositej Obradović, for example.

A final comment on the translations: special care was taken to face the problems presented by nearly 700 years of language and a variety of dialects. After the work was done, and the selections had been put into English, I felt that for the first time I truly appreciated the literary and intellectual quality of some of these works. Previously, a pervasive consciousness of form–either of the "quaintness" of the dialect or of the antiquity of the language, had persistently intruded itself in the creative process which always takes place between author and reader, so that it had been impossible for me to give the author my undivided attention.

I want to take the opportunity to express my thanks to several specialists on Serbian and Croatian culture, as well as to native speakers of Serbo-Croatian, for their help on individual problems of interpretation. Professor Albert B. Lord of Harvard University was very helpful, both in reading my translations of the folk songs, and in making valuable suggestions on interpretation and style. Helpful on questions of language were Nada Rajnvajn Toomey of Madison, Wisconsin (now deceased), as well as Milan Radović, Robert Gaković, and Joseph Strmečki of the University of Wisconsin Memorial Library, and Catherine Edmunds of Harvard University (Serbian Church Slavonic). I would also like to thank Professor Thomas Magner of Pennsylvania State University for his continuing encouragement, and Professor Ladislav Matejka, the editor of this volume, for his kind suggestions, patience, and faith.

Finally, I want to thank my wife Julia, an intelligent and dedicated reader, who read the entire manuscript, including the introductory notes, and made many helpful suggestions.

Thomas Butler
Harvard University

Illustration from a Serbian *aprakos*

INTRODUCTION

We have no relics of Serbian and Croatian writing dating earlier than the twelfth century. In spite of the lack of such written evidence, however, it seems reasonable to assume that 10th and 11th century Croatian and Serbian monks and priests were copying and utilizing the Church Slavonic texts passed on to them by the disciples of the apostles to the Slavs, Saints Cyril and Methodius.

Almost from the beginning of their conversion the Croats began to experience cultural pressure from the Roman Catholic Church, with its closely organized structure and its various orders of missionary priests and monks providing both the institutions and the personnel for the diffusion of Catholic influence among the Croats along the coast and in the hinterlands. These accepted the Roman Catholic Church but resisted the Latin liturgy that was being forced on them by the high clergy, which condemned Methodius's translations into Slavonic as heretical. Although the Split synods of 925 and 1060 passed resolutions against the use of the Slavic liturgy, the Croatian clergy complained that many of their priests could not learn Latin, and so the "glagoljaši" priests continued to thrive until well into the seventeenth century. In time the Old Church Slavonic base of this liturgical language became altered under the influence of the čakavian dialect spoken by the priests; these changes were accelerated after the Lateran Councils in the first half of the thirteenth century, when it was resolved that different varieties of language and ritual (including the Slavonic) could exist in the Catholic Church, with the stipulation that all Biblical and liturgical texts be revised in conformance with the Latin Vulgate. For the Croats this meant that a whole set of new translations had to be done, this time under the heavy influence of contemporary spoken čakavian. Such translation activity undoubtedly contributed to the development of a čakavian liturgical koiné, vital to the flowering of čakavian secular literature in the fourteenth and fifteenth centuries, when many of Europe's important literary works were translated, some of which were later adapted into Serbian Slavonic.

The Serbs had not developed a strong state until Stefan Nemanja (ruled 1169-1196) united their local tribal chieftains in the state of Raška. It is from this period that we have the first dated relics of Serbian literature. When Stefan's son Sava established an independent (autocephalic)

Serbian Orthodox Church, he simultaneously laid the foundation for the flourishing of Byzantine-Slavic culture in the Serbian kingdom. Serbian kings were exceptionally generous to their church, contributing to the building and maintenance of churches and monasteries, including the monastery of Hilandar on Mount Athos, which was a center for the diffusion of Byzantine-Slavic writing during the Middle Ages. That the new Serbian culture also embodied some Western elements can be seen not only from the architecture of some of its churches, such as at Dečani, but also in the ornamentation of the *Miroslav Gospel* (ca. 1180), which featured Western-style initials and miniatures of the type produced in the Benedictine scriptoria on the coast.

Perhaps the most original works of Serbian literature during the medieval kingdom (from the twelfth to the fifteenth centuries) were the hagiographic *Lives* (Žitija) of the Serbian rulers. This tradition was begun by Sava and his brother Stefan Prvovenčani ("First Crowned") with their *Lives* of their father, *(Life of Saint Simeon)* and continued by the gifted Teodosije *(Life of Saint Sava),* Archbishop Danilo II *(The Lives of the Serbian Kings and Archbishops),* Grigorije Camblak *(Life of Stefan Dečanski)* and Konstantin of Kostenec *(Life of Stefan Lazarević).* Most of these works were written in Serbian Church Slavonic, with the exception of Camblak's and Konstantin's writings, which were in the revised Bulgarian Slavonic style of the Trnovo school. Serbian Church Slavonic, in spite of certain orthographical changes reflecting Serbian usage, had remained reasonably close to the language of the original Slavic translations of Cyril and Methodius and their disciples. This Serbian literary language changed little from the thirteenth to the seventeenth centuries, and it was so similar to the language used by Bulgarian, Rumanian, and Russian writers that in practice Church Slavonic was to the Slavic Orthodox world what Latin was to the Roman Catholic West.

Although the Croats and Serbs had taken very different approaches to the development of their medieval literary languages (the Croats toward vernacularization, and the Serbs toward petrification), and although the increasing polarization of relations between Rome and Constantinople after the schism of 1054 could not help but adversely affect Croatian and Serbian cultural relations, still there is ample evidence that in the fourteenth and fifteenth centuries there was a significant exchange of manuscripts. Major works of medieval secular literature, such as the *Story of Alexander of Macedonia,* the *Tale of Troy,* and the *Story of Barlaam and Josaphat* existed in both Serbian-Slavonic and Croatian čakavian versions. That there was a literary exchange between the Croats and Serbs was attested by Vatroslav Jagić, who pointed out that the čakavian Roudničky manuscript of the *Story of Alexander* stemmed from a Serbian Slavonic version, which in turn could be traced to a Greek original. The *Tale of Troy,* on the other hand, entered the Balkan area from the opposite

direction, via a čakavian translation of an Italian source. There were also cases of separate provenance for the čakavian and Serbian Slavonic versions, as with the *Story of Barlaam and Josaphat,* which entered Serbian literature from an originally Greek source, and Croatian literature from a Latin or Italian source.

One of the salient features of Serbian and Croatian literature from the medieval period until Romanticism is its lack of a continuous tradition: the glagolitic čakavian school, which had developed a smooth and flexible literary language, one quite capable of turning into a modern literary language for the Croats, faltered and gradually died out (except for occasional use in the liturgy) in the seventeenth century; the Serbian Slavonic tradition lost its vitality after the fifteenth century, with the notable exception of Gavrilo Venclović and a few others. As these two traditions died, a third literary school arose during the fifteenth and sixteenth centuries in the cities and towns along the Dalmatian coast, from Split to Dubrovnik, and on some of the islands. This tradition seems to have borrowed little from the glagolitic-čakavian school of the Croatian Littoral, or from the Serbian Slavonic writers of the interior; instead, the Dalmatian writers turned toward Italy for their inspiration, sharing in its humanism and its Renaissance. Nor were the Dalmatian writers merely imitators of their Italian models. The humanist Marko Marulić of Split (1450-1524) was known through Europe for his *De Institutione Bene Vivendi Per Exempla Sanctorum* (On the Manner of Living Well by the Example of the Saints, Venice, 1506) and for his *Evangelistarium* (Venice, 1516). *De Institutione* alone was published twelve times during the sixteenth and seventeenth centuries.

While Split and other cities on the Dalmatian Coast fell under the rule of Venice, Dubrovnik preserved its precarious freedom as the only enclave on the coast free of outside dominion, and it was in Dubrovnik that the Dalmatian Renaissance writers were most active. Many of its writers completed their education in Italian universities, where they were influenced by the Petrarchan revival, as well as by the new political ideas that were the vogue in Europe, such as the utopian dream of Thomas More. Yet it seems safe to say that these Dalmatian students brought with them to Italy one idea that burned more strongly in them than anything they acquired abroad, namely, that the Turkish presence in the Balkans had to be destroyed and that their brother Serbs and Croats had to be liberated from the Ottoman yoke.

It has often been conjectured that it was consciousness of his brother Slavs' plight that led Marko Marulić to choose the biblical theme of Judith (Judita) for his master work in the spoken language. Marulić, a man of strong faith, may have chosen this theme to assure his countrymen that God was on their side, just as he was on the side of the Jews, and that from Judith's destruction of Holofernes they should gain hope in the

eventual destruction of the Turks and their own deliverance. Hanibal Lucić also takes up the theme of liberation, in his *Robinja* (*The Captive,* 1557), a play with a happy ending, but a serious drama nonetheless, since its story deals with the Turkish capture and sale of Christians as slaves. Gundulić's *Osman* (1637), written nearly a century later and not long after the defeat of the Turkish army at Hotin (1621), sounds a strong note of optimism, giving voice to the conviction that the Turkish days in the Balkans are numbered.

Folklore and the language of the "puk" (the common people) make their way into literature for the first time, via the Dalmatian Renaissance. The plays of Marin Držić, particularly his *Dundo Maroje* (*Uncle Maroje,* 1550) bring us the lively, everyday speech and wit of the common man. And the best poems in the *Ranjinin Zbornik* (*Ranjina's collection,* begun in 1507) are not those which imitate the Italian Petrarchists, but rather those which are either pure folk poetry or close imitations (see, for example, the poem "Vila je moma tri vjenačca" in this book). It was in this period, too, that the first folk poems were published, when Petar Hektorović included two bugarštice (folk ballads) in his versified account of a three-day fishing trip with two local fishermen: *Ribanje i ribarsko prigovaranje* (*Fishing and Fishermen's Conversation,* Venice, 1558).

Had Dalmatian poets drawn more deeply from the oral folk tradition, and had political and economic conditions been favorable, it is quite possible that Croatian poetry would have had a more extensive "Golden Age" in the sixteenth and seventeenth centuries. But this did not happen; instead, the coastal literature lost its vitality in the seventeenth century, and this school slipped beneath the waves, much as the North Croatian glagoljaši and the Serbian Slavonic school had done earlier.

Eighteenth Century Serbian and Croatian literature showed a dim, but nonetheless important reflection of the European Enlightenment, most notably in the works of Andrija Kačić-Miošić, Matija Reljković, and Dositej Obradović. All three were infused with the Enlightenment's conviction that the general well-being (common weal) of a nation could be raised by educating its common man, who was innately good and perfectable. All three were passionate idealists who loved their countrymen, and who wrote not for profit but for the edification of all. For this reason, too, they wrote in their spoken language. Although Kačić's and Reljković's devout Catholicism did not permit them to embrace the freethinking of the Enlightenment on religious matters, the former Serbian monk Dositej was both willing and able, in his *Život i Priključenija* (*Life and Adventures,* Leipzig, 1783) and elsewhere, to express himself quite openly on the need to strip religion of its ritualistic trappings.

Like their ninth and tenth century ancestors, these eighteenth century writers saw a vernacular-based literary language as the fundamental tool for the education of their people and the preservation of their ethnic

identity. Dositej is quite explicit in the "Letter to Haralampije," which prefaces his *Život,* when he states that Church Slavonic is no longer suitable as a Serbian literary language, and that Serbs should write as they speak. And Kačić, in his *Korablica* (*The Ark,* 1760), reminds his countrymen not to be ashamed to speak in their own language when they are in the midst of foreigners: "Nemoj se dakle stiditi u tvoj slavni jezik govoreći, kakono se ne stide Grci ni Latini govoreći u jezike njihove" ("Don't be ashamed, then, to speak in your glorious language, just as the Greeks and Italians are not ashamed to speak in theirs.") He also cautions them not to tell the Italians they are "šćavon" because "schiavo" means "slave" in Italian; rather, they should say "Ja sam Dalmatin, Rvat, Bošnjak, oli Slovinac, jer smo od starine slavni a ne šćavi ni šćavoni rečeni" ("I am a Dalmatian, a Croat, a Bosnian, or a Slovene, because from the days of old we were called 'slavni' [glorious] and not 'šćavi' or 'šćavoni'.")

The first half of the nineteenth century saw the beginning of the extirpation of the Ottoman Empire from the Balkans, with the consolidation of the Montenegrin state and the creation of the Serbian Principality, following the two Serbian insurrections of 1804 and 1815. It was Vuk Stefanović Karadžić, a veteran of the first Serbian Insurrection, who laid the foundation for a new Serbo-Croatian literary language based on the spoken language of the peasant. Vuk also perfected a modified Cyrillic alphabet, phonetically-based, with one letter for one sound; his Croatian counterpart, Ljudevit Gaj, devised a modified Latin alphabet, using diacritical marks, in the manner of the Czechs. Vuk and Gaj were revolutionaries, but their ideas were not revolutionary, expressing as they did the same yearning that their ancestors had felt for a written language in their own tongue, with a symbolism of their own choosing.

Nor does it seem any coincidence that the two chef d'oeuvres of the Romantic period, Ivan Mažuranić's *Smrt Smail-Age Čengića* (*The Death of Smail-Aga Čengić,* 1845) and Petar Petrović Njegoš's *Gorski Vijenac* (*The Mountain Wreath,* 1847) focus on the theme of Turkish oppression and Slavic (Montenegrin) resistance. Njegoš's work, really a long epic poem in dramatic form, tells the history of the Montenegrin struggle with the invader. Mažuranić, on the other hand, focuses on one small event in the continuing fight between the Turks and the Montenegrins, the ambush of the Moslem champion, Smail-Aga, and his slaying by a band of Montenegrins in revenge for his slaughter of some Christians. As in Marulić's *Judita,* the execution of the oppressor is experienced as a catharsis for centuries of brutal indignities.

That the Catholic Croat Ivan Mažuranić should pick an Orthodox milieu for his heroic poema gives evidence that the feeling of brotherhood between Croats and Serbs that motivated Kačić-Miošić in the middle of the seventeenth century was still alive among the Croatian and Serbian intelligentsia of the mid-nineteenth century. In choosing a theme of

resistance to oppression Ivan Mažuranić found a focus that was common to both the Croatian and Serbian experience. In portraying the Montenegrin captives of Smail-Aga as brave "Christians" and nothing more, Mažuranić rose above the narrow prejudices that some South Slavs had inherited from their oppressors, and in seeing their separate national experiences as aspects of one and the same phenomenon he was able to give his work a universality that assured it a place, along with Njegoš's *Mountain Wreath,* as one of the first great works of modern Croatian and Serbian literature.

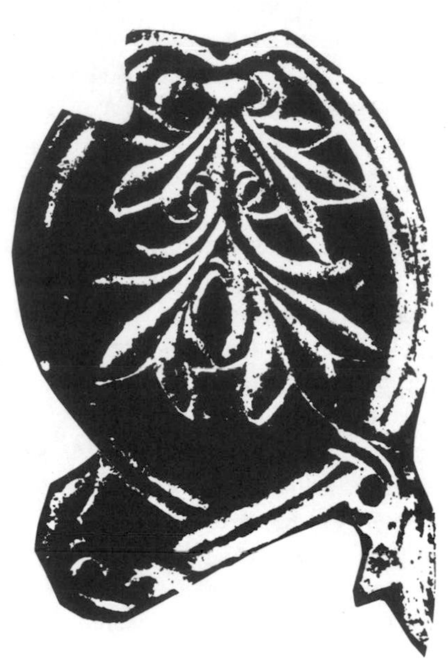

I

CHURCH SLAVONIC MATERIALS AND EARLY LEGAL DOCUMENTS

Silver cross from a 9th century Slavic grave

The Proglas

It is appropriate to begin this anthology with one of the earliest and most beautiful of Slavic written poems, the PROGLAS ["Prologue"] to the Gospels, believed to have been written by Constantine-Cyril, the Apostle to the Slavs (827-869). Originally a native of Salonika, where Slavic as well as Greek were spoken, Constantine had a broad education, studying at the Imperial University in Constantinople such subjects as philosophy, rhetoric, grammar, Homer, music, and dialectics. After graduation he served first as librarian (chartophylax) *to the Patriarch Photius, his patron, and then as professor of philosophy. He was also sent on important missions to both the Arabs and the Khazars, and in 863 he went to Great Moravia, along with his brother Methodius and others, in answer to a request from the Moravian Prince Rastislav to the Byzantine Emperor Michael III for teachers and priests who could provide religious instruction in Slavic.*

It was in connection with his mission to the Moravians that the learned Constantine devised the first Slavic alphabet, called glagolitic, *and began to translate the gospels and other religious texts into Slavic with the help of his brother and their disciples. This was the first time that church writings were being translated into a spoken language in the West, where it was commonly held that only Greek, Latin, and Hebrew were the divinely sanctioned languages for Holy Writ. The brothers were strongly criticized for their promulgation of the Slavonic liturgy, particularly by the Frankish clergy, who jealously guarded the Moravian church as part of their sphere of influence. It is against the background of this fight for Slavic religious autonomy that one should read Constantine's* Prologue, *which is a spirited defense of the Slavic translations, as well as an exhortation for their use by all Slavic Christians.*

St. Constantine-Cyril died in Rome in 869, after successfully defending the Slavic gospels and liturgy before Pope John VIII. Following the death of Methodius in 885, the disciples of the Slavic apostles were driven from Moravia, but they found a friendly welcome in the Bulgarian kingdom of Boris and his son Symeon, during whose reign (893-927) Church Slavonic writing enjoyed a Golden Age. The Life *of St. Clement of Ohrid (died 916) tells us that in the Ohrid diocese alone there were some*

3500 people involved in the translation and copying of religious texts and in the conversion of the Macedonian population. It was during the rule of Symeon, who was himself highly educated in Hellenic culture, that the Church Slavonic language instituted by Constantine and his followers was both expanded and refined, primarily through the translation of Greek texts. Eventually Church Slavonic became the lingua franca *of all the Orthodox lands, and texts written in this language were considered the property of all Slavs, the narrow concept of "national" literatures then being unknown.*

It is precisely because of the communality of Church Slavic literature that the Proglas *has been included in this anthology, as well as other works of medieval Slavic literature not specifically Serbian or Croatian. The inclusion of this poem seems particularly appropriate, however, since of the four extant copies of the* Prologue *three are in Serbian Slavonic manuscripts. Our text is from the oldest preserved copy of the* Proglas, *a thirteenth-century Hilandar manuscript.*

In the past there has been some discussion about the authorship of the Prologue, *some Slavicists preferring not to ascribe it to Constantine-Cyril himself, but to Constantine of Preslav, a disciple of Methodius. The fact that all three Serbian Slavonic versions of the poem begin with the words "A Homily by Our Beloved Teacher Constantine the Philosopher" is not conclusive, but it does indicate that traditionally the poem was believed to have been written by St. Cyril. Roman Jakobson (see his article "St. Constantine's Prologue to the Gospels," in St.* Vladimir's Seminary Quarterly, *Summer 1954), Father Francis Dvornik (*Byzantine Missions Among the Slavs: SS. Constantine-Cyril and Methodius, *Rutgers University Press 1970, 118) and Emil Georgiev (*Dve proizvedenija na Sv. Kirila. *Studia historico-philologica serdicensia, supplementi, vol II, Sofia 1938, 6) do not hesitate to ascribe the poem to St. Cyril. Rajko Nahtigal, who did a long study as well as a reconstruction of the original poem, states emphatically that the* Proglas *was definitely written during the Moravian-Pannonian period, either by Cyril or one of his disciples. In conclusion, there seems to be no reason not to ascribe this poem to St. Constantine-Cyril himself,* not *only because of its highly skillful adaptation of the Byzantine twelve-syllable line (Cyril was known for his poetic gifts, and was called "the melodious nightingale"), and not only because the manuscripts themselves attribute the* Proglas *to him, but more because this poem uses the same arguments that Cyril employed in defending the Slavic gospels and liturgy against the "three-language heresy," at the synod in Venice in 868, and because it is imbued with a sense both of immediacy and of urgency, as though the gospel translations had just been completed.*

Блаженаго оу

чителꙗ нашего Ко

стантина философо

фа слово

Проглась ѥсть стго

ѥулиꙗ. ꙗкоже

пррци прорекли

соуть прѣжде. Хсь

БЛ҃ЖЕНАГО ОУ
ЧИТЕЛꙖ НАШЕГО КО
СТАНТИНА ФИЛОСО
ФА СЛОВО

Проглась ѥсть с҃тго
ѥѵ҃лиꙗ. ꙗкоже
пр҃роци прорекли
соуть прѣже. х҃ъ
гредеть ѩзыкы събра
ти. свѣть бо ѥсть
всемоу мироу. рѣ
ше бо сѧ ни слѣпии
прозрѧть. глоусии оу
слышеть слово боукъ
вное. б҃а познаѭть
ꙗко достоить. тѣ
мже оуслышите сло
вѣни вси. дарь бо ѥ
сть ѿ б҃а съдань. да
рь бж҃ии десныѩ чѧ

сти ѥсть. дарь бж҃ии
д҃шамь николи же гибѣ
ѭ. д҃шамь тѣмь иже
и приимоуть. се же
ѥсть дарь. матѳеи
маркъ лоукa иѡань
оучеть вьсь народь глаѭ
ще. ѥлико лѣпотоу
своиа имать д҃шѧ. вн
ди те любите и радоуи
тесе. ѥлико же хоте
ть грѣхь тмоу ѿврѣ
щи. на мира сего тлю
ѿложити. ѥлико
ма тне раискоѥ ѡбрѣ
сти. и избѣжати ѿ
огнꙗ горещаго. вьнь
мѣтени ѿ всего оу
ма. слышите слово
нꙑнѣ народь вьсь.
слышите слово ѿ б҃а

A HOMILY BY OUR BLESSED TEACHER
CONSTANTINE THE PHILOSOPHER

THIS IS A PROLOGUE TO THE HOLY GOSPELS.
JUST AS THE PROPHETS HAD FORETOLD BEFORE,
CHRIST IS COMING TO GATHER THE NATIONS,
FOR HE IS A LIGHT TO THE WHOLE WORLD.
NOW THEY SAID: THE BLIND WILL SEE,
AND THE DEAF WILL HEAR THE WRITTEN WORD;
THEY WILL KNOW GOD AS THEY SHOULD.
THEREFORE, LISTEN ALL SLAVS:
FOR THIS GIFT IS GIVEN BY GOD,
A DIVINE GIFT FOR THE RIGHT SIDE,
A DIVINE GIFT FOR SOULS, NEVER DECAYING,
FOR THOSE SOULS THAT ACCEPT IT.
AND THIS IS THE GIFT: MATTHEW, MARK, LUKE AND JOHN.
THEY TEACH ALL THE PEOPLE, SAYING:
THOSE OF YOU WHO SEE THE BEAUTY OF YOUR SOULS
LOVE ONE ANOTHER AND REJOICE.
AND THOSE OF YOU WHO WISH TO CAST OFF THE DARKNESS OF SIN
AND TO PUT ASIDE THE CORRUPTION OF THIS WORLD,
AND WHO WISH TO ATTAIN LIFE IN PARADISE
AND TO ESCAPE THE BURNING FIRE,
PAY ATTENTION NOW WITH ALL YOUR MINDS!
HEAR, ALL YOU SLAVIC PEOPLE,
HEAR THE WORD, FOR IT COMES FROM GOD,

бо приде. слово иже
крьмить дше у члвть
весник. слово же иже крѣ
пить срдца ноумы.
слово обѣса готовалы ба
познати. ѣко бо без
свѣта радость не боу
деть. тако оу видещи
бжию тварь всю. нь
вес ни лѣпо ни видин
может. тако и
душа всяка безь боу
кови. не видещи бжи
я закона добрѣ. за
кона книжна дховна
го. закона раі бжний
ѣвляющие. кыи бо
слоух грома наготоу
тна не слышавь мо
жеть ба быти не. но
зарнице пакы нцвѣта

неоухающии. тако
разоумѣютъ бжии
ю. оуста бо иже вла
дкане чюють. тако
капляна творетъ члв
ка. паче же сего дша
безбоукована. мерт
ѣвляетсѧ въ члвцѣх
еже весе алы братие
засылышлающе. гл
аль свѣть повабающь.
еже учлвки вне отлоу
чить отжитии ско
тская похоти. да не
оуаль и алоуще нера
зоумнь. тоужнина
езыко аль слышаще
слово. ѣко медна
звона сла слышите.
се бо сты павль оуче
ре. матвоу свою вь

THE WORD WHICH NOURISHES MEN'S SOULS,
THE WORD WHICH STRENGTHENS HEARTS AND MINDS,
THE WORD WHICH PREPARES ALL TO KNOW GOD.
FOR JUST AS THERE CAN BE NO JOY WITHOUT LIGHT
FOR THE EYE SEEING ALL GOD'S CREATION,
BUT INSTEAD EVERYTHING IS NEITHER BEAUTIFUL NOR VISIBLE,
SO, LIKEWISE, EVERY SOUL WITHOUT LETTERS
DOES NOT SEE GOD'S LAW WELL,
THE SACRED LAW OF THE SCRIPTURES,
THE LAW REVEALING DIVINE PARADISE.
FOR HOW CAN HEARING THAT HAS NOT HEARD THE THUNDER'S ROLL
BE AFRAID OF GOD?
AND NOSTRILS THAT HAVEN'T SMELLED A FLOWER–
HOW CAN THEY SENSE GOD'S WONDER?
AND A MOUTH THAT HAS NO TASTE FOR SWEETNESS
MAKES A MAN LIKE A STONE.
EVEN MORE DOES THE UNLETTERED SOUL
APPEAR DEAD IN MEN.
AND WE, BRETHREN, REFLECTING ON ALL THIS,
GIVE YOU THE PROPER ADVICE,
WHICH WILL FREE ALL MEN FROM THE LIFE OF CATTLE AND FROM
LUSTFUL DESIRE;
LEST HAVING AN UNENLIGHTENED MIND,
AND LISTENING TO THE WORD IN FOREIGN TONGUE,
YOU HEAR IT LIKE THE VOICE OF A COPPER BELL.
FOR SAINT PAUL, IN TEACHING, SAID THIS:
"IN OFFERING MY PRAYER UP TO GOD

здаѥ іпрѣжебоу · ꙗко
хощю словесь петь
изрещи · да и вси бра
тиꙗ разоумѣють ·
не же тѣмоу словесьне
разоумѣвынь · ѥсыи и б
чьтыи сь неразоумѣѥ
ть · ѥсыи не приложи
ть притъчамоударыі
ѥ · сказающа бесѣды
правинамъ · ꙗко бо
тлꙗ пльтехъ настои
ть · вьсе тлещи паче
гноꙗ гноѥщии · ѥгда
своѥго брашна не и
мать · тако душа вьсꙗ
ко падаѥть жизни ·
бжиꙗ не имоуща жи
вота · ѥгда словесе бжи
ꙗ не слышить · и моу
жьлꙗѥсꙗ притъчю моу

дроу зѣло · да глаголемъ
чтѣбцимъ любещеѥ · хо
теще растиб жиѥмъ
растомъ · ѥ тобо вѣры
сеѥ не бѣсть правы ·
ꙗко овѣщеме падающа
наи вѣ · та ѥсо на срци
хъ чтѣбуещѣхъ · требоу
ющемъ бжии боуѥ
вь · да възрастеть пло
дъ бжии паче · ѥто мо
жеть притъчевые · облич
ающе безъисмигѣзы
ки · не выглеѣ салыемь
нѣгдоюща · ни аще к
зыкси вьсоуемѣѥть ·
можеть сказати нем
щьсихъ · собаче свою
притъчю да приставлю ·
многъ оумь бывалѣ
рѣчисаме · назибо

I WOULD RATHER SPEAK FIVE WORDS
THAT ALL MY BRETHREN UNDERSTAND,
THAN A MULTITUDE OF INCOMPREHENSIBLE WORDS.
NOW WHAT MAN DOESN'T UNDERSTAND THIS?
WHO WILL NOT MAKE USE OF WISE PARABLES
TELLING US RIGHT COUNSEL?
FOR JUST AS CORRUPTION AWAITS THE FLESH,
EVERYTHING DECAYING AND PUTREFYING WORSE THAN PUS,
WHEN IT DOESN'T HAVE ITS NOURISHMENT,
SO, TOO, DOES EVERY SOUL PERISH
WHEN IT DOESN'T HAVE DIVINE LIFE,
WHEN IT DOESN'T HEAR THE WORD OF GOD.
BUT LET US RELATE ANOTHER PARABLE, A VERY WISE ONE,
O MEN LOVING ONE ANOTHER
AND WISHING TO GROW IN GOD!
FOR WHO DOES NOT KNOW THIS TRUE FAITH?
LIKE THE SEED FALLING ON THE FERTILE GROUND
IT FALLS IN THE SAME WAY ON THE HEARTS OF MEN
WHICH NEED THE RAIN OF GOD'S LETTERS
SO THAT THE DIVINE FRUIT MAY GROW.
WHO CAN *TELL* ALL THE STORIES
WHICH EXPOSE NATIONS WITHOUT BOOKS,
SPEAKING IN AN UNINTELLIGIBLE VOICE?
EVEN IF ONE KNOWS ALL LANGUAGES
ONE CANNOT EXPRESS THEIR POWERLESSNESS.
BUT LET ME ADD MY OWN PARABLE,
IMPARTING MUCH WISDOM IN A FEW WORDS:

вси безъ книгъ ꙗзыци·
братие не могоуще
безъ ѡроужиꙗ· въ
противникомъ дати
нашихъ· готовивъ
плѣнъ моукы и бѣтны
ѥ· иже бо ꙗзыци не
любите врага· брати
мѣсе мыслеще с никамь
зѣло· ѿвръзѣте при
лежно оумоу добри·
ѡроужие приимаше
твьрдыниꙗ· ѥже исо
ють книгы гнѣ·
главоу троуще непрі
ꙗзни велми· боуѥ
вибосние иже приимае
ть моудрость хсь гле
ть· и даше ваше ерѣ
пить· а пакыже въпра
кы вси· иже бо сихъ

ело вельми глаголюще· побні
боудоуть врага оуби
ти· побѣдоу прино
сеще къ богоу доброу·
пльть и бѣжеще тлѣ
гноѥ вныи· пльтѥ
ѥже животь ꙗко
въ снѣ· не падающе
прѣ покоместоѥще·
боу ꙗвльщесе ꙗко
храбри· стоѥще ѿ
десноую оубѣжища прѣ
стола· ѥгда ѿгнѣвли
соудить ѧзыкомъ·
ꙗдоующесе съ аггелы въ
вѣкы· прѣ побѣдела
вещема тиваго· вс
гда ѥси нужныи мнѣ гѣ
ми· боупающе тебе
моловоующе моу·
ꙗко томоу побать

NAKED ARE ALL NATIONS WITHOUT SCRIPTURES,
WEAPONLESS, UNABLE TO FIGHT
WITH THE ADVERSARY OF OUR SOULS,
READY FOR THE PRISON OF ETERNAL TORMENT.
BUT YOU NATIONS THAT DON'T LOVE THE ENEMY,
AND TRULY INTEND TO FIGHT AGAINST HIM,
OPEN DILIGENTLY THE DOORS TO YOUR MINDS,
HAVING RECEIVED NOW THE STURDY WEAPONS
FORGED BY THE SCRIPTURES OF THE LORD,
WHICH IRRITATE THE DEVIL'S HEAD VERY MUCH.
FOR WHOEVER ACCEPTS THESE SCRIPTURES–
TO YOU CHRIST SPEAKS HIS WISDOM
AND STRENGTHENS YOUR SOULS,
TOGETHER WITH THE APOSTLES AND ALL THE PROPHETS.
AND WHOEVER SAYS THEIR WORDS
WILL BE CAPABLE OF KILLING THE ENEMY,
BRINGING TO GOD A FINE VICTORY,
AND FLEEING THE STINKING DECAY OF THE FLESH,
OF THE FLESH WHOSE LIFE IS LIKE A DREAM.
NOT FALLING, BUT STANDING FIRM,
THEY WILL APPEAR BEFORE GOD AS COURAGEOUS MEN,
STANDING AT THE RIGHT SIDE OF GOD'S THRONE,
WHEN WITH FIRE HE WILL JUDGE NATIONS,
REJOICING WITH THE ANGELS THROUGH ALL AGES,
ETERNALLY PRAISING THE MERCIFUL GOD,
ALWAYS IN PSALMS FROM THE SCRIPTURES,
SINGING TO GOD WHO IS MERCIFUL TOWARD MAN:
BECAUSE TO HIM IS PROPER EVERY KIND OF GLORY,

велiка слава. быть
же и хвала бж̃твнѣи выі
ноу. съ ѿц̃емъ и съ
стыімъ дх̃омъ. въ вѣ
ки вѣкомъ ѿ всея
твари. ами̃нь ∴

HONOR AND DIVINE PRAISE ALWAYS,
TOGETHER WITH THE FATHER AND THE HOLY SPIRIT,
THROUGH ALL AGES, AND FROM ALL CREATION.
AMEN.

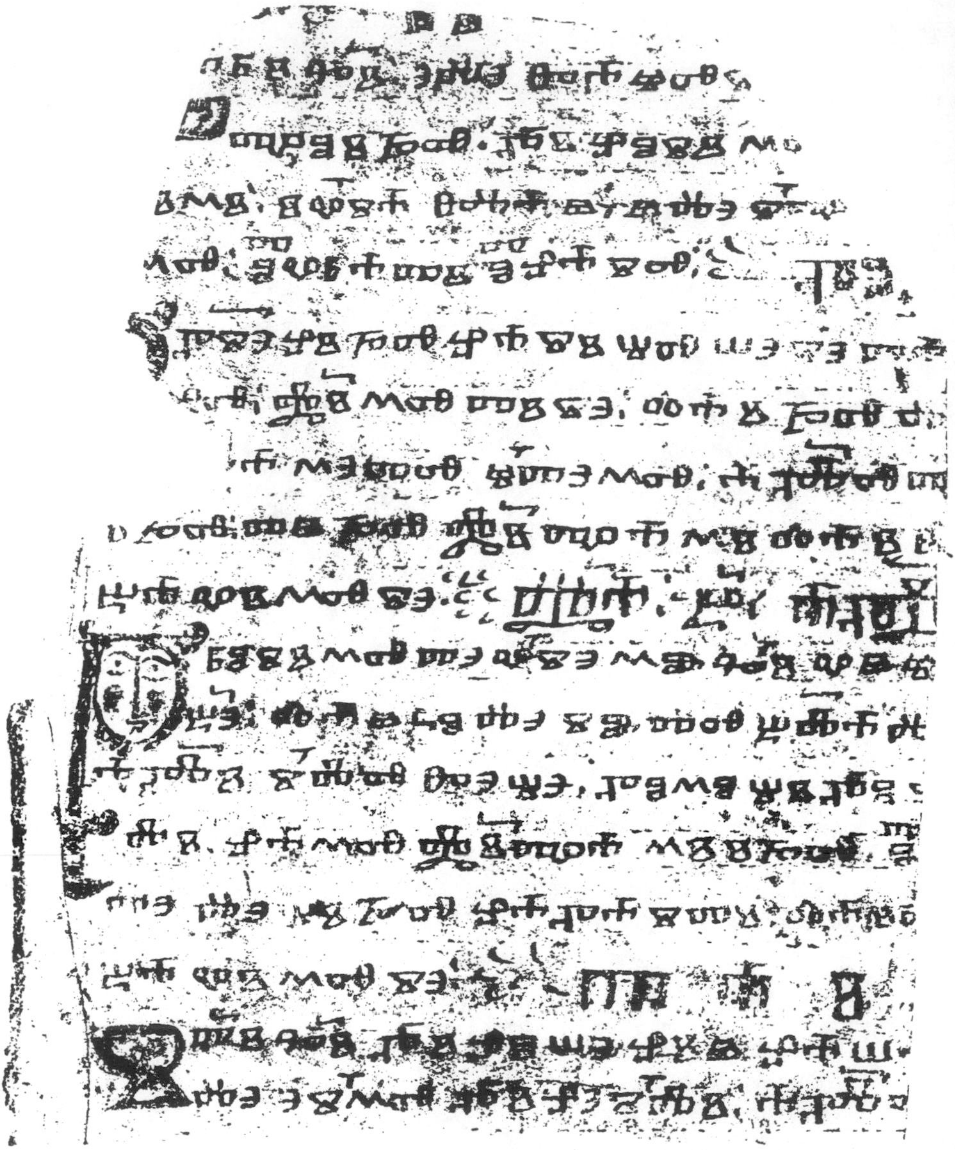

Fragment from a 12th century Croatian glagolitic text

The following prayers are from a fragment of a very old Croatian Mass book or missal, published and analyzed by Vatroslav Jagić in 1890 (Vienna: Kaiserliche Akademie der Wissenschaften, Denkschriften der phil.-hist. Cl. XXXVIII Bd., II Abh., 1-26). *According to Jagić, the fragment dates from the twelfth century, and it represents a transition between the Old Church Slavonic glagolitic writing of Cyril and Methodius and their followers, and the native Croatian glagolitic that flourished along the Dalmatian coast and on its nearby islands from the twelfth to the seventeenth centuries. The roundness of its letters links this fragment to the more ancient style of writing, whereas its language and its content (Roman rather than Byzantine ritual) tie it to the later Croatian glagolitic tradition. Jagić claims that the twelfth-century Croatian missal, plus the earlier West Church Slavonic Kievan missal, likewise based on a Latin original, give evidence of the coexistence during Methodius's episcopacy of two competing Church Slavonic liturgical traditions, one based on the Byzantine rite and the other on the Roman.*

A Croatian glagolitic fragment

Although the glagolitic alphabet did endure in Croatian Dalmatia, alone among the Slavic lands, the Church Slavonic language itself was gradually altered under the influence of the spoken language and through error. Croatian Church Slavonic was subjected to a particularly disastrous revision as a result of the seventeenth and eighteenth century "reforms" of Levaković and Karaman, who mistakenly tried to purify it on the model of contemporary Russian Slavonic. It wasn't until the growth of Slavic studies in the late eighteenth and early nineteenth centuries that some scholars were able to distinguish between the older forms of Slavonic and the more recent corruptions. One of the leaders in the revival of Croatian knowledge of the glagolitic tradition was Ivan Brčić, a priest from Zadar, who published in Prague an Old Slavonic Reader (Čitanka staroslovenskoga jezika, 1859 and 1864), *really an anthology of glagolitic texts. Brčić's book was the first to present examples of both the original old-style glagolitic (oval-shaped) and the native Croatian (angular lettering).*

Jagić tells us that when Father Brčić was consecrated a Catholic priest in Vienna, the Viennese Church hierarchy did not permit him to say the Mass in Slavonic, as was his right as a priest of the Zadar Archdiocese. Thus the struggle between the Germano-Latin culture and the Slavonic, begun in these lands in Cyril and Methodius's time, and perhaps even earlier, still plagued the Church one thousand years later. (For more on Brčić, see Vatroslav Jagić's introduction to Dvie službe rimskoga obreda za svetkovinu svetih Ćirila i Metuda izdao Ivan Berčić. *Zagreb: JAZU, 1870, IV.)*

. . . . . . ТАИ . . . .

(Да)ри г҃и : еже за чьс(ть ап҃ль)
твоихь . приносимь (м҃стивь)
(при)ими : и вса злаѣ, ѣже ств(о)
мь : ѿврати ѿ нась : ПО(БРАШ)
Сп҃сенихь насицьше се та(и)
нь : м҃лимь ти се : да ихьж(е)
(п)аметь чтемь : ап҃ль т(во)
ихь : тѣхь м҃литвами да из
бавимь се : МША : Б : АПЛМ
Просимь те всемоуги вѣч(ьни)
б҃е : да ѣкоже соуть бл҃аж(ени)
ап҃ли сльзеще . помощи прос(и)
ли . намь м҃литвами ихь . ѿ (на)
лежещихь напасти . да из
бавимь се : ТАИ
С҃ти г҃и : приношениѣ наш(а ѣ)
же . есмь принесли : ап҃л . .

. . . . . . *SECRET* . . . . . .

THE GIFTS, O LORD, WHICH WE BRING

IN HONOR OF THINE APOSTLES

MERCIFULLY RECEIVE, AND ALL EVIL WE HAVE DONE

TURN AWAY FROM US. *POST COMMUNION:*

SATIATED BY THY SAVING MYSTERIES

WE PRAY THEE THAT WE MAY BE SAVED

THROUGH THE PRAYERS OF THOSE

WHOSE MEMORY WE HONOR, THINE APOSTLES:

A SECOND MASS OF THE APOSTLES .

WE IMPLORE THEE, ALL-POWERFUL ETERNAL GOD,

THAT AS THE BLESSED APOSTLES

IN TEARS HAVE IMPLORED THY HELP FOR US,

SO MAY WE BE SAVED BY THEIR PRAYERS

FROM THE TEMPTATIONS THAT LIE IN WAIT. *SECRET*

BLESS, O LORD, OUR GIFTS

WHICH WE HAVE BROUGHT

(AND THROUGH THE INTERCESSION) OF THINE APOSTLES . .

Illustration from
the *Miroslav Gospel*

The Miroslav Gospel

From the beginning of the medieval Serbian Nemanjić dynasty (1169-1371) there existed a strong bond of cooperation between the state and the church. This relationship was given a solid foundation by Sava, son of Stefan Nemanja, the founder of the dynasty. Sava established an autocephalous Serbian Orthodox Church, which became a powerful ally of the monarchy.

With the rise of an independent church, Serbs engaged in a flurry of building, erecting new churches and monasteries, including scriptoria (copying centers) whose main function was to replace the many manuscripts that had been burned during the anti-Bogomil inquisition of Byzantium. It was at a scriptorium in Hum (today's Hercegovina) that Miroslav, the prince of Hum and brother of Stefan Nemanja, had copied for him the priceless gospel known today as the "Miroslavljevo Jevandjelje."

The Miroslav Gospel *seems to have been written by two copyists, Varsameleon (the chief copyist) and Gligorije (see St. M. Kul'bakin:* Paleografska i jezička ispitivanja o Miroslavljevom jevandjelju. *SKA Posebna izdanja, knj. LII, 1925, p. 111). According to Vladimir Mošin, their writing exhibits a definite Russian influence, owing perhaps to the close cooperation between Russian and Serbian monks on Mount Athos during the late twelfth and early thirteenth centuries (see his "O periodizacii russkojužnoslavjanskix literaturnyx svjazej X-XV vv.,"* Trudy otdela drevnerusskoj literatury, *XIX, Moskva-Leningrad. Izd. AN SSSR, 1963, 70-71). But while its cyrillic writing may show Russian influence, the priceless miniatures and initials of this manuscript seem to have been done by a Western artist, perhaps by a Benedictine monk from the Dalmatian coast (see Josip Vrana,* L'Évangéliaire de Miroslave. *Mouton: Slavic Printings and Reprintings, XXV, 1961, 90).*

The Miroslav Gospel *is one of the treasures of medieval European manuscript writing.*

Illustration from
the *Miroslav Gospel*

THE GOSPEL ACCORDING TO SAINT MATTHEW

And great crowds of people followed Jesus, from Galilee and Decapolis, from Jerusalem and Judaea, and from the other side of the Jordan. And seeing the great crowds he went up onto a mountain, and after he had sat down his disciples came to him, and opening his mouth he was teaching them, saying:

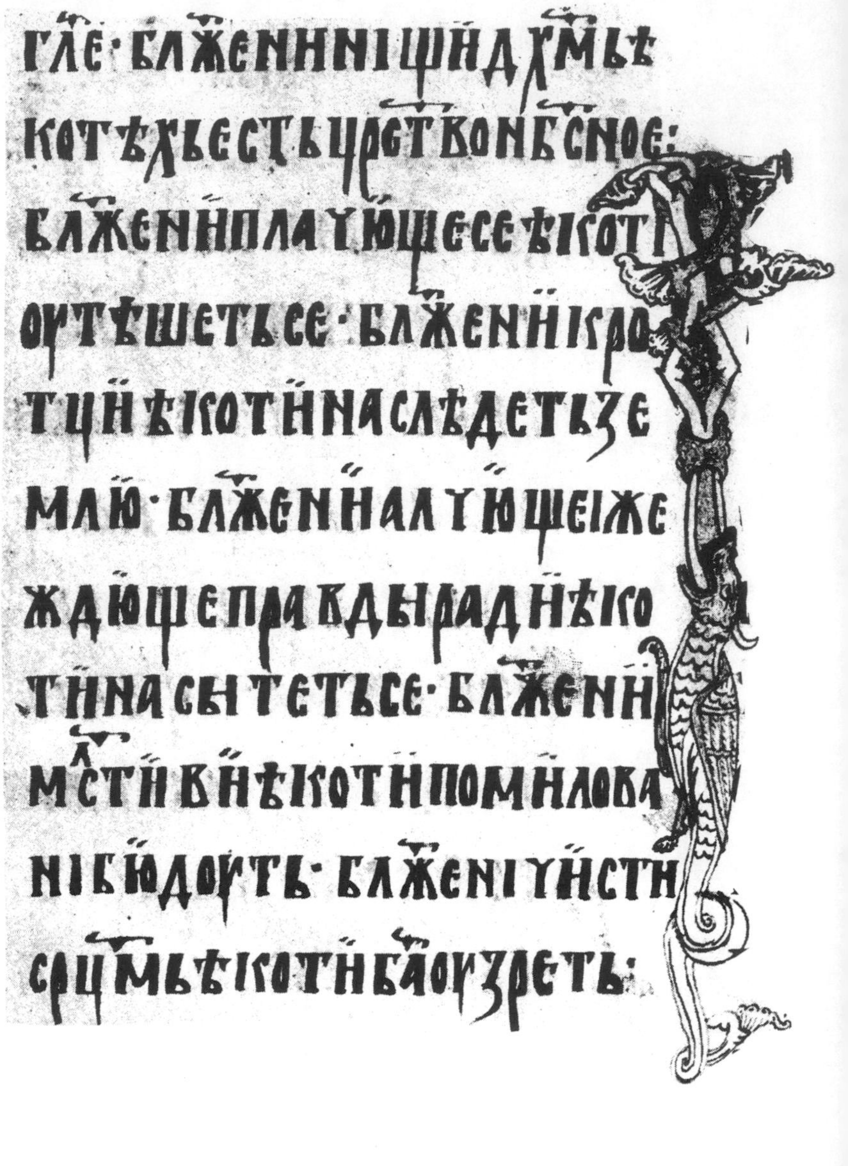
гле· блажени нищи дхмь ѣ
ко тѣхь есть црство нбсное·
блажени плачюще се ѣко ти
оутѣшеть се· блажени кро
тции ѣко ти наслѣдеть зе
млю· блажени алчющеиже
ждющеправды ради ѣко
ти насытеть се· блажени
мсти ви ѣко ти помилова
ни бюдоуть· блажени чистии
срцмь ѣко ти бга оузреть:

Blessed are the poor in spirit, because theirs is the kingdom of heaven;
Blessed are those who mourn, because they will be comforted;
Blessed are the humble, for they shall inherit the earth;
Blessed are they who hunger and thirst for justice's sake, for they will be satisfied;
Blessed are the merciful, for they will receive mercy;
Blessed are the pure of heart, for they will see God;

БЛЖНИ СЬМИРѢЮЩЕИ ѢКО
ТО СНВЕ БЖИ НАРЕКѪТЬ СЕ·
БЛЖНИ ИЗГНАНИ ПРАВДЫ
РАДИ ѢКО ТѢХЬ ЕСТЬ ЦРСТВО
НБСНОЕ· БЛЖНИ ЕСТЕ ЕГДА
ПОНЕСЮТЬ СЕ ВАМИ· И ЖДЕ
НЮТЬ ВЫ И РЕКЮТЬ ВСѢКЬ
ЗЬЛЬ ГЛЬ· НА ВЫ ЛЖЮЩЕ
МЕНЕ РАДИ· РАДИ ТЕ СЕ И ВЕ
СЕЛИТЕ СЕ· ѢКО МЬЗ
ДА ВАША· МНОГА ЕС
ТЬ НА НБСѢХЬ·

Blessed are the peacemakers, for they will be called the sons of God;
Blessed are those persecuted for justice's sake, for theirs is the kingdom of heaven;
Blessed are you when they will carry on against you, and persecute you, and say all kinds of evil lies against you, because of me.
Rejoice and be happy, because your reward is great in heaven.

Illustration from a glagolitic text

The Mihanović Homiliar

This excerpt is taken from a homily by the famous fourth-century Greek preacher St. John Chrysostom, who was such an eloquent speaker that he was given the name"Chrysostomos"which means "Gold Mouth" in Greek; in Serbo-Croatian he is known as Ivan Zlatousti, which has the same meaning.

The sermons of John Chrysostom were very popular with the early Balkan converts to Christianity. Vatroslav Jagić points out that the Old Church Slavonic Codex Suprasliensis *contains twenty of Chrysostom's sermons, and that John's sermons outnumber all others in the thirteenth century Serbian* Mihanović homiliar. *What Jagić says of Chrysostom's popularity with the Bulgarians, during the Golden Age of Tsar Simeon (died 927 A.D.), could also be said of his acceptance by the Serbs: "John Chrysostom from earliest times took a very special place in Old Bulgarian literature; his practical, simple, and lucid manner of interpreting Holy Writ was especially suited to serve as a model for Old Bulgarian teachers in the teaching and preaching of God's word." (Vatroslav Jagić.* Historija književnosti naroda hrvatskoga i srbskoga. *Zagreb, 1867, 75).*

Saint John Chrysostom lived and preached long before the schism between the Eastern and Western branches of Christianity, and he is recognized as a saint by both churches. Today's multi-volume translations of his sermons into English, French, German, Russian, Spanish and other languages, as well as the continuing publication of studies of his life and works, attest to his importance as one of the great Christian theologians. In choosing to translate many of Chrysostom's sermons into their native recension of Old Church Slavonic, Serbian monks showed ultimate taste and wisdom. Chrysostom's style and language must have had considerable influence on the language and style of native Serbian writers from the eleventh through the fourteenth centuries. Nor was his popularity with Serbs limited to this period; Dositej Obradović mentions in his Život i priključenija *that Chrysostom was one of his favorite writers when he was at the monastery of Hopovo.*

Our text of Saint John's "Homily on the Beheading of John the Baptist" is from the thirteenth century Mihanović homiliar, *as photoreproduced by R. Aitzetmüller (Editiones monumentorum slavicorum veteris dialecti, 1957). R. Nahtigal has stated his belief that the* Mihanović zbornik *stems from an original manuscript of Methodius, while Vatroslav Jagić opined that the* Mihanović homiliar *was based either on the Old Church Slavonic* Codex Suprasliensis *(cyrillic) or the Clozianus manuscript (glagolitic), or a third document similar to the two (Jagić,* Historija, *75).*

ON THE TWENTY-NINTH DAY
OF THE SAME MONTH
A HOMILY OF SAINT JOHN CHRYSOSTOM
ABOUT THE BEHEADING
OF JOHN THE BAPTIST

We have been of a tranquil state of mind, like a man who enjoys the wilderness and who sits in the shade of some wooded place, by the water's edge, and the place resounds with the melodious chirping of birds, and the water's rush. But when the evangelist tells about Herod's fury and that woman's shamelessness, and about the banquet of madmen and the loathsome banquet table, and the unlawful gift, and the burial of an

honorable body, I become dumb, my beloved. When I bring before my eyes the things that were done by Herod, how can I mention these things and the destruction which he caused? "At that time," he says, "when Herod the Tetrarch heard of Jesus, he said to his men: 'This will be John, the one whom I beheaded. He has arisen from the dead, and that is why he is performing miracles.'" He admits the murder of the prophet whom he could not deceive. And he knew that he had killed a prophet and a holy man. For if he did [not] know, he would not have said that he had risen from the dead and that was why he was performing miracles. O,

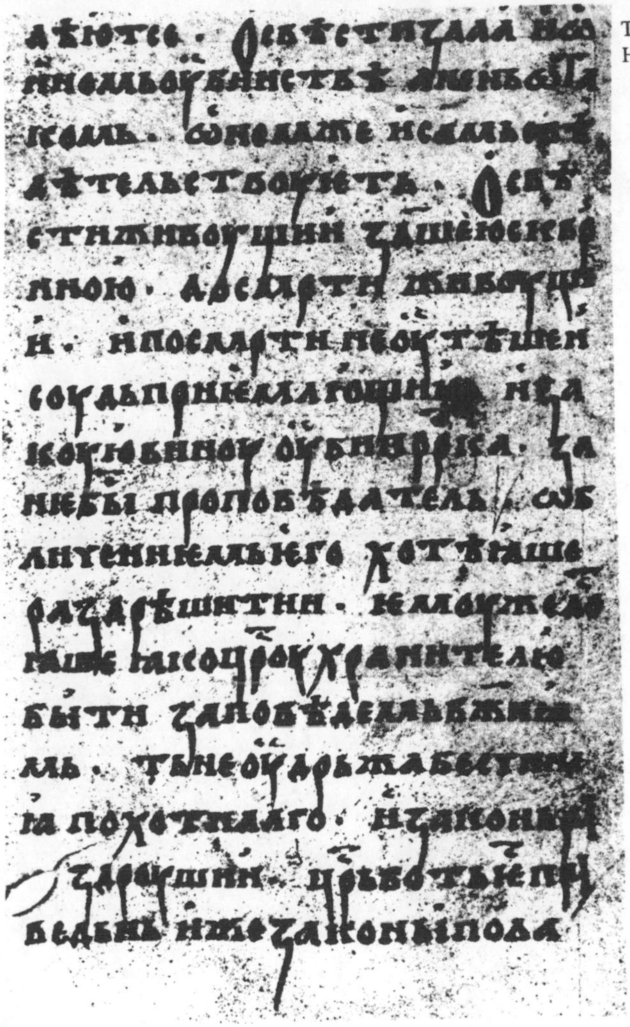

The Mihanović Homiliar

evil conscience! And no other murder but this one, and he himself bears witness to it! O conscience living with a rotten soul, living that way before death, but after death receiving an irredeemable judgment! And for what crime did he kill the prophet? So that he wouldn't preach; because he [John] wanted to free him by exposing him. For it was incumbent on him, as ruler, to be the preserver of God's laws, and not to support lustful carousing, and not to break the law. For that ruler is righteous who,

when establishing laws, is himself the first to observe them. And how else could he maintain good order amongst his subjects, if he did not keep the unrestrained human race in check with just laws, like reins. But Herod is the ruler not of people, but of desires. "And whoever is defeated by them is their slave." Not only did he violate God's law, but he also committed an unjust murder. And whom did he kill? A righteous man, him about whom the Lord himself gave witness. John was living in a barren and grassless desert. He wasn't fleeing his tribe and his human

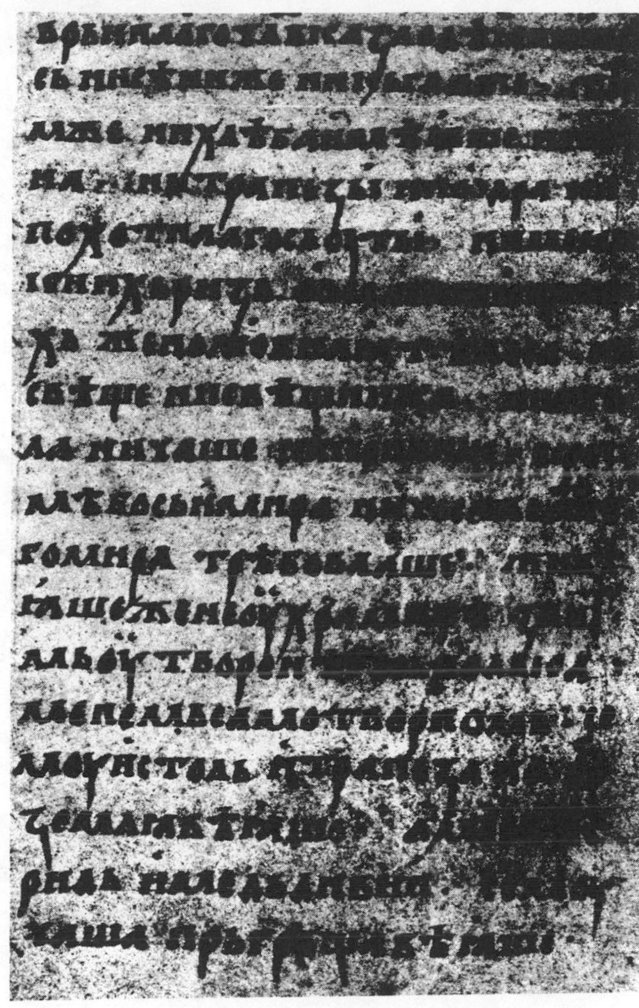

The Mihanović Homiliar

nature, but he was fleeing the sights and sounds of loathsome human crimes. This man never sowed, and therefore he never had any bread; neither did he have wine, nor a dining table, nor a bed, nor a servant at his pleasure, nor soft robes which weaken effeminate bodies; neither a candle did he have nor a candleholder, neither a table, nor a cup, nor goblet. And being removed from the world he needed nothing from this world. He was living not in a house adorned with gold, but under natural stone. For this one the ground was his chair, and his dining table, and his bed. And his meat was the grasshopper, and his honey was wild. For this

one his palm was his cup, and he drank pure water flowing from a rock
"And having seized this John, he bound him and he threw him into priso
for the sake of his brother Philip's wife." O what a repugnant thing
John had wanted to free his [Herod's] soul from its sinful bonds, b
exposure, but he bound the one who was freeing him. But even thoug
bound, John talked, and even though cast into prison he exposed hin
For he was accomplishing what was written: "I spoke concerning Th
teachings before emperors, and I was not ashamed." For John was nc

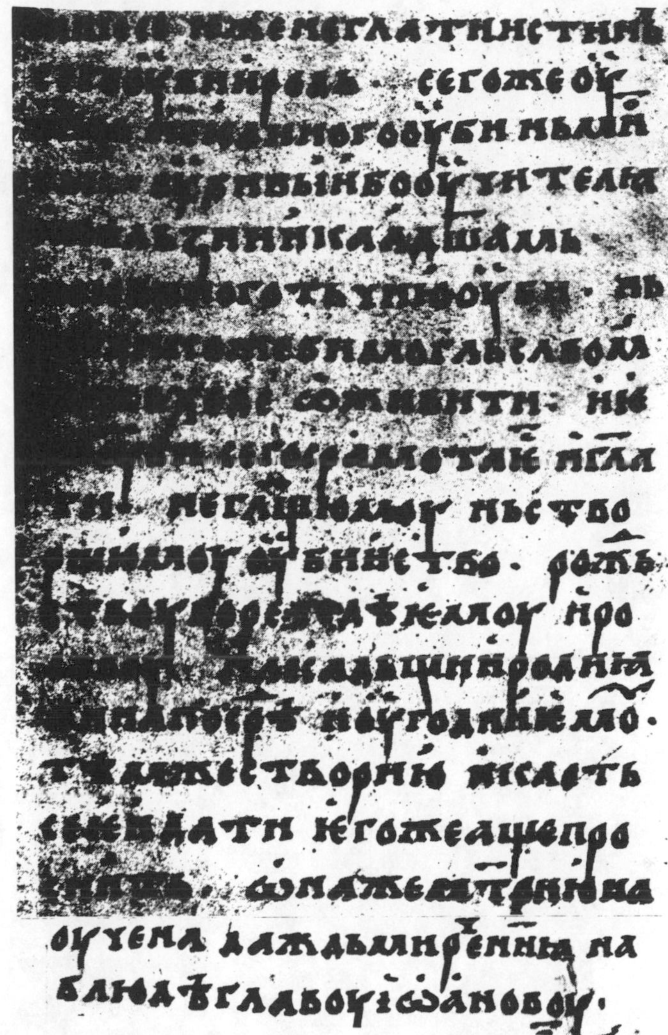

The Mihanović Homiliar

afraid of death, but he was afraid not to speak the truth. This one Herod killed. And in killing him he did not kill one person, but many. For in killing the teacher and healer of souls he did not kill him alone, but all those to whom he could have brought life, had he remained alive. And when did he kill him? It would be a shame even to say–not for the one who would say it, but for the one who committed the murder. "And they were celebrating," he says, "Herod's birthday, and the daughter of Herodias was dancing in their midst, and she pleased him, whereupon he made an oath to give her whatever she asked. And she, having already been coached by her mother, said: 'Give me the head of John on a platter.' "

Stefan Nemanja

The Life of Nemanja

Hagiography, the writing of the lives of saints, was a common literary activity during the Middle Ages, both in the Eastern and Western branches of Christianity. The earliest known attempts at hagiography in Serbia were the Lives *of Stefan Nemanja (St. Simeon) by his sons Sava and Stefan Prvovenčani. Some scholars believe that there were earlier* Lives *written in the Serbian lands, such as that of Saint Vladimir, whose story has come down to us in Latin in the* Ljetopis Popa Dukljanina *(see elsewhere in this anthology), but this has not been confirmed.*

The Žitija *of Stefan Nemanja, as written by his son Sava (about 1208) and Stefan (about 1216), are amplifications based on the short biographical materials given in the charters (chrysobulla) of 1198 and 1200 to the Serbian monastery of Hilandar, on Mount Athos. The two brothers approached the writing of their father's life very differently: Sava writes of his father's good works, and with much emotion he describes Nemanja's last years together with him at Hilandar, particularly his death; Stefan Prvovenčani, as a ruler, is more interested in Nemanja's work as unifying head of the new Serbian state, in his successful liquidation of the Bogomil heresy, and his miraculous posthumous interventions in the affairs of the Serbian kingdom. In spite of the difference in their approach to Stefan's life, both these* Lives *are permeated with the beginnings of a dynastic ideology, with the already strong conviction that God has looked with favor on the efforts of the Nemanja family to consolidate and expand the Serbian kingdom.*

Sava's and Stefan Prvovenčani's Lives *of their father laid the groundwork for a life-writing tradition in medieval Serbian literature. Henrik Birnbaum has written of this tradition: "The literary genre of biography, developed to a level of high sophistication, can be considered perhaps the most eloquent expression of medieval Serbian civilization." ("Byzantine Tradition Transformed: The Old Serbian Vita", in* Aspects of the Balkans: Continuity And Change, *H. Birnbaum and S. Vryonis, editors. The Hague-Paris: Mouton, 1972, 243-284.) The most important corpus of such medieval biography was the* Životi kraljeva i arhiepiskopa srpskih *(Lives of Serbian Kings and Archbishops), written by the Archbishop Danilo II and his continuers. In this collection, each king is a saint, regardless of the actual facts of his life.*

The Serbian monastery of Studenica

Нашь с(ве)тыи монастирь сы, ꙗко вѣдѣти вамь, ꙗко поустоу мѣстоу семꙋ бывшоу ловища ѕвѣремь бѣхоу; пришьд(ь)шоу же въ ловитвоу г(оспо)д(ин)оу нашемꙋ и самодръж'цоу, ц(а)р(ь)ствоующоу въсеѥ сръб'скыѥ землѣ, Стефаноу Немани, ловещꙋ ѥмоу здѣ и изволи се ѥмꙋ въ поустѣмь семь здѣ мѣсте оустворити монастирь сы на покой и на оумножениѥ ѥдинокыхь чина. Сего бо трьбл(а)женнаго по истинѣ г(оспо)д(ин)а ны и ѿ(ть)ца да вѣдомо боудеть въсѣмь нами же и инѣмь, ꙗко б(ог)ъ, творей на бол'ша чл(овѣ)кωмь не хотѣ чл(овѣч)ьской гыбѣли, постави сего самодръж'наго г(оспо)д(ин)а ц(а)р(ь)ствовати въсею сръб'скою землѥю, нареченнаго Стефана Неманю. И ѡбновив'шоу ѿ(ть)чиноу дѣдиноу и болше оутвръдившꙋ б(о)жиѥю помощиѭ и своѥю моудростиѭ данною ѥмоу ѿ б(ог)а, и въздвиже погывшоуѭ своѭ дѣдинꙋ и приобрѣте ѿ помор'скыѥ землѥ Зетоу и съ градовы, а ѿ Равна Пилота ѡба, а ѿ гръчьскыѥ землѥ Пат'ково, Хвост'но въсе и Под(ь)римиѥ, Кострьць, Дръжьковиноу, Ситницꙋ, Лабь, Липлꙗнь, Гльбочицоу, Рѣкѣ, Оуш'коу и Поморавиѥ, Загрълатꙋ, Лѣв'че, Бѣлицю; та вса моудростиѭ

This our holy monastery, as you know, once was a desolate place and a hunting ground for wild animals; and our lord and autocrat Stefan Nemanja, ruler of all the Serbian lands, came here hunting, and while he was hunting here he thought it would be good to build in this barren place a monastery for the peace and increase of the monastic order. For all of us, and others too, should know that God, who guides people toward what is better, not wishing man's ruin, appointed this thrice-blessed man, truly our lord and father, named Stefan Nemanja, to rule over all the Serbian land as autocratic lord. And he restored his patrimony and he consolidated it further, through God's help and through his own God-given wisdom, and he raised up his ruined patrimony, and of the coastal land he acquired Zeta, together with its cities, and from Albania he got both Pilots, and from the Greek land he got Patkovo, all of Hvosno and Podrimlje, Kostrac, Draškovina, Sitnica, Lab and Lipljan, Dubočica, Reke, Uška and the Pomoravlje, Zagrlata, Levče, and Belica; through

ӥ троу́дѡмь своимь сїа̀ въса̂ прио̂брѣте, погы́бшоую некогда̀ ѿ наси́лїа своее ѐмоу̂ дѣдины, достоинаа ѐмоу̂ срьбскые землѥ. Ӥ поспѣше́нїемь б(о)жїемь ми́рь и тиши́ноу въспрїе́м'шоу вл(а)д(и)чьствоу ѐго ѿ въсо́удоу, въ ӥстиноу бо̂ сы ди́в'нь ӥ стра́шнь быс(ть) въсѣ́мь жи́воущїимь о̂кр'сть се́бе, вл(а)д(и)чьствоу бо̂ ѐго̀ бывшоу ҃лз лѣтъ съхра́нѥноу ӥ цѣлоу ӥ ни ѿ ко́гоже невр̊ѣжденꙋ. Что бо̀ се́го нарече́мь? Бл(а)д(и)кꙋ ли па́че ӥ оу̂чителꙗ? Оу̂тврьди бо̀ ӥ въразоумѝ въсѣхь ср(ь)д(ь)ца ӥ наста́ви ны ка́ко подобаеть правовѣ́рнымь хр(и)стїа́нѡмь дрьжати пра́воую вѣ́роу къ б(ог)оу; собо́ю прьвѣе бл(а)говѣ́рїе показа̀, по то́м' же ӥ ӥнѣх(ь) наста́ви, цр(ь)кви ѿс(ве)ти, монасти́ре създа̀, с(ветите)лѥ въ сла́сть послоу̂шае, ӥере́е ч'тѐ, къ мни́хѡм же велико смѣре́нїе ӥ лю́бовь ӥма́е, ненадѣ́ющим се наде́жда, оу̂бѡгымь застоу̂пникь, ни́щимь кръми́тель, на́гые въ домь свой въво́де ӥ ѡ̂дѣ́ваше, си́рые въспи́та, в'до́вице о̂пра́вда, слѣ́пымь ӥ хрѡ́мымь ӥ немѡ́щнымь ӥ глоу̂хымь ӥ нѣмымь вь ӥстиноу ма́ти быс(ть);

his wisdom and hard work he acquired all these places which were part of his patrimony and belonged to him as Serbian land, but which had been lost because of war. And with God's assistance his kingdom enjoyed peace and quiet everywhere, for in truth he was both wonderful and terrifying for all who lived in his vicinity, and his state was preserved whole and intact for thirty seven years, and it wasn't infringed upon by anyone. Now what should we call him? Our lord, or even more, our teacher? Because he strengthened and sobered the hearts of us all, and he taught us how true-believing Christians should keep the true faith with respect to God; he first of all showed true faith in himself, and then he taught others. He consecrated churches, built monasteries, listened to the bishops with delight, respected priests, and had great humilty and love in his relations with monks; he was the hope of those who were without hope, the defender of the poor, the nourisher of the destitute; he brought the naked into his home and he clothed them, he fed the orphans, he justified widows, and to the blind and the crippled and the feeble and the deaf and the mute he was a true mother . . . .

Нє́мањини Life by Sava

Са́м' же създа мѡнастꙑ́ре: и҆ пр҄ьво оу҆ Топли́ци с(ве)таго ѿ(ть)ца Нико́лꙑ, и҆ дроу҆гꙑ та́можде с(ве)тоу б(огоро)ди)цꙋ оу҆ Топлици; по том жде па́кꙑ създа̀ монастірь св(ет)аго Геѡ́ргіа въ Ра́сѣ. И҆ въсѣ́мь тѣмь мѡнастꙑремь сътво́ри оупра́воу ꙗ҆кож(е) подобаеть. Послѣ́ди же тѣ́хь сꙑ на́шь с(ве)тꙑи монастꙑ́рь създа̀, е҆го́же и҆ наре́че въ и҆ме прѣс(ве)тꙑе вл(а)д(и)ч(и)це на́ше б(огороди)це бл(а)годѣ́тельнице, създа́вь ѡть ма́ла и҆ до вели́ка, и҆ се́ла прѣда́вь и҆ съ и҆нѣми пра́вдами монасти́рю, и҆кѡ́нꙑ и҆ съсꙋ́дꙑ ч(ь)ст(ь)нꙑми и҆ книгꙑ и҆ ри́зꙑ и҆ завѣ́сꙑ и҆ ꙗ҆̀же сꙋть пи́сана въ злато печат'нѣи по́вели е҆го̀, паче же и҆ въ црькви напи́сано на стѣнѣ и҆ съ кле́твою и҆ съ заоу҆зою, ꙗ҆ко да никто̀ не потво́рить е҆го́ва прѣда́нїа, ꙗ҆коже слꙑшите и҆ въ кни́гах(ь) си́хь напрѣ́ди ѡ҆ то́мь сло́во.

He himself built monasteries: and the first was that of our holy father Nikola in Toplica, and the second was in the same place, the monastery of our Blessed Mother in Toplica; and again later he built the monastery of Saint George at Ras. And he established the appropriate administration for all these monasteries. And after them he built this holy monastery of ours, which he named after our Lady, Our Blessed Mother the Benefactress; and he built it from top to bottom, and he ceded villages to the monastery, along with other things that pertain to a monastery, such as icons and holy vessels, books and robes and curtains, and those things which are written down in his charter with the gold seal, and what's more, he had written on the wall of the church, together with a curse and with a binding obligation, that no one should change his bequest, which you will hear about in the following chapters.

The Serbian monastery of Mileševa

Nemanja's *Life* by Stefar

Пришьд(ь)шоу же ѥдиномоу ѿ правовѣрныих. воинь ѥго и поклонь колѣнѣ свои сь оумилениѥмь и смѣрениѥмь многомь г(лаго)лаше ѥмоу: „Г(оспод)и, азь ѥдинь ѿ хоуждьшихь слоужещих' ти мьни ѥсьмь, видѣвь срьдобольство твоѥ, ѥже кь вл(а)д(и)цѣ твоѥмоу г(оспод)оу Іс(оусоу) Х(ри)с(т)оу и кь прѣч(и)стѣи вл(а)д(и)ч(и)ци б(огороди)ци и кь симь с(ве)тымь оугод'никомь ѥю побор'никомь твоимь, иже крѣп'кою дланию под(ь)дрьжеть власть твою неврѣдимоу, др'зноухь вьзвѣстити дрьжавѣ твоеи, ѥже нелюбещаꙗ ти вѣра и трьклетаꙗ ѥресь юже оукорѣнѧѥт' се вь вл(а)д(и)чьстви твоѥмь. Єн же прѣпод(о)бны с(ве)ты мои г(осподи)нь, ни мали зак'снѣвь, скоро призвавь своѥго ар'хиѥреꙗ Ѥв'димиꙗ г(лаго)лема и чрьн'це сь игоумени своими и ч(ь)ст(ь)ныѥ иѥреѥ, стар'це же и вел'моуже своѥ ѿ мала и до велика ихь, г(лаго)лаше с(ве)т(ите)лю и чрьн'цемь соущимь и в'сѣмь сьбраныимь с ними:

And there came to him one of his true-believing soldiers, and neeling before him he said with much agitation and humility: "Lord, am the least among your worst servants, and when I saw your zeal oward the Lord Jesus Christ and toward our most pure Lady, the Mother of God, and toward their holy saints, your defenders, who in the strong alm of their hands maintain your power undefiled, I have made so bold s to report to your majesty that that faith and thrice-cursed heresy which ou find odious is already taking root in your kingdom." And my most enerable and holy lord, without any delay, quickly called in his archriest, named Jeftimije, and the monks with their abbots, as well as the oly priests, and his magnates large and small, and he said to the bishop nd to the monks and to all who were gathered there with them: "Come

„Придѣте и видѣте, ѡ(ть)ци и брат(и)ꙗ, ѥже аще и хоуждь-
ши ѥс'мь ѿ брат(и)ѥ своѥѥ, нь г(оспод)ь б(ог)ь и пр(ѣ)ч(и)-
стаꙗ вл(а)д(и)ч(и)ца б(огороди)ца м(а)ти ѥго, не зри на
лице чл(о)в(ѣ)че, нь спод(о)би мене хоуждьшаго вѣроующа
вь ѥдиносоущ'ноую нераздѣлимоую троицоу сьблюдати сиѥ
прѣданоѥ ми имь стадо, ѥже и вид(и)те н(и)нꙗ, ꙗко не вьсѣ-
ꙗти се плѣвелоу злокьзнаго и неприꙗзньнаго диꙗвола, и никако же мнѣти ми ѥже быти томоу вь ѡбласти моѥи, юже
бо н(и)нꙗ слышоу вькорѣнившоу се вь малѣ злокьзномоу
и хоулоу приносеща на с(ве)ты д(оу)хь и раздѣлꙗща недѣ-
лимоѥ б(о)ж(ь)ство, ѥже г(лаго)лаше безоумны Арии прѣсѣ-
каѥ ѥдиносоущ'ноу троицоу, ѥже прорекоше с(ве)ти и б(о)го-
носни ѡ(ть)ци: „Кто ти, сп(а)се, ризы раздра?“ „Арии“, реч(е),
„безоумны, иже троицоу прѣсѣче“. Тѣм' же и си безоум'ни
послѣдоують того оучению не вѣдоуще ѡкании, ꙗкоже сьни-
ти имь вѣровав'шимь и сь ѡнѣмь трьклетымь вь дно адо-
вьѣ скровищь“. Сиже г(лаго)лющоу с(ве)томоу семоу и распри

and see, fathers and brothers, that even though I am the worst among my brothers, nevertheless the Lord God and our most pure Lady, the Mother of God, His mother, overlooking my human side, chose me, the worst one, who believes in the consubstantial and indivisible Holy Trinity, to watch over their flock which they gave me, and which you see here now, so that the cockle of the evil and hostile devil might not be sowed among them; and in no way did I think that it was in my territory, but now I hear that the evil one has taken root in no time at all, bringing blasphemy against the Holy Spirit and dividing the indivisible divinity, speaking like the insane Arius when he was splitting the consubstantial Trinity; and when the holy and godfearing fathers said: 'Who, Savior, has rent your garments?' he answered: 'Arius, the insane one, who has split the Trinity.' And in the same way these insane people follow his teaching, not knowing, poor miserable creatures, that because they believe in this manner they will descend with that thrice-cursed one to the bottom of hell's recesses." And while the holy one was saying this,

ѥлницѣ бꙑв'ши, прииде дъщи ѥдиного вельможь ѥго · право-
ѣр'ныхь ѡброучена бꙑв'ши за моужь ѿ кривовѣр'ныхь тѣхь
соущи вь нихь и сьблюд'ши неч(и)стыѥ мрьзости ихь и
и мали прикоснoув'ши се вѣрѣ ихь и припад'ши кь ногама
(ве)томоу исповѣдаше ꙗсно г(лаго)лющи ѥмоу: „Г(оспод)и,
(оспод)и мои, се ѥже кождоу стезающоу се вл(а)д(и)чьствию
твоѥмоу ѡ вещи сеи мрьз'кыѥ и неприꙗзнин'ныѥ вѣры. Истиною, г(оспод)и мои, испрошена быхь по законоу брачномоу ѿ
о(ть)ца моѥго, раба твоѥго, мнещоу ѥдиновѣрьство соущоу
вл(а)д(и)чьствию твоѥмоу, и быхь оу законопрѣстоуп'ных(ь)
тѣхь, и видѣхь истиною, г(оспод)и, слоужеще ихь ѿпад'-
шоумоу славы б(о)жиѥ, самомоу сотонѣ. И не могоущии трь-
пѣти смрада глоухихь коумирь и мрьз'кыѥ ѥреси, истрьг'ши
се из роукы их(ь) и прибѣг'ши вьпию дрьжавѣ твоѥи, порази
кр(ь)стомь коpoущих' се с нами, да навик'ноуть неч(ь)стиви
врази, како можеть вѣра твоꙗ, г(оспод)и".

С(ве)ты же из'ведь сию прѣд(ь) с'борь свои сьбраны
на ѥресь тоу лоукавоую. Изьѡбличивь кривовѣриѥ ихь и сьбе-

nd while there was a great quarrel going on among them, there came orward the daughter of one of his true-believing magnates, who was narried to one of those heretics, and since she was living among them he had observed their impure abomination, while not being in the least it tainted by their belief; and falling at the feet of the holy one she nade a clear confession, saying: "Lord, my lord, behold I see that your overnment is investigating the matter of this rotten and evil faith. In ruth, my lord, I was sought in lawful matrimony from my father, your ervant, who believed that there was unity of religious belief in your ingdom, and I lived with those law-breakers and I saw, lord, that they eally do serve that renegade from God's glory, Satan himself. And not eing able to stand the stink of their deaf idols and their hateful heresy, tore myself away from their hands, and fleeing here I cry out to your tate: defeat with the cross those who oppose us, so that these accursed nemies may learn how powerful your faith is, lord!"

And the holy one brought this woman before his council, convened ecause of this cunning heresy. And when he had exposed the wrongness

сѣдовавь се сь с(ве)т(ите)лиемь си Іѳв'димиемь и сь ч(ь)ст(ь)-ными чрьн'ци и сь вельможами своими, и ни мали закьснѣвь, посла на не вьѡроужикь ѿ слав'ныхь своихь, г(лаго)ле: „Рев-ноуе поревновахь по г(оспод)ѣ б(о)зѣ в'седрьжители". Ꙗкоже иногда пpор(о)кь Илиꙗ на бестоудьние иерее вьставь и ѡб-личи без'б(о)жьствые ихь и ѡвыихь иждеже, и дроугыхь казньми различными показа, иныхь ѡземльствии ѿ вл(а)д(н)-чьствиꙗ своего и домове ихь и имѣниꙗ их' в'се сьбькоу-пивь разда ꙗ прокажен'нымь и нищиимь; оучителю же и на-чел'никоу ихь езыкь оурѣза оу грьтани его не исповѣдаюци Х(рист)а, с(и)на б(о)жиꙗ. И книгь его нечьстикыие иждеже и того вь из'гнании створии, запрѣщ' неисповѣдати ни поме-новати ѿноудь трьклетаго имене. И ѿноудь искорѣнии про-клетоую тоу вѣроу, ꙗкоже ни поменовати се ей ѿноудь вь влад(н)чьствѣ его, нь славити се единосоущнѣи и нераздѣл'-нѣи и животворещеи троици ѡ(ть)цоу и с(и)ноу и с(ве)томоу д(оу)хоу всегда и н(ы)нꙗ и пр(и)сно и вь в(ѣ)кы вѣкомь, ам(и)нь.

of their belief, and after he had consulted with Bishop Jeftimije and with his venerable monks and his magnates, he didn't delay a bit but he sent an armed force of his best soldiers against them, saying: "Zealously strove for the Lord God Almighty." Just as the Prophet Elijah once rose up against the shameless priests and exposed their godlessness, so did he burn some and he punished others with various punishments, and a third group he expatriated from his kingdom, and he distributed their houses and all their possessions to the lepers and to the poor. He cut the tongue from the throat of their teacher and leader, who did not confess Christ, the Son of God. And he burned his impious books, and when he had banished him he forbade that that thrice-cursed name be either professed or mentioned henceforth. And he completely uprooted that cursed faith, so that it was not even mentioned again in his kingdom but rather there was praise of the consubstantial and indivisible and life giving Trinity: the Father, the Son, and the Holy Spirit, always, now and forever, through all ages, Amen.

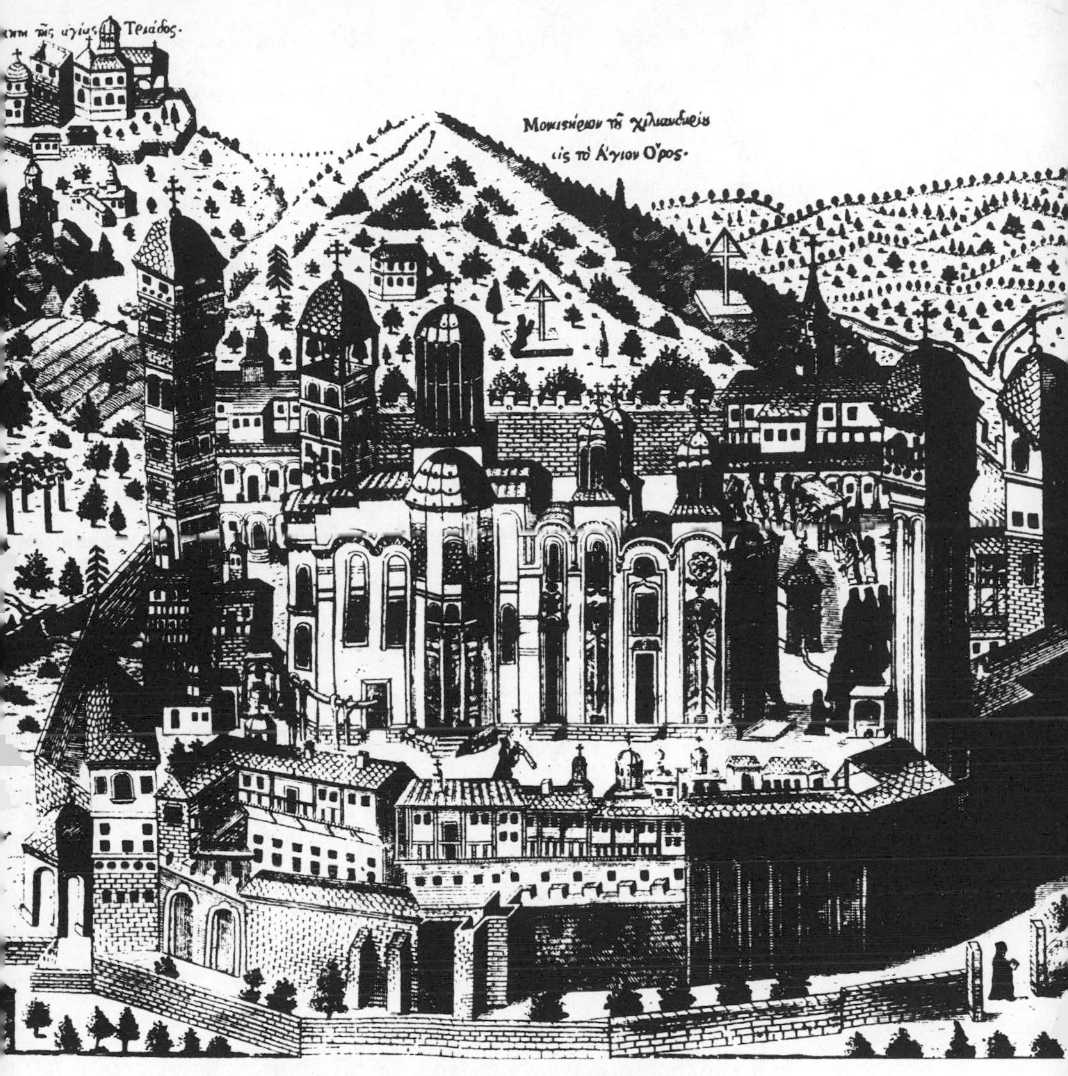

In 1196, after having ruled his state for thirty seven years, Stefan Nemanja abdicated his throne in favor of his son Stefan, and he became a monk, taking the name Simeon. He stayed first at the monastery Studenica, which he had founded, and in 1197, at the age of eighty three, he travelled to Mount Athos, to be with his son Sava. Together they supervised the reconstruction of an old monastery, which was to become the Serbian monastery of Hilandar. After three years on Mount Athos, Nemanja died. The following excerpt from Sava's life of Stefan Nemanja (Saint Simeon), describes Nemanja's death in a language that reflects both filial and religious piety.

Пришьд(ь)шоу же того м(ѣ)с(е)ца и҃і д(ь)нь рече къ мн
„Чѣдо моѐ, посли ми по ѿ(ть)ца д(оу)хо́внаго и҆ по вс
ч(ь)ст(ь)ные ста́рце Свѣ́тые Го́ры, да пріидоуть къ мнѣ҇, оу
бо приближает се д(ь)нь и҆схо́да моѐго". И҆ и҆спльнившоу
повелѣ҇нію ѐго҇, приде мно́жьство чрьньц(ь) ꙗ҆ко бл(а)гово́ных(
цвѣ́тьц(ь) цвьтещих(ь) вь тои с(ве)тѣи поустыни. И҆ приш
д'шоу же къ нѥ́моу ми́рь и҆ бл(аго)с(ло)ве́ніе пріе́мше дру
ѿ дроу́га и҆ не да́с(ть) имь ѿти́ти ѿ себе, г(лаго)ла
и҆мь: „Прѣбоу́дѣте оу҆ ме́не дондеже тѣло моѐ с(ве)тыми
чьстными ва́шими пѣс(ьн)ми опѣ҇вше и погребете". Бл(а
жены же ста́р'ць ѿ з҃го на і҃ д(ь)не, да́же и҆ до пок
ѐмоу҆ не вькоу́си хлѣ́ба ни во́ды, тьчію на вьсакь д(ь)
причещаше се с(ве)т(ы)хь и҆ прѣч(и)стых(ь) та́инь, тѣ́ла
кръве г(оспо)да б(ог)а и҆ сп(а)са на́шего І҆с(оуса) Х(рист)а.

And when there came the 18th day of that month [February he said to me: "My child, send for the spiritual father and for all t pious elders of the Holy Mountain, so that they might come to me, becau the day of my departure is already approaching." And when his ord had been fulfilled, there came a large number of monks, like fragra flowers blooming in that holy wilderness. And as each one came up him, they exchanged the sign of peace and blessed one another, and would not let them leave him, saying to them: "Stay with me until yo have sung your holy and pious songs over my body, and laid it to rest And the blessed old man, from the 17th day of the month right u until his death, did not taste bread or water, only partaking every da of the holy and most pure mysteries of communion, the body and blo of our Lord God and Savior Jesus Christ.

Nemanja's *Life* by Sava

Въ кв҃ д(ь)ны пришьд(ь)шоу того м(ѣ)с(е)ца рече: „Чѣдо
оѐ, принеси ми прѣс(ве)тоую б(огороди)цоу, тако бо имамь
бѣтованїе, ꙗко да прѣд' нею испоущоу д(оу)хь мои". И
створеноу бывшоу повелѣнїю, къ в(е)черю бывшоу, г(лаго)ла:
Чѣдо мое, сьвр'ши любовь, вьзложи на мѐ расоу, еже ес(ть)
огребенїа моего и оустрои ме съврьшено образом(ь) с(ве)тымь,
ако и вь гробѣ ми вьзлещи. И простри рогозиноу на
емли и положи ме на неи и положи камикь под(ь) главоу
ою да тоу лежю до[н]деже посѣтить ме г(спод)ь вьзети
сoудоу". Аз' же вьса испльнивь—сьтворих(ь) повелѣна
и имь. Вьсѣмь же намь зрѣщимь и плачющимь се гор'ко
рѣщемь на семь бл(а)женемь стар'ци таковаа неизр(е)чен'наа
(о)жїа смотренїа, ꙗко бо и здѐ проси оу б(ог)а и дасть
моу вь дрьжавѣ его, тако и до сего часа не вьсхоте ни
дине вещи лишити се д(оу)ховные, нь вьса б(ог)ь испльни
моу. Вь истиноу бо, братїе моа любимаа и ѿ(ть)ци, чюдо
ѣ зрети: егоже боꙗхоу се и трепетахоу вьсе страноу тъ ви-
димь бѣ ꙗко единь ѿ стран'ных(ь), нищь, расою ѡбит',
лежещь на земли на рогозинѣ и камы емоу под(ь) главою,

... And when the twenty-second day of that month came, he said to e: "My child, bring me the icon of the Blessed Mother of God, for I ve promised that I would give up my spirit in her presence." And his mmand was carried out, and when it was nearly evening he said: "My ild, do me a favor, place over me the robes which are meant for my rial, and lay me out in a completely holy manner, just the way I shall in the grave. And spread a reed mat on the ground and put me on it, d put a stone under my head so that I may lie there until the Lord sits me, to take me away from here." And in doing all these things fulfilled his commands. And all of us who were looking on were crying tterly at the sight of such inexpressible divine concern for such a blessed d man, for just as here [in Serbia—trans.] he asked God and it was ven to him during his rule, so, too, even to this hour he did not want be deprived of a single spiritual thing, and God fulfilled everything for m. For in truth, my beloved brothers and fathers, this was a wonder to e: he who had caused fear and trembling on all sides, now appeared e some stranger, destitute, wrapped in a monk's robe, lying on the ound on a reed mat, with a stone under his head, bowing to everyone

въсѣ́ми кла́нѣемоу и҆ оу҆ми́лѣющꙋ се и҆ просе́щꙋ оу҆ въсѣ́х(ь)
проще́нїа и҆ бл(аго)с(ло)ве́нїа. Но́щи же бывши прости́в'шим
се и҆ бл(аго)с(ло)вив'шим се оу҆ не́го въсѣ́мь, ѿтидо́ше в
ке́лїе слоужбы тво́рити и҆ нѣколико ма́ло покоа̀ въкоу́сити.
А҆з' же и҆ є҆ди́нь и҆е҆ре́й о҆ста́вихь съ собо́ю и҆ прѣбы́хѡвѣ оу҆
не́го въсоу̂ тоу̂ но́щь. Полоуно́щи же бы́в'шоу втиша бл(а)
же́ны ста́рць и҆ к то̂моу неѥ̀ г(лаго)лати къ мнѣ; бывш
ж(е) врѣ́мени оу҆трънıе и҆ зачь́ншоу пѣ́тїю цр(ь)ков'номоу а҆бї
просвѣти с(е) лице бл(а)же́номꙋ стар(ь)цꙋ и҆ въздви́гь на н(е)б
и҆ реч(е): „Хвали́те б(ог)а въ с(ве)тых(ь) є҆го̀, хвали́те є҆го и҆ н
оу҆твръждени си́лы є҆го̀“. А҆з' же рѣ́хь є҆моу̂: „Ѿ(ть)че, ко́г
ви́дѣ говóриши?“ О҆н же възрѣ́вь на мѐ г(лаго)ла ми
„Хвали́те є҆го и҆ на си́лах(ь) є҆го̀, хвали́те є҆го и҆ по прѣмнѡ
гомоу вл(а)д(и)чьст[в]їю є҆го̀“. И҆ се̂ ре́кшоу є҆моу̂ а҆бїе прѣ
б(о)ж(ь)ственыи д(оу)хь свои̂ и҆спꙋсти́вь оу҆спѐ о҆ г(о)с(по)дѣ.

А҆з' же па́дь на ли́ци є҆го̀ пла́ках се го́рко на дльг
ча́сь и҆ въста́вь бл(а)годарих(ь) б(ог)а о҆ си́кои кончи́нѣ ви́дѣв
се́го пр(ѣ)п(о)д(о)бнаго моу́жа.

and seeking their good graces, asking forgiveness and blessings from a
As it was night, everyone said goodbye to him and received his blessin
and they went off to their cells to carry out their duties and to rest a bi
But I remained, and I kept a priest with me, and we stayed with him a
that night. When it was midnight the blessed old man became silent, an
he didn't speak to me again; but when it was time for the matins, and th
church singing had begun, suddenly the blessed old man's face becam
suffused with light, and raising his hands to heaven he said: "Praise th
Lord among his saints; praise him in the firmament of his powers." An
I said to him: "Father, whom did you see when you were talking?
And looking at me, he said: "Praise him in his powers, praise him in h
most powerful rule." And when he had said this, he immediately gave u
his most holy spirit, and he rested in the Lord.

And I fell on his face and wept bitterly for long hours, and whe
I got up I thanked the Lord that I had been able to see such a death
this saintly man.

The Life of Saint Sava

If there is one figure in Serbian history who best epitomizes the Serbian ethos, it is that of Stefan Nemanja's son, Rastko, who is generally known by his monastic name of Sava. It was under his influence that the Serbian state of Raška, which previously had vacillated between Rome and Constantinople, committed itself irrevocably to Byzantine culture and Orthodoxy.

Rastko Nemanjić (1169-1235) lived during the High Middle Ages, a time of intense religious fervor throughout Europe, when noblemen and their ladies helped haul the stone to build the great Gothic churches such as Notre Dame of Paris and Chartres, and when learning and commerce were revived as a result of the interaction between East and West created by the Crusades.

An outgoing young man, but inclined to immerse himself in the lives of the saints and in other religious texts, Sava is said to have fled his royal home at the age of seventeen, travelling to Mount Athos, where he became a monk. Since he was the first son of a royal house to live in this monastic center of Orthodoxy, Sava's presence on Athos attracted attention throughout the Orthodox world. He applied himself vigorously to his calling, enduring long fasts and isolation, eventually impairing his health permanently. In time, Sava used his father's wealth to rebuild and maintain some of the monasteries on Athos, thus enhancing Serbia's prestige, as well as his own.

Less than two years after Stefan Nemanja abdicated his throne (in 1196), becoming a monk and taking the name of Simeon, he joined Sava on Mount Athos, where together they made plans for the establishment there of the Serbian monastery of Hilandar. Nemanja sent Sava to Constantinople in 1198, to obtain a charter for Hilandar from the Emperor Alexius III, whose daughter was married to Nemanja's son Stefan, the new ruler of Serbia. Sava was successful in his mission, and in time the monastery of Hilandar became the most important Serbian cultural center of the Middle Ages.

Eight years after the death of his father (in 1208) Sava returne to Serbia, to restore peace between his brother Stefan and their olde brother Vukan. Sava also brought with him the myrrh-giving body of the father, which he buried at the monastery of Studenica. Sava remained i Serbia, becoming active not only in church affairs, but in matters of stat as well. He succeeded in persuading the Hungarian king Andrew to ca off an offensive against Serbia. He also dealt with the Macedonian leade Strez, a former vassal of Stefan who now posed a serious threat to Easter Serbia. Although Sava could not persuade Strez to return to the fold, h was able to talk with some of Strez's deputies, who killed the rebel chie shortly after Sava left. Teodosije gives the impression (contrary to that pro vided by an earlier biographer, Domentijan) that Sava eventually turned h back on his brother Stefan, as the latter began to pursue an increasingl pro-Western policy, following the capture of Constantinople during th Fourth Crusade, in 1204. Stefan divorced his Byzantine wife and marrie the daughter of the Venetian doge Dandolo, and in 1217 he accepted crown from the legate of Pope Honorius III, whence he received the sobr quet "first-crowned" (prvovenčani). According to Sava's biographer Teo dosije, the body of Saint Simeon ceased to give off its miraculous myrrh and the people took this to mean that "Simeon has left Serbia." Sava le Serbia, too, returning to Hilandar in protest against his brother's actions.

It may be that Sava felt that if Serbia aligned herself too close to the West she would one day be annexed, as Croatia was by Hungar after the merger of 1102. It also seems likely that twelve years of monast life on Athos had left him with a strong allegiance to Orthodoxy, an probably impelled him to seek a pro-Byzantine solution. In 1219 he wen to Nicaea, refuge of the deposed Patriarch of Constantinople, Manue and of the exiled Emperor Laskaris. Aided by Laskaris, Sava persuade the Patriarch to grant autonomy to the Serbian Church, with Sav becoming its first archbishop. This was a great diplomatic coup, whic not only made possible the establishment of an independent nation church, but also considerably enhanced the prestige of the Serbian stat It was, moreover, the single most important event in Serbian cultur life during the Middle Ages, because it laid the groundwork for an ind pendent development of Serbian culture, at a time when cultural lif including education, was largely the domain of the Church. Sava returne to Serbia in triumph, eventually crowning his brother at the newly-bui monastery of Žiča. The partnership between church and state now wa sealed for the lifetime of the Serbian kingdom. Sava completely reo ganized the Serbian Church, creating new dioceses and appointing ne bishops responsible to him. He established monastic schools, and h decreed that each diocese would be given only one master copy of eac religious text, from which all other copies would be made. In this wa he hoped to prevent error and unwitting heresy.

Sava made two pilgrimages to the Holy Land, in 1229 and 123 the latter at the request of King Asen of Bulgaria, who wished to gain th

consent of the patriarchs of Jerusalem, Antioch, and Alexandria to the formation of a Bulgarian patriarchate. During his successful mission Sava also managed to visit many countries of the Near and Middle East. He was the guest of the Sultan of Cairo, visited Mount Sinai, and stopped in Armenia on his way home. He died at Trnovo, Bulgaria, in 1235. His body was returned to Serbia in 1237 and buried at Mileševa, where it is said to have remained whole and intact for centuries, the object of veneration of Moslem as well as Christian Slavs. His grave became a symbol of Serbian national feeling, which may explain why a local Ottoman ruler, Sinan Pasha, had Sava's body removed and burned, in 1595.

There is much folklore about Saint Sava. There are many stories, legends, and ballads about him, and it sometimes seems that his figure has been grafted over those of earlier, pre-Christian culture heroes. For example, there are legends about how Sava taught various tradesmen their trades, including saddlemaking, ropemaking, and cheesemaking. Perhaps because he was such a tireless traveller, both within Serbia and abroad, he often appears in folk stories disguised as an itinerant beggar, who tests the hospitality of a particular village. He is stern and even cruel with villages which are inhospitable, sometimes destroying them and creating lakes in their place. In some stories and ballads he has the power of a mythological hero, as in the ballad about Hasan Pasha, where he cripples Hasan with a glance. He can appear and disappear at will, and he controls lightning.

Many books have been written about Sava, including Bishop Nikolaj D. Velimirović's The Life of Saint Sava, *published by the Serbian Eastern Orthodox Diocese at Libertyville, Illinois (1957). Two of the more scholarly books on Sava are Stanoje Stanojević's* Sveti Sava *(Belgrade, 1927) and Vladimir Ćorović's* Sveti Sava u narodnom predanju *(Beograd, 1927). A photographic reproduction of Teodosije's* Life of Sava, *as published by Djura Daničić in 1860, was issued by Djordje Trifunović in 1973:* Teodosije Hilandarac. Život svetoga Save *(Dj. Trifunović, Beograd, ul. Geršičeva, 18). Father Mateja Matejić of Ohio State University has also recently published an interesting book on Sava (*Saint Sava; *Columbus, Ohio, 1976), which will be particularly useful to English readers.*

As for the author of Sava's Life, *the gifted monk Teodosije, we know practically nothing about him, except that he lived at Hilandar during the second half of the thirteenth century, and that he based his book on an earlier* Life *of Sava, written by the monk Domentijan.*

Saint Sava

THE LIFE OF SAINT SAVA BY TEODOSIJE

SYNOPSIS: Stefan Nemanja, founder of the Serbian medieval dynasty, and his wife Anna had not had a child for several years. They both prayed to God that he might give them one more child, who would be a consolation to them in their old age. God listened to their prayers, Anna became pregnant, and in due time she gave birth to a son, Rastko (Sava). The fond parents showered their son with love, and as he grew older he delighted all with his gentleness, sense of joy, and remarkable intelligence.

вьзраста же дошьдь лѣть еі., ѡтьдѣлнше емоу рωднтеліе страноу нѣкою дрьжавы своее, ѡтьходнтн емоу ѡть отьца на поглоумленіе сь вельможамн н сь благорωдными юнωішамн веселнтн се. юноша же вь вькоусь пришьдь разоума светынхь кннгь; паче честѣе снхь проучитааше, н ѡть (с)оудоу оубѡ зачело прѣмоудростн пріимаше божіи страхь, н сьвьспріимааше се божьственые любве дьнь ѡть дьне, ѡгнь кь ѡгню прилагае желаніемь несытнымь, царство н богатство, славоу же н свѣтлость н вьсаю благодьньствіе мнωгометежно н нестоıателно разсоуждааше, добрωть зрнмынхь н житіа обилїе ıако сѣнь

And when he had reached fifteen, his parents alloted to him a part of their state, a place where he could go to play sports with the magnates and to have a good time with the young men of noble birth. But the young man had developed a taste for the wisdom of the sacred books, and reading them more and more frequently, he gained from them the beginning of great wisdom – the fear of God, and he was receiving divine love day after day, laying fire on fire with insatiable desire; he was coming to understand that power and wealth, glory and brilliance, and every sort of happiness were very unsettling and impermanent, and he considered the visible beauties and riches of this life a shadow, so that when he

вьмѣнꙗаше, мнωгопиштїе и веселїе и вьса єлика чловѣчьскаа на ꙁемли соуєтнаа и несоуштнаа раꙁоумѣвь, десnаго поута ꙗемлꙗет се, поoучєнїємь книгь оупражнꙗает се, вь црькви по вьсе слоужбы не лѣнит се стоати, поштенїє любить, соуꙗго праꙁнословиꙗ и смѣха беꙁгоднаго иꙁбѣгаε, скврьнословесnыих же и врѣдныихь пѣснїи юношьскаа- го желанїа ωслаблꙗюштихь доушоу до коньца ненавиде, благь, кротькь, вьсѣмь оувѣтливь, ништелюбивь аште кто дроугыи, иноучьскыи же чинь иꙁ лиха почитає, ꙗко и самѣма рωдителюма его ꙁаꙁрѣти се и оустыдѣти се таковааго ωпасенїа и оустава благонравна видеште вь юнинѣ вьꙁрастѣ, и не ꙗко ωть нихь рожденна, ꙗко по истинѣ ωть бога данна непиштеваахоу. (Лѣ)тоу же ꙁı-тноу пришьдьшоу вьꙁраста его, рωдителꙗ же его пооучаста се бракоу ꙁаконномоу причетати и. молитвою же богоданныи божьствныи юноша присно желааше како и коимь оухыштренїємь мира иꙁбѣжати и ωть всѣхь кь богоу оупраꙁнити се. слышал бо бѣ ω светѣи горѣ Афона и о постештих се вь нюмь и о про-

understood that heavy eating and fun-raising, and all things human on this earth were vain and unreal, he took the right road and he studied the teachings in books, nor was he too lazy to stand through the whole service in church, he loved fasting, shunned idle talk and inappropriate laughter, despised indecent and harmful songs about youthful desires, which weaken the soul completely. Gentle and meek, kind to everyone, loving the poor like few before him, he had such great respect for the monastic order that even his parents felt ashamed and embarrassed when they saw such zeal and moral character in one so young, and they did not look on him as though he were their offspring, but rather as though he were truly a gift from God.

And when he had reached seventeen, his parents began to discuss how they might marry him in lawful matrimony. And the godly youth, given by God in answer to their prayers, was forever wishing somehow and in some way to flee the world, and to free himself from everyone and devote himself to God. For he had heard about the holy Mount Athos and about those who were fasting there, and about other desolate

ѵїнхь мѣстѣхь поустынныхь. прнхождахоу бо кь отьцоу его ѡть вьсоудоу прїимати трѣбоуемаа нмь, дроугоици же й самь посилааше кь светаа мѣста на раздааніе прѣподобно живоуштнхь, бѣ бо моужь благь, милоуе и дае ꙗко многo. богь же готовь кь молитвѣ и желанїю рабь своихь и семоу сьврьшае нзволиеніе, подвизаеть его прїнти сь роднтелюма ѡть страны даниые емоу, и пристоу бывшоу сь великою любовїю и сь благорωднимн его сь·нимь пришьдьшимь, безмѣрнон же радости и весеаїю и пироу великоу сьтвараемоу о пришьствин вьз-люблиеннаго сына кь рωднтелюма, и миωгодьневно веселештим се, и се ꙗко богомь подвигноути соуште прїидоше нѣкои ииωци ѡть светые горы Аѳона кь рωднтелюма его принети трѣбоуемаа нмь ништете поможеніе. слоучи же се едииь ѡть нихь роусинь родωмь. сегоже ѡсобь ськрнвь божьствиыи юноша о семь испыташе ꙗже о светѣи горѣ, прѣжде оутврьдивь закѣштаніемь не повѣдати таи-ноу его никомоуже. ѡн же сказаеть емоу вьса по ѵииоу поустыньскомоу, како вь мωнастырихь

places. For these people were coming to his father from everywhere, to get what they needed, and besides that he himself was sending things to the holy places for distribution to those who live most piously, because he was a gentle and compassionate man, and he gave very much. And God, who is ready to answer the prayers and wishes of his servants, fulfilled his desire too, and He moved him to leave his part of the kingdom and to visit his parents. And they received him and the noblemen who came with him with great love, and there was immeasurable joy, gaiety, and feasting because of the arrival of the beloved son at his parents' home. And they had been celebrating for many days, when lo and behold, as though sent by God, there came to his parents some monks from Holy Mount Athos, to receive the help they needed in their poverty. And it happened that one of them was a Russian by birth. And taking this person aside, the godly young man was secretly questioning him about the Holy Mountain, after first making him promise that he would tell no one his secret. And the monk told him everything about the ascetic

ѡбьштно прѣбыванїє и ѡсобно по двѣма или трємь коупнодоушно и ѡтьходно оуєдинѥнїємь вь поштенїи мльчаливѣ живоуштихь, ѡ вьсѣхь скаꙁавь ємоу иꙁештнѣ. бѣ бо и ть чрьньць не прость нь искоусьнь скаꙁаємымь, рекоу же, богомь послань бѣ. юноша же слыша ꙗже ѡ житїи иноучьскомоу и кь богоу попечєнїꙗ и добраа ихь оупражнѥнїа, рѣкою сльꙁь, источника иꙁливаахоу се ѡть очию єго. поꙁдє нѣколи ѡтьдыхавь, глагола кь старцоу: виждоу, ѡтьче, ꙗко богь провѣдыи вьса и видѣвь болѣꙁнь срьдьца моєго, посла твою светость оутѣшити мене грѣшнааго. нынꙗ оутѣши се срьдьце моє и доуша моꙗ вьꙁвесели се радостию неиꙁглаголанною. нынꙗ раꙁоумѣхь чесомоу желатель бываахь непрѣмѣнꙗємь. блажени и трьблажени таковомоу беспечалномоу и неметежномоу сподобльше се житїю. что же аꙁь створоу, ѡтьче, како вьꙁмоглъ быхь оубѣжати мнѡгометежнааго мира. сего житиꙗ и таковые жиꙁни аггелские сподобити се? єда коли родителїє мои вьсхотеть бракоу причетати ме, и любопльтїємь оудрьжань не достигноу

rule: about the communal life in the monasteries and about the separate life, with two or three living together, and also about the solitary life of those who go off and live alone, fasting in silence; he gave him an excellent account of all this, because this monk was no ordinary person, but an expert on the subject, and as I said, he was sent from God. And the young man listened to what he had to say about the monastic life and about their zeal toward God, and about their good works, and the tears were streaming from his eyes. Later, after he had got hold of himself, he said to the old man: "I see, father, that God who knows all, saw the pain in my heart and sent your holiness to comfort me, a sinner. Now my heart has been comforted, and my soul has rejoiced with an inexpressible happiness. Now I understand what it is that I have been continually desiring. Blessed, and thrice blessed are those who have merited such a carefree and untroubled life. So what should I do, father, how could I manage to escape the very turbulent life of this world and merit such an angelic life? For if my parents should marry me off I will be prevented from attaining such a life, because of lust for the flesh; after

таковааго житїа, и ни єдинь дьнь хотѣл быхь по
семь ꙁде прѣбывати, да не како любосластїє мира
сего кь мнѣ косноувши се, и не хотєштоу ми
ѡтьвлѣчеть доушоу мою таковые любьве аггелска-
го житїа, ꙗкоже оучиши, отьче. хотѣл же быхь
бѣжати, и поути не вѣдѣ, ѐда како ꙁаблоуждаю-
штоу ми на мноꙁѣ, постигь ѡтьць мои ꙗко мошт-
но моу соуштоу и вьꙁвратит ме, и вь скрьбь ѡтьца
вьложоу, и себе вь стоудь многь, и по сихь не
оуправлѥнь боудоу таковомоу рачению. Вьсприем
же старць слово глагола ємоу: желанна ѥсть люби родитель, ѡ доблии, и сьоуꙁь ѥстьства нерѣ-
шима, и милостно братиѥє єдиньство и вь коупь
хождениє. нь оубо и владыка и сихь оудобь прѣ-
обидѣти повелѣваєть, и крьсть вьꙁети на рамо, и
томоу оусрьдно послѣдовати, и вьса оудобь стра-
дати, єже ꙁа ни страсти єго подобешти се, не
вь мекыихь красовати се, не тѣлесныи искати покои, паче же наготѣ и алъчбѣ, бдѣнїю же и молитвѣ прилежати, оумилєнїю же и плачю сь
вьꙁдыханїємь и срьдьца ськроушенїємь вьнимати.

this conversation I would not want to remain here a single day, lest I be affected somehow by love for the delights of this world, which against my will might divert my soul from the love for the angelic life that you teach, father. I would like to flee, but since I don't know the way and I might wander far afield, my father could catch me, as he is capable, and turn me back, which would cause my father pain and me shame, and after that I would not achieve what I desire.

And the old man began to speak, saying: "O most exemplary young man, parental love is desirable, it is an unbreakable natural bond, but the unity and communal living with one's brothers is most benign. For the Lord has commanded us to despise these things easily, and to take up the cross on our shoulders and zealously follow after him, and to suffer all things effortlessly, imitating his passion for our sake, and he has also commanded us not to adorn ourselves in soft clothes, but to apply ourselves to nakedness and hunger, vigil and prayer, and to respond to unhappiness and lamentation with sighing and contriteness of heart. . . . .

Радости

же великыѥ ѡ сихь исплынь бывь, и ни мала ѡть-
ложь, кь рѡдителюема вьходить, оукрадаеть ѡть-
поуштеніѥ, просить по ѡбычаю молитвоу и бла-
гословеніѥ, глаголѥ: господїе мои, вь ѡнои горѣ,
и име ѥи приложь, повѣдаше ми ѕвѣрїе соуште
мнѡгы. аште ѡбрѣть милость, благословень боудоу ками и ѡтьпоуштень боудоу ловити, и аште
оукьснымь, не прогнѣванию боудемь повинни,
идеже оубо мнѡгые елене слышахь. Ѡтьць же
его оугодне емоу творе, господь с тобою, глагола, чедо, да благословит те и исправить поуть
твои. И мати же, ꙗко матери обычаи, обьемши
и целовавши любьѕно, ѡтьпоустише и сь мирѡмь,
ѕаповѣдавша скоро вьѕвратити се. не бѡ вѣдѣ-
аста ꙗко не елене хоштеть оуловити, нь источника животнаго Христа, ꙗко напоити оуелениѥноу
доушоу его, ѕапалившоую се ѡгниѥмь желаннымь
любве его. на оувѣреніѥ же родителю посилаеть
вь горoу лѡвештихь, на се оуготованнѡмь, ꙗко
сьгнати ѕвѣры, самь рекь: подь горою до оутрѣи

And being filled with a great joy because of all this, and not delaying at all, he went to his parents and tricked them into letting him go, and he asked for their prayers and blessing, saying: "My lords, I have been told that in such and such a mountain, and he gave the name, there are many wild animals. Please be so kind as to give me your blessing and your leave to go hunting; and if we are late in returning please don't be angry at us, because I have heard that there are many deer there." And his father approved, saying: "The Lord be with you, my son, and may he direct you toward what is right." And his mother, as is the way with mothers, embraced him and kissed him nicely, and gave him her leave with peace, commanding him to return quickly. For they did not know that he was not going to hunt deer, but Christ, the fountain of life, that he might slake his deer-like soul, which burned with the fire of longing for his love. To reassure his parents he sent hunters to the mountain, and dressed as though he were going hunting he said to them: "I will wait for you at the foot of the mountain until morning." And

вась ѡжидаю. и ношти соушти иже сь нимь бла-
горѡдныимь веселештим се и оусноувшимь, сь
своими малыми хранештими таиноу его, прѣдь-
водештааго ихь бога сь инокѡмь имоуште, бѣгомь
бѣжеште оубѣжаше. дьню же освьтшоу,- благо-
рѡдныи ѡни вьзыскаахоу господїна своего, и се не
бѣ где видѣти и, ни обрѣсти. глаголахоу: еда по-
глоумлѥе се намь, кь ѡтьцоу вьзврати се? поискавше
же и мниха, иже бѣ сь нимь, и проуїихь ѡть слоугь
его, и ни сихь ѡбрѣтше, глаголаахоу: что иже ѡ
нась оужась сь? камо се дѣ господинь нашь?

when it was night, and the noblemen who were with him had enjoyed themselves and gone to sleep, he fled at top speed, together with the few who knew his secret, guided by God and monk. And when it was daybreak the other noblemen looked for their lord, and lo and behold, he was nowhere to be seen or to be found. And they said: "Can it be that he is playing a trick on us, and that he has already returned to his father's house?" And they also looked for the monk who had been with him, and for his remaining servants, and when they did not find them they said: "What terrible thing has happened to us? Where has our lord disappeared?"

[Rastko made good his escape to Mount Athos, where he was tonsured and became a monk, taking the name Sava. In time, his aged father abdicated his throne and joined his son at Athos, where they built the famous Serbian monastery of Hilandar. Sava eventually became the first archbishop of an independent Serbian Orthodox Church. He died in Bulgaria, on his return from a trip to the Holy Land. Although his remains were eventually removed from the church of the forty martyrs in Trnovo, Bulgaria, where he was first buried, his tomb continued to be the source of miraculous cures, as in the following story about the cripple Neofit.]

Вь томже монастыри царевѣ бѣше нѣкын инокь Неѡфить нарицаемь. ть оубо ѡть многыхь лѣть слоукь сы, и ни мала могын кьздвигноути се, царем же повелѣнь бѣ вь монастыри его хранити се. светомоу же егда еще вь живѡтѣ вь монастырь ть пришьдьшоу многоу милость чловѣкѡлюбно кь немоу показавшоу, на колѣноу бо и на дрѣвїахь роукама опирае се, по земли пльже, зѣло страдално житїе прохождаше. по прѣставлѥнїи же и по прѣнесенїи моштеи светаго нѣкыимь страннымь вь монастырь ть пришьдьшимь, и сего Неѡфита любовїю бога ради на трапезоу прїемшимь, и доволно оугостившимь того и напоившимь, ꙗко не мошти емоу свое рогозины допльзѣти и покои полоучити, страннїим же изьшьдьшимь, и сего Неѡфїта вь припратѣ црьковнои ѡставившимь, ѡн же виномь отегоштень, и не вѣды что

In that same imperial monastery there was a certain monk named Neofit. Now he had been crippled for many years, and he couldn't straighten up even a little, so the Emperor commanded that he be fed in his monastery. And Saint Sava, when he was still alive and used to come to that monastery, was very kind to that man, because he used to creep along the ground, supporting himself on his knees and on crutches and he led a very painful existence. After the passing away of the Saint, and the transfer of his relics, some foreigners came to the monastery and they accepted Neofit at their table, out of love for God, and they gave him so much to eat and drink that he couldn't creep away to his reed mat to rest; and when the foreigners had gone out and left this Neofit in the church refectory, loaded with wine and not knowing what

не соумне се творить, възлег бо на камень, иже бѣ врьхоу гроба светаго, и на нюмь спе покои прїимаше. кь полоуноштїю же ѩко се нѣкымь свѣтлымь възбоуждень бывь, и вь незаапоу ѡть гроба светаго вьскоуь, абїе и прость на ногахь своихь стое себе разоумѣвь, оужасом же оудивлѧше се вь себѣ глаголе: Гоубω азь ли есьмь Неωфїть? и аште азь есмь, како прость стою, и ходе есмь? не вчера ли азь бѣхь на колѣноу и дрѣвїахь по земли пльже, и нынѧ прость и безь вьсакое споны есьмь ходити? что оубω о мнѣ оужась сьи? не вѣдѣ аште азь есьмь. Оувѣрити же се хоте вештїю, аште ть самь ѥсть Неофїть, и възыскавь дрьвїа, на нихже роукама ωпирае се по земли прѣсмикаше се, и сихь идеже бѣ лежаль на гробѣ светаго обрѣть, ωсезав же се по колѣнома, и сихь пльстїю и кожею ωшвенѣхь разоумѣвь глагола: ѩко вь истинноу безь всакое пре азь есмь Неωфїть, се бо и ωбразы еже по земли страданїа моего извѣствоують ме ѩко самь азь есмь. Весел же и зѣлω радостьнь ω своемь

to do, he didn't think twice about it, but he lay down on the stone slab over the saint's tomb, and he went to sleep. Toward midnight he was awakened as though by some shining being, and he suddenly jumped up from the saint's tomb, and all at once he realized that he was standing on his own; and he was filled with wonder and awe, as he said to himself: "Is this really me, Neofit? And if it is me, then how is it that I am standing on my own and can move about? Wasn't it just yesterday that I was creeping along the ground, on my knees and using crutches, and now I can walk on my own, without any support? What sort of horror has happened to me? I don't know if this is me." And wanting to make sure that he was himself, Neofit, he looked for the crutches on which he used to lean while creeping along the ground, and he found them on the tomb of the saint, where he had lain down. And touching his knees he felt the felt and the hide that covered them, and he said: "Really, there's no use arguing, I am Neofit, for this evidence of my suffering along the ground shows me that I am me." Happy and very joyful about his cure,

ꙁдрави бывь бога похвалꙗше. кь гробоу же светаго главою біє, и оумилꙗє се, глаголаше: кыими благодѣтми дароносивь азь ништїи к тебѣ, ѡтьче, ꙗвлю се? коими ли почьстми чюдодѣистьвныи светыи твои гробь оукрасити вьꙁмогоу? благопохвалꙗю те, благыи ѡтьче Саво, ꙗко вь живѡтѣ сыи, чловѣкѡлюбно милостїю по ꙁемли страждоущоу ми помилова, и кь господоу ѡшьдьшоу ѡть нєго дрьꙁновенїємь ѡть ꙁемлѥ пльꙁанїа проста ходити вьꙁдвиже ме. мнѣ бо страждоущомоу ѡгнємь ѡть бога сьжеженоу быти подобнѣ, или бѣсѡмь вьданоу быти моучити ме, или ꙁемли повелѣнїємь єго пожрѣти ме, ꙁа нєже многомь оупитїємь беꙁвѣстно на светѣмь гробѣ твоємь вьꙁлегша и спавша, ты же вь (ѡть)мьштенїа мѣсто и ѡть свеꙁавшаго мене доуха ѡтьрѣшь, ꙁдрава оустроиль єси, и кь ꙁлобѣ благоѡдатлив ми бысть. блаже и пакы оублажаю те, светьче божїи, доидеже и гроб ме прїиметь. по истинѣ благаго и беꙁлобиваго истиннаго єси бога оученикь, и ꙁаповѣди єго сьблюдае, сице о мнѣ

he was praising God and beating his head against the tomb of the saint, and he became upset, saying: "With what good things can I, a poor man, appear before you, father, bearing gifts? With what honors can I decorate your miraculous, holy tomb? I thank you most gratefully, gentle father Sava, for being so kind to me when you were alive and I used to creep along the ground; and when you went away to the Lord, you, with His permission, raised me from creeping along the ground to walking on my own. But it would be more fitting that I, a sufferer, be burned with fire by God, or handed over to devils to be tormented, or swallowed up by the earth at his command, because I drank too much and lay down on your tomb without knowing it, and I slept there, but instead of getting even with me, you liberated me from the spirit that had bound me, and you made me whole, and so you met malice with generosity. I praise you, and I will praise you again and again, O saint of God, until the grave shall receive me. Truly you are the disciple of the gentle, kindly and true God, and it is in keeping his commandment that you have done

сьтворилъ еси. Сими пооучающтоу се глаголы, и сь сльзами молештоу се оу гроба светаго реченномоу Неофїтоу, и авїе вь оутрьни парамонарь црькве светыихь .м. моученикь вьжешти кандила вь црьковь вьниде. видѣв же чловѣка оу гроба светаго стоешта, оубоꙗв се ѕѣлѡ и страхомь смете се, непштеваше бо призракь быти или татїе вьшьдьше вь црьковь. вь себѣ же бывь, глаголаа: кто ты еси? и ѡть коудоу прѣжде вьсѣхь вь црьковь вьшьль еси? ѡн же припадь на ѕемлю, поклони се емоу глаголѥ: аѕь есьмь грѣшьныи Неофїть, иже до вчера слоукь и на колѣноу валꙗх се. Видѣв же его парамонарь проста вьсего и ѕдрава ходешта, вештьшимь страхомь обьеть бывь, мнѣвь мьчтанїе нѣкое быти, ѕнаменїемь же крьстнымь оукрѣпив се, глагола кь нѥмоу: аште ты еси слоукыи Неофїть, ꙗкоже глаголѥши, то како еси прость, и сь всакою крѣпостїю ныниꙗ ходиши? Глагола ѡнь: не вѣдѣ, ѡтьче, богь вѣсть, едино вѣмь ꙗко вь вчерашныи дьнь страннїимь ѡнѣмь пришьдьшимь и доволно любовїю на-

this for me." And the aforesaid Neofit was edifying himself with these words and was tearfully praying at the tomb, when suddenly there entered the church for matins the sexton of the Church of the Forty Holy Martyrs, to light the candles. And when he saw a man standing at the tomb of the saint, he became very much afraid and he was overcome with fright, for he thought it was a ghost, or a thief that had entered the church. And getting hold of himself he said: "Who are you? And how is it that you have entered the church before everyone else?" But falling to the ground he bowed before him, saying: "I am the sinful Neofit, who until yesterday was crippled and hobbled along on my knees." Seeing him completely whole and walking normally, the sexton was gripped by an even greater fear, thinking that this was some trick, and making the sign of the cross for protection, he said to him: "If you are the cripple Neofit, as you say you are, then how is it that you are healthy and moving around with full power?" He said: "I don't know, father, God knows. I only know that yesterday, when those foreigners came and kindly gave

питавшимь ме и оупоившимь, ꙗко не мошти ми рогозины мое доплъзевшоу покои полоучити, вьсклоних же се кь гробоу светаго Савы срьбина, и безвѣстїемь врьхоу его вьзлегь спахь. кь полоуноштїю же свѣтьль нѣкыи кь свештеннаа и свѣтлаа одѣань сь жьзломь надь спешта ме пришьдь, и потикае ме глагола: на гробѣ моемь спиши; вьставь скоро сьниди. аз же ѡть свѣтлости его оубоꙗв се, и безь вьсакое споны ѡть гроба по глаголоу его вьскочихь, и сьноу же страхомь ѡть мене ѡшьдьшоу, абїе разоумѣх се прость оу гроба светаго стое. много же стоꙗхь плаче се кь светомоу, и моле се ѡ помиловани моего ѡкаанства, дондеже и ты вьниде, ѡтьче. Парамонар же сїа ѡть нѥго слышавь, чюдесе оудивлѥнїемь страхь измѣнивь, глагола кь нѥмоу: аште тако ѥсть, ꙗкоже глаголѥши, то дрѣвїа, на нихже ѡпирае се по земли страдаль еси, хоштоу видѣти ихь, и ѡть сихь оувѣрити се. Ѡн же близь гроба светаго лежештихь сихь оуказавь, и колѣнѣ же свои пльстїю и кожею ѡбвезанѣхь показавь, оувѣри се емоу ꙗко истиноу глаголѥть.

me food and drink, I couldn't creep back to my reed mat to rest, so I made my way to the tomb of Saint Sava the Serb, and without knowing it I lay down on it and went to sleep. But toward midnight some shining person, dressed in a priest's clothes and radiant, with a scepter, leaned over me while I was sleeping, and pushing me he said: "You are sleeping on my tomb; get up at once, and come down off it." And that light scared me, so as soon as he said it I jumped off his tomb, without leaning on anything. And now wide-awake because of my fear, I immediately realized that I was standing by myself at the tomb of the saint. And for a long time I stood crying to the saint, and praying to him for having had mercy on me in my misery, until you entered, father." When the sexton had heard these things from him, he changed from fear to wonder at the miracle, and said: "If it is as you say it is, then I would like to see the crutches you used to lean on when you struggled along the ground, and then I will be convinced." And he pointed them out to him, lying near the tomb of the saint, and he showed him his knees, wrapped with felt and leather, and he convinced him that he was telling the truth.

славн ѿбѣгноувь славоу ѡбрѣтеса
такло ѿюдоу слава іавнсе родоу; ✕
ода свѣтлость вѣры свѣтлость прѣ
зрѣ, тѣкьже родоу свѣтнло іавнсе
всеклоу; ✕ хлава высата санавы
сѡтоу свьрьже, тѣкь оубо оук
выше доброту стиже.
слова славн савѣ сьплете снлоуан

Siluan's Song to Saint Sava

This brief but intricate poem of praise to Saint Sava is a rare jewel in medieval Serbian literature. The text of the poem refers to Sava's flight from his royal home to Mount Athos, where he became a monk; in shunning the light of secular power, the poet says, Saint Sava became a model ("a beacon") for all his people. The poem is patterned after the twelve-syllable Byzantine line, with obligatory caesura after the first hemistich of seven syllables (for further discussion of its poetics, consult Roman Jakobson's article in Zbornik za filologiju i lingvistiku, *knj. IV-V, 1961-62, 131-139).*

Just who the poet-monk Siluan was is not clear, since it appears there were several fourteenth and fifteenth-century Hilandar monks with that name, as was pointed out by Dragoljub Pavlović and Radmila Marinković in their book: Iz naše književnosti feudalnog doba *(Beograd: Prosveta, 1968). We only know that these verses were first found in a fifteenth century manuscript collection belonging to the monastery of the Holy Trinity at Plevlja, and that the poem was first published by the Serbian printer Božidar Vuković, in 1536-1538, in a praznični minej (a holy day menaion or book of readings from the lives of the saints).*

Saint Sava

С ла́вы ѿбе́гноу[illegible]

Слави отбегнув, славу обрете, Саво,
Тамо отјуду слава јави се роду.
Рода светлост вери светлост презре,
Тем же роду светило јави се всему.
Ума висота сана висоту сврже,
Тем убо ума више доброту стиже.
Слова слави Саве сплете Силуан.

SILUAN'S SONG TO SAINT SAVA

Fleeing glory, you found glory, Sava,
There whence glory appeared to your people.
The light of faith for your people, you scorned the light,
And thereby you appeared as a beacon to all your people.
Loftiness of intelligence superseded loftiness of position,
Thereby achieving a virtue beyond intelligence.
Siluan composed these words of praise to Sava.

The Serbian monastery of Dečani

The Life *of Stefan Dečanski, Serbian king from 1321-1331, with its heart-rending story of the blinding of Stefan by his father, King Milutin, offers an unforgettable reminder of the dynastic rivalry that plagued the Serbian Empire and speeded its downfall.* *The Life of Stefan Dečanski*

Grigorije Camblak (1364-1418), Stefan Dečanski's biographer, was a Bulgarian, born and raised in Trnovo. A churchman, Grigorije Camblak was educated in the famous school of Euthymius of Trnovo at a time when the hesychastic movement had reached its peak of influence in the Bulgarian Orthodox Church, and when Euthymius was leading a revision of Church Slavonic writing, known as "ispravlenie knig" (the correction of books). The latter current aimed at the restoration of certain archaic features of Old Church Slavonic writing, as well as the incorporation of some highly stylized syntactic arrangements known as the "pletenie sloves" (word weaving).

After the fall of Bulgaria to the Turks (1393), Grigorije lived in Constantinople, Mount Athos, Serbia, Moldavia, and Russia. He wrote the Life *of Stefan Dečanski (ca. 1405) while he was abbot of the Monas-*

*tery of Dečani, near Peć. Dragoljub Pavlović (*Srpska književnost u sto knjiga, *I) believes that Camblak wrote the* Life *"to promote as much as possible the cult of Stefan Dečanski as a martyr-saint and as a miracle worker." It seems also likely that Camblak, a well-educated man and acquainted with medieval secular as well as religious literature, perceived the human interest that the story of Dečanski was certain to evoke through such story elements as: Stefan's high station as king's son, his fall from favor through a woman's treachery, his ruthless blinding by his father's henchmen, his miraculous cure, and his eventual accession to the throne. Judging from the many manuscripts of Dečanski's* Life *still extant, particularly in Russia, Camblak was not wrong in his estimate of the popularity this story would enjoy in the Orthodox lands.*

Grigorije Camblak was an outstanding Slavic Orthodox writer of the early fifteenth century; of his writings there have come down to us some twenty-seven homilies, a sermon on the translation of the relics of Saint Paraskeva or Petka Trnovska from Vidin to Serbia, an adaptation of Euthymius's Life *of Paraskeva, and the* Life *of Stefan Dečanski). He was also noteworthy as a church administrator, as well as an international activist for a reconciliation between the Orthodox and the Roman Churches. Having already seen his own homeland fall to the Turks, along with large parts of Serbia, Camblak may have understood the full gravity of the Turkish threat more clearly than many statesmen of his time. Šafařik states that Camblak led a delegation of Lithuanian boyars to Rome and Constantinople, in an effort to heal the rift between the two branches of Christianity; Camblak failed, and Constantinople fell to the Turks some thirty years later (*Glasnik društva srbske slovesnosti, *knj. XI, Beograd 1859, 37).*

Camblak's Life *of Dečanski is also interesting for its attempt to explain how evil sometimes triumphs in the world and how the all-powerful hand of Providence fails to prevent a misdeed, even though an omniscient God knows about it even before it takes place. Grigorije's explanation is that such evil deeds as the blinding of Stefan Dečanski by his father are meant to be a test of man's faith.*

The biographer of Stefan's father, King Milutin (ruled 1282-1321), differs with Camblak as to the reason for Milutin's cruel punishment of his son: Danilo sees this act as a punishment for Stefan's "disobedience" and his plotting with other nobles against his father, whereas Camblak attributes the whole tragedy to the weakness of a woman, Milutin's wife, who turned father against son, at the devil's urging.

Njegoš probably had this incident in mind when, in Gorski Vijenac, *the kolo sings of Serbian rulers who persecuted one another, "one putting out the eyes of the other."*

Месеца Поемвріа. а҃і. житїе и жителство светаго великомоученика въ царехь Стефана сръбьскаго. иже въ дѣчахъ съписано григорїемь минхωмь и прѣзвитерωмь, игоуменωмь бывшимь тоежде ωбытѣли.

Благослови ωтьче.

Бѣше и се великааго и славнѣишааго сръбьскаго ѥзыка. не тъкмо конистиьными силами дроугыхь ѥзыкь прѣвъсхωдити. и славою и бωгатьствωмь. и мѣста красотою и величьствомь. иже ωкрьсть соущихь прѣодолѣвати. нъ и царьми благочьстывѣишими и прѣмоудрїими красовати се и похвалити. къ нимь же и паче ꙗко имѣе любовь.

Корѣнь оубо благь сїи ꙗко же рѣхь Сумеωнь, доволнїи наслѣдникы изьостави царствїю. вь свое врѣмѣ ωть сихь которагождω наслѣдство прѣемлюща. не ꙗко же великааго Костантина синове же и нетїе възмоущающе црьковь еретичьскыими влънами. и еллинскыими скварами же и

The eleventh of November: the life and feats of the holy great artyr, who among emperors was called Stefan the Serbian, whose reains are at Dečani; written by Grigorije, the monk and priest, who was bbot of that same cloister

Bless us, Father!

He was of the great and most glorious Serbian nation. Not only id it surpass other nations in military forces, and overcome those in s vicinity with its glory, and its wealth, and the beauty and majesty of e place, but it was also graced and praised for its most pious and wise mperors, with whom it even seemed to be in love . . .

Now the root of these blessings, Simeon, as I said, left sufficient eirs to his kingdom, who took over its rule, each in his time. Unlike the ons and nephews of Constantine the Great, who were stirring up the hurch with waves of heresy, Hellenic inanities, and fables, they were

басньми. нъ благочьстивѣ и богомоудрьнѣ же и боголюбьзнѣ правеще воинствное и прочее вѣроученое стадо.

Начинающоу же ми повѣсть о великомȣченицѣ и цари. вънимати ȣсрьдно молю. боголюбьзныихь[5] ваших дȣшахь прѣдложенїе. и аще что недостатъчно боудеть. прошоу вась милости сподобити ме. иномоу инако повѣдающимь ми и которомоу же сихь своа оутврьдити хотѣщȣ. нъ азь на мȣченика оуповавь, ни ѡнѣмь ни ѡнѣмь благодеть исповѣдоую, нъ того помощи надѣавь се, къ того похвалномоу житїю ȣстрьмихь повѣсть.

Милоутинь иже по великомоу сумеѡнȣ четврьти раждаеть Стефана, великаго благочьстїа стльпа и царьствїа веньць. и юже вь съврьшеноу мѣроу възраста бѣше, текоущȣ на мноѕѣ врѣмени. ѡбрадованьнь же и свѣтль къ въсѣмь. страхоу господню поучаше се присно. и тѣмь ѡть вьсакого оукланѣше се ѕлаа. и многаа оубѡ иже ѡть юности моужа исправленїа благопристоупнь

piously, and prudently, and reverently directing the army and the re[st] of the flock entrusted to them.

In beginning my story about the great martyr and emperor, [I] sincerely beg your reverent souls to pay attention to what is offered her[e] and if something should be incomplete I beg you to favor me with yo[ur] kindness. Different people tell a story differently, each one wishing [to] support his own point of view. But I, trusting in the martyr, do n[ot] profess the advantages of one over the other, but rather I hope for th[e] help of the one whose praiseworthy life I have striven to tell.

Milutin, who was the fourth in line after the great Simeon, sire[d] Stefan, the great pillar of piety and the crown of the kingdom. And h[e] had already reached his full growth, having spent much time being joyf[ul] and cheerful towards all, continually edifying himself with fear of th[e] Lord, and in this way avoiding every kind of evil. And he [made] man[y] courageous self-improvements during his youth. He was polite to tho[se]

кь бесѣдоующимь. тихь словωмь. милостивь къ страждоущїимь. грьдиие же толико възгноушаше се. ꙗко таковомоу иниже поне тωго ωчима ꙗвлꙗти се. тѣмь и въсѣмь срьдца и разоуми къ тωго любвы распалꙗхоу се. и вьсь бѣше вышнꙗго положивь помощника себѣ, и кь томоу единомꙋ зрѣше. нъ что пострада. завысть дїавωль пωдвиже доброе присно ненавидеи. слоуженїю же такову. жена тωго вьслоужитель ω мнохь сльзь. аще прѣродителюко къ раи великомоудрїе прѣможе женскаа лъсть. здѣ что нехотѣше сътворити ω тьщаемыхь. и слышите. Приходить царица кь цароу. лице показоуеть дреxло. неоукрашень и неωбычнь вьхωдь. слъѕы испоущаеть. и иже ωть вьноутрь пламенемь прѣсѣцаеть глась. и да съкратикь рекоу. на ослѣплюенїе ωтьца подвижеть прьвородномоу синꙋ. Сиioу въ истиноу пωдобноу Ïсаакоу. благопокоренїемь и послоушанїемь. не невѣдѣаше оубω онь ꙗже ω немь оумышлꙗемаа. нъ и множаишїими ωть кнеѕовь и вельмоужїи таино оучимь бѣше, кь некоеи ωть иже тамо странахь съ множьствωмь

who talked with him, soft-spoken, and merciful to the suffering; and he loathed only those who were proud, as though he didn't want even to lay eyes on such a person. For this reason the hearts and minds of all were enflamed with love for him. And he had fully established the One on high as his helper, and he looked toward Him alone. But why did he suffer? The Devil put envy to work, he who especially hates the good. And the instrument for such a purpose was his wife. O my tears! If a woman's deceit could overcome our forefather's wisdom in paradise, what could it not do to the zealous here. And hark! The Queen comes to the Emperor. She shows a sad face. She makes an ugly and uncustomary entrance. She lets the tears fall, and her voice cracks from inner emotion. And to make it brief, she moves the father to blind his first-born son, a son in truth like Isaac, both in submissiveness and obedience. Now he himself did not know about the things that were planned against him, but he was advised secretly by very many princes and magnates to take refuge, with many of his soldiers, in one of the countries there, and to

вои оуклонити се. и ѡть иже оубо нань сьши-вaемїе избѣжати льсти. съкрьшене же вь все съ-дрьжанїе царьствїа ѡдѣати се. нъ невьсхотѣ сихь послоушати. болше соудивь божїе еже ѡ нюмь ѡкръмлюнїе.

„Владико всехь“ глаголю „и боже. видимїе же и невидимїе твари едине сьдѣтелю. вѣси срьд-ца свѣдѣтелствованиыихь . вѣси прѣжде вься бытїа ихь. помишлюнїе члoвеческо исповѣсть се тебѣ ...
Выждь аще юсть неправда вь срьдци моемь. виждь аще поуть безаконїа въ мнѣ. испитаеи срьдца и оутробн боже праведно. виждь аще истинна соуть ѡ ихь же оглаголоують ме. и соуди праведна. и оутиши неправедно на ме ожесточившоую се родителноую оутробоу. и прѣѡбрати на миловaнїе милости, движоущее се стрьмлюнїе,

flee from the plot that had been shaped against him, and to take o
himself the full trappings of the Empire. But he didn't care to pay hee
to them, judging that God's direction was better . . .

“Lord of all,” he was saying, “and God, the sole Creator of wha is visible and invisible: You know the hearts of those whom You hav created, You know their whole lives in advance, men's thoughts ar known to you(. . .) See if there is any injustice in my heart, see if th road to lawlessness lies within me; O God, who righteously tests ou hearts and emotions, see if what they are saying against me is true, an judge justly, and calm my parent's emotions, which have become un-justly infuriated against me, and turn this gathering onslaught into lovin mercy . . .”

The *Life* of Stefan Dečanski

Сице доблѥствныи стефань тѣснотоу срьдца своего богоу єдиномꙋ вѣдомо творе и нань вьсоу надеждоу спасенїа възлагае. въ царьскыихь хождаше благоговѣииѣ оубѡ и благочинииѣ. радѡстьнь кь вьсѣмь показоуе обычаи ѥстьствныи. Въ прѣдстоаныи же иже кь ѡтьцоу смѣрень нѣкаковь и своиствнь образь имѣе по истинѣ. нь оумльча промышлѥнїа сила о таковѣмь начинанїи, ꙗко да и неправедною ꙗзвою искоушень бывь, праведнымь вѣнцѣмь ѡть живоначелнїе вѣнчаеть се роукы. Єго же кромѣ троудѡвь и потовь єже о истинѣ, невъзможно спѡдѡбыти се комоу. Что иже ѡть здѣ. достоинаа оумилѥнїа и слъѕамь повѣсть прѣодоле женскаа лъсть: побѣди се царева прѣмоудрость. женьскыимь оухыщренїемь. подклониисе ѡтьчаа моудрѡсть женскои слабости. оугасе родителнаа топлота жени бестоудїемь. еть бываеть праведни неправедно. незлобывїи навѣтомь лютѡмь. милостивїи немилостивно. и ѡ безмѣстїа , ѡчїю лишаеть се.

Thus did the brave Stefan make known to the one God the anxiety in his heart, placing all his hopes for salvation in Him. In the Imperial Court he walked piously and with composure, displaying his natural, joyful ways toward everyone. In truth, he had a certain modest and self-composed mien when standing before his father. But the power of Providence became silent in the face of such plans, so that he might be tested by an unjust wound, so that he might be crowned by the life-giving hand with the crown of the just, which it is impossible for anyone to merit except through labor and toil for the truth. And what happened next? Feminine deceit, worthy of pity and cause for tears, triumphed: imperial wisdom was defeated by female trickery, fatherly wisdom submitted to female weakness, parental warmth was extinguished by a woman's shamelessness, the just was taken unjustly, the unmalicious by a cruel trap, the merciful unmercifully, and O, what impropriety, he was deprived of his eyes! . . .

Ꙗко оуко стефань сїе пострада оумилѥнное лишенїе ѕрака. мѣсто же бѣше идѣ же сїѥ сьдѣа се, полѥ овчее именоуемо . идѣ же и храмь молитвнїи бѣше, великомоу архїерархоу хрїстовоу николаꙋ. и лютѣ ѡть болѣѕни страдалцоу пробадаемоу, и иѕнемогшоу послѣднѥе и лежещоу не безь мала мрьткоу. нощи скончавающи се сьномь тьнкомь обьѥть бываеть. и ѕрыть моужа прѣдставша емоу, свещеннолѣпно видѣнїе имоуща. светителъскою же ѡдѣждею оукрашена соуща. благодети же свѣтлость на лици моужоу сїаше. носеща на дѣснои своѥи длани ѡбѣ его иѕвръженнїе ѡчи, и глаголюща къ нѥмоу. „не скръбы стефане. Се бо на длани моеи твои ѡчи.“ и съ слѡвомь покаѕокалше емоу носимое. ѡнь же ꙗко мнѣше се глагола къ нѥмоу. и ктѡ еси тыи господи мои иже толикое о мнѣ прилѣжанїе твореи. и ꙗвлѥи се азь есмь рече николае, мирїиликыискыихь епископь.

Thus did Stefan suffer this touching deprivation of sight, and the place where this took place was called "the sheep field," where there also was a shrine to Christ's great archpriest, Nicholas. And then the sufferer, who was fiercely pierced with wounds, and who had been weakened in the extreme and was lying not far from death, fell into a light sleep as night was drawing to a close. And he saw a man standing before him, who had a saintly appearance, and who was adorned in a bishop's robes. And the light of grace was shining in his face, and he was carrying in his right palm both the removed eyes, and he said to him: "Don't be sad, Stefan. For look, your eyes are in my palm." And having said this he showed him what he was carrying. And he, as though he were just imagining it, said to him: "And who are you, my lord, to take such pains for my sake?" And he who had appeared said: "I am Nicholas, the Bishop of Myra."

The Vinodol Law Code

*Vinodol, or "Wine Valley" (*Vallis Vinearia *in Roman times), is located near the North Croatian Coast. Some time after the settling of the Croats in this region, in the sixth or seventh century, the towns and villages of Vinodol grouped together in a loose confederation. Although we have no information on the functioning of the Vinodol communal government, we can speculate about its chief offices, some of which are mentioned in the* Vinodol Law Code of 1288. *There we find cited a common council, consisting of all the voters of the valley; the local judge* (sudac); *the chief clerk or mayor of a town (*satnik, *from the čakavian word for "one hundred," similar perhaps in origin to the Roman centurion); a clerk (*graščik, *from* grad, *likely the community fiscal officer); and the crier* (buščik). *Other, minor officers mentioned are the* pristavi, *who were court officers as well as oral notary publics, and the* porotnici, *who acted as character witnesses at trials; since both of these offices are also cited in the Serbian Emperor Dušan's* Law Code of 1349, *this may be an indication of their common Slavic provenance.*

The autonomy or semi-autonomy that the Vinodol community enjoyed both before and during the Croatian Kingdom (924-1102), and perhaps for a century after the merger with Hungary, eroded precipitously after 1225, when King Andrew II of Hungary gave the valley to Vid, the Count (Knez) *of Krk. The resultant loss of the community's autonomy is clearly reflected in the* Vinodol Law Code of 1288, *whose main function was to legitimize the feudal relationship that had developed during the preceding sixty years between the "Counts of Krk, Vinodol, and Modruš" (later known as the "Frankapani") and the remaining population of the valley. That the code was written on behalf of the* knezovi, *and not on behalf of the people (as the preamble would have us believe), can be deduced from the fact that the great majority of the crimes listed are treated as though they were crimes against the count, for it is he who receives all or part of nearly every fine or penalty. For example, if a woman is caught at witchcraft* (vračanje), *she has to pay 100 libras to the count, or be*

burned at the stake. (This fine, which was the equivalent of the wergeld, was heavy indeed, if Marko Kostrenčić is correct in stating that at the time the price of an ox was 8 libras. See Rad, *227, JAZU, 1923, 188, note 98). Arsonists, likewise, are required to pay 100 libras to the count, plus damages to the injured party. And if a woman is raped, she is to receive 50 libras in compensation, unless the rapist can "straighten the matter out with her in some other way," and the* knez *is also to receive 50 libras!*

The preeminence of the count and his court in Vinodol can also be seen from the fact that penalties for crimes against one of the knez's *men were far more severe than for the same crime committed against anyone else in the valley, including priests, judges, and other officials. For example, the penalty for assault on a commoner* (kmet) *was 2 libras, to be paid to the* knez, *plus 2 head of cattle to the injured party, plus the cost of medicine. If one of the count's men were beaten, however, the penalty was 25 libras to the count, and if the victim lost the use of a limb as a result of the attack the count could exact any punishment he wished. The extent to which the Counts of Vinodol regarded the valley as their possession can be ascertained from the fact that no judgment could be handed down by the courts without the approval of the count or one of his men, nor could there be any public gatherings in Vinodol to discuss community business, unless one of the count's men were present. And as if the first 74 articles of the code had not made the* knez's *powers clear enough, the concluding article (75) states: "The Lord Count has the right and full power, with respect to punishment, penalties, and arbitrary decisions, both over noblemen and churchmen and the common people, and over all other people, as stated above." It may be true, of course, as scholars have pointed out, that there are traces of old Slavic tribal law in the Code–for example, in the payment of the wergeld* (vražda) *to the children and relatives of the murdered man, and the assumption of the burden of paying the wergeld by the heirs and relatives of the murderer, if he should escape. But such traces of tribal customs seem minimal and their significance should not be exaggerated.*

Because of its importance as one of the oldest law codes in a Slavic language, the Vinodolski zakon *has been subjected to intensive study, complicated by the fact that it was written originally in a thirteenth century čakavian dialect, with many terms that are unclear to linguists and jurists today. There is only one complete manuscript of the* Code, *dating from the fifteenth century; this copy has some omissions, which have been completed by scholars, on the basis of a later code (that of Trsat). Some of the more noteworthy studies and publications of the* Code *have been by Antun Mažuranić (*Kolo, *Zagreb, 1843, sv. 3, 52-83), Vatroslav Jagić (*Izdanija obščestva ljubitelej drevnej pis'mennosti, *vol. 54, St. Petersburg, 1880), Franjo Rački (vol. 1 of* Monumenta historico-juridica Slavorum meridionalium . . . *Zagreb: JAZU, 1890), and in more recent times, by Marko Kostrenčić (cited earlier). The excerpts from the* Code *given below are from Kostrenčić's publication.*

THE LAW CODE OF VINODOL

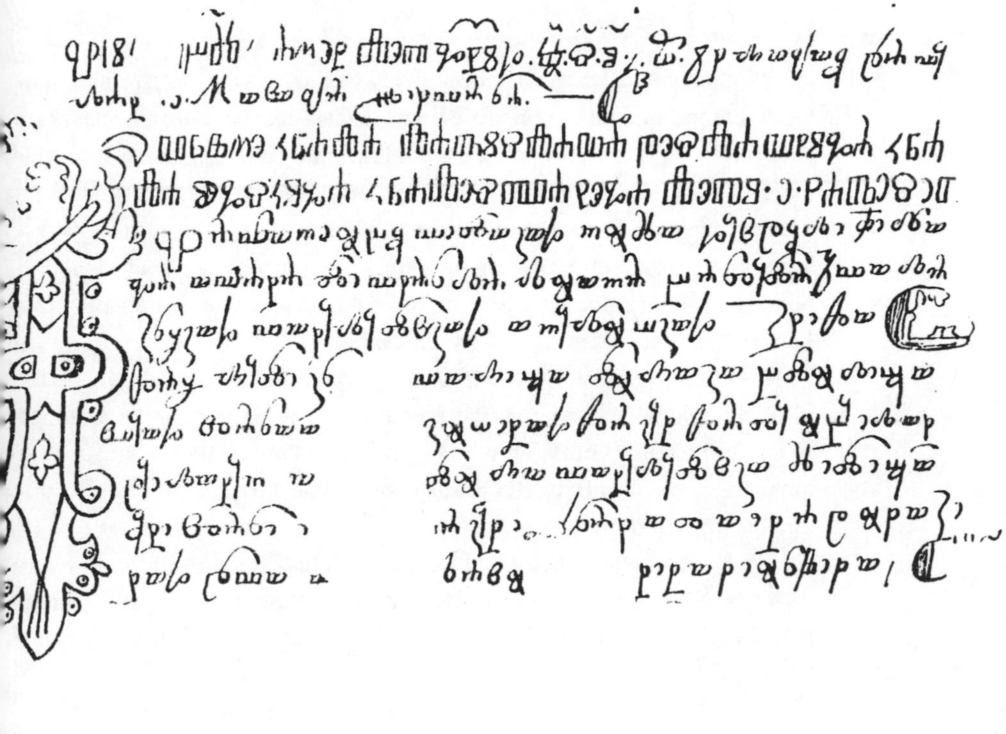

VINODOLSKI ZAKON

Vь ime b(o)žie. Amen. Let g(ospod)nih 1288. indicio prvo, dan 6. miseca jenvara.

Vь vrěme krala Ladislava, preslavnoga krala ugrskoga, kralestva nega leto 6 na deset(e).

Va vrime ubo velikih muži gospode Fedriga, Ivana, Levnarda, Duima, Bartola i Vida, krčkih, vinodolskih i modruških knezi.

Zač do(vo)le kr(at) videći ludi ki bludeći svojih starii(h i is)kušenih zakon, zato ubo edin po edinom i (vsi) ludi vinodolski želeći one stare d(obre z)akone shraniti e na puni, ke nih prvi v(sag)da su s(hran)ili neurěeni–skupiše se vs(i) na kup (tako) crikveni tako priprošći ludi sveršeněm (iměju)ć zdrave svet u Novom Gradu pred obrazom (t)oga istoga kneza Leonarda zgora imenovana isbraše se od vsakoga grada vinodolskoga ne vse st(a)riiši na vkup, na ke viahu, da se bole spominahu v zakonih svoih otac i od svoih ded ča bihu slišali.

I nim narediše i ukazaše tesnim zakonom da bi vse dobre, stare, iskušene zakone u Vinodol činiti položiti v pisma, od kih bi se mogli spomenuti ili slišati od svoih otac i ded zgora rečenih, tako od sada naprid mogu se uleći bluenja te riči i nih detca vrime ko pride, da nimaju primisalja v tih zakonih.

Ki ubo buduć izbrani na to od tih istih ludi vinodolskih:

z Novoga Grada: Ćrna, dvornik vsega Vinodola i od knezi zgora rečenih, Petar plovan i Vlkona Pribohna satnik; Ranac Saražin, Bogdan Vlčnić;

z Ledenic: Ratko prvad i Radoslav, popove, Dobroša satnik;

iz Bribira: Dragoslav arhiprvad i Bogdan pop, Zlonomer satnik, Jurislav Gradenić;

z Grižan: Luban i Petar, popovi, Domian satnik, Dunat i Dragoljub i Vidomir Vlčić;

iz Drivenika: Dragolub satnik i Mikula Dragolub i Pribinig;

THE LAW CODE OF VINODOL

In God's name. Amen. In the year of Our Lord, 1288. In the first of the Indiction, on the sixth day of January.

In the time of King Ladislav, the most glorious Hungarian king, in the sixteenth year of his rule.

And in the time of the great men, Lords Fedrig, Ivan, Leonardo, Dujam, Bartol, and Vid, the Princes of Krk, Vinodol, and Modruša.

Since they have often seen people who observe their old and time-tested laws, therefore, the Vinodol people, both individually and collectively, wishing to preserve in their entirety those good old laws which their forefathers had always preserved in an unsystematic way,—they all gathered together in an assembly, both clerical and lay persons, and after they had made good counsel in Novi Grad, in the presence of the same above-mentioned Prince Leonardo, men were selected from each Vinodol town for a council; these were not all elders, but also such men who were known to be well versed in the laws of their fathers, as well as in what they had heard of the law from their grandfathers.

And they were ordered and commanded by strict authority to put in writing all the good, old, time-tested laws in Vinodol, which could still be remembered or which they had heard about from the above-mentioned fathers and grandfathers, so that from now on it would be possible to avoid errors in this matter, and so that their children in times to come would have no doubts about these laws.

And from these same people of Vinodol there were selected for this task:

from Novi Grad: Črna, chancellor of all Vinodol and of the above-mentioned princes; Petar the curate and Vlkona Pribohna, mayor; Ranae Saražin, and Bogdan Vlčinić;

from Ledenice: Ratko the presbyter and Radoslav, priests; Dobroša, mayor;

from Bribir: Dragoslav the archpresbyter and Bogdan the priest, Zlonomer the mayor, and Jurislav Gradenić;

from Grižane: Ljuban and Petar, priests, Domjan the mayor, Dunat and Dragoljub and Vidomir Vlčić;

from Drivenik: Dragoljub the mayor, and Mikula Dragoljub and Pribinig;

a iz Hrilina: Raden plovan, i Ivanac satnik, Živina sudac i Kliman Nedal;

iz Bakra: Krstiha plovan i Grubina pop, Ivan satnik, Derga Vlčina i Nedrag;

iz Crsata: Vazmina plovan i Nedrag satnik, Dominik sudac i Vieka;

iz Grobnika: Kirin plovan i Slavan satnik i Domian Kinović, Paval i Slavina Vukodružić.

I ti vsi pisani na vkup skupleni, od vole općinske i edinim pristanenem i nareenjem sabranim vse općini vinodolske... ke budu zdola pisane vola ke su slišali od svoih stariih.

Čl. 1. Najprvo, da ako ka od crikav općinskih z Vinodola imaju se kerstiti vola ih bude kerstiti g(ospo)d(i)n biskup, v koi biskupii est crikav rečena–nima imiti od keršćenja rečenoga neveće vernez benetačkih soldini 40, tr 1 obed tr 1 večeru, a navlašćno od onih, ki učine tu crikav kerstiti.

Žakan ubo, ki za biskupom stoi v toi istoj crikvi, zove se hrvatski malik, a vlaški macarol, nima imiti od toga istoga keršćenja neveće bolanač 15 vernez benetačkih.

Čl. 2. Ošće: zverh crikav, opatii vola molstirov općinskih rečenih g(ospo)d(i)n biškup ne more položiti vola vzeti ali zapovidati, neveće ono, ča bi otili dati kaštaldi tih istih crikav nemu svoju volu dobru.

* * * * * * * *

Čl. 5. Ošće: ako g(ospo)d(i)n knez u Vinodolu vola rečeni biskup, kada bi pošal po knežstvu po vinodolskom i v ki god bi grad prišal ki od niju, more činiti ěti i k sebi činiti priti po ruki satnika onoga grada za svoe jidenje i za svoe obiteli, od kih koli goved i brav, ke se mogu naiti naibliže, tako od skota kmetšćega, tako od plemenitih ludi, tako od popi i od inih vsakih ludi. Ništar manie za ne imaju platit g(ospo)d(i)n knez gdi se koli i mogu od svoih perman činit ěti za se i za svoju obitel i za vas svoi dvor ot naibližnago skota te iste općine, budući koga godi zgora imenovanih.

Čl. 6. Ošće: ako bi ki rubani (učinil) na puti ili gdi indi: da plati knezu libar 50.

Čl. 7. Iošće: ki bi v gradu hram razbil v noći, vola ako bi ukral u nem,

and from Hreljin: Raden the curate and Ivanac the mayor, Živina the judge and Kliman Nedal;

from Bakar: Krstiha the curate and Grubina the priest, Ivan the mayor, Derga Vlčina and Nedrag;

from Trsat: Vazmina the curate and Nedrag the mayor, Dominik the judge and Vieka;

from Grobnik: Kirin the curate and Slavan the mayor, and Domjan Kinović, Paval and Slavina Vukodružić.

And all the above-mentioned, having gathered together in assembly according to the will of their communities, by individual agreement and by a decree passed by all the Vinodol community [they have put together these laws] which are written below, or they have heard them from their elders.

Art. 1 First of all, if one of the churches of the Vinodol communities has to be consecrated, and if it should be consecrated by the Lord Bishop in whose bishopric the said church is located, he should not receive for consecrating the said church any more than forty soldin in Venetian vernezi, and one dinner and one supper, and precisely from those who are having the church consecrated. And the deacon who stands behind the Bishop in this same church–he is called *malik* in Croatian, and *macarol* in Italian–should not receive for this consecration more than fifteen bolanča in Venetian vernezi.

Art 2 Further, with regards to the churches, abbeys, and monasteries of the said communities, the Lord Bishop can give no commands, nor can he take or order anything other than what the castellans of those same churches want to give him of their own free will.

* * * * * * * *

Art. 5 Further, when his Lordship the Prince of Vinodol, or the said bishop travels through the Vinodol Principality, in whatever city either of them should come they can order through the local mayor of that town that food be brought for themselves and for their company, whatever oxen and cattle are closest at hand, whether from the common people's cattle or from that of the nobility, or from the priests, or from all other people. By the same token his Lordship the Prince has to pay for them when he has some of his own men get them for him and his company and his whole court, from the nearest cattle of that same community, from any one of the above mentioned people.

Art. 6 Further, if someone commits robbery on the highway, or anywhere else, let him pay the Prince fifty libras.

Art. 7 Further, if someone should break into an establishment in the city at night, or if he should steal from it, and if someone should cry

ter ako bi klical „pomagaite": platit ima knezu libar 50 (i škodu duplu). Vapiuć ubo „pomagaite" esu verovani, ako reku s rotu, da esu onoga zlotvorca poznali.

Ništar mane, ako nij onde klicano, nima platit nego soldini 40, ter škodu, kakoi više izrečeno. I ako tu hudobu va dne učini: nii držan platit neveće soldini 40, ako se more pokazati po verovanu svedoku.

* * * * * * * *

Čl. 12. Iošće: ako ki prime nikoga zgonika toga knezžtva vola ako bi im (dal) jisti ili piti ili inu ku pomoć vola svet, platit ima knezu libar 50.

* * * * * * * *

Čl. 15. Ošće: vsaki pop držan je stražu strići v noći v gradu, kako ini č(lovi)k.

* * * * * * * *

Čl. 18. Iošće: dobra edna žena i dobra glasa pomaknena za svidočastvo ako ni veće svedoki, verovana e od ženi k ženi, tako od psosti ězika kako od bienja i ot ranenja.

* * * * * * * *

Čl. 24. Iošće: more zvati vsaki „pomagaite", ako vidi delajuć niko zlo i zato se nima kaštigati niednu penu.

Čl. 25. Ošće: od bienja, ranenja i od stučenja meju kmeti nij band nego soldini 40, ke krivac ima platiti knezu, a onomu ki bude bien 2 brava ter likariju. A to takoe od satnika i grašćika i busovića, ki v sih esut pod zakon i pod pravdu kmetsku, a ne od s(lu)žabniki i po zakonu kmetšćkomu sudet se i nim est za uraženě za dovole učineno.

* * * * * * * *

Čl. 27. Ošće: ako bi muž ženi zvergal hoverlicu ili pokrivaču z glave va zli voli, ter bi se moglo prikazati trimi dobrimi muži volia ženami: plati libar 50, ako e tužba s toga; od kih g(ospo)d(i)n knez imii soldini 40, ona koi je vašćina učinena 40 i 8 l(i)b(a)r.

Da ako žena ženi sverže pokrivaču više rečenu: plaća 2 libre

"help": he has to pay the Prince 50 libras (and double damages). And those who cry "help" are to be believed, if they say under oath that they recognized that criminal.

By the same token, if no one cries out he has to pay only forty soldin, plus the damages as stated above. And if he did this crime by day he has to pay no more than forty soldin, if it can be proved by a reliable witness.

* * * * * * * *

Art. 12 Further, if someone should shelter someone who has been banished from this Principality, or should give him something to eat or drink or some other help or counsel, he has to pay the Prince fifty libras.

* * * * * * * *

Art. 15 Further, every priest has to stand guard at night in the city, just like any other man.

* * * * * * * *

Art. 18 Further, a good woman of good reputation, brought forward as a witness when there are no other witnesses, is to be believed when there is a dispute between women, whether it be for cursing, beating, or wounding.

* * * * * * * *

Art 24 Further, everyone can call "help", if he sees that some evil is being done, and he should not be penalized for that by any fine.

Art. 25 Further, for beating, wounding, and brawling between commoners, no judgment will exceed forty soldin, which the guilty one has to pay the Prince, and he has to pay the one whom he beat two head of cattle, plus the cost of medicine. And this holds true for the local mayor, the castellan, and the town crier, who in such matters come under the law and justice of the common people, and not under administrative law, and they are to be judged according to the common people's law, and in this way are they to receive satisfaction for injury done them.

* * * * * * * *

Art. 27 Further, if a man should pull the kerchief or covering from a woman's head with evil intent, and this can be proven by three good men or women, he has to pay fifty libras if a complaint has been filed because of that. Of these fifty libras his Lordship the Prince receives forty soldin, and the woman who has been shamed—forty eight libras.

If a woman pulls the above-mentioned head covering from a woman, she pays two libras to the court, and two sheep to that woman.

dvoru, a onoi 2 ovci. Ako ubo onde nisu svedoci dobri, prisezi, ki tai, da nij to učinil, budi prost.

* * * * * * * *

Čl. 29. Iošće: ako bi ki ubil od podknežinov ili od slug od obiteli kućne g(ospo)d(i)na kneza, od permanov, ter bi ušal i ne mogal se eti, da knez vazme vražbu, to e zagovor vrnezi kakov i kolik bude otil; zverh plemene zlotvorca koliko za polovicy, zač pleme ni držano nere od pol, a zločinac drugi pol. Da ako se ěme ta zlotvorac š nega ima ta isti knez ili niki mesto nega učiniti ko godi mašćeni bude hotil, a nega pleme nišće se nebosujuje.

* * * * * * * *

Čl. 31. Ošće: ako bi ki ubil nikoga kmeta ili od roda kmet, da bi se ne mogal ěti, vpadi v osud lib(a)r 100 bližikam, onoga grada, ki e ubien, općini libri 2. Od tih libar 100 ima imiti: dica ubienoga, ako ima ditcu, imaju imit polovicu, a drugi pol nega bližiki. Ta osud krivac plati.

Ako ubigne, imaju nega bližike osud platit pol, a pol nega redi, ako e ima.

Da ako se ěti more pria ner se vražba plati vola ako e učinena naprava, budi od nega mašćeni, a nega bližiki budite prosti.

* * * * * * * *

Čl. 56. Iošće: ako bi ki učinil silu ženi koi jebući ili bi hotil jebati ima knezu platit libar 50, a toi ženi tolikoe, ako se ne bude mogal napraviti š nu po niki zakon.

Vola ako od rečene sili nima svedoki: verovana e; nišće mane ima priseći položivši ruku zverhu knig tičuć samo 25 od rečene sile zvrhu onoga, od koga se bude tužiti.

Ke porotnike ta žena naidi kako bole vi. Ako porotniki nima vola ih toliko ne more imiti, ta žena priseći e držana za onih ki joj mankaju.

Priseguć ubo š nu ali ona sama po prvom tratě imaju taknuti ruku i reći v tu rotu. I vsi ne porotnici imaju biti žene. I ka se onde rota, da ne odgovornik ima odgovoriti: „Da, s onu rotu prisegu". A ona ima priseći, kako je zgora rečeno.

I ako ta ista žena ili niki od ne porotnikov umankal bi ča e zgora rečeno: on suprotiv komu govori budi odrišen od toga griha više rečenoga.

If there are no good witnesses there, let the defendant swear that she didn't do it, and let her go free.

* * * * * * * *

Art. 29 If someone should kill one of the Prince's assistants, or one of the servants of his Lordship the Prince's household, or one of his aides, and he should run away so that he can't be caught, let the Prince take the wergeld, that is, a fine in vernezi as large as he wishes to make it; he takes one half from the criminal's tribe, since the tribe doesn't have to pay more than one half, and the criminal pays the other half. And if that criminal should be caught, that same prince or someone in his place can take whatever revenge he should wish, but his tribe is not liable.

* * * * * * * *

Art. 31 Further, if someone should kill a common man or someone of common birth, and he can't be caught, let him be fined one hundred libras for the dead man's kin, and the council of the victim's city should receive two libras. Of these one hundred libras the children of the victim, if he had children, should receive one half, and the second half should go to his kin. The guilty one pays this penalty.

If he should flee, his kin have to pay half the penalty and his heirs have to pay half, if he has any heirs.

And if he can be seized before the wergeld is paid, or if an arrangement can be made, then let the revenge be taken on him and let his kin be free.

* * * * * * * *

Art. 56 Further, if someone should use force on a woman and have intercourse with her or intend to have intercourse with her, he has to pay the Prince fifty libras and the same amount to the woman, if he cannot straighten the matter out with her in some way.

And if the said rape should have no witnesses, she is to be believed; but by the same token only twenty five character witnesses have to swear, putting their hands on the book, concerning the rape and against the accused.

Let the woman find witnesses as best she can. If there are none, or if she cannot find enough, that woman must swear for those whom she lacks. Those who swear with her, but with her in first place, have to touch the book with their hands and say the oath. And all her witnesses have to be women. And when a woman is being sworn in her respondent has to answer: "Yes, I too will swear by this oath." And she has to swear as is stated above.

And if that same woman or any of her character witnesses should make a mistake in any of the above, let the one against whom she is speaking be cleared of the above mentioned crime.

Čl. 57. Ošće: niedno viće općinsko ili navlašćno v gradu ili indi ne mozi biti od niednih del, ke bi pristojale k općini, ako ne bude onde knezova č(lovi)ka; i ako ka dela suprot učine zgublaju vse svoe blago i budi knezu zgora rečenomu.

* * * * * * * *

Čl. 59. Iošće: ako bi se ka žena našla tvarnica ter bi se mogla skazati svedočastvom verovanim: za prvo ostani knezu libar 100 vola se sažgi, ako bi se ne imelo od česa platiti.

A od sada naprid ako bi učinila g(ospo)d(i)n knez ju kaštigai po nega voli.

I takoi v toi istoj peni ako se ki muž naide v tom grihu, da se kaštigai.

* * * * * * * *

Čl. 62. Iošće: ako bi ki položil v kuću ogan, ili v hram vola v ničji osik: za požgane za prvo ostani v osud dvoru 100 libar, ter škodu platiti onomu, komu (j)u učini vola budi osuen na život, ako nima odkud platiti. I ako to veće učini osudi se na život i na smert.

Ako bude ondee požgano od nikoga č(lovi)ka vola od nikih ludi, a on zlotvorac ne bi se mogal jeti: plati se vražba za vsako požganje, kako zgora od vražbi est izrečeno.

Art. 57 Further, no meetings, either municipal or private, may be held in the city or anywhere else, concerning any business whatsoever pertaining to the community, unless one of the Prince's men is there. And anyone who does anything against this will lose all his property, which goes to the above-mentioned Prince.

* * * * * * * *

Art. 59 Further, if a woman should be found to be a sorceress, and if this can be proven by reliable testimony, the first time she has to pay the Prince 100 libras, or let her be burned if she has nothing with which to pay.

And from then on if she does it, let his Lordship the Prince punish her as he wishes.

And let a man likewise be punished with the same punishment if he be found guilty of that sin.

* * * * * * * *

Art. 62 Further, if someone should set fire to a house or an establishment or someone's stable, for the first arson let him pay the court 100 libras, plus damages to the person to whom he has done that, or let him be condemned to corporal punishment if he has nothing with which to pay.

And if he does it again, let him be condemned to both corporal punishment and to death.

If an individual or several people are the victims of arson, and it is impossible to catch the criminal, then the wergeld is paid for each burning, as is stipulated above concerning wergeld.

The Emperor Dušan

The Law Code of the Emperor Stefan Dušan *(1349 and 1354) was written when medieval Serbia was at the peak of its power, nearly twenty years after the battle of Vel'bužd (today's Kustendil), where the young Dušan, together with his father King Stefan Uroš III Dečanski, had won a major victory over a combined Byzantine and Bulgarian army. Dusan, who was involved in the murder of his father a year later (in 1331), took over the Serbian kingdom, consolidating and expanding its power over Albania, Epirus, Macedonia, and Northern Greece. Within a decade he was threatening the conquest of Constantinople itself, so that the Byzantine Emperor felt constrained to call Turkish mercenaries from Asia Minor for help. And thus was prepared the eventual downfall not only of Serbia, but of Byzantium as well.*

The Dušan Law Code

In 1349 Stefan Dušan already regarded himself as the true heir to the Byzantine throne and the leader of Orthodoxy. As he himself says in the Epilogue to his Zakonik:

> *. . . And so (God) in his mercy changed me from King to Orthodox Emperor. And he gave everything into my hands, as he had done for the Great Constantine, the Emperor: the lands, and all the countries, and the sea coasts, and all the cities of the Greek Empire. . . . And I was crowned Emperor with the God-bestowed Imperial Crown, on the fourteenth of April, 1346 . . . on Easter Sunday.*

Dušan's assumption of imperial status helps to explain why he felt it necessary to revise the legal system established by his grandfather, King Milutin (1282-1321), borrowing heavily from the Byzantine laws in Blastares' Sintagmat *(1335) and from the corpus of Byzantine constitutions, known as the* Basilica. *The reliance on Byzantine legal sources underlined the fact that Dušan considered himself the Emperor of the Greeks as well as of the Serbs; indeed the new* Zakonik *was often combined*

with a Serbian Slavonic translation of the Sintagmat (in abbreviated form, and a copy of the Greek agrarian code, known as "the Emperor Justinian's Law Code," so that together they formed a tripartite codex for the use of the courts. (See Vladimir Mošin's Vlastareva sintagma i Dušanov zakonik u Studeničkom 'Otečniku,' an offprint from Starine 42, Zagreb: JAZU, 1949.)

Dušan's Law Code gives a picture of a complex social and political system undergoing rapid change. Unlike the Code of Vinodol, where the knez's power has already been consolidated, the Zakonik seems to reflect a strong tension and struggle for power between the new Emperor and the magnates or great nobles. Although Dušan confirms with this code the hereditary rights of nobles to their lands (baštine), and although he absolves them from all feudal obligations except for the land tax and the provision of troops in time of war, still he threatens them with divestiture of their estates if they cause harm or damage to another locality, or if they show disrespect for one of the imperial judges. Dušan is particularly hard on the kraištniki (margraves), who hold border fiefs (pronija) in return for guarding the frontiers against marauding bands. In the first section of the Code (1349) he threatens to force them to make restitution for all damage caused by bands that penetrate the Empire via their territories, and in the supplement to the Code (1354) he increases the penalty to seven times the value of such damage.

Another group to which the Zakonik devotes much attention, particularly in the supplement of 1354, is the serfs (meropasi). The meropasi were obliged to give their lords two days' work per week, in exchange for the use of land, and for protection. The Code is insistent that the serfs remain on the estates to which they are attached, and that no other lord should receive them, under penalty of being punished as "a traitor to the Empire." Since there are several articles dealing with this situation, one may assume that runaway serfs were common and that the resultant shortage of labor was causing economic problems. Paradoxically, while tying the meropasi to the land, the Code does guarantee them their right to go to court against their lord, even if he be the Emperor or the Church. Slaves (otroci) are also mentioned in the Code; they were considered chattel, and both they and their children could be inherited from one generation to the next. Freemen (sebri) are also referred to in a few articles, but we know little about their status, except that they had no right of assembly, and were considered inferior to the nobility in the eyes of the law.

Besides the nobility, a second privileged class in Dušan's empire was the Church, which had been a strong support of the Nemanjić dynasty since Sava's time. The Serbian hierarchy was both prosperous and influential, playing a leading role, together with the nobility, in the Serbian Sabor, and directly influencing decisions on grave matters of state. The monasteries owned huge landed estates, worked by meropasi, who were responsible to them alone. The influence of the Church, as well as the

nportance which the Empire attached to religion and orthodoxy, may be een from the fact that the first 38 articles in the 1349 Codex (out of a otal of 135) are devoted to religion and the Church. The very first article peaks about the necessity of "purging Christianity," which reflects a ertain intolerance toward Roman Catholic subjects, who elsewhere are eferred to as "latini" and "poluverci" (half-believers). This intolerant ttitude toward Catholics, which may be a legacy from the schism between the two churches (1054) and the capture of Constantinople by the 'ourth Crusade, with the resultant establishment there of the Latin Cingdom (1204-1261), may have reflected an "official" state attitude oward Catholicism, one that was honored more in the breach than in fact, or it somewhat contradicts the protective spirit of the Code toward ravelling Dubrovnik merchants and immigrant Saxon miners, for example, ll or most of whom were Catholics.

The main instrument of imperial control seems to have been the ystem of circuit courts, to which the Code devotes much attention. As as already been stated, judges were protected by the law from the actions of irate landowners; also protected were their retinue, including their ooks (who ensured them against poisoning) and their beadles, who acted s body guards. The preeminence of the Law over everyone, including the Emperor himself, is expressly stated in two articles of the Supplement of 1354, wherein the Emperor proclaims:

> If I should write a letter, whether from anger, or from love, or from mercy toward someone, and that letter should undermine the Law Code, and should not be according to justice and the law, . . . then the judges should put no faith in that letter, but instead they should judge and act according to justice.

And in the next article the Code states:

> All judges should judge according to the Code, correctly, as it is written in the Code, and they should not judge in fear of me.

In this affirmation of the principle of legality (zakonitost) the Law Code of Emperor Stefan Dušan reflected the highest spirit of Byzantine law, thus showing that the Emperor and his advisors had seriously prepared themselves to assume the leadership of the Orthodox lands. But the Serbian imperial idea was not to be tested in the crucible of history, for Dušan died in 1355, unexpectedly, and the Empire disintegrated rapidly under his successor Uroš V, torn apart by the centrifugal forces which the Code had attempted to harness and contain.

Until recent times, at least, the definitive study and edition of the Code was by Stojan Novaković (Zakonik Stefana Dušana Cara Srpskog

1349 i 1354, *2nd edition, Belgrade, 1898.) According to Nikola Radojčić who published a new edition of the Code in 1960 (Belgrade: SANU) Novaković erred in not basing his edition on one of the older manuscripts, such as that of Athos or Struga. Novaković's accompanying Serbo-Croatian translation also tends to amplify and explain some of the more murky passages, Radojčić complains, instead of letting the Code speak for itself. The* Zakonik *has been translated into English by Malcolm Burr (*The Code of Stephan Dušan: Translation and Notes. *London:* Slavonic and East European Review, *1950. An offprint.) Burr relied on Novaković's 1898 edition when making his translation. The following excerpts from the Code are from Radojčić's publication.*

A word about language: the Zakonik *is written in a Serbian Slavonic that is closer to the spoken language, both phonetically and syntactically, than the language one would find in a religious text of the same period.*

Закѡн благовѣрнаго цара Стефана. Вь лѣтѣ ·≠ѕѡнз· индиктиѡн ·в· вь праздникь вьзнесенија господнија ·мѣсеца маїа ·ка· дьнь.

Сїи же законыкь поставлјаемь ѡт православнаго сьбора нашего· сь прѣѡсвѣщеньнымь патрїарьхѡм кvрь Іѡаникїемь, и вьсѣмы архїереи· и црьковникы малимы и великыми· и мною благовѣрьнымь царемь Стефанѡм· и вьсѣмїи властели царства ми, малїими же и великїими·

Закѡнѡмь же симь сложенїа быше:

Law code of the pius Emperor Stefan. In the year 6857, the second of the indiction, on the feast day of the Ascension of Our Lord, the twenty first day of May.

This law code is established by our Orthodox Synod, including the most holy patriarch, Lord Joaniccius, and all the archpriests and clerics, minor and major, and me, the pius Emperor Stefan, and all the nobles of my Empire, minor and major.

And the regulations of this law code are as follows:

1. Ѡ хрїстїанствѣ:

Наипрьво за хрїстїаньство • симьзи ѡбразомь да се ѡчи
хрїстїаньство:

2. Ѡ женитвѣ:

Властѣле и прочїи людїе • да се не жене не благословив
се оу своего арьхїереа • или оу техзїи да се благослове, кое
поставили изьбравьши доуховьнике архїереие.

3. Ѡ свадьбѣ:

И ниедина свадьба да се не оучины без вѣньчанїа • ак
се оучины безь благословенїа, и оупрошенїа црькве • так
да се разлоуче.

4. Ѡ доуховномь дльгоу:

И за доуховнїи дльгь • всакь чловѣкь да има пови
венїе, и послоу[ша]нїе кь своемоу архїереѭ • аколи се кто ѡбрѣ
сьгрѣшивь црькви • или прѣстоупивь что любо ѿ сиега зак
воломь • али[1] и нехотѣнїемь да се повинѣ и исправы црьк
аколи прѣчюе и оудрьжи се ѿ црькве • и не вьсхощет исп
вити повелѣнїа црькви • потомь да се ѿлоучи ѿ црькве.

1. Concerning Christianity:
   First, concerning Christianity. Christianity should be purifie in the following manner:
2. Concerning Marriage:
   Noblemen and other people should not get married withou having been blessed by their archpriest, or else they should b blessed by those whom the archpriests have appointed, when they chose them for priests.
3. Concerning the Wedding:
   No wedding should be made without a marriage ceremony, an if it is done without the blessing, and without an inquiry by th Church, let such people be separated.
4. Concerning the religious obligation:
   And as for the religious obligation, let every man submit to hi archpriest and obey him. If there should be someone who has sinned against the rules of the Church, or who has violated any thing in this law code, willingly or unwillingly, let him humble himself and absolve himself with the Church; and if he should turn a deaf ear and keep away from the Church, and if he shall not desire to fulfill the Church's commands, then let him be excommunicated from the Church.

5. Ѿ проклети христїаньскомь:

И светителїе да не проклинаю христїань, за сьгрѣшениѥ доуховно. нь да пошлѥ дващи, и трищи кь ѡномоузи, и да га ѡбличи. да а кѥ не слоуша. и не оусхокѥ исьправити се заповѣдию доуховною потомь да ѡтлоучит се.

6. Ѿ ереси латиньскои:

И за ересь латиньскоу: що соу ѡбратили христиꙗне вь азимьство. да се вьзврате ѡпет вь христиꙗньство. а кѥ[ли] се кьто ѡбрѣте прѣслоушавь и не вьзвратив се. вь христиꙗньство. да се каже како пише оу законѣ светыхь ѡтцьь.

7. Ѿ ереси латиньскои:

И да постави црьковь великаа протопопе, по всѣх градовѣх и трьговѣх. да вьзврате христиꙗне ѡт ереси латиньске. кои се соу ѡбратили вь вѣроу латиньскоу. и да имь дадоу заповѣдь доуховноу: и да се врати всакы вь христїаньство.

Dušan's Law Code

5. Concerning the Anathematization of Christians:
And let not the Bishops anathematize Christians for a spiritual transgression, but let them send messengers to that person two and three times, and expose him, and if he shall not want to reform in accordance with religious command, then let him be excommunicated.

6. Concerning the Latin heresy:
And as for the Latin heresy, and that Christians have turned to taking communion with unleavened bread, let them return again to Christianity, and if there should be someone who pays no heed and doesn't return to Christianity, let him be punished as is written in the law of the holy fathers.

7. Concerning the Latin heresy:
And let the Great Church appoint head priests for all the cities and market places, to turn from the Latin heresy those Christians who have converted to the Latin faith, and let them be given the religious command: that everyone should return to Christianity.

10. Ѡ еретизе:

И кьто се ѡбрѣте еретигь живе вь христиꙗнехь· да с
жеже по ѡбразоу· и да се прожене· кьтоли га име таити
тьзи да се жеже.

20. Ѡ ресницѣхь: кои тѣлеса мрьтьвыихь жегоуть:

И люди, кое с вльховствомь изимаю изь гробовь, тере
ихь сьжижоу· този село да плати враждоу· кое тои оучини·
и ако боуде попь на този дошьль· да моу се оузме поповство·

21. Ѡ проданїи христїаньскомь:

И кто прода христїанина вь иновѣрноу вѣроу· да моу
се роука ѡтсѣче и езыкь ѡтрѣже.

53. Ѡ насилованїи:

Аще кои властелинь, оузме владыкоу по силѣ· да моу
се ѡбѣ роуцѣ ѡтсѣкоуть, и нось оурѣже· ашели севрь оузме
по силѣ владыкоу, да се ѡбѣси· аще ли своюо дроугоу оузме
по силѣ. да моу се ѡбѣ роуцѣ ѡтсѣкоу и нось оурѣже.

10. Concerning the heretic:
And if there should be some heretic living among Christians, let him be branded on the face and driven off, and if anyone should hide him, let that person be branded too.

20. Concerning soothsayers, who burn the bodies of the dead:
And people who take bodies from their graves, in connection with sorcery, and burn them, let the village which does that pay the wergeld, and if a priest should be present, let his priesthood be taken from him.

21. Concerning the sale of Christians:
And whoever sells a Christian into a different faith, let his hand be cut off and his tongue cut out.

53. Concerning rape:
If some lord takes a noble woman by force, let both his hands be cut off, and his nose slit; if a freeman takes a noble woman by force, let him be hung; if he takes one of his own kind by force, let both his hands be cut off and his nose slit.

96. Ѡ оубїиствоу:

Кто се ѡбрѣте оубивь ѡтца или матерь или брата или чедо свое да се тьзи оубица ждеже на ѡгьни.

97. Ѡ брадѣ властѣѡскои:

Кто се ѡбрѣте ѡскоубь брадоу властелиноу или доброу чловѣкоу· да се томоузи ѡбѣ роуцѣ ѡдсекоу.

98. Ѡ скоубѣжоу себровоу:

И ако се ѡскоубета два себра да ѥст мѣхоскоубина ·ѕ· перьперь.

112. Ѡ соужних:

Кои чловѣкь оутече изь соужьньства· сьчимь прїидеть на дворь царевь· или ѥст царевь чловѣкь· или црьковныи· или властельскы· с темьзи· да е свободьнь· аще ѥст ѡтбѣгль оу тогази чловѣка комоу ѥст оутекьль· този да ѥст комоу ѥст оутекьль.

Dušan's Law Code

96. Concerning murder:
Whoever should kill his father or mother or brother or child, let that murderer be burned in the fire.

97. Concerning a nobleman's beard:
Whoever should pluck the beard of a nobleman or of a good man, let such a person have both his hands cut off.

98. Concerning the plucking of a freeman's beard:
And if two freemen pluck each other's beards, the beard plucking fine is six perpera.

112. Concerning captives:
Whatever man flees from captivity, once he reaches the Emperor's castle, whether he be a vassal of the Emperor, or of the Church, or of a noble, by this act he is free; if he has taken something from the man from whom he has fled, that belongs to the man from whom he has fled.

113. Ѡ соужнѥ:

Кои се соужьнь дрьжїи оу дворoу царьства ми, т оутече на дворь патрїарьшь да ѥст свободьнь· и тако на дворь царевь да ѥст свободь[нь].

149. Ѡ гоусари и татѣ:

Симьзи ѡбразѡмь да се каже тать и гоусарь ѡбличь И такози вь ѡбличениѥ· ако се що где [лицемь оухвати] них· или ако их оухвате оу гоусѣ или краги· или их пр жоупа или села· или господари, или властелѥ кои соу нимии· како ѥст выше оуписано· тизи гоусариѥ и тати се не помилоую· нь да се ѡслѣпе и ѡбѣсе.

166. Ѡ пиꙗницах:

Пиꙗница откоудоу греде· и зарьве кога или посѣ или ѡкрьвави, а не досьмрьти· таковомоу пиꙗницѣ· моу се око изме и роука ѡтсѣче· аколи пиꙗнь задере· капоучь комоу скине· или иноу срамотоу оучини· а не ѡк вави· да га бию· да се оудари стапы·р· крати· и да врьже оу тьмницоу· и потомь да се изведе ис тьмнице да се пакы биѥ, и поусти.

113. Concerning a captive:
Whatever captive is kept in a castle of my kingdom, and then flees to the patriarch's manor, let him be free; and also if he flees to the Emperor's castle, let him be free.

149. Concerning the bandit and thief:
In this manner are punished the proven thief and bandit. And the following is the proof: If the goods themselves (corpus delicti) are found on their person, or if they are seized in the act of banditry or thievery, or if they are handed over by the county or villages, or lords, or noblemen who are over them, as is written above, these bandits and thieves are to receive no mercy, but they are to be blinded and hung.

166. About drunks:
A drunk who comes out of some place and challenges someone to a fight, or cuts him up, or bloodies him, but not so as to cause death, for such a drunk let one of his eyes be removed and a hand cut off. If a drunk should tear someone's clothes or remove someone's hat, or shame him in some other way, but does not bloody him, let him be beaten, let him be struck with canes 100 times, and let him be thrown into jail, and afterwards let him be led out of jail, and let him be beaten again and released.

It is characteristic of the Adriatic Sea that its western or Italian coastline is flat and has few good ports, whereas its eastern or Yugoslav shore is generally rocky and has many natural harbors. Dubrovnik (Ragusa), on the southeastern shore of the Adriatic, was especially favored as a trade center during its approximately one thousand years as a city-state, because it was the last major port between the Adriatic and the Mediterranean. Not only was it the last secure stopping point and haven for ships proceeding from Venice to the Levant, North Africa, and Western Europe, but it was also the terminus for land routes to the interior of the Balkans: to Hercegovina (Hum), Serbia (Raška), Bulgaria, and Constantinople. *Dubrovnik Treaties*

*The city of Ragusa is said to have been founded in the seventh century A.D., by the Romanized inhabitants of Epidauros, a former Greek colony some ten miles distant, which had been destroyed by a marauding band of Avar-led Slavs. The Byzantine Emperor and historian, Constantine Porphyrogenitus, who was the first to write of the city, in 949 A.D. (*De Administrando Imperio, *chapter XXIX), says that it got its name from the Latin word for the original site,* laû *("cliff"), which became* lausaioi *("those living on the cliff"), then* rausaioi, *and finally* ragusa. *The Slavic name for the city, "Dubrovnik," probably developed from a derivative of the word for oak* (dub). *The earliest known use of the name "Dubrovnik" was in a commercial treaty between the city and Kulin, the governor of Bosnia (1189), which would indicate that by the twelfth century the descendants of the original Latin settlers had begun to merge with the Slavic population dwelling on the outskirts of the walled city. The co-existence of the names* Ragusa *and* Dubrovnik *throughout much of the city's history symbolizes her combined Latin and Slavic roots, as well as her dual orientation, both westward and eastward.*

Unlike the other cities of the Dalmatian coast, which were overcome by foreign armies and navies, Dubrovnik, whose motto was "Non bene pro toto libertas venditur auro" ("freedom is not to be sold at any

price"), managed to maintain her independence, while acknowledging the suzerainty at various times of the Byzantine Empire, Venice, Hungary, and the Ottoman Empire. Her internal government, which had earlier been of the communal type, gradually was taken over by a wealthy noble class, which jealously guarded its privileges, allowing only its own members to be elected to the great council (consilium maius), *small or executive council* (consilium minus) *and the senate* (consilium rogatorum). *This mercantile oligarchy also appointed the prince or rector, who was titular head of the city for a term of one month (after 1358). The remaining population of Dubrovnik, largely composed of craftsmen, merchants, and seamen, was concentrated in guilds* (esnafi) *and trade associations (bratovštine). When most of the Dubrovnik senate perished during the calamitous earthquake of 1667, the surviving nobility invited some leading merchant families to join it.*

Because of her unique and often precarious position as a "middleman" between the Christian West and the Moslem East, as well as her role as a flourishing trading nation (in the middle of the sixteenth century she had a larger merchant navy than England), the city-state of Dubrovnik maintained an intensive commercial and diplomatic correspondence with representatives as far apart as London, Istanbul, and Goa. Much of this correspondence, as well as the deliberations of her three governmental bodies, has been retained in the precious state archives, which have documents dating from as early as the eleventh century. The seven thousand volumes and one hundred thousand separate acts of the archives are a mine of information about the political and economic situation in Europe, North Africa, and the Byzantine and Ottoman Empires, from the fourteenth through the eighteenth centuries. Since Latin was the official state language, the majority of the documents are in that language, although a significant number are in Italian, Slavic, and Arabic. The earliest documents concerning Dubrovnik's relations with the Balkan Slavic states are in Latin, one being a peace treaty with Stefan Nemanja and his brothers Stracimir and Miroslav (1186), and the other the already-mentioned trade agreement of 1189 with the Bosnian leader Kulin. The Dubrovnik Slavic documents excerpted in this anthology refer to trading rights and other privileges granted to merchants by local rulers in Serbia and Zeta (Montenegro); they were originally published by Franz Miklosich in his Monumenta serbica spectantia historiam Serbiae Bosnae Ragusii *(Vienna, 1858).*

An inventory of the types of documents in the Dubrovnik archives can be found in Francis W. Carter's comprehensive work: Dubrovnik (Ragusa): A Classic City-State *(London/N.Y.: Seminar Press, 1972; 601-661). Bariša Krekić has published a small but excellent book:* Dubrovnik in the 14th and 15th Centuries: A City between East and West *(Norman: Univ. of Oklahoma Press, 1972), while Dr. Anton Kolendić has written a fine handbook,* Dubrovnik *(Beograd: "Jugoslavija" Pub. House, 1965; transl. Dorian Cooke). There have been some specialized studies of*

)ubrovnik, as well, including Konstantin Jireček's work on her medieval rade (Die Bedeutung von Ragusa in der Handelsgeschichte des Mittelalters) Vienna, 1899), Jovan Radonić's superbly annotated volumes of)ubrovnik's diplomatic documents (Dubrovačka akta i povelje, I-II, 3eograd, 1934-35).

The titles of other works are sufficient alone to give an idea of he once far-reaching influence of "the Pearl of the Adriatic"; for examle, Bariša Krekić's Dubrovnik (Raguse) et le Levant au Moyen Age Paris: Mouton, 1961), Radovan Samardžić's Veliki Vek Dubrovnika (The ;reat Age of Dubrovnik; Beograd: Prosveta, 1962), Nicholas Biegman's 'he Turco-Ragusan Relationship (The Hague/Paris: Mouton, 1967), Iarriet Bjelovučić's The Ragusan Republic: Victim of Napoleon and Its)wn Conservatism (Leiden: Brill, 1970), Momčilo Spremić's Dubrovnik i ıragonci: 1442-1495 (Dubrovnik and the House of Aragon); Beograd: 'avod za izdavanje udžbenika SFRJ, 1971), and Veselin Kostić's Dubrovik i Engleska, 1300-1650 (Dubrovnik and England . . . ; Beograd: SANU, 975).

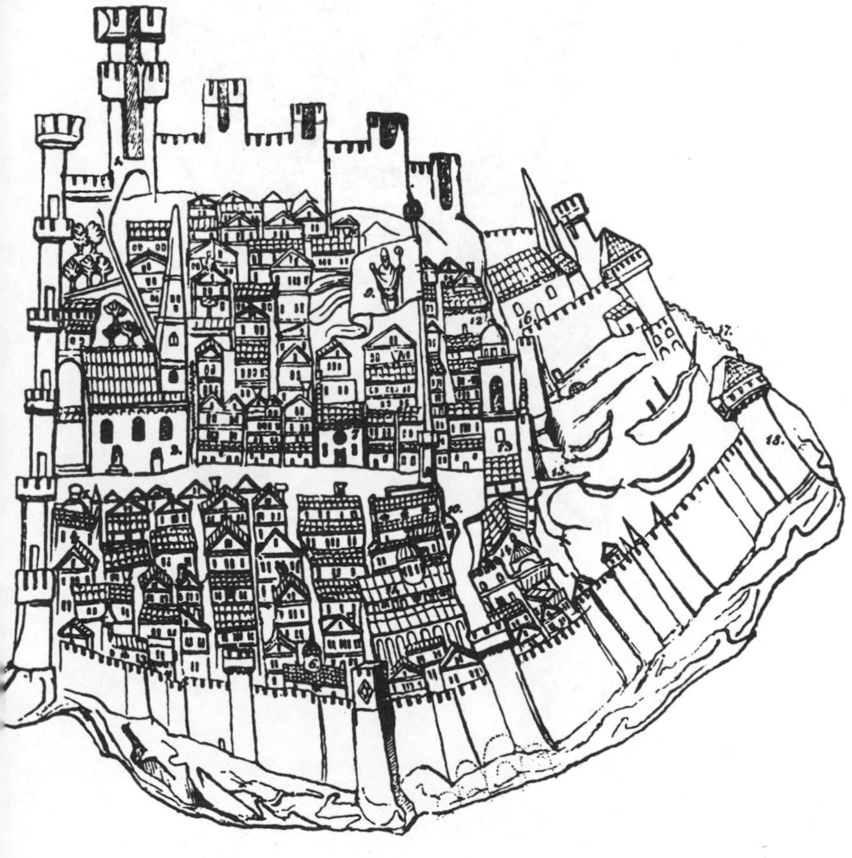

COAT OF ARMS OF THE REPUBLIC OF DUBROVNIK

† Ꙗ Балша, милости божиѡмь дȣка драчки и ѡще,
імамь хотениє, пишȣ и повелевамь, да есть вь сведение
ксакомȣ чловекȣ, како доге кь мнѣ поклисиꙗрь Мате Жȣрь-
'овикь ѡдь града Дȣбровника, и говори ми за работе и за
трьговце и за слободȣ и за повелиє господина ми и брата ми
Гюргꙗ и мое, и ꙗ видевь негово добро говорениє ѡдь приꙗ-
тель моихь властель (града) Дȣбровника хотеки, да есть
любовь стара мегȣ нами, паче потврьгюю (пове)лиє брата ми
Гюргꙗ и мое, како да сȣ тврьде и непоколебиме, и како да
ходе нихь трьговци по моѡи земли, да слободно кȣпȣю и
продаю безь ние(дне за)баве; и ако (имь) кто ȣзме що любо
силомь, ꙗ да плакю ѡдь мое кȣкиє, а ꙗ да ищȣ (кривца);

I Balša, by God's mercy Duke of Drač and elsewhere, do desire, write, and command that it be known to every man that there has come to me the messenger Mate Žurković from the city of Dubrovnik, and he talked to me about business activities and about merchants and about freedom, and about the charters of my lord, and of my brother George, as well as my own, and I having taken note of his good discourse, which comes from my friends the lords of the city of Dubrovnik, and wanting that there be love between us as of old, so do I once more confirm the charters of my brother George as well as my own, that they be firm and unshakeable, and that their merchants may go throughout my land, and that they may buy freely and sell without any interference whatsoever; and if someone takes anything [from them] by force, I shall pay for it from my house, and I shall look for [the guilty party]; and merchants

и трьговци, кои минꙋю ꙋ Срьблие на Данию, да не плате ни-щл, ни да плакꙗю... царине ни бродове, кое нѣсꙋ имали законь ꙋ цара Стефана и ꙋ Гюргꙗ; и що се наге да сьмь дльжьнь трьговцемь дꙋбровачкимь, да имь испралю; и ако се слючи, да се разьбие дрѣво дꙋбровчко ѡ мощи землѣ, да нѣсть никто волнь що ꙋзети или закавити. и (кто) ли дрьзне потворивь сие више ꙋписано, такови да плати .є̄. сьть перьперь, и да ми е невѣрьнь; и такои даю вѣрꙋ мою и моихь властель, да не потворꙋ сие пи-сание до мога живота. а писа се сиꙗ повелꙗ вь лѣто рождьства христова на тисꙋкю и .т҃пє., мѣсеца априлꙗ .к҃д. дьнь, ꙋ Тꙋзѣхь близꙋ Плоче. а томꙋ милостникь про-този(с)тарь Филипь.

who do trade with the Serbs in Danj will pay nothing, neither will they pay... tariffs nor ferry taxes which were not in effect with Emperor Stefan nor with George; and if it should happen that I owe the Dubrovnik merchants something, I will straighten it out with them; and if it should happen that a Dubrovnik ship be shipwrecked on my territory, no one is free to take anything or to destroy it, and whoever should dare to do any of the above, let such people pay 600 perpera, and let him be regarded as unfaithful to me; and likewise I give my pledge and that of my lords that I will not alter this writ while I am alive. And this charter was written in the 1385th year after the birth of Christ, on the twenty fourth day of April, at Tuzi, near Ploča. And the witness to this was the protovistar Filip.

По неизреченнѡмꙋ милосрьдию и чловѣколюбию моѥгѡ
адкагѡ ми Христа и по неизреченнѡмꙋ и веле милостив-
(о)мꙋ его призрению ѥже на господство ми ꙗкоже и на прь-
ихь светихь и правѡславнихь царихь такожде благодеть
ѣсветаго своѥгѡ дꙋха на господство ми излиꙗ, и поста-
и ме господина земли срьпскои и поморию и странамь по-
ꙋнавьскимь. азь вь Христа бога благовѣрни и самодрь-
авни по милости божиѥи Стефань кнезь Лазарь и госпо-
инь, сьдрьжещꙋ ми сиꙗ вса, богꙋ ѡ семь благоволещꙋ, и
ако присла кь господствꙋ моѥмꙋ владꙋщи и властеле гра-
а Дꙋбровьника своѥ властели, на име Николꙋ Гꙋндꙋликꙗ и
кова Бавжеликꙗ, и молише господство ми, како щѡ имь
били записали прьва господа вса срьпска простагме и зако-
, да имь господство ми потврьди: и господство ми по-

By the ineffable mercy and charity of my sweet Christ, and by his ineffable and most merciful tutelage which, along with the grace of the Holy Spirit, he has lavished on my kingdom, as he did on that of the first holy and Orthodox emperors, I in Christ God the faithful and autocratic by God's mercy Stefan Prince Lazar and lord, holding all that which God wills, now whereas the governors and lords of the city of Dubrovnik have sent to my government their lords named Nikola Gundulić and Jakov Bavželić, and they have asked my government that just as the first all-Serbian lords had written down for them the rules and laws, so might my government confirm them for them: and my government

тврьди, како щѡ сȣ имали законе ȣ прьве господе срьпске и
цара Стефана, тѣзи законе да имаю ȣ господства ми, да
имь се не потвори ни за щѡ. и ѡще имь створи милость господство ми, како си сȣ и прѣге имали. и ако се ȣчини кои
пра мегȣ дȣбровчани и срьбли, да се постави половина сȣди
дȣбровьчкихь а половина срьбль, да се прѣд ними прѣ, и
да ѥ порѡта дȣбровчанинȣ негова дрȣжина дȣбровчане, кои
сȣ ѡндези, или кои се нагȣ дȣбровчане ȣ наиближнемь ме-
стȣ; ако ли ȣзьхѡтѣ ѡбоѡи сведочбȣ, кои се прѣ, да поставе половинȣ дȣбровчань а половинȣ срьбль; а ѡдь ѡнех-
зи сведѡкь да нѥ вольнь побеки ниѥдань. ако ли ȣзимак
кою прȣ саси з дȣбровчани, такогерѣ да се сȣде како и срьбле:
половина сась сȣдии а половина дȣбровчань. и да не позива
срьбинь дȣбровчанина на сȣдь никамо тькмо прѣдь ѡнези
сȣдие. такогерѣ и сасинь да се прѣ прѣдь ѡнемизи сȣдиꙗми.
и да се не мȣче прѣдь господство ми ни прѣдь кефалию. и ако
кои дȣбровчанинь кȣпи конꙗ, и ѡногази конꙗ ако ȣхвати
срьбинь или сасинь, и рече: ȣкраденꙿ ми ѥ или гȣшень, да
се ѡдкльне дȣбровчанинь, како нѥ светьца ѡномȣзи коню
ни гȣсе ни татбе, нȣ га ѥ кȣпиль; ако кȣде драгѡ срьбинȣ

has confirmed them; and just as they had laws under the first Serbian lords and Emperor Stefan, so let them have these laws under my government, and may they not be changed for any reason. And my government has granted them another privilege that they had before. And if there should be some dispute between citizens of Dubrovnik and Serbs, let half of the appointed judges be from Dubrovnik and the other half Serbian, and let it be argued before them, and let the jury for a Dubrovnik person be his own people, Dubrovnik citizens who are from that place or from the nearest location; if both of the contestants desire testimony, let half of the witnesses be Dubrovnik people and the other half Serbs; and let none of these witnesses be free to run off. If Saxons should become involved in a dispute with Dubrovnik people, let them be judged as with the Serbs: one half of the judges will be Saxons and one half will be natives of Dubrovnik. And let no Serb summon a Dubrovnik citizen to court except before these judges. Also, a Saxon should plead complaints before such judges. And let them not be tortured before my government nor before the *kefalija* [head magistrate]. And if some Dubrovnik citizen should buy a horse, and if a Serb or a Saxon should seize that horse and say: it has been stolen or rustled from me, let the Dubrovnik citizen swear under oath that he was not aware that the horse had been stolen or rustled and that he had bought it; if he got the horse from

ȣзєти свога конꙗ или сасинȣ, щѡ бȣдє даль дȣбровчанинь за ѡногази конꙗ, този да мȣ вратѣ, а конꙗ личнєга да нѥ зѡльнь ȣдрьжати. и гдє станє дȣбровчанинь на станȣ, ако бȣдє ѡнь прѣгє сталь на ѡно(мȣ)зи станȣ, да нѥ вольнь срьбинь стати ѡньдєзи безь нєгѡва хтѣниꙗ. и кои годє дȣбровчанинь идє сь [своимь трьгомь] или с тȣгимь по трьгов(ѣ)хь господства (ми) и по (зєм)ли, како имь ѥ биль законь прѣгє ȣ прьвє господє и ȣ цара Стєфана, такози и сьда имь ѥ законь. и щѡ даа дȣбровчанинь ср(ьбинȣ) своѥ иманиѥ ȣ вѣрȣ, ако мȣ за(пши) срьбинь, и рєчє: нє си ми даль, да рєчє дȣбровчанинь своѡмȣ вѣромь и д(ȣшомь), щѡ мȣ ѥ даль добитка, да мȣ плакꙗ. и кȣдє идȣ дȣбровчанє по зємли господства ми с трьгѡмь, гдє га ȣбиѥ гȣса, или ако га пок(рад)ȣ ȣ сєлє, да имь плакꙗ ѡколина, щѡ имь ȣзмє гȣса, и щѡ имь сє ȣкрадє; ако ли ѡколина нє плати, да плати господство ми, (щѡ) имь сє ȣзмє. и да нѥ намєта дȣбровчаномь ȣ трьговєхь господства ми. и ко(и) сє ѥ дȣбровчанинь забащиниль ȣ Новѡмь Бр(ьдȣ), тьзи да зигє градь, и да чȣва; кои ли сȣ гостиє, и нє сȣ сє забащинили, да имь ѥ на

some Serb or Saxon, let that person return to him what he has given for the horse, and let him not be free to keep his own horse. And where a Dubrovnik citizen stays in a dwelling place, if he has previously dwelled in that place, then no Serb is free to stay there without his permission. And whatever Dubrovnik citizen goes with [his merchandise] or with another's through the markets of my kingdom and my land, just as the law was for them before, under the first lords and under Emperor Stefan, so let the law be now. And if a Dubrovnik person should give his property in trust to a Serb, and if that Serb should withhold it from him, saying: "you didn't give it to me", let the Dubrovnik person swear by his faith and by his soul, and let whatever property he gave him be paid to him. And wherever Dubrovnik people travel through my kingdom with merchandise, and if a robber should kill him [sic] or rob him in a village, then let the locality pay what the robber has taken from them and what has been stolen from them; and if the locality doesn't pay, then my government will pay what has been taken from them. And any Dubrovnik citizen that acquires a residence in Novo Brdo should build a wall around it and should take care of it; but those Dubrovnik citizens who are guests,

вѡли, що имь гѡдє. и ако сє разбиѥ дрѣво дȣбровчко ȣ
приморию ȣ владанию господства ми, кои ѥ законь биль за
този ȣ прьвиѥ господє и ȣ цара Стєфана, тьзи законь да
єсть и сьди. и кто люби ити изь моѥ зємлє ȣ Дȣбровникь
или срьбинь или влахь или чи г(одє) човѣкь на кȣплю,
всак(ь) да грєдє слободнѡ, да га нє ȣсталꙗ господство ми
ни кєфалиꙗ господства ми, и що имь ѥ биль за(к)онь при
царȣ Стєфанȣ, тои и сьди. и за трьговє помѡрскє, кои сȣ
ȣ владанию господства ми, а сланицѣ, кȣдє сȣ били трьговє ȣ прьвє господє и сланицѣ ȣ цара Стєфана, тȣдєзи да сȣ
и сьда, а индє нигдє да нє бȣдȣ. и що сє прѣ мєгȣ собомь
дȣбровчанє, или сє бȣдє ȣчинило ȣ Срьблихь или ȣ Дȣбров-
никȣ, да сє прѣ прѣдь кȣньсȣлѡмь дȣбровчкимь и прѣд
нихь сȣдиꙗми, и що сȣди кȣньсȣль и нєговє сȣдиє, на томь
да стоѥ: ако ли би нє хтѣль дȣбровчанинь стоꙗти на
ѡномзи сȣдȣ, да ѥ во(льнь) кȣньсȣль и нєговє сȣдиє ·ѡ(нога)зи свєзати и дрьжати, до гдє плати, ȣ що ѥ ѡсȣгєнь. а
да тогаи закона ниѥ вольнь (потворити ни) кєфалиꙗ ни вла-
далць. и ако сє слȣчи смрьть к(омȣ) дȣбров(чанинȣ) ȣ зємли

and who have not acquired a residence, are free to go as they please. And if a Dubrovnik ship should be shipwrecked on the coastal territory under the jurisdiction of my government, whatever law was in effect for such a circumstance under the first lords and under Emperor Stefan, let that law hold now, too. And whoever wants to go from my land to Dubrovnik, whether he be Serb or Vlah or whatever, in order to trade, let each one go freely, and let not my government nor my chief magistrates prevent them, and what the law was for them under Stefan so let it be now. And as for the coastal markets which are under the jurisdiction of my kingdom, and the salt concessions, where there were markets under the first lords and where there were salt concessions under Emperor Stefan, let there be such now, and let there be none anywhere else. And if Dubrovnik citizens should have a dispute among themselves, whether it be about something that happened in Serbia or in Dubrovnik, let it be tried before the Dubrovnik consul and before their own judges, and let them agree to abide by what the consul and judges decide: if a Dubrovnik citizen is unwilling to accept such a judgment, then the consul is free, as are the judges, to tie that person up and to detain him until such time as he pays the judgment against him. And let it be that neither the chief magistrates nor the ruler are free to change this law. And if death should befall some citizen of Dubrovnik while in my kingdom,

оcподства ми, що ѥ негова иманиꙗ [да за тои не] има
нocла господство ми ни кеф[алиꙗ госпоства ми ни ин . .
гко сȣ ȣ земли госпоства ми], тькмо да си е, комȣ га да ѡнзи
на смрьти [дȣбровчанинȣ. и да ние дȣбровчаномь посноно-
'а дара. и ако слȣчи господствȣ ми, те]ре се сваге з Дȣ-
бровникомь, да имь приповемь [на .ѕ҃. мѣсеца прѣге тога,
како да си изидȣ вси дȣбровчане с иманиѥмь своѥмь из] земле
господства ми свободнѡ, по толе да ихь ратȣѥ го[спод-
ство ми. и молю, ѥгоже изволи богь по мене бити господина земли срьпскои или кога ѡдь син]овь моихь или ѡдь
рода господства ми или ино[го кого, ѥгоже изволи богь,
семȣи више писанномȣ не потворенȣ бити, нȣ паче по]-
тврьжденȣ, ꙗкоже и ми не потворисмо прѣ[ге нась бивши-
хь. и сеи се повелениѥ господина Лазара писа се мѣсеца ген-
вара .д҃. дань ȣ слав]номь градȣ господства ми Крȣшевцȣ
вь лѣто . ҂ѕ҃ѡч(е). и сиемȣ повелени[ю госпоства ми милостникь логофеть Ненада и Петарь жȣпань и челникь] Михо
и кефалиꙗ Гоиславь.

let not my government nor the chief magistrates of my government nor anyone else have anything to do with his property, but let it belong to whatever Dubrovnik citizen he leaves it at his death. And let it not be a gift for Dubrovnik citizens. And if my government should happen to quarrel with Dubrovnik, then I should advise them four months in advance, so that all Dubrovnik people may leave my kingdom freely, with their property, in as much as my kingdom is at war with them. And I beseech whomever God chooses to be lord of the Serbian land after me, whether it be one of my sons, or a member of my family, or someone else whom God chooses, that what is written above not be changed, but rather that it be confirmed, just as we did not change what was written by those before us. And this order of Lord Lazar was written down in the month of January, on the ninth day, in the glorious city of my kingdom, Kruševac, in the year 1387, and the witness to this order of my government is chancellor Nenad and count Petar and chieftain Miho and chief magistrate Gojislav.

Illustration from the *Hrvoje missal*

The "Apocalypse" or revelation of Saint John the Evangelist, *The Apocalypse* *a canonical document in both the Eastern Orthodox and Roman Catholic Churches, was a favorite with early Christian heretical sects as well.*

Our selection is taken from a Bosnian cyrillic manuscript, copied by a Bogomil "heretic" named Hval, for the Bosnian Duke Hrvoje in 1404. The entire "Apocalypse" was reproduced by Djura Daničić in Starine *("Apokalipsa iz Hvalova Rukopisa,"* Starine *IV).*

Bogomilism seems to have taken root first in Bulgaria, in the tenth century. As a movement directed against the established Church it became strong after the Golden Age of Tsar Simeon (died 927 A.D.), when a regression toward paganism seems to have taken place among the newly converted Bulgaro-Slavic-Thracian population. Bogomilism was attractive to the common people because it adopted certain pagan folk beliefs, while giving them a Christian patina. Its opposition to service to the state, as well as its expressed antagonism toward an elaborate church hierarchy, made this heresy as much a social movement as a religious one.

The Bulgarian churchman Kozma, toward the end of the tenth century, wrote a strong attack against the Bogomils: Beseda na novopojavivšuju se jeres bogomilju, *in which Kozma identified the leader of this sect as Jeremiah, the man who is elsewhere referred to as "Bogomil." Kozma describes the Bogomils as follows: "Externally the Bogomils are like sheep: timid, humble, and quiet, their faces are pale from their hypocritical fasting; they don't utter a word; they don't laugh loudly; they are not inquisitive; they avoid the gaze of the stranger, and on the outside they do everything so that one might not distinguish them from Orthodox Christians, but on the inside they are like wolves and birds of prey." (V. Sl. Kiselkov:* Prezviter Kozma i negovata beseda protiv bogomilite, *Karnobat, 1921, 34).*

Although the Bogomils are often called Manicheans or dualists, such a designation is not accurate, as Franjo Rački pointed out in his very thorough study, Bogomili i Patareni *(SKA,* Posebna izdanja, *87, Beograd, 1931). According to Rački, the Bogomils more often believed in one supreme God, who created the spiritual world (i.e., men's souls); the material world, including the human body, was supposedly the handiwork of a fallen angel, either Satan or Lucifer. Bogomils also believed that Christ never became incarnate (took on a real human form), nor did they believe that Mary was his physical mother. They likewise did not believe that Christ suffered on the cross, since his body was only an illusion, nor did they recognize communion as a sacrament, although they broke bread in honor of the Last Supper. Bogomils were also opposed*

to marriage, and they looked upon sexual intercourse as a vile activity which only stirred up the destructive forces in man.

An espousal of most of the above beliefs could get a person burned at the stake during the Middle Ages, as was often the case with the Bogomils and their co-believers in Italy and France, the Patareni or Catharists. The threat to the established Church and State was so great that it provoked anti-Bogomil purges by the Byzantine Empire in the eleventh and twelfth centuries and by the Serbian Veliki Župan, Stefan Nemanja toward the end of the twelfth century. (See elsewhere in this anthology Nemanja's biography by his son Stefan, where he discusses his father's successful effort to eradicate the heresy in the Serbian lands.) But the Bogomils became strongly entrenched in Bosnia, where they succeeded in converting the ruling class. We know that the Bosnian Ban Kulin (late twelfth century) and his wife were Bogomils, as was his sister, who was married to Prince Miroslav of Hum (for whom the famous Gospels were copied). In the fifteenth century the Grand Inquisitor Juan de Torquemada wrote a treatise against the Bosnian "manichei," in which he rebutted fifty points of belief of the Bosnians (See Fr. Rački, "Dva nova priloga za poviest bosanskih Patarena," in Starine, XIV, Zagreb, 1882).

There seems no doubt that the Bogomils had their own religious tracts, as well as folk songs to make their doctrine more readily comprehensible to the uneducated, but unfortunately such literature seems to have been totally destroyed during the various purges that took place. We do know that they were very fond of apocryphal literature, such as "O dreve kr̆stnem " (Concerning the tree of the Cross), "O Gospode našem Isuse Hriste kako v popu stavlen"(About Our Lord Jesus Christ, how he was made a priest); and "Čto Hristos plugom oral" (How Jesus Christ plowed with a plow). Many of these apocryphal works, attributed to the priest Jeremiah (Bogomil), are listed on the Index in the fourteenth century Pogodinski Nomokanon, as well as in other Nomokanons. In Russia these apocryphal stories were known as "Bulgarian fables," and Jagić believes that the reference to "babunska reć" in the Law Code of Tsar Dušan is directed against the same type of literature. (Vatroslav Jagić, Historija književnosti naroda hrvatskoga i srbskoga, I, Zagreb, 1867, 83.)

For further information on the Bogomil heresy, the following books might provide a good beginning: The Bogomils by Dmitry Obolensky, Cambridge University Press, 1948 (very sketchy on Yugoslav Bogomilism); Bogomilski knigi i legendi by Iordan Ivanov, Fototipno izdanie BAN, Izd. Nauka i Izkustvo, 1970 (has much on apocryphal literature), Bogomilskoto učenie i istorija na bogomilstvoto by Anton Glogov, Sofia, 1948 (purports to be a translation of Bogomil tenets from Turkish documents); Le traité Contre les Bogomils de Cosmas le Prêtre: Traduction et Étude by Henri-Charles Puech and André Vaillant (introd.), Paris, 1945. Also to be consulted, of course, are the works of Rački and Kiselkov, cited earlier.

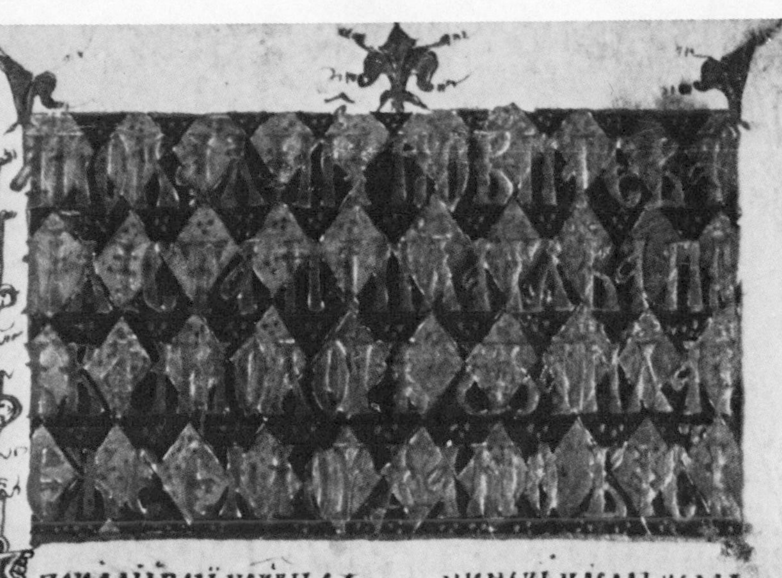

The first page of the Hval Apocalypse

Апокаліпсї Іована еванђеліста и апостола.

I

Апокалыпсы исоухристовы, еже дасть емоу богь показаты рабомь
своимь, имьже подобаеть вь скоры бїти, и сказавь пославь анђеломь
своимь рабоу своемоу Іованоу, 2 иже свыдытельствова слово божїе и
свыдытельство исоухристово, еже вѣды. 3 блажень чтеи и слышеште
словеса пророчьствиѣ и сьблоудаюште напысаниѣ вь немь, врѣме бо
близь. 4 Іовань седмы црькквамь соуштимь вь Асыи благодить вамь и
мѣрь ѡть соуштаго, иже бысть и гредоуштаго и ѡть седмы доухь,
иже соуть прѣдь прѣстоломь его, 5 и ѡть Исоуса Христа, иже
ѥсть свыдытель вѣрань и прьвынаць изь мрьтвыхь и кнезь царемь
земльнимь, ло(ү)бештоумоу ны и раздрѣшьшоумоу ѡть грѣхь нашыхь
крьвыю своею; 6 и створыль есть намь царьсткые, и ерые богоу и
отьцоу своемоу; томоу слава и дрьжава оу вѣкї вѣкомь. ам(и)нь. 7 се
гредеть сь облакы и оузрыть всако око иже и прободоше, и плачь и
вьпаль створеть о немь вса колына земльна. амынь. 8 азь есамь альпа и
о, начетакь и конаць, глаголеть богь, се, бысть и есть и греды, все-
дрьжитель. 9 азь Іовань, брать вашь и обаштиникь вь печалехь и царь-
ствы и трьпыны їсоухристовы, бѣхь вь отоцы нарицаемы Патомы за
слово божые и за свыдытельство исоухристово. 10 быхь доухомь вь
дань недыльны, и слышахь за собою глась велыи ѣко троубыѣ глаголоу-
шты: 11 еже выдышы напиши вь кныгы и послы седмы (rkp. седимы)
црькквамь вь Ефессь и вь Измоурыю и вь Перьгамь и вь Тыатырь и
вь Сарьдыю и вь Пиладокыю и вь Ладокию. 12 и обратих се вѣдїти
глась иже глаголаше сь мною, и обрашть се вѣдихь .з. св(ѣ)тыльникь
златыхь гороушть, 13 и по срѣды седмы свытильникь подобань сыноу
чловѣчьскомоу обльчень вь подырь и прѣпоѣсань при сасьцоу поѣсомь зла-
тымь; 14 глава же его и власы бѣли ѣко и ѣрына и ѣко снѣгь, и очы
его ѣко пламень огньны, 15 и нозы его подобиѣ мѣди лыванові ѣко
вь пешти раждежени, и глас его ѣко глась водь многыхь текоушть;
16 дрьже вь роуцї своеи звыздь .з., из оусть его мачь обоюдоу остарь
изострень исходеи, и лыце его ѣко сль(нь)це сиѣеть вь силы своеи. 17 и
егда выдыхь, падохь прѣдь ногама его ѣко мрьтавь; и положы роукоу
свою десноую на миѣ глаголе: не бои (rkp. пои) се, азь есамь прьви
и послѣдны, 18 и жывь, быхь ѣко мрьтавь, и се живь есамь оу вѣкы
вѣкомь. ам(и)нь. имамь клоучь смрьты и адоу. 19 напыши оубо ѣже
вѣды и ѣже соуть, имьже подобаеть по сыхь бїти; 20 таина .з. звыздь,
еже вѣды вь десници моеи, и .з. свыт(и)льникь златихь: .з. звѣздь ан-
ђелоу .з. црькавь соуть и .з. свыт(и)льникь, еже вѣды, .з. црькавь ѥсть.

THE APOCALYPSE OF JOHN THE EVANGELIST AND APOSTLE

The apocalypse from Jesus Christ, which God allowed him to show to his servants, concerning what must soon be; and he made it known by sending an angel to his servant John, who had given witness to God's word and to Christ's testimony, which he had seen. Blessed be he who reads and hears the words of the prophecy and heeds what is written in it, for the time is near. John wishes grace and peace to the seven churches which are in Asia, from him who is, who was, and is to come, and from the seven spirits who are before his throne, and from Jesus Christ who is the true witness and the first-born to rise from the dead and the prince over earthly kings, who loves us and who absolved us from our sins by his blood; and he created for us a kingdom, and he made us priests for God, his father; glory and power be to him through all ages, Amen. Behold he comes with clouds about him, and every eye that has pierced him will see him, and all the tribes of the earth will wail and lament because of him. Amen. I am the alpha and the omega, the beginning and the end, says God; he who was, and is, and is to come, the Almighty. I, John, your brother and sharer in your sorrows and in your kingdom, as well as in your endurance in Christ, I was on the island called Patmos because I preached God's word and gave testimony concerning Christ. I was in the power of the spirit, on the Lord's day, and I heard behind me a great voice, like that of a trumpet, saying: "Write down what you see in a scroll and send it to the seven churches: to Ephesus, and Smyrna, and Pergamum, and Thyatira, and Sardis, and Philadelphia, and Laodicea." And I turned around to see the voice which was talking to me, and as I turned I saw seven gold candlesticks burning, and in the midst of the seven candlesticks one who was similar to the son of man, dressed in a long garment and girded with a gold belt around his chest. His head and his beard were white like wool and like snow, and his eyes were like a fiery flame. And his feet were like molten copper when it is heated in the crucible, and his voice was like the voice of many flowing waters; he was holding in his hand seven stars, and from his mouth there extended a sword, sharpened on both edges, and his face was like the sun shining in full force. And when I saw him I fell at his feet, as though I were dead; and he put his right hand on me, saying: "Don't be afraid, I am the first and the last, and even though alive I was as dead, and behold I am alive through all ages. Amen. I have the key to death and to hell. So write down what you see, both what is, and what is to come later; the secret of the seven stars which you see in my right hand, and the seven gold candlesticks, is this: the seven stars are the angels of the seven churches, and the seven candlesticks which you see are the seven churches."

И видыхь сыдештаго на прѣстолы вь десницы кныги написане вьни-
юдоу и вьноутрьюдоу прѣдь и задь запечатлени .з. печатї. 2 и в(и)дыхь
ины анђель крѣпакь проповыдаюшть гласомь велынмь: кто достоѣнь разагноутн книгы и разрѣшыти печаты ихь? 3 и никтоже не можаше
на небесы ни на земли ни подь беѕадною разагноутн книгь ни раз-
дрѣшыти ихь. 4 и плакахь се много, ѣко никтоже не обрѣте се достоѣнь разагноуты книгь и раздрѣшити ихь. 5 и глагола мы ѥдань
ѡть стар(ь)ць: не плачи се, се побыдыль ѥсть ѡть колына июдова
корень давидовь разагноуты кныгы и седамь печаты ихь. 6 и в(и)-
дыхь по срѣды прѣстола .д. животна, и по срѣды старьць агнаць сто
ѥшть ѣко заколень, имоушть рогь .з. и очесь .з., иже соуть .з.
доухь божихь посланихь кь всоу землоу. 7 и прыде прыетї книги ѡть
десниц̑е сѣдештаго на прѣстолы. 8 и ѥгда приеть кнїги, и .д. животна
и .к. и .д. старцы падоу ниць прѣдь прѣстоломь и прѣдь агньцемь, имоуште
каждо ихь гоусли и пиѣлы златы пльни тамыѣна, ѥже соуть молытвы
светыхь. 9 и поють пѣсань новоу глаголоуште: достоѣнь ѥсы прыети
книгы и ѡтьврѣсты печати ихь, ѣко заколень бысть, искоупї ни богови
своѥю крьвию ѡть всакаго колына и лоуды и ѥзикь и племень, 10 и стко-
рыль ѥсї богоу нашемоу царе и ѥрие, и вьцареть се на земли. 11 и
видыхь и слышахь гласъ анђель многь окрьсть прѣстола и животныхь
(и) стар(ь)ць; и бы число ихь тмы тмамы и тысоуште тысоуштамы,
12 глаголоуште гласомь велнкимь: достоѣнь ѥсть агнаць заколень прїеты
силоу и богатьство и прѣмоудрость и крѣпость и часть и славоу и
благословление. 13 и всако сьзданїе, ѥже ѥсть на небесихь и на земли
и подь землею и на мори и соушта вь нихь вса, и слышахь пакы глаголоушть сѣдештаго на прѣстолы агньцоу благословление и часть и
слава и дрьжава оу вѣкы вѣкомь. аминь. 14 и .д. жывотна аминь глаголахоу, и старьцы падоу ниць, и поклонише се.

I в(и)дыхь ѥгда ѡтьврьзе агнаць ѥдиноу ѡть .з. печаты, и слышахь ѥдино ѡть .д. жывотань глаголоуште ѣко гласъ громань: греды и
выждь. 2 и се конь биль, и сѣден на немь имаше лоукь, и дань ѥмоу
бысть вѣнаць, изыде побиждае и да побыдїть. 3 и ѥгда ѡтьврьзе дроугоу печать, и слышахь дроуго животно глаголоуште: греды и виждь.
4 изыде конь рыждь, и сѣдештоумоу на немь и дано ѥмоу бысть вьзеты
мѣрь ѡть земле, да оубыють дроугь дроуга, и дано ѥмоу бысть ороужые
велие. 5 и ѥгда ѡтьврьзе печать третыю, и слышахь третие жывотно
глаголоуште: греды и выждь. и се конь врань, и сыдеи на немь дрьжаше мѣрыло вь роуци своеи. 6 и слышахь гласъ по срѣды .д. жїво-
тань глаголоуште: хоуниз пшеннце пѣнезоу, и .г. хоуниз ѥчмень пѣ-

And I saw the one sitting on the throne, in his right hand a scroll written on the inside and outside, sealed front and back with seven seals. And I saw another angel, one robust, who was saying in a loud voice: "Who is worthy to open this scroll and break its seals?" And no one, either in heaven, or on earth, or beneath the abyss, was able to open the scroll or break the seals. And I wept much, because no one could be found worthy to open the scroll and to break them. And one of the elders said to me: "Don't cry, behold one who has won the right to open the scroll and its seven seals; he is from the tribe of Juda, from the stock of David." And I saw in the center of the throne area four living figures, and in the midst of the elders a lamb was standing that appeared to have been sacrificed; he had seven horns and seven eyes, which are the seven spirits of God sent throughout the whole earth. And he came to take the scroll from the right hand of the one sitting on the throne. And when he took the scroll, both the four living figures and the twenty four elders fell prostrate before the throne and before the lamb, each one having a harp and a gold bowl filled with incense, which is the prayers of the saints. And they sang a new song, saying: "You are worthy to receive the scroll and to open its seals, because you were sacrificed, and with your blood you redeemed us for God, out of every clan, and people, and language, and tribe. And you have made us kings and priests for our God; and he will reign on earth." And I saw and heard the voices of many angels, who were surrounding the throne and the living figures and the elders; and they numbered myriads of myriads and thousands of thousands, saying in a loud voice: "The sacrificed lamb is worthy to receive the power and the riches and the wisdom and the strength and the honor and the glory and the blessing." And every creature that is in heaven and on earth, and under the earth, and on the sea, and all that are in it, I heard to say: "Blessing and honor and glory and power through all ages to him who sits on the throne and to the lamb. Amen." And the four living figures were saying "Amen," and the elders fell prostrate and worshipped him.

And I saw the lamb break open one of the seven seals, and I heard one of the four living figures say with a thunderous voice: "Come and see." And behold, there was a white horse, and its rider had a bow, and he was given a crown, and he rode out victorious, and to win victory. And when he broke open the second seal, I heard a second living figure say: "Come and see." A red horse came out, and its rider had been empowered to take peace away from the earth, so that men would kill one another, and he was given a great weapon. And when he opened the third seal, I heard the third living figure say: "Come and see." And behold, there was a black horse, and its rider was holding a scales in his hand. And I heard a voice from the midst of the four living figures, saying:

неꙃоу, вына и олыѣ не врѣды. 7 и егда ѡтьврьꙃе печать .д.-оу, и слышахь .д.-о жывотно глаголоуште: греды. 8 и видыхь, и се конь блѣдь,
иже сидыаше на немь, име емоу смрьть, и адь идѣаше вь слѣдь его, и
дана емоу бысть область на .д. честы ꙃемле оубыты ороужыемь и гла-
домь и смрьтыю и ꙃвырьмы ꙃемльнымы. 9 ї егда ѡтьврьꙃе печать .є., и
в(и)дыхь подь олтаремь доушь чловѣчьскыхь иꙃбиенихь ꙃа слово божые и
ꙃа свыдетельство исоухристово, еже имахоу. 10 и вьꙃоупише гласомь
велыкымь глаголоуште: до колы господы светы истиньни (rkp. истьньни)
не соудышы и не мастышї крьвы наше на живоуштыхь на ꙃемли?
11 и дани быше комоуждо ихь рыꙃы били, и речено бысть имь да по-
чыють еште мало врѣме, до ньдыже сконьчають се чысла клеврѣть ихь
и братые ихь хотештихь иꙃбиени бити ѣкоже и ты. 12 и егда ѡтьврьꙃе
.ѕ. печать, бысть троусь велыкь, и сль(нь)це бысть мрачно ѣко врѣ-
тыште власимыто, и мѣсець бысть ѣко и крьвь, 13 и ꙃвыꙃды спадоу
с небесе на ꙃемлоу ѣко смоковница ѡтьмытающты поупы свое ѡть
вѣтра велиѣ движїма; 14 и небо ѡтьлоучы се ѣко свытакь свываемы,
и всака гора и отокь ѡть мѣсть своихь двигноуше се; 14 царые ꙃе-
мльсцы и вельможане и тисоуштинцї и богаты и крѣпцы и всакы рабь
и свободни скрише се оу пеќехь и оу камени горьсцымь 16 глаголоуште горамь: покрите ни, и каменню: падыте на нась ѡть лица сиде-
штаго на прѣстолы и ѡть лица агньча, 17 ѣко приде дань велики
гнѣва его, и никтоже не може статы протывоу емоу.

Н по томь выдихь .д. анђелы стоеште на четирехь оуглыхь ꙃемле
дрьжеште .д. вѣтре ꙃемльне, да не дышеть вѣтарь на ꙃемлоу ни на
море ни на всако дрѣво. 2 и в(и)дыхь ини анђель исходешть ѡть ꙃемле,
имѣе печать бога жываго; и вьꙃоупы гласомь великимь кь .д.-мь анђеломь, имьже дано бысть врѣдыты ꙃемлоу и море, глаголе: 3 не врѣдыте
ꙃемле ни мора ни всакаго дрѣва, до ньдыже ꙃапечатлыемь рабы бога
нашего на челыхь ихь. 4 и слышахь чысло ꙃапечатленихь ѡть всакаго
колѣна сыновь иꙃраилевыхь. 5 .а. ѡть колына июдова .ві. тїсоуштї ꙃапечатленихь; .в. ѡть колына роу(ви)мова .ві. тисоушты ꙃапечатленихь;
.г. ѡть колына гадова .ві. тисоушты ꙃапечатленихь; 6 .д. ѡть колѣна
асоурова .ві. тысоушты ꙃапечатленихь; .є. ѡть колѣна нептали̇мова .ві.
тисоушты ꙃапечатленихь; .ѕ. ѡть колѣна манасїина .ві. тысоушти ꙃапечатленихь; 7 .ꙁ. ѡть колина семеонова .ві. тисоушты ꙃапечатленихь;
.и. ѡть колѣна левгынина .ві. тисоушты ꙃапечатленихь; .ѳ. ѡть колѣна исахарова .ві. тысоушты ꙃапечатленихь; 8 .і. ѡть колѣна ꙃаве-
лона .ві. тысоушты ꙃапечатленихь; аі. ѡть колѣна иосыпова .ві. тысоушты ꙃапечатленихь; .ві. ѡть колына веньѣминова .ві. тисоуштї
ꙃапечатленихь. 9 и по сихь видыхь, и се народь многь, егоже ны-

"A silver piece for a quart of wheat, a silver piece for three quarts of barley; but don't damage the wine and the oil." And when he opened the fourth seal, I heard the fourth living figure say: "Come." And I looked, and behold there was a pale horse, and its rider was called Death, and hell followed in its tracks, and he was given sway over the four quarters of the earth, to kill with weapons, and hunger, and death, and wild beasts of the earth. And when he opened the fifth seal I saw beneath the altar the souls of men killed for God's word and for having borne witness of Jesus Christ. And they cried out with a loud voice, saying: "How long, o Lord, the holy, the true, before you will pass judgment and take vengeance for our blood on those who are living on earth?" And to each of them was given a white robe, and they were told to rest a little while longer, until their numbers were completed by their fellow servants and their brethren who would be killed as they had been killed. And when he opened the sixth seal, there was a great earthquake, and the sun became as dark as sackcloth and the moon was like blood, and the stars fell from the sky onto the earth, like a fig tree shaking loose its blossoms when it is shaken by a great wind, and the sky was peeled off like a rolled up scroll, and every mountain and island moved from its place; the kings of the earth, and magnates, and colonels, and the rich and the strong, and every slave and freeman hid in caves and amidst mountain rocks, saying to the mountains: "cover us," and to the rocks: "fall on us [and hide us] from the person sitting on the throne and from the face of the lamb, for there has come the great day of his wrath, and no one can stand against him."

After that I saw four angels standing at the four corners of the earth, holding back the four winds of the earth, so that the wind could not blow on the earth or on the sea or on any tree. And I saw another angel coming out of the earth, holding the seal of the living God, and he cried out with a loud voice to the four angels who were empowered to do harm to the earth and the sea, saying: "Do not harm the earth, or the sea, or any tree, until we put the seal on the foreheads of those who are servants of our God." And I heard the number of those who were sealed from every tribe of the sons of Israel. First, from the tribe of Juda twelve thousand were sealed; second, from the tribe of Ruben twelve thousand were sealed; third from the tribe of Gad twelve thousand were sealed; fourth, from the tribe of Aser twelve thousand were sealed; fifth, from the tribe of Nephthali twelve thousand were sealed; sixth, from the tribe of Manasse twelve thousand were sealed; seventh, from the tribe of Simeon twelve thousand were sealed; eighth, from the tribe of Levi twelve thousand were sealed; ninth, from the tribe of Issachar twelve thousand were sealed; tenth, from the tribe of Zabulon twelve thousand were sealed; eleventh, from the tribe of Joseph twelve thousand were sealed; twelfth, from the tribe of Benjamin twelve thousand were sealed. And after this

ктоже не можеть исчисти ѡть всѧкаго колѣна и езыкь ї лоудї и племень стоештихь прѣдь прѣстоломь и прѣдь агньцемь облъчены вь рызи
былы, и финикы вь роукахь ихь. 10 и вьзоупыше гласомь велыимь
глаголоуште: спасение бога нашего сѣдештаго на прѣстолы агньчы.
11 и вси анђелы стоѣхоу окрьсть прѣстолѧ и старцы и .д. животна падоу
прѣдь прѣстоломь ницѣ, и поклониише се богоу нашемоу сѣдештоумоу
на прѣстолы и агньцоу глаголоуште: аминь. 12 благословление и прѣмоудрость и слава и часть и сила и хвала и крѣпость бога нашего оу
вѣки вѣкомь. аминь. 13 и ѡтьвештавь единь ѡть стар(ь)ць глаголѧ мы:
си облъчены вь рызї бѣли кто соуть, и ѡть коуда приидоуть? 14 и
рѣхь емоу: господы мои, ты вѣси. и рече мы: сы соуть гредоуште
ѡть скрьбы великые, испраше ризы свое, и оубѣлыше е оу крьвы
агньчы. 15 и сего ради соуть прѣдь прѣстоломь божиимь, и слоужеть
емоу д(ь)нь и ношть кь црькви божыи; сѣдеи на прѣстолы вьселыть
се ва не. 16 и не ваз(ал)ьчоуть се к томоу, ни каждеждоуть се, ни
имать пасты на нихь сльнце ни всѧкы зиои. 17 ѣко агнаць иже по
срѣды прѣстолѧ оупасеть е, и наставыть е на жывы источникь водны,
и ѡтьиметь богь всѧкоу сльзоу ѡть очыю ихь.

И егда ѡтькрьзе .з. печать, бысть безмльвие на небесы ѣко поль
годынї. 2 и видыхь .з. анђель, иже прѣдь богомь стоѣхоу, и дано бысть
имь .з. троубни. 3 и дроугы анђель приде имые кадылницоу златоу;
и даны емоу быше тамыѣни мнози, да дасть молытвамы светыхь всїхь
на олтары соуштыхь светїхь прѣдь прѣстоломь его. 4 и вьзиде днмь
кадильни молытвамї светыхь роукою анђелокою прѣдь бога, 5 и вьзеть
анђель кадылницоу, и напльни ю ѡть огнѧ соуштаго на олтарї, и положы на землї; и биише громы и блыстаниѣ и гласи и троуси. 6 и
.з. анђель, иже прѣ(дь) богомь стоѣхоу, имыѧхоу .з. троубыи, оугото-
ваше се да троубеть. 7 и прьвы анђель вьстроубы, и бысть градь и
огнь смѣшень сь крьвыю, и паде на землоу, и третыѣ часть земле
погорѣ, и третыѣ часть ѡть дрѣвѧ погоры, и всѧкѧ трава (rkp. драва)
злачна погорѣ. 8 и дроугы анђель вьстроубы, ѣко гора велїѣ жегома
огнемь вьврьжена бысть вь море, и бысть третыѣ часть мора кры-
вью. 9 оумрѣть и третыѣ часть зданиѣ вь моры имоуштихь доушь и
.г.-ѣ часть корабль погыбе. 10 и .г. анђель вьстроубї, и паде с небесе
звѣзда велыѣ гороушта (rkp. гоуроушта) ѣко свыщта, и паде на тре-
тиѡ часты рѣкь и на источникы водные. 11 име звѣзды глаголеть се
аспинь, и бїсть третыѣ часть водь ѣко и пелѣнь, и мнози ѡть чловѣкь оумрѣше, ѣко горькы быше. 12 и .д. анђель вьстроубї, и ѣзвена
бысть третыѣ часть сльнца и .г. часть лоуны и третыѣ часть звѣздь,
и .г. да оумрькнеть, и .г. часть дне да не свытыть, и .г. часть свое
ношти такожде. 13 и видихь и слышахь единь анђель парешть по срѣди
небесь, глаголоушть гласомь велыимь три крать: горе, горе, горе живоу-
штимь на земли ѡть прочыхь глась троубнихь трехь анђель хотештихь
троубыти.

I looked, and behold I saw a multitude of people, which no one could count, from every clan and language and people and tribe, standing before the throne and before the lamb, dressed in white robes, and with palm branches in their hands. And they cried out with a loud voice, saying: "Salvation is from our God, sitting on the throne of the lamb." And all the angels who were standing around the throne, and the elders and the four living figures, fell prostrate before the throne, and they worshipped our God who was seated on the throne, and the lamb, saying: "Amen. Blessing and wisdom and glory and honor and power and praise and strength be to our God through all ages. Amen." And turning, one of the elders said to me: "Who are those who are dressed in white robes, and whence do they come?" And I said to him: "My Lord, you know." And he said to me: "These people are coming from great sorrow; they have washed their robes and made them white in the blood of the lamb. And for this reason they are in front of God's throne, and they serve him day and night in God's temple; seated on the throne he takes joy in them. And they will not be hungry nor will they thirst, nor will the sun beat down on them, nor will they sweat. For the lamb, who is in the centre before the throne, will be their shepherd, and he will lead them to the living spring of water, and God will remove every tear from their eyes(...) And when he broke open the seventh seal there was silence in heaven for about half an hour. And I saw seven angels who were standing before God, and they were given seven trumpets. And another angel came, bearing a gold censer; and he was given much incense, that he might make an offering of the prayers of all the saints at the altar before his throne. And the smoke from the censer in the angel's hand rose up before God like the prayers of the saints. And the angel took the censer and he filled it with fire from the altar, and he laid it on the earth; and there was thunder and lightning and voices and earthquakes. And the seven angels who were standing before God, and who had the seven trumpets, made ready to sound them. And the first angel blew his trumpet, and there was hail and fire mixed with blood, and it fell onto the earth, and a third of the earth burned up, and a third of the trees, and all the golden grass burned up. And a second angel blew his trumpet, and it was as if a great mountain burning with fire was thrown into the sea, and a third of the sea was like blood. And a third of all the living creatures in the sea died, and a third of the ships were lost. And the third angel blew his trumpet, and a great star fell from heaven burning like a candle, and it fell on a third of the rivers and on the sources of water. The name of the star is Wormwood, and a third of the water was like wormwood, and many men died because it was bitter. And the fourth angel blew his trumpet, and a third of the sun and a third of the moon and a third of the stars were struck by it, and they became dark so that one third of the day was without light, and a third of the night also. And I saw and heard an angel, who was flying across the middle of heaven, saying three times in a loud voice: "Woe, woe, woe, to those living on earth, from the trumpet blasts of the three angels who have yet to blow their trumpets."

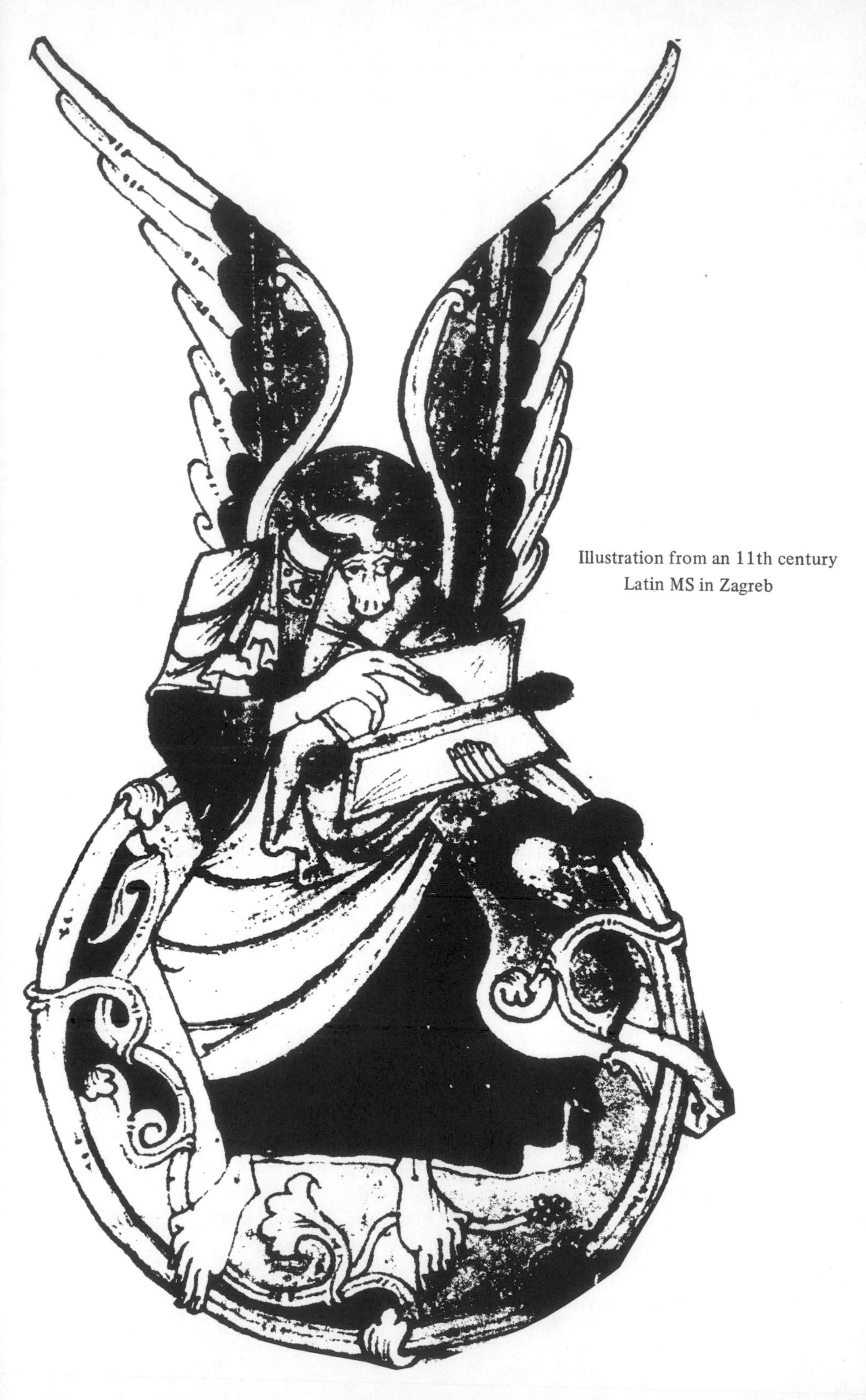

Illustration from an 11th century
Latin MS in Zagreb

II

MEDIEVAL BELLES LETTRES

A Croatian king

The Priest of Duklja

*The tragic love story of King Vladimir of Duklja and his wife Kosara is from the twelfth-century Chronicle of the Priest of Duklja (*Ljetopis popa Dukljanina*). Duklja or Doclea was a tenth and eleventh century Slavic kingdom, which included part of today's Montenegro (Zeta), the southern Dalmatian coast, and part of Albania. Its capital was located not far from today's city of Titograd.*

The twelfth century chronicler of Duklja wrote in Latin, basing his account on a Slavic document and on oral tradition. We know that the Latin chronicle was later translated into Slavic, since in the year 1510 Dmine Papalić found at Makarska a version of the Ljetopis *written "harvackim pismom" ("in Croatian writing"). Papalić claims to have copied this document word for word, and at his request the distinguished Split writer and scholar, Marko Marulić (see the excerpt from his* Judita *in this book) translated it into Latin (really a paraphrase), so that those who did not know Serbo-Croatian might become acquainted with the early history of the Slavs in the Balkans. In the introduction to his translation Marulić calls the* Ljetopis *"res certe digna relatu et quam non solum nostrae vernaculae linguae gnari, sed etiam Latini intelligant" ("A subject certainly worth telling, and not only to those who know our native language, but also to those who understand Latin." Quoted from Ferdo Šišić's excellent study:* Ljetopis popa Dukljanina. *Beograd: SKA, posebna izdanja LXVII, 1928, 157.)*

The oldest published version of the Ljetopis *is the Italian translation of Mavro Orbini, a Dubrovnik Benedictine priest, who gave his work the title* Il regno degli Slavi oggi corrottamente detti Schiavoni. *(Pesaro, 1601.) Šišić, in his study of the* Chronicle, *gives both Orbini's translation and a variant of the original Latin manuscript, published by Ivan Lucić (or Lucije) in Amsterdam, in 1666 (*De regno Dalmatiae et Croatiae libri sex.*) Šišić points out that Lucić and Orbini did not use the same Latin variant for their publications, and that Orbini's source was superior in detail.*

That the saintly King Vladimir and his Bulgarian wife Kosara actually lived in the period given in the Chronicle *has been corroborated by Byzantine sources, among others. The strong cult of Saint Vladimir, which persisted among Slavs and Albanians right into the twentieth century, is a possible indication that he was indeed a generous and restrained ruler, and that his subjects felt his martyrdom as a personal loss.*

The story of Vladimir and Kosara, as given in the Ljetopis popa Dukljanina, *has literary qualities which are reminiscent of the best of Western medieval literature. Although its background is strongly religious, there is a minimum of supernatural intervention, and the basic story is not marred by long biblical quotations and learned digressions.*

An interesting sidelight on the relationship between oral and written literature is the fact that Kačić-Miošić, whose Razgovor ugodni *is excerpted in this book, put the story of Vladimir and Kosara into ballad form (using Orbini's version of the* Chronicle*), whence it found its way into folklore.*

VLADIMIRUS ET COSSARA

Post haec rex Petrislavus genuit filium, quem Vladimirum vocavit et in pace quievit. Sepultus est in ecclesia sanctae Mariae, in loco qui dicitur Craini.

Puer autem Vladimirus, accepto regno, crescebat decoratus omni sapientia et sanctitate. Tempore itaque eodem, dum Vladimirus esset adolescens et regnaret in loco patris sui, supradictus Samuel Bulgarinorum imperator, congregato magno exercitu, advenit in partibus Dalmatiae supra terram regis Vladimiri. Rex vero, qui vir sanctus erat et nolebat aliquem de suis perire in bello, secessit humiliter et ascendit in montem, qui Obliquus dicitur, cum omni gente sua. Veniens post haec imperator cum exercitu et cernens, quod regi praevalere non posset, partem sui exercitus ad montis pedem reliquit partemque secum ducens ad expungnandam civitatem Dulcinium perrexit. Erant praeterea per montem Obliquum igniti serpentes, qui statim ut aliquos percutiebant, absque ulla tarditate moriebantur caeperuntque magnum damnum facere, tam de hominibus, quam de animalibus. Tunc rex Vladimirus orationem fudit ad dominum cum lacrimis, ut deus omnipotens liberaret populum suum ab illa pestifera morte. Exaudivit deus orationem famuli sui et ab illo die nullus ex eis percussus est, sed et usque hodie, si homo aut aliqua bestia in monte illo a serpente percussus fuerit, sanus et absque ulla laesione perseverat. Fueruntque in illo monte ab illo die, quo oravit beatus Vladimirus, quasi sine veneno serpentes usque in hodiernum diem. Interea misit imperator nuncios Vladimiro regi, ut cum omnibus, qui cum eo erant, de monte descenderet. Sed rex non acquievit. Iupanus autem eiusdem loci, Iudae traditori similis effectus, misit ad imperatorem dicens: "Domine, si tuae placet magnitudini, ego tibi tradam regem," cui remisit imperator: "Si hoc agere praevales, ditatum te scies a me et magnificum valde." Tunc rex congregatis omnibus qui cum eo erant, taliter eis locutus est: "Oportet me, fratres carissimi, ut video adimplere illud evangelii versiculum, ubi dicitur: "Bonus pastor animam suam ponit pro ovibus suis." Melius est ergo, fratres, ut ego ponam animam meam pro omnibus vobis et tradam corpus meum sponte ad trucidandum seu occidendum, quam ut vos periclitemini fame sive gladio." Tunc postquam haec et alia plurima eis locutus fuisset, resalutatis omnibus, perrexit ad imperatorem. Quem imperator statim relegavit in exilium in partibus Achridae, in loco qui Prespa

VLADIMIR AND KOSARA

After that King Petrislav sired a son to whom he gave the name Vladimir, and he rested in peace. He is buried in the Church of Saint Mary, in the place called Krajina.

And the young lad Vladimir, having received the kingdom, was growing up endowed with every kind of wisdom and sanctity. At that time, while the young Vladimir was ruling in his father's place, the above mentioned Emperor of the Bulgarians, Samuel, having gathered a large army attacked the Dalmatian area, the land of King Vladimir. And the king, who was a saintly man and didn't want any of his people to die in war withdrew meekly and climbed the mountain which is called Oblik with all his people. Subsequently, when the Emperor came with his army and saw that he could not conquer the King, he left one part of his army at the foot of the mountain and the other part he took with him to conquer Ulcinj. On Mount Oblik, however, there were poisonous snakes, and whomever they would bite would immediately die, and so they wrought great harm not only to the people but also to their animals. Then King Vladimir, in tears, prayed to the Lord that Almighty God might deliver his people from that pestilential death. God heard the prayer of his servant, and from that day on no one was bitten, and even today if a snake should bite some man or animal on that mountain he remains healthy and without any injury. And from the day that Saint Vladimir prayed, the snakes on that mountain have been as though poisonless right up until today. In the meantime the Emperor sent his deputies to King Vladimir with the message that he should come down off the mountain with all those who were with him. But the King wouldn't agree. And the *župan* of that place, like the traitor Judas, sent a message to the Emperor saying: "Lord, if your highness wishes, I shall betray the King to you;" whereupon the Emperor answered: "If you succeed in doing that, know that I will make you rich and exalted." Then the King, having gathered all those who were with him, said to them: "It is necessary, dearest brethren, that I see how there will be fulfilled in me that verse in the New Testament which says: "The good shepherd lays down his life for his sheep." It is better, therefore, brethren, that I give my soul for you, and that I voluntarily surrender my body to torture and murder, rather than that you should suffer hunger or the sword." Then, after he had said this to them and a lot more besides, he said goodbye to them all and he went off to the Emperor. The Emperor immediately banished him to the Ohrid region, to a place called Prespa, where the palace of this same Emperor was also located. After that he

dicitur, ubi et curia eiusdem imperatoris erat. Post haec congregato exercitu, debellavit Dulcinium longo tempore, sed eum capere nullatenus valuit. Inde ascendit iratus, caepit destruere, incendere ac depraedare totam Dalmatiam, Decatarum autem atque Lausium civitates incendit nec non et vicos et totam provinciam devastavit, ita ut terra videretur esse sine habitatore. Pertransivit imperator sic devastans tam maritimas quam et montanas regiones usque Jadram; postea per Bosnam et Rassam reversus est in locum suum.

Interea Vladimirus tenebatur in vinculis, ieiuniis et orationibus vacans die noctuque. Apparuit et in visione angelus domini confortans eum et nuncians ei ea, quae ventura erunt, quomodo eum deus liberaret de ipso carcere et quomodo per martirium perveniret ad regna coelorum et acciperet immarcescibilem coronam et praemia vitae aeternae. Tunc beatus Vladimirus de visione angelica roboratus, magis ac magis vacabat orationibus atque ieiuniis. Quadam itaque die imperatoris Samuelis filia Cossara nomine, conpuncta et inspirata a spiritu sancto, accessit ad patrem et petivit ab eo, ut descenderet cum suis ancillis et lavaret caput et pedes vinculatorum et captivorum, quod ei a patre concessum est. Descendit itaque et peregit bonum opus. Inter haec cernens Vladimirum et videns quod esset pulcher in aspectu, humilis, mansuetus atque modestus et quod esset repletus sapientia et prudentia domini, morata locuta est cum illo. Videbatur namque ei loquella illius dulcis super mel et favum. Igitur non causa libidinis, sed quia condoluit iuventuti et pulchritudini illius, et quoniam audiret eum esse regem et ex regali prosapia ortum, dilexit eum et salutato eo recessit. Volens post haec a vinculis liberare eum, accessit ad mperatorem et prostrata pedibus illius taliter locuta est: "Mi pater et domine, scio quia daturus es mihi virum sicuti moris est. Nunc ergo, si tuae placet magnitudini, aut des mihi virum Vladimirum regem, quem tenes in vinculis, aut scias, me prius morituram, quam alium accipiam virum." Imperator haec audiens, quia valde diligebat filiam suam et quia sciebat Vladimirum ex regali progenie ortum, laetus effectus est, annuit fieri petitionem illius; statimque mittens ad Vladimirum et balneatum vestibusque indutum regiis iussit sibi praesentari; et benigne intuens atque osculans coram magnatibus regni sui, tradidit ei filiam suam in uxorem. Celebratis itaque nuptiis filiae suae more regali, constituit imperator Vladimirum in regem et dedit ei terram et regnum patrum suorum totamque terram Duaracenorum. Deinde misit imperator ad Draigimirum, patruum regis Vladimiri, ut descenderet et acciperet terram suam Tribuniam et

gathered an army and beseiged Ulcinj for a long time, but in no way was he able to take it. He went away angry, and he began to destroy, burn, and lay waste the whole of Dalmatia, and he burned the cities of Kotor and Dubrovnik, and he so devastated the villages and the whole province that it appeared as though it were uninhabited. And laying waste in this way, the Emperor passed through the maritime and mountainous regions as far as Zadar, and then he returned via Bosnia and Raška to his own territory.

Vladimir and Kosara

In the meantime they were keeping Vladimir in chains, and he spent his days and nights in fasting and in prayer. Once an angel of the Lord appeared to him in a vision, and encouraging him he announced to him that God would free him from that prison, and that he would attain the heavenly kingdom through martyrdom, and he would receive the unfading crown and the reward of eternal life. Then blessed Vladimir, fortified by the vision of the angel, gave himself more and more to fasting and prayer. But one day the daughter of the Emperor Samuel, Kosara by name, moved and inspired by the Holy Spirit, went to her father and asked him to let her go down into the prison with her servant girls to wash the heads and feet of those who were in chains and were captives, and her father allowed her to do that. And so she went down, and she performed a good deed. Meanwhile she noticed Vladimir, and seeing that he was handsome in appearance, humble, kind, and modest, and that he was full of knowledge and the Lord's wisdom, she stopped to talk with him. It seemed to her that his speech was sweeter than honey and the honeycomb. And she fell in love with him, not out of passion but because she was sorry for one so young and so handsome, because she had heard that he was a king and of royal birth; and after saying goodbye to him she went away. After this, wanting to liberate him from his chains, she went to the Emperor, and throwing herself at his feet she spoke in this manner: "My father and lord, I know that you will give me a husband, as is the custom. Now then, if it please your Highness, either give me for my husband King Vladimir, whom you are keeping in chains, or know that I shall be happier dead than to take anyone else as my husband." When he heard this the Emperor rejoiced, because he loved his daughter very much and because he knew that Vladimir was of royal birth; and he gladly agreed that her request should be granted. And he immediately sent for Vladimir, and he ordered that he be bathed and dressed like a king before they brought him to him. And looking kindly at him and kissing him before the nobles of his kingdom, he gave him his daughter for a wife. After his daughter's wedding had been celebrated in a royal manner, the Emperor made Vladimir a king and he gave him the land and the kingdom of his fathers and the whole of the territory of Drač. Then the Emperor informed Dragomir, the uncle of King Vladimir, that he should come and receive the land of Trabunja, and

congregaret populum et inhabitaret terrant, quod et factum est.

Vladimirus itaque rex vivebat cum uxore sua Cossara in omni sanctitate et castitate, diligens deum et serviens illi nocte ac die; regebatque populum sibi commissum cum timore dei et iustitia. Post non multum vero temporis defunctus est imperator Samuel et filius eius Radomirus accepit imperium. Qui fortis extitit viribis commisitque praelia multa cum Graecis tempore Basilii imperatoris Graecorum obtinuitque totam terram usque Constantinopolim. Timens autem Basilius imperator, ne forte imperium ammitteret, misit oculte legatos ad Vladislavum, consobrinum Radomiri, dicens: "Quare non vindicas sanguinem patris tui? Accipe aurum et argentum a me, quantum tibi visum fuerit estoque nobiscum pacificus et accipe regnum Samuelis, qui patrem tuum et fratrem suum interfecit. Et si praevales, occide filium eius Radomirum, qui nunc tenet regnum." Quo audito Vladislavus consensit et quadam die, dum Radomirus iret venatum, ipse cum eo equitans percussit eum atque intefecit. Et sic mortuus est Radomirus et regnavit in loco eius Vladislavus, qui occidit illum. Accepto itaque imperio misit nuncios ad regem Vladimirum, ut ad eum veniret. Quo audito Cossara regina tenuit eum dicens: "Mi domine, noli ire, ne—quod absit—tibi eveniat sicut fratri meo, sed dimitte me, ut eam et videam e audiam, quomodo se habet rex. Si me vult perdere, perdat; tu tantum ne pereas." Igitur voluntate viri sui perrexit regina ad consobrinum suum, quae honorifice ab eo suscepta est, tamen fraudulenter. Post haec misit legatos secundo regi, dans ei crucem auream et fidem, dicens: "Quare venire dubitas? Ecce, uxor tua apud me est et nil mali passa, sed a me et a meis honorifice habetur. Accipe fidem crucis et veni, ut videam te, quatenus honorifice cum donis revertaris in locum tuum cum uxore tua." Cui remisit rex: "Scimus, quod dominus noster Jesus Christus, qui pro nobis passus est, non in aurea vel argentea cruce suspensus est, sed in lignea; ergo, si vera est fides tua et verba tua vera sunt, per manus religiosorum hominum crucem ligneam mitte mihi, et fide et virtute domini nostri Jesus Christi spem habendo in vivificam crucem ac pretiosum lignum, veniam." Tunc accersitis duobus episcopis et uno heremita, mentiendo illis maligne fidem suam, dedit illis crucem ligneam misitque eos ad regem. Qui venientes salutaverunt regem et fidem atque crucem dederunt. Rex vero accipiens crucem pronus adoravit in terra et deosculatam recondidit in sinu suo assumptisque paucis secum perrexit ad imperatorem.

Interea iusserat imperator per viam ponere ei insidias, ut transeunte eo insurgerent ex adverso et interficerent eum. Deus autem omnipotens,

he should gather his people and settle there, and this was done.

And so King Vladimir lived with his wife Kosara in full sanctity and chastity, honoring God and serving him day and night. And he ruled the people entrusted to him with justice and with fear of God. After a short time the Emperor Samuel died, and his son Radomir inherited the Empire. He was powerful and brave, and he waged many wars with the Greeks during the time of the Emperor Basil, from whom he seized all the land up to Constantinople. Now the Emperor Basil, fearing that he might lose his empire, secretly sent emissaries to Vladislav, the nephew of Radomir, saying: "Why don't you avenge your father's blood? Take as much gold and silver as you desire from me and be at peace with us, and you will receive the Empire of Samuel, who killed your father, his brother. And if you can, kill his son Radomir who now rules." When he heard this Vladislav agreed, and one day while Radomir was hunting and he himself was riding with him, he struck him and killed him. And thus died Radomir, and Vladislav ruled in his stead, who had killed him. And after he had taken over the empire he sent deputies to King Vladimir and invited him to come visit him. But when Queen Kosara heard that she restrained him, saying: "My lord, don't go, lest—God forbid—lest what happened to my brother should also happen to you; but let me go instead, so that I may see and hear what the King has on his mind. If he wants to kill me let him kill me, just so that you don't die." With her husband's permission, therefore, the Queen set out to visit her cousin and she was received with honors, but hypocritically. After this he sent deputies a second time to the King, giving him a gold cross and a pledge of safe conduct, saying: "Why do you hesitate to come? Look, your wife is here with me and no harm at all has befallen her; on the contrary, my people and I have treated her with dignity. Accept my pledge on the cross and come, that I may see you, so that afterwards you may return to your place with honors and gifts, and with your wife." The King answered: "We know that our Lord Jesus Christ, who suffered for our sake, was not crucified on a cross of gold or silver, but of wood; therefore if your pledge and your words are true send me a wooden cross with some of your churchmen, and then by the faith and power of our Lord Jesus Christ I shall come, trusting in the life-giving cross and the holy wood." Then he called in two bishops and a hermit, and concealing from them his bad faith he gave them the wooden cross and sent them to the King. When they arrived they greeted the King, and they gave him the pledge and the wooden cross. And the King accepted the cross, bowed deeply to the ground, kissed it and placed it in his bosom; and taking a few of his people with him he set off to visit the Emperor.

Vladimir and Kosara

Meanwhile the Emperor had given orders for ambushes to be set up along the way, so that when the King would be passing by they might attack him from the side and kill him. But almighty God, who had de-

qui ab infantia custodivit famulum suum, noluit extra homines dormitationem accipere. Nam misit angelos suos, qui eum custodirent. Cumque transiret per loca quo insidiae erant, videbant insidiatores comitari milites regem, quasi alas habentes manuque trophaea gestantes; et cum cognovissent, quod angeli dei essent, timore perteriti aufugerunt quisque in locum suum. Rex vero venit ad imperatoris curiam, in loco qui Prespa dicitur moxque ingressus est, ut ei mos erat, orare caepit deum coeli. Ut autem cognovit imperator advenisse regem, ira magna iratus [est]. Proposuerat nempe in corde suo, ut in via occideretur, antequam ad eum veniret, ne videretur consors vel consentien neci eius, eo quod iurasset et in episcoporum et in haeremitae manibus crucem dedisset et hac de causa per viam insidias illi imposuerat. Sed cum iam videret denudatum opus suum nequissimum, sedens ad prandium, [Vladislavus] misit gladiatores, qui eum decollarent. Orante interea rege, milites circumdederunt eum. Ut autem cognovit rex, vocatis episcopis et haeremita, qui ibidem aderant, dixit: "Quid est domini mei? Quid egistis? Quare me sic decepistis? Cur verbis et iuramentis vestris credens sine culpa morior?" At ipsi prae verecundia vultus eius non audebant aspicere. Tunc rex facta oratione et confessione, accepto corpore et sanguine domini, crucem illam quam ab imperatore acceperat, manibus tenens dixit: "Orate pro me, domini mei, et haec venerabilis crux una vobiscum sit mihi testis in die domini, quoniam absque culpa morior." Deinde osculata cruce, dans pacem episcopis et flentibus omnibus egressus est ecclesia moxque a militibus ante ianuam ecclesiae percussus; decollatus est XXII die intrante maio. Episcopi vero tollentes corpus eius in eadem ecclesia, cum hymnis et laudibus sepelierunt. Ut autem dominus declararet merita beati martyris Vladimiri, multi diversis languoribus vexati, intrantes ecclesiam orantesque ad eius tumulum, sanati sunt. Nocte vero videbatur ibi ab omnibus lumen divinum et quasi plurimas ardere candelas. Uxor vero beati Vladimiri flevit cum fletu magno ultra quam dici potest diebus multis. Videns autem imperator mirabilia, quae ibi deus operaretur, poenitentia ductus, satis timuit concessitque consobrinae suae tollere corpus eius et sepelire honorifice quocumque vellet; tulitque denique corpus eius et asportavit in loco, qui Craini dicitur, ubi curiae eius fuit et in ecclesia sanctae Mariae recondidit. Iacet corpus eius integrum et redolet quasi pluribus conditum aromatibus et crucem illam, quam ab imperatore accepit, manu tenet; congregaturque multitudo populi in eadem ecclesia omni anno in festivitate eius, et meritis

fended his servant from his childhood, did not choose to slumber over men's acts, but instead He sent his angels to protect him. And when he was passing through the places where ambushes had been set, those who were waiting in ambush noticed that the King was accompanied by soldiers who seemed to have wings and who were holding in their hands emblems of victory, and when they realized that these were angels of God they took fright and fled, each to his own place. And the King arrived before the Imperial Palace, at the place called Prespa, and when he entered there he began to pray to God, as was his custom. When the Emperor learned that the King had arrived he became furious. For in his heart he had assumed that the King would be murdered along the way, before he could arrive at his place, and thus he would not have seemed to have been a participant in his murder or to have approved it, for he had taken an oath and had given a cross to the bishops and the hermit, and that was why he had set the ambush along the route. But when he saw that his filthy deed had been exposed, while seated at dinner he sent his assassins to behead him. While the King was praying the soldiers surrounded him. When the King noticed this he called the bishops and the hermit who were there, and he said to them: "What is this, my lords? What have you done? Why have you deceived me so? Why should I die without any fault, for having believed in your words and your oaths?" And they were so ashamed that they didn't dare to look him in the face. Then the King prayed to God and made his confession, and he received the body and blood of the Lord; and holding in his hand the cross that he had received from the Emperor he said: "Pray for me my lords, and may this holy cross and you be my witness on judgement day that I am dying without fault." Then he kissed the cross, took leave in peace with the bishops, and while everyone was crying he went outside the church, and the soldiers immediately killed him in front of the church doors; he was beheaded on the twenty-second day of May. And the bishops took his body and buried it in the same church, with hymns and praises. And the Lord, so that he might make known the merits of the blessed martyr Vladimir, granted that many people suffering with various illnesses should recover as soon as they entered the church and prayed over his grave. And at night there they all saw a divine light, as though a multitude of candles were burning. And the wife of the blessed Vladimir wept bitterly for many days, more than can be described. When the Emperor saw the miracles that were being performed there by God, he repented and became very much afraid, and he allowed his cousin to take his body and to bury it where she wished. She at last took his body and transported it to the place called Krajina, where his palace was located, and she buried him in the church of Saint Mary. His body lies whole and intact and smells as though it were annointed with many scents, and he holds in his hand the cross which he received from the Emperor. On his feast day many people gather in that same church, and through his merits and

et intercessione eius praestantur ibi multa beneficia recto corde petentibus usque in hodiernum diem. Uxor vero beati Vladimiri Cossara, sanctimonialis effecta, pie et sancte vivendo, in eadem ecclesia vitam finivit ibique sepulta est ad pedes viri sui.

Eodem itaque tempore, quo translatum est corpus beati Vladimiri de Prespa in Craini, imperator Vladislavus, congregato exercitu, venit possidere terram beati Vladimiri et civitatem Durachium, ut promissum ei fuerat ab imperatore Basilio, propter homicidia quae perpetraverat. Manens itaque ante Durachium, quadam die dum coenaret et epularetur, subito apparuit ei miles armatus in effigie sancti Vladimiri. Et terrore percussus magnis vocibus clamare caepit: "Currite mei milites, curite et defendite me, quia Vladimirus occidere me vult." Et haec dicens surrexit de solio suo, ut fugeret. Statimque percussus ab angelo corruit in terram et mortuus est corpore et anima. Tunc principes et milites eius et omnes populi, magno terrore percussi et metu, succenso igne per castra, eadem nocte fugerunt omnes per loca sua. Sicque factum est, ut nequissimus homicida, qui sedens ad prandium beatum Vladimirum decollari iusserat et martyrem facerat, ipse hora coenae percuteretur, ut angelus satanae efficeretur.

Quantas et quales virtutes et prodigia deus operare dignatus est per beatum Vladimirum, famulum suum, qui scire desiderat, librum gestorum eius relegat, quo acta eius per ordinem scripta sunt et agnoscet profecto, quod ipse vir sanctus unus spiritus cum domino fuit et deus habitavit cum eo, cui honor etc.

intercession many good things are granted there right up to this very day, to all those who pray with a pure heart. And the wife of the blessed Vladimir, Kosara, became a nun, living a pious and holy life; and she finished her life in that same church and was buried there at the feet of her husband.

Vladimir and Kosara

And at the time when the body of the blessed Vladimir was being moved from Prespa to Krajina the Emperor Vladislav, gathering an army, came to take the land of the blessed Vladimir and the city of Drač, since the Emperor Basil had promised it to him for the murder he had committed. And while encamped before Drač he was having supper and entertaining one day, when there appeared unexpectedly before him an armed soldier in the likeness of Saint Vladimir and struck with terror he began to shout in full voice: "Run here, my soldiers, run here and defend me, because Vladimir wants to kill me." And when he said this he jumped up from his seat to flee. But an angel struck him down at once, and he collapsed to the ground and died both in body and in spirit. Then the princes and his soldiers and all the people were struck with great terror, and they set fire to the camp, and that same night they flew back to their own territory. And so it happened that this most repulsive killer, who while seated at dinner had given the order for Vladimir's beheading and had made him a martyr, was himself killed and made an angel of Satan while at supper.

Whoever wishes to know how many and what kinds of good deeds and miracles God deigned to perform through the blessed Vladimir, let him read the book about his deeds, wherein his deeds are described in succession, and he will be convinced that this holy man was of one spirit with the Lord and that God dwelled with him, to whom honor, etc.

A page from the Croatian glagolitic *Žgombič Compendium*

The following *Legend about St. John Chrysostom* was popular during the Middle Ages, versions of it appearing in many languages, including Greek, Latin, French, German, English, and Slavic. In France the story was called: "De l'érmite que le diable enivra" ("About the hermit whom the devil got drunk"); this tale was later adapted into a miracle play: "Miracle de Nostre-Dame de St. Jean le Paul érmite . . ." ("Miracle of Our Lady for St. John the Hermit . . ." In English St. John's story was transformed into "The Legend of St. Alban."

The Legend of St. Chrysostom

Our version of the "Legend" dates perhaps from the late fifteenth or early sixteenth century. It is from the Croatian *Žgombić Compendium,* as published by Stjepan Ivšić (*Prilozi za književnost, istoriju, i folklor,* knj. XI, 1931.) Written in glagolitic script, its language is spoken čakavian with a strong admixture of Church Slavonic forms. In his transcription of the glagolitic original, here reproduced, Ivšić writes the words in their full form, even where the copyist had abbreviated them. If the copyist indicated an abbreviation Ivšić adds the missing letters in parenthesis: *kap(i)t(u)l*; where no abbreviation is indicated he puts the missing letters in brackets: *c[r] norizac.*

The "Legend about St. John Chrysostom" also appears in the Dubrovnik manuscript *Libro od mnozijeh razloga* (1520), a štokavian-jekavian document (with some čakavisms), written in *bosančica,* a type of Cyrillic miniscule. The *Libro* was edited and published by Milan Rešetar in *Zbornik za istoriju, jezik i književnost . . .* (XV, Sr. Karlovci, 1926). Its version of the "legend" is sketchy and generally inferior to that of the *Žgombić Compendium*, which follows.

Biše | *j*eterь kraļ velmi krepakь i vzmožan' silo*ju* veliko*ju* zelo, i *j*edan' dan' vshote poiti loviti v dalečni*j*e gori svo*j*e, iskati zveri velikih'. I reče vitezem' i slugam' svo*j*im', da napravet se i vazmut' sa sobu potrebnaê *j*imь'. On že imeše kćerь svo*ju* *j*edinočedu, krasnu i lipu velmi vzorь; ka prišad'ši pred cara o(t)ca svo*j*ego i reče ńemu: „O(t)če moi, prošu te, da i mene poimete s vami, i da pogledam' kraļev'stva i visokih' gorь i zveri čudnih', ki sutь v gorah' va-

THE LEGEND ABOUT SAINT JOHN CHRYSOSTOM

SYNOPSIS: Troubled by the immoral life led by some of the monks in his monastery, John obtains the permission of his abbot to leave the monastery. Taking with him only ink and paper, John travels forty days into the wilderness, where he builds a little hut and spends his time praising God. One day, while John is writing lauds to the Blessed Virgin, the devil steals his inkpot and runs away with it. Undaunted, John continues to write, spitting on his pen and using his saliva for ink. His writing turns to gold. An angel comes to him, and tells him that henceforth he will be called "John Gold Mouth" (in Slavic "Ivan Zlatousti").

In praying to the Lord, John often asks that He save him from the little sins of thought and word, and he promises that he, John, will guard against the major ("mortal") sins himself, since he knows how to do that well. In order to show John that he has been praying poorly, the Lord sends an angel who chides John, and asks him to decide which of three sins is the least serious, and to choose one of the three: to get drunk, to commit murder, or to rape a virgin. John chooses to get drunk, because he reasons that if he gets drunk he will be able to go to bed and do no harm to anyone. The angel tells him that he has chosen the greatest sin of all, since in getting drunk he will end by committing all three sins. The angel then leaves John and goes back to Heaven.

One day, when John had already forgotten about his meeting with the angel, the following took place:

There was a certain king, very strong and with very great power, and one day he desired to go hunting in some distant forests of his, to look for big game. And he told his knights and servants to make ready, and to take with them what they needed. Now he had a daughter, his only child, beautiful and very fair to see, who came before the emperor, her father, and said to him: "My father, I beg you to take me with you, too, so that I may see the kingdom and the tall forests and the amazing

ših'". On že reče ńei: „Kći moê predragaê i lipa, ne hoću, da ideš' s nami ni*j*ednim zakonom'".

Izašad' kraļ' van' is polače svo*j*e*j*e k slugam' svo*j*im' i reče ńim', da skoro priprave końe svo*j*e i oružiê i vsa, ka ńim' potreb'na *j*esu. I tagda g(ospo)dična način' plakati se velmi i sa slzami prošaše moleći o(t)ca svo*j*ego, êko da poimet' *ju*. On že smiliv' se na ńu slz' radi ńe*j*e i reče ńei, da napravit' se sa vsimi službenicami svo*j*imi i idet' š' ńimi. Ona že vzveseli se radost*iju* veli*j*e*ju* zelo, i skoro tekši v komoru svo*ju* i obleče se v sviti svo*j*e prekrasni*j*e, a mati ńe*j*e žalostna bi velmi ńe*j*e radi. I vazamši dvi kokošě, *j*ed | nu pečenu, a drugu kuhanu, i kruha nekoliko i vloži v *j*edne bisagi i priveza na końa ńe*j*e; vze že sa sobu i vina v *j*ednom' sasude krasne i velice.

I poidoše v put' svoi. I kada pridoše k velikim' goram', v keh' behu zveri čud'ne velikosti: lefan'ti, lavi, medvedi, *j*eleni i zveri proči, i *j*egda pridoše na sredu gorь teh', i naidoše zveri mnogi*j*e i čudne velikosti, kakovih' ne bihu nigdarь videli. I tud*ij*e videv' *j*e kraļь i vsa voiska ńegova poidoše v sled' ńih' s meči i sa strelami i s kop'*j*i svo*j*imi, rastekoše se *j*edan' od' drugoga daleko, tako da naiti se ne možahu me*ju* sobo*ju*. Osta že takmo *j*edina sama gospodič'na v gorah' oneh' bludeći.

Noć' že v skore pris'pevaše, i dažь gotovaše se, i bi noć' črna i gusta, i dažь mnogь i gromi i mlni*j*e m<n>oge. Ona že sedeći na końe svo*j*em' bluêše, i postavši na *j*ednom' mesti sliša glas' lava rovuća i medvedi i inih' zveri, i uboê se vel'mi i s plačem' gorkim' govoraše: „G(ospod)i B(ož)e moi, stvori me vid(e)ti li *j*ednoga č(love)ka kr*šć*ena v pustińe ovoi i tud*ij*e videv'ši ga umreti!" I se rekši vide v *j*ednom' mesti ogań' bliska*juć*' se i poče jizditi k ńemu govoreći: „Vi*ju*, êko stvoren*ij*e č(lověča)sko *j*estь on'dě". | I *j*egda približi se k mestu onomu, vide *j*ednu pěć' i v ńei ogań' goreć', i z'sed'ši s końa svo*j*ego lah'ko i pristupi bliže i poče prigledati vnutarь hoteći videti, čto bilo bi si*j*e, êko ogań', gorit' i nikogože ne slišit'. I vide vnutre č(love)ka

wild animals which are in your forests." But he said to her: "My most dear and beautiful daughter, in no way do I want you to go with us."

The king went out of the palace to his servants, and he told them to ready their horses and weapons and everything which they needed. And then the young lady began to weep a lot, and while asking her father to take her along she was also imploring him with her tears. Now he took pity on her because of her tears, and he told her to make ready, together with all her servants, and to go with them. She was overjoyed, and running quickly to her chamber she got dressed in her most beautiful clothes; but her mother was very saddened on her account. She took two chickens, one roasted and the other boiled, and some bread, and she put them in her daughter's saddlebags and tied them to her horse; the girl also took with her some wine in a vessel beautiful and large.

And they set out on their journey. And they came to large forests in which there were wild animals of amazing size: elephants, lions, bears, stags, and other wild animals; and when they reached the center of those forests they found many wild animals of an amazing size, such as they had never seen before. And as soon as they sighted them the king and all his army began to pursue them with swords and arrows and spears, and they became widely separated from one another, so that they couldn't find one another. And so the young lady herself was left alone, wandering aimlessly in those forests.

Now night was quickly setting in, and it was beginning to rain; and the night was thick and black, and there was much rain and thunder and lightning. And she, seated on her horse, wandered about, and stopping at one place she heard the sound of a roaring lion and of other wild animals, and she became very frightened; weeping bitterly she said: "Lord, my God, grant that I may see one baptized person in this wilderness and that I may die as soon as I have seen him." Having said this, she saw a fire glowing in one place, and she began to ride toward it, saying: "I see that there is something human over there." And when she drew near to that place, she saw a cave with a fire burning inside it, and lightly dismounting from her horse she stepped closer and began to peer inside, wanting to know what this might be, since there was a fire burning but she could hear no one. And she saw a man inside, kneeling and praying

*j*ednoga klečeća na kolenu svo*j*e*j*u i molitvu tvoreća B(og)u. Ona že zveseli se velmi, načet' s radost*iju* zvati *j*ego, êko da otvorit' ńoi. On' že ne hote otvoriti *j*ei, takmo otveća reki: "Idi, proklet'če dêvle, posramļen' ot mene silo*ju* s(ve)tago križa". Mnogo bo krat' dêv(a)l' prihoêše k ńemu va obraze žen'sce*j*em', a nekada v podob'stve an'j(e)lsce*j*em, zato tako od'govori *j*ei. Ona že odgovori *j*emu: „Nisam' dêvalь, da krstênińa *j*esam, i kršćena *j*esam' v ime Oca i Sina i D(u)ha s(ve)tago". On' že slišav' si*j*e veselь bě, i šad otvori ńoj dvari. Ona že všad'ši v dom' sta pri ogńi i poče svlačiti sviti svo*j*e s sebe, ke zmočila běše na sebe; drugi*j*e, ke imeše na końe svo*j*em' suhe, <vnese>,' i vazam'ši *j*e obleče se v suhi*j*e sviti svo*j*e; vnese že i bisažice svo*j*e, v kih' imeše kruh' i meso i vino svo*j*e. I sede poli ogań' i poče griêti se, i vazam'ši kruh' i vino i meso i poče jisti i piti; poče že i ńega pr | ositi, da bi jil'ь š' ńu. On' že ne hote, ona že počet' prositi ńego, da bi pilь š ńe*ju* jedino*ju* vina, koga imeše sa sobo*ju* v sasude *j*etere*j*em'. On' že veliki*j*e radi proš'ńi ńe*j*e priêm' vino i pit', i *j*egda piv' *j*edino*ju* opi sě, piv' že drugovice*ju* i razide se vino po žilah' *j*ego, i sed' na zemļi i počet' gledati ńe*j*e v lice ńe*j*e i čuditi se lepoti ńe*j*e, êko krasna běše velmi i lipa vzorь. I paki priêm' vino i piv' tretice*ju* i važga se v pohot' ńe*j*e i silu stvori ńoi. I kada paki usnuvь i prospav' se i počet' misliti, čto stvoril' bi, i pomislivь v sebe i reče: „Čto stvoru od' se*j*e gospodič'ni, êko otac' ńe*j*e počnet' iskati *ju* za*ju*tra s l*ju*dmi svo*j*imi, i našad' *ju* poli mene i ubi*j*et me? Izvol*ju* ubiti *ju*". I priêm' nožić' ńe*j*e i zakla *ju*. Iz'vleče *ju* van' is kućice svo*j*e*j*e, ku imeše v pustińi toi, i privleče *ju* v *j*edan' dolac' i položi *ju* me*ju* dve stene, i tu položi *ju* i vsa imen*i*ê ńe*j*e položi š ńe*ju*, i sa svitami ńe*j*e pokri *ju* i kameni*j*em' pozida *ju*, końa že ńe*j*e pusti samogo v gore toi, i zveri gorь tih' razdreše ga. I vrati se Ivan' v kućicu svo*ju*, i pre*j*e neže vnide va ńu, an'j(e)lь G(ospo)dańь

to God. She was overjoyed, and she began happily to call to him to open up for her. But he didn't want to open up for her, and he answered: "Go away, cursed devil, thwarted by me through the power of the Holy Cross." Because many times the devil appeared to him in the form of a woman, and sometimes in an angel's likeness, and that is why he answered her in this way. She answered him back: "I am not the devil, but I am a Christian, and I was baptized in the name of the Father, and the Son, and the Holy Spirit." Now when he heard this he was happy, and he opened the door for her. And entering the house, she stood by the fire and began to take off the clothes which had become wet on her; she brought in other dry ones, which she had on her horse, and she dressed in these dry clothes. She also brought in her saddlebags, in which there was bread and meat and her wine. And she sat by the fire and began to warm herself, and taking the bread and wine and meat she began to eat and drink; she also began to ask him to eat with her. But since he didn't want to eat, she began to entreat him to drink one glass of the wine which she had with her in that vessel. And because of her great urging he took the wine and drank it, and when he had drunk that one glass he was drunk, and when he had drunk a second glass the wine spread through his veins, and sitting down on the ground he began to look into her face and to marvel at her beauty, for she was very beautiful and fair to see. And again taking the wine he drank a third glass, and he became enflamed with desire for her, and he raped her.

And when now he had fallen asleep and had slept for a while, he began to think about what he had done and he said to himself: "What will I do with this young lady, since her father will begin to look for her tomorrow morning with his people, and when he finds her with me he will kill me? I had better kill her. And taking her knife he slew her. He dragged her out of his hut, which he had in that wilderness, and he dragged her into a little valley and he placed her between two boulders, and here he put her and all her possessions with her, and he covered her with her clothes and he walled her up with stones; but he let her horse go loose in that forest, and the wild animals there tore it to pieces. And John returned to his hut, and before he entered it the angel of the Lord

v | zvapi glasom' veli*j*em' reki: „Ivane, Ivane Zlatousti! Proklet' ti *j*esi v prošen*j*i tvo*j*em' i v dele tvo*j*em, êko izvoli opiti se mne*juć*i naimańi greh' opiti se i v ńem' vsa isplnil' *j*esi. Od'sele *ju*že ne uslišiši glasa mo*j*ego govoreća k tebe v pustińi ovoi, ni ot ruku mo*je*ju primeši piće, dokle ne poka*j*eši se od' toga, ča si učinilь".*

cried out with a great voice saying: "John, John Gold Mouth! You are cursed in your praying and in your work, because you chose to get drunk, thinking it the smallest sin, but by getting drunk you have done it all. From now on you won't hear my voice in this wilderness, nor will you drink from my hands, until you repent what you have done."

Barlaam and Josaphat

In the introduction to his publication of the Ethiopian version of Barlaam and Josaphat, *E. A. Wallis Budge writes that this story is really a "Christianized version of a very ancient spiritual romance, which was composed in India and first written down in an Indian language by Buddhist propagandists." (*Baralam and Yewasef, II, *Cambridge, 1923.)*

The name Josaphat itself seems to be a corruption of the Hindi word Bodhisattva, *which means "he who is to become a Buddha (an awakened one)" and the resemblance between the story of Josaphat and the life of Gautama Buddha is close enough to have convinced scholars that the former is really a Christian adaptation of the life of Buddha. As for the parables recited by the ascetic Barlaam while instructing his royal convert, these have been traced to various Indian collections of stories, including the* Panchatantra.

It has been traditionally held that it was Saint John of Damascus (676-749) who adapted this story into Greek, using an eighth century Arabic source, but David Lang, in his publication of a Georgian version of the story, states that the legend went from an Indian language into Arabic between 800 and 900 A.D., and that it was Saint Euthymius of Athos who later did the Greek adaptation. (David Lang. The Wisdom of Balahvar. A Christian Legend of the Buddha. *London (Unwin) and New York (Macmillan), 1957.)*

Both Barlaam and Josaphat were treated as Christian saints in Jacobus de Voragine's thirteenth-century Legenda Aurea, *but they weren't officially recognized until January 14, 1584, when a revised* Martyrologium Romanum *was published by the Roman Catholic Church. Their feast day has traditionally been celebrated on November 27 in the Roman Catholic Church, and November 19 in the Orthodox Church. Thus did Buddha, in disguise, become a Christian saint!*

There are more than eighty versions of the story of Barlaam and Josaphat extant; it first entered the English language via Caxton's translation and publication of the Legenda Aurea *at Westminster, in 1483.*

(Barlaam's parable of the three caskets,as retold in Shakespeare's Merchant of Venice, *comes from Caxton's book.) The story entered Serbian and Croatian literature from separate sources, being translated into Serbian Slavonic from Greek, and into čakavian from either Latin or Italian.*

Those who wish to read more complete versions may consult Stojan Novaković's Barlaam i Joasaf *(*Glasnik srpskog učenog društva, *knj. L., Beograd, 1881), which includes both a Serbian-Slavonic text and a scholarly introduction, or G. R. Woodward and H. Mattingly's* St. John Damascene: Barlaam and Iosaph *(Cambridge: Harvard University Press, 1953), which gives the Greek text with a parallel English translation. Lang's book, cited earlier, seems to afford the most up-to-date scholarly treatment of the whole subject.*

BARLAAM AND JOSAPHAT
THE RHINOCEROS STORY

SYNOPSIS: In India there once lived an emperor named Avenir, who loved the pleasures of this life, and whose one sorrow was that he had no children. Avenir worshipped pagan idols, and when Christianity began to spread throughout his kingdom, along with Christian asceticism and monasticism, he gave orders that the monasteries should be destroyed and all Christians should either renounce their religion or be subjected to torture. A reign of terror ensued, in the midst of which Avenir's first child, Josaphat, was born. The emperor called in astrologers to foretell the child's future; all the wise men, except for one, predicted that the boy would be the greatest ruler India had ever had. But the astrologer who was most noted for his wisdom said that the boy would not rule his father's kingdom at all, and that he would become a Christian.

To avoid such a possibility, Avenir had a special palace built for Josaphat. He ordered that the palace be closely guarded at all times, and that the boy should be surrounded by beautiful young people, and that he should never hear of illness and death, or of Christ. But when Josaphat became a young man he persuaded his father, in a very emotional scene, to allow him to go outside the palace, so that he might become acquainted with the aspects of life he had never experienced. And in spite of Avenir's orders to Josaphat's retinue that the boy should see only beauty on his walks, and that he should be met by singers and dancers along the way, the young prince met a blind man, a cripple, and a feeble old man, and thus he became aware of the existence of misery, disease, and death. Josaphat began to ask questions about the meaning of this life, and whether there was a life beyond the grave.

One day a Christian monk named Barlaam came to India; acting under divine inspiration he sought out Joasaphat, pretending to have a very precious jewel to show the young prince. When he was admitted to Josaphat's chamber, Barlaam first ascertained that he was fertile ground in which to implant the jewel of faith, and then he proceeded to instruct him in the foundations of the Christian religion. Barlaam illustrated his teaching with parables, such as the following one about the rhinoceros, which shows the plight of people who are tied to the things of this world.

Подобни ти мню моужеви бѣгающтоу оть лица инорога, иже не трьпе гласа вьплѧ юго и страшныхь юго рыканїи нь крѣпко бѣгаше, да не боудеть томоу вь снѣдь, вьнегда же течаше быстро вь великоу нѣкою вьпаде пропасть. Вьнегда же вьпасти юмоу вь ню и ꙁа древо нѣкою похитивь се крѣпко дрьжаше се и на расосѣ нѣкоеи ноꙁѣ оутврьдивь мнѣше се прочеѥ вь мирѣ быти и вь тврьдыни. Вьꙁрѣвь оубо видѣ два мыша, бѣль бо юдинь, а дроугыи же чрьнь, подгриꙁающтїи же непрѣстанно древо, югоже бѣше оухытиль се, и юликоже оуже вь малѣ приближающтема се има сїе искоренити. Посмотривь же вь дно пропасти видѣ ꙁмїа страшна видѣнїемь, огнюдышоущта и ꙗро иꙁвирающта се, оуста же страшно раꙁ'ꙁинокаше, и пожрѣти єго грѣдоущта. Вьꙁрѣвь же пакы на степень онь, на нюмь же бѣше ноꙁѣ свои оутврьдиль, видѣ четири главы аспидовы оть стѣны иꙁникше, на неи же стоаше, и вьꙁревь оуима видѣвь оть вѣтвїи древа оного мало меда каплющта. Оставивь оубо пешти се о одрьжештїихь юго бѣдахь, како вьнѣюдоу оубо инорогь лютѣ неистове се иштеть снѣсти юго, долоу же горкыи ꙁмїи ꙁиѧеть по-

And in my opinion these people are like the man who fled before the face of a rhinoceros; he could not stand the sound of its shrieking and its terrible grunting, and so he fled at top speed, not wanting to be eaten by that animal; but as he was running quickly he fell into a great pit. And as he was falling, he grabbed a tree and was holding on to it with all his might, and bracing his feet in a cleft of the tree he thought that he would continue to live in this world, and on a firm basis. And then he looked and saw two mice, one white and the other black, incessantly gnawing away at the tree he had grabbed, and already close to cutting it down. And peering into the bottom of the pit he saw a dragon, a terrifying sight, breathing fire and coiling itself fiercely, and it was opening its jaws in a horrifying manner and preparing to swallow him up. And now he looked at the footing on which he had planted his feet, and he saw four serpent heads sticking out of the cleft on which he was standing, and then looking up he saw with his own eyes a bit of honey dripping down from the branches of that tree. And thus he stopped worrying about the troubles that surrounded him, about the rhinoceros outside that was going into wild frenzies while seeking to devour him, and the awful dragon below that was opening its mouth to swallow him up, about the

жрѣти юго, дрѣво же, ꙁа нюже се бѣше оухытиль юлико же вь малѣ искоренити се хотѣше, ноꙁѣ же на пльꙁ'цѣ и невѣрнѣ степени оутврдиль бѣше: и — толикыхь и таковихь ꙁль ꙁабывь — оустрьми се кь сладости маллаго меда оного! Се юсть подобїе прѣльстїи житїа сего прѣльштаюштихь, югоже сказанїе нынѣ рекоу ти. Инорогь оубо образь юсть сьмрьти, гонештаа оубо постигноути гредоуштии адам'скыи родь, пропасть же мирь юсть, испльнь сыи всачьскыхь ꙁль и сьмртоносныхь сѣтїи, дрѣво же юже оть двою мышоу непрѣстанно подгризаюмое югоже оухытивше дрьжимь се, врѣме юсть коюгожде жиꙁни, ськраштаваюмо и сконьчаваюмо дьнемь и ноштїю и кь посеченїю по малѣ приближаю се. Четыри же аспиды иже оть четырехь прѣльстныихь сьставь сьставлюнїе чловѣчьскааго тѣлесе наꙁнаменоують, имже беꙁ'чинно носимомь и метештимь се, тѣлесное раꙁдроушають се сьставлюнїе. И кь симь же огнюобраꙁныи онь и неистовыи ꙁмїи страшноую проображають адовоу оутробоу, ождаюштоую приюти мира сего красна паче боудоуштїихь благь иꙁволшїихь; медовнаа же капла сладость ꙗвлають мира сего сладкыихь, ими же ть прѣльштають своѥ дроугы, не оставлають ихь о своюмь пештисе спасенїи.

fact that the tree he had grasped would in a short time be cut down, and that he had planted his feet on a slippery and unsure footing: and forgetting about all these misfortunes he sought after the sweetness of that little bit of honey! Now this is like the temptations of this world which deceive people, as in the story which I have just told you. Thus the rhinoceros is the symbol of death, impelling us to catch up with those of Adam's clan who have gone before us, and the pit is the world, filled with all kinds of evil and with fatal traps, and the tree which is incessantly being gnawed away by the two mice and which we grasp and cling to, is the span of a person's life, which night and day is being shortened and brought toward its close, and its end comes in a short while. And the four snakes represent the four concupiscent elements of the human constitution, and when these are not kept in check and are turbulent, the human constitution is destroyed. And what's more, the fiery and furious dragon represents the terrible bowels of hell, which wait to receive those who choose the beauties of this world over future riches; and the drop of honey is the sweetness of the sweet things of this world, which the world uses to deceive its friends, not allowing them to concern themselves about their salvation.

Illustration from the *Serbian Alexander* (15th century)

The story of the Macedonian Emperor Alexander the Great (ruled 336-323 B.C.) was perhaps the most popular work of medieval secular literature. Composed by a man known today as Pseudo-Callisthenes, at some time between the second century B.C. and the second century A.D., this story gradually evolved over the centuries into four separate literary traditions, one of which is generally called "The Serbian Alexander" (F. P. Magoun: The Gests of King Alexander of Macedon, *Harvard University Press, 1929, 37). The Serbian Alexander traces its origins from a Greek text, as Jagić points out in the Introduction to his publication of the Roudničky manuscript (*Život Aleksandra Velikoga, *Zagreb, 1871, 11). Jagić also proves that the Roudničky text, which is čakavian, descends from the Serbian Alexander.*

The Story of Alexander

The selection in this book is taken from a Serbian-Slavonic manuscript published by Stojan Novaković (Glasnik srpskog učenog društva, *IX, Beograd, 1878, 1-93). This manuscript, plus other Alexander manuscripts, was later destroyed, during the bombing of Belgrade in 1941. Radmila Marinković has published a study of the basic Serbian text:* Srpska Aleksandrida. Istorija osnovnog teksta *(Beograd: Filološki fakultet Beogradskog univerziteta, monografije, XXXI, 1969). C. A. Van den Berk has printed two versions of the story, one Serbian and the other Russian, in his* Der "Serbische" Alexanderroman *(Fink Verlag, München, 1970).*

Алексен'дроу же вь тоу ношть іави се пророкь Іереміа сь философомь Іерусалимскымь, и кь ніемоу рекоста: дрьзаи, чедо Алексен'дре, самь се поклисарь сьтворь, и кь Дарію поиди, и сходи іего, и виждь воискоу великоу, юже ведеть Даріе на те, и аште оувѣдѣнь боудеши, имаи помошть бога Саваоѳа, и избавить те. Вьставь же царь оть с'на Ан'тіохоу и Потоломею сьнь свои сказа. И походе кь нимь рече: аште тамо мнѣ сьмрьть прилоучить се, в'са земльнаа царствіа имате раздѣлити, макіедон'скыи же плькь добрѣ сьблюдите. Они же сь плачемь дрьжахоу іего, глаголюште: аште сіе мыслиши сьторити, прьво намь главѣ изьотсѣцаи. Онь же кь нимь рече: аште промыслоу божію годе мене оубити, ви вьси не можете ме оухранити; аште ли іемоу годе боудеть сьблюсти ме, в'се пер'скые роукы не могоуть ме оубити.

И се рекь кь Дарію отиде писание носе. Об'лѣкло же пер'ско на се вьзьмь и сьврьхоу плашть финичьскыи, на главѣ же клобоукь макіедон'скыи сь аспидовѣми рози и златѣми печат'ми. Даріе же парастась великь сьтвори, іако да чюд'нь

поклисароу Алексен'дровоу іавить се. И тако Алексен'дрь кь Дарію вьшьдь, писание давь, и рече: господинь мои Алексен'дрь, царь царемь, тебе, пер'скомоу цароу Даріоу, мною посламь іесть радовати се. Писаніе прочьть, мнѣ дроуго одпиши. Даріе же сѣдѣше на мѣстѣ высоцѣ. Около ніега іако лица аггелскаа сьтворен'на бѣхоу. Вьса же полата оть злата свѣт'ла сьтворен'на бѣше, и іако лица аггел'скаа томоу іако богоу прѣдстоіахоу. Стльпове злати каменіемь многоцѣн'нымь оукрашен'ны бѣхоу; четири же камены на четири оугле тоіе полати бѣхоу, иже вь ношти іако ог'нь вь мѣсто свѣшть свѣтехоу. Писаниіе же Алексен'дрово приіемь, Даріе див'іаше се крьз'ноу іего и клобоукоу. Писаниіе же велегласно повелѣ чисти. Пер'шанинь же нѣк'то начеть чтати, иже оумѣіаше макіедон'скаа словеса. Іепистоліа же писан'на бѣше сице: Алексен'дрь, царь надь

THE STORY OF ALEXANDER OF MACEDONIA

SYNOPSIS: Alexander is waging war against the Persian Emperor Darius. He has taken Babylon, and now is preparing for the final battle with Darius. Alexander has a dream in which he sees the Prophet Jeremiah, who gives him some advice:

That night the Prophet Jeremiah appeared to Alexander, together ith a Jerusalem philosopher, and they said to him: "Be daring, child lexander; disguise yourself as a messenger and go to Darius and spy on im, and see the large army which Darius is leading against you, and if ou are found out you will have the help of the God of the Sabbath, and e will save you. And getting up from his sleep the Emperor told his ream to Antioch and Ptolemy. And going to them he said: "If death hould befall me there, you have all the earth's kingdoms to divide up, ut take good care of the Macedonian regiment. And they, in tears, vere holding him, saying: "If you intend to do this thing, first cut off ur heads." But he said to them: "If it pleases God's Providence to kill ie, then all of you cannot save me; but if it pleases Him to look after ie, all the Persian arms cannot kill me."

And having said this he went off to Darius, bearing a letter. And e put on Persian clothes, and he wore a Phoenician cloak over them, ut on his head he had a Macedonian helmet with serpent horns and gold mblems. And Darius had staged a great spectacle so that he might dazzle lexander's messenger. And so, going in to Darius and giving him the etter, Alexander said: "My master Alexander, the Emperor of Emperors, as sent you, the Persian Emperor Darius, the message to be happy. Vhen you have read the letter write me out another." Now Darius was eated in a high place. Those around him were made to appear like angelic ersonnages. And the whole palace was made of burnished gold, and hey stood before him like angelic personnages before a god. The gold illars were embellished with very precious stones; and there were four tones at the four corners of that palace, which shone like fire at night, nstead of candles. Having taken Alexander's letter, Darius was admiring is fur pelt and his helmet. And he ordered that the letter be read in a oud voice. And some Persian, who knew how to read Macedonian writing, egan to read. And the letter was as follows: "I Alexander, Emperor over

цари и всемоу свѣтоу царь выш'нıаго промысла изв
лıениıемь, Даріоу цароу пишоу радовати се. Помни
ли, Даріıе цароу, кьдь даньк приимаше оть отьца м
ıего, оть Макıедоніань, и томоу оумьр'шоу мене на пр
столѣ остави, ты же поноуждень бысть лоукав'ство
своимь мене оть прѣстола и отьчьства изьгнати и ино
вь мѣсто мене поставити ? Сіа видѣвь божіе в'севид
штеıе око, иже вьса видить и помышлıеніа срьдьчи
знаıеть, и мѣрами правед'ними вьз'мѣраıеть тебѣ дьньс
мене же, ими же вѣсть соудбами, господина отьчьство
моемоу и вьсѣмоу свѣтоу сьтвори. Ты же повелѣль бѣ
кь себѣ привести ме; азь же самь прііидохь. И ıакож
ты хотеıаше свемоу нашемоу господинь назвати се, т
кожде и азь свемоу твомоу господинь хоштоу назват
се. Нь не тако азь немилостивь ıесьмь, ıакоже те
мнить се быти; нь прѣклони непрѣклон'ноу свою гр
дыню мнѣ, поклони се, и дани мнѣ даи, и боуди г
сподствоуıе. Аште ли ти се неугодно ıесть, то Пер'со
ты низ'матарь ıеси, и симь заклати се радь ıеси оть М
кıедоніискога мьча. Боуди готовь сь в'сѣми своими
бои .ег. дьнь, на Ар'сопор'скои рѣцѣ". Писаниıе же Д
ріıе слышавь, кь своимь си рече: надѣıаше ли се к'
таковеи подвижи и таковеи ıарости оть Макıедоні
изыти? Алексен'дрь же, стоıе прѣдь нимь, рече: не чюд
аште Макıедоніане свѣтомь обладають. Даріıе же рече
по ч'то? Алексен'дрь рече: по ч'то соуть вьси ıедино
срьди и храбри безь кон'ца и моудри же и любим
Пер'сенинь же нѣкто рече: по ч'то тако великомоу царо
глаголıеши? Онь же рече: сил'на господина вол'нь по
клисарь. И то рекь, отстоупи. Даріе же рече: боуди оу нас
на вечери, дон'деже писаніıе Алексен'дроу одпишоу

И тако, Даріоу на ве
чероу сѣд'шоу, Алексен'дра посади на поклисар'ском
мѣстоу прѣмо ıемоу. И ıегда начеше слоужити, Алек
сен'дрь златоу чашоу испивь, скри вь нѣдра. Тогда слоуг
Даріоу повѣдѣ. Даріıе же рече дроугоу ıемоу налиıати
Онь же и тоу испивь, ськри вь нѣдра. Іединь же от
вел'моужіи Даріıевѣхь рече ıемоу: не подоба на цар-

mperors and ruler of the whole world by the design of heavenly Providence, write Emperor Darius to be happy. Do you remember, Emperor arius, when you used to receive tribute from my father, from the Macedonians, and when he died he left me on the throne, but you were comelled by your trickery to drive me from the throne and to put another ne in my place? These things were seen by God's all-seeing eye, which es all things and knows the heart's thoughts, and which measures you oday with justice's scales; and it made me, whose fate is known to it, aster of my fatherland and of the whole world. And you had comanded that I be brought to you, but I have come on my own. And just as ou wanted to be called lord over all that is ours, so, too, do I want to be alled lord over all that is yours. But I am not as merciless as you intend to e; so bend your unbending pride to me, pay homage and give me tribute, nd continue to rule. If you don't agree to this, then you are the enemy of he Persians, and for this reason you deserve to be slain by a Macedonian word. Be prepared, with all your men, for a battle in fifteen days at the igris River." And hearing this letter Darius said to his men: "Did anyne ever expect such boldness and ferocity to come out of Macedonia?" ow Alexander, standing before him, said:: "It should be no wonder Macedonians rule the world." And Darius said: "For what reason?" lexander said: "Because they are all of one mind, and infinitely brave, nd wise, and loving." And some Persian said: "Why do you talk in his manner to the great Emperor?" And he said: "I am the free messenger f a powerful lord." And when he had said this he stepped back. And arius said: "Stay with us for dinner while I write an answer to Alexander."

And so when Darius had sat down to dinner he seated Alexander the messenger's place opposite him. And when they had begun to serve, lexander drained a golden goblet and hid it in his bosom. Then the ervant informed Darius of this. And Darius told him to fill a second one or him. And when he had drained this one, too, Alexander hid it in his osom. Now one of Darius' magnates told him that it was not proper to ct in this manner while seated at the Imperial table. But he said: "At my

скомь столѣ сѣде тако творити. Онь же рече: оу господина мога Алексен'дра прьвоу и вьторoу чашоу всакы поклисарь себѣ оузимать. Се же слышав'ше Перси оудивише се. Кан'дар'коусь же, іегоже бѣше Дарііе в Макіедонию послаль, сь вечере вьставь, Дарію рече: вѣси, цароу, іако дьньсь в'соу волю твою бози сьтворише. Онь же рече: како? Ть же рече: сы поклисарь самь Алексен'дрь іесть. Даріе же радости испльнивь се рече: аште се истына, то азь свемоу свѣтоу царь, и тако честь тихомь лицемь кь мнѣ обраштати се начеть. Нь семоу не вѣровавь рече: вьсѣхь главь глава не обѣшаіеть се, в кон'ци. Кан'дар'коусь рече: аште се истына не боудеть в'сеіе чьсти да оулишоу се, и главоу мьчемь отсѣци. Александрь же, домысливь се, прѣжде оухвакіевіа прьстень вь тобол'ци врьхов'ныи вьзеть, иже бѣ вь Трои вьзель Клеопатре егупьт'ске царице. Іегда ть прьстень на роукоу став'лїааше, оть всѣхь невидимь бываше. И вь роукоу іего вьз'мь, хоте искоусити Дарііево малодоушіе. Даріе же кь піемоу рече: приличпа ми те кь Алексен'дроу кажоуть. Онь же рече: прилики ради любить ме господинь мои, приличьнь бо іемоу іес'мь, и мнози мнѣ поклонише се, мнѣв'ше ме Алексен'дра. И тако Даріе в раз'мышлїеніе выпадь, пе рече оухватити іего. Трапезо же ногою риноувь, оу ложницоу отиде, сьвѣштаваіеть како оухватити іего. Свѣшт'никы сь царемь однесоше Алексен'дрь же сь властели оу великои коуки оста. В т'мѣ сьвлѣче сь себе многоцѣн'но крьз'но и [македонски клобоукь, прьстень же на роукоу положивь вльхов'ныи И тако кь вратомь градоу отиде, чашоу златоу изь нѣдра изьмь, дасть вратароу, рекь: вьзми сію чашоу и храни Даріе царь посла ме страже наредить. И отвори іемоу Пришьдь на дроуга врата, дроугоу чашоу изьмь, дасть вратароу, рекь: дрьжи чашоу сию; царь бо посла ме воіеводѣ призвати, да страже оутврьдеть. И тако отвориш іемоу скоро. Изь града же изьшьдь, и на великога коні вьсѣдь, на Синор'скоу рѣкоу тьк'мо сь свѣтомь дошьдь и сию помрз'шоу обрѣть, прѣиде цѣль. И тоу чекахоу іего Ан'тıохь и Филонь и Ан'тиногень. И повѣда имь вьса, іаже сьлоучише се іемоу вь Пер'сидѣ.

d Alexander's, every messenger takes for himself the first and second blet." And when they heard this the Persians were amazed. But Kan-rkus, whom Darius had once sent to Macedonia, arose from the dinner ble and said to Darius: "You should know, Emperor, that today the ds have done your will." And he said: "How?" And that one said: 'his messenger is Alexander himself." And Darius, full of joy, said: f this be true, then I am emperor of the whole world and thus has rtune begun to turn my way with a gentle face." But not believing is, he said: "The head of all heads does not hang by a thread." Kandar-s said: "If this should not be the truth, may I be stripped of all my nors and may my head be cut off with a sword." Now Alexander ught wise, and before he could be seized he took from a pouch a magic g which [the magician] of Cleopatra, the Egyptian Queen, had got in oy. When he would put this ring on his hand he was invisible to every-e. And taking it in his hand, he wanted to test Darius' lack of courage. ow Darius said to him: "They tell me that you resemble Alexander."

d he said: "Because of this resemblance my lord loves me, for I look e him, and many have bowed to me, thinking me Alexander." And Darius fell into a deep revery, and he didn't tell anyone to seize him. shing the table with his foot, he went off to his bedchamber to discuss w they could seize him. They took the candles away with the Emperor, d Alexander remained with the magnates in the great house. In the rkness he removed his very precious fur and his Macedonian helmet, st having put the magic ring on his hand. And so he went out to the tes of the city, and taking a gold goblet from within his bosom he ve it to the gatekeeper, saying: "Take this goblet and guard it; Emperor rius has sent me to arrange the guard."And he opened the gates for n. When he arrived at a second gate he took out the second goblet d gave it to the gatekeeper, saying: "Hold this goblet, for the Emperor s sent me to call in the commanders, to strengthen the guard."And so opened the gates for him quickly. Now he left the city, and having ounted a large horse, he arrived at the Tigris just at daybreak, and ding it frozen he crossed it in safety. And waiting for him there were ntioch and Filon and Antinogen. And he told them about everything at had happened to him in Persia.

а се парнмь пробаде єдїного щита внте за

Семоуже снцу бывшоу ::

И потомь прѣнмоу шыкрал оучнннн зборъ.
И рече прѣ всѣ зборомь . кто мн хощеть по
магатн оу боисꙗ созлѣлѣ помагачимн.
хоке ємоу дати рыд олѣ тла . нслы
шаса спато два дїавола земльна. пе
боушь н непїтомоушь. нцѣ ннота
сь шнм. бѣше пебоушь гоусльникь

The Tale of Troy

The "Roman o Troji," or "Rumanac Trojski," as it is known in ɐ glagolitic Petrisov zbornik *(1468), probably was translated on the oatian Littoral, from an Italian source, during the late Middle Ages. ke "The Story of Alexander of Macedonia," this work served as a primer chivalry, incorporating medieval notions about courtly behavior.*

Although they deal with the ancient Greek theme of the siege Troy, the Serbian and Croatian versions do not trace their origin to omer's Iliad, *but rather to the accounts of two supposed eyewitnesses the Trojan War, Dictys of Crete (*Ephemeris Belli Troiani*) and Dares e Phrygian (*De Excidio Troiae Historia*), both of whose stories we have Latin translation, the original versions having disappeared.*

Since Dares and Dictys claimed to have participated in the Trojan ar, their stories were given more credence in the Middle Ages than was omer's Iliad. *In the twelfth century Benoit de Sainte Maure wrote the* oman de Troie, *based on Dares and Dictys, but with a background at reflected prevailing French customs, religion, and military procedures. uido de Columnis later prepared an abbreviated Latin adaptation of enoit's work, which became more popular than the original. It was anslated into Czech, as well as into Italian and other European languages. he story of Troy became known in English through Lydgate's* Troy ook *(1412-1420), a much expanded rendition of Guido's work (30, 7 lines!). Caxton's* Recuyell, *a translation of Raoul Lefèvre's collecon of Trojan stories (*Recueil*), was the first book to be printed in English 1474).*

*Useful information about the origin and dissemination of the ojan story is given by Margaret R. Scherer (*The Legends of Troy in rt and Literature, *Phaidon Press, New York, 1963) and Arthur M. Young* roy And Her Legend, *University of Pittsburg Press, 1948). Our text from the Serbian-Slavonic version in Allan Ringheim's* Eine Altservische rojasage. Text mit linguistischer und literarhistorischer Charakteristik. *rague-Upsal: Publications de l'Institut Slave d'Upsal, 1951).*

И потом изиде Ѥкторь краль оу грьчкоу воискоу и оучи великоу сьмрьт ѿт грьчке воиске. И посласта ѡба ц<а>ра Теоуце и Оурикшиша молит<и> Аньцилеша, еда би приѥль ѡрѹжїѥ сво и пошьль противоу Єкторoу кралю. И ѡна га молꙗхота мно и ѡнь нымь ница не ѿтгавараше(!). И потом реч<е> Брижеида г<о п<о>гꙗ: „Грьчсци оурове, пошлѥте мене! И кю брьже мога г<о>с<поди>на оумолит<и> нерѣли лѣпе рѣчи Теоуцера и Оурикшиша. И ц<а>рїѥ послаше Брижендоу г<о>сп<о>гю, и ѡна придѣ кь А цилешоу и поклекноувь прѣд Анцилешем и говораше к нѥмо „Анцилешоу г<о>с<поди>не, що се срьчиши? Прими ѡроужиѥ сво и походи прѣма Ѥкторoу кралю! Илы не слышишь или не в д<и>шь коликоу крьвь проливат Єктѡрь крал на дроужиноу тво Да хоцїет ѡнаи крьвь прѣд б<о>гомь оузоупит<и> на тебе, ако ю ѡсвѣтишь. И можеши се на то срьчит<и>, ерѣ сьм кривена была твоѥга лица, да м<о>лю те, г<о>с<поди>не Анцилешоу: прими л к себѣ! И прими ѡроужїе свое и походи прѣма Єкторѹ кралю!" И Анцилешь к нои ницарѣ не ѿтвѣща. И пот<о>мь прїидѣ к нѥмо Потроколоушь, доичикь еговь, и молꙗше га и правлꙗше: „Анци лешоу г<о>с<поди>не, вид<и>ш ли коу крьвь пролива Ѥкторь кр ѿт дроужине твоѥ? Походи прѣма Ѥкторoу!

Ако ли не хокѥшь ти поити прѣма Ѥкторѹ кралю, мол те, г<о>с<поди>не: даи мнѣ свога парїжа и своѥ ѡроужїе и сво знаменїе, да погю га под твоим именем, ѥда быхь ѡслабыль Ѥкто

THE TALE OF TROY

SYNOPSIS: Paris has abducted Helen, the wife of Emperor Menelaus, and has taken her to Troy, his home city; Menelaus and his brother, Emperor Agamemnon, gathered forces from throughout Greece to march against Troy. The shrewd Ulysses ("Urikšis"), not wanting to go to war, pretends to be insane, but he is unmasked and has to go. Hector ("Jektor"), the Trojan hero, kills many Greeks and demoralizes their ranks. The two Greek Emperors send for Achilles ("An'cileš"), who is in hiding, disguised as a girl; the sly Ulysses unmasks Achilles through a subterfuge, and Achilles, too, goes to join the Greek army. When Emperor Agamemnon takes Achilles' concubine, Briseis ("Brižeida"), Achilles becomes enraged and refuses to fight the Trojans. Hector continues to raise havoc in the Greek lines, and the Greek cause appears desperate in this, the tenth year of the fighting.

And then King Hector went forth against the Greek army, and he caused much death in the Greek ranks. And both Emperors sent Teucer and Ulysses to plead with Achilles to take up his arms and to go against King Hector. And they did much pleading with him, but he would not answer them at all. And then the Lady Briseis said: "Greek lords, send me! I shall persuade my lord more quickly than the beautiful words of Teucer and Ulysses." And the Emperors sent Lady Briseis, and she came to Achilles, and kneeling before Achilles she said to him: "Lord Achilles, why are you angry? Take up your arms and go against King Hector. Either you haven't heard, or else you haven't seen how much blood King Hector is spilling in your company. But that blood will cry out before God against you, if you don't avenge it. And you can be angry because I was hidden from your person, but I beg you, Lord Achilles: take me to you! And take your arms and go against King Hector!" And Achilles wouldn't answer her at all. And then there came to him Patroclus, who had shared the same wet nurse as a child, and he was pleading with him, saying: "Lord Achilles, do you see what blood King Hector is spilling from your company? Go against Hector!

If you don't want to go against King Hector, then I beg you, Lord: give me your horse and your weapons and your banner, that I

рово рьваніе.“ И реч<е> моу Анцилешь: „Ѡ Потроколоушоу, ꙗ т
не браню мога паріжа и мога ѡроужіꙗ и мога знаменіꙗ. Да ѥ
ти добрѣ говороу: ако поидешь прѣма Ѥкторoу, не хокеш с
ѡпет оузвратити.“ И пода моу ѡроужіе и паріжа своѥго. И тьд
изидѣ Ѥкторь крал на рьванію, и Потроколоушь ороужа се и
оусѣд<ѣ> на паріжа и поидѣ прѣма Ѥкторoу. И видеше га Трѡ-
ꙗне / и белѣгь Анцилешевь и начеше бежати како ѡвце прѣд
вькоомь. И ѡбрати се к ниемоу Ѥкторь крал и мнеше га, да
ѥс<т> Анцилешь, и реч<е> моу: „Ѡ Анцилешоу г<о>с<поди>не, що
поугꙗшь ѡвце сіе н<и>нꙗ и оубиꙗеши ихь? Чти оу том ниѥдне
не имашь, ноу ѡбрати се к мене, ерѣ сьм дѣсница троискога
град<а> и врат. Ако мен<е> прѣможешь, тебѣ хоте вса троиска врат<а>
ѡтворена бит<и>.“ И ѡнь то за срамотоу имаше, ако би моу
оустоупиль: ѡгрьдѣл би Анцилешевь глас. И оудри се сь Ектором
кралѥмь и прободѣ га Ѥкторь краль на дроугоу страноу. И реч<е>
Ѥкторь привезати га кь фарижоу нѥговоу за ѡпашь, и реч<е>
га повлекы оу Трою и влачи га по Трою и вес<е>лꙗше с<е>. Мнѣше
моу се, да ѥс<т> Анцилешь оубиѥнь. И слыша то Анцилешь, како
оуби Ѥкторь Потроколоуша доичикꙗ, и бы моу много жалоос<т>
и скрьбьн ѡ нѥм мног<о>, нерѣ моу бѣше ѡроужіе оузель.

И оуслыша то Анцилешь, како оубы Ѥктѡрь крал Потроколоуша, доичикꙗ нѥгова, ѡсоумори се вел<е> и посла кь Ѥктѡроу
кралю и говораше моу: „Ѡ кралю Ѥкторе, сьда вес<е>лиши се и
оузнесл се ѥси мне, да си мене Анцилеша оубиль. Оубил си мога
драгога дроуга Потроколоуша, ноу да знашь: хокеш се плакати
и хокешь плакати то ѡроужіе, коѥ си на нѥм оузель, ерѣ два
детикꙗ, кога соу едноу сьсцоу сала, м<и>л<о>стива хокета мегю
собом быти и хоще єдінь дрꙋгога пожалит<и>.“ И тогда посла Ан-

might go forth under your name, that I might weaken Hector's fighting." And Achilles said to him: "O Patroclus, I won't refuse you my horse and my weapons and my banner. But I will tell you straight: if you go against Hector, you won't return again." And he presented him with his weapons and his horse. And then King Hector went out to battle, and Patroclus armed himself and mounted his horse and went towards Hector. And the Trojans saw him and Achilles' crest, and they began to run like sheep before the wolf. And King Hector turned toward him, and thinking that it was Achilles he said to him: "O Lord Achilles, why do you frighten these sheep now and kill them? You gain no honor from that, but face me instead, because I am the right arm of the Trojan city and of its gates. If you defeat me all the Trojan gates will be opened to you." And he held it to be a disgrace if he were to back off from him: he would have sullied Achilles' reputation. And he clashed with King Hector and King Hector ran him through. And Hector told them to tie him to the tail of his horse, and he told them to pull him into Troy; and he dragged him through Troy and he was enjoying himself. He was thinking that Achilles had been killed. And Achilles heard how Hector killed Patroclus, his milk brother, and he was grief-stricken, and he was sorry because he had taken his weapons.

And Achilles heard how King Hector had killed Patroclus, his milk brother; he became very sombre and he sent a message to King Hector, saying: "O King Hector, you are enjoying yourself and you have become arrogant, thinking that you have killed me, Achilles. You have killed my dear friend Patroclus, but I want you to know that you will weep for yourself, and you will weep for those arms which you took from him, for two children who have nursed on the same teat will be kind to one another and will mourn one another." And then Achilles

цилешь кь матери своѥи Тетише г<о>ⷭп<о>гѥ и правлѥше: „Ѡ Тетише г<о>ⷭп<о>гѥ, оудаи ми ѡнака ѡроужїа, каконо ми беше и прѣгѥ оудала била, ерѣ ѥⷭ<т> оубыль Ѥкторь кра̂ мога драгога Потроколоуша доичикꙗ, ерѣ, г<о>ⷭп<о>гѥ, знаⷨ: печална си ѡ моѥи сьмрьти, да какова годе хокю ѡроужїа наити, и поити хокю прѣма Ѥктороу кралю и рьвати се хокю ѡ ниⷨ и понести хокю свою главоу пⷣо троиⷭкы граⷣ.“ И мати ѥго печална бы много и поиде оу ѥтероу гороу кь Ельканоушоу ковачю, пⷣо ко бехоу .п҃з. дробныⷯи враговь, кои га ѹчахоу. / И Тетиша г<о>ⷭп<о>гꙗ ѡбетова ѥмоу силно златѡ, да оучини Ꙗнцилешоу ѡнакво ороужїѥ, каконо бѣше и прѣгѥ оучиниль. И оучини оу скорѣ ѡнакво ѡроужїѥ и посла га кь Ꙗнцилешоу. И то чювь Ѥкторь кра̂ и посла кь Ꙗнцилешоу: „Да знаⷷшь: чюваи се ѿ мене колико можешь наивекма, ерѣ гⷣе те кю наити, знаи що ти хокю оучинити!“ И слышаста то ц<а>ра пристависта .в҃і. витеза чювати Ꙗнцилеша. И изиде Ѥкторь кра̂ и оучини великоу сьмрьⷮ оу грьⷱской воисцѣ.

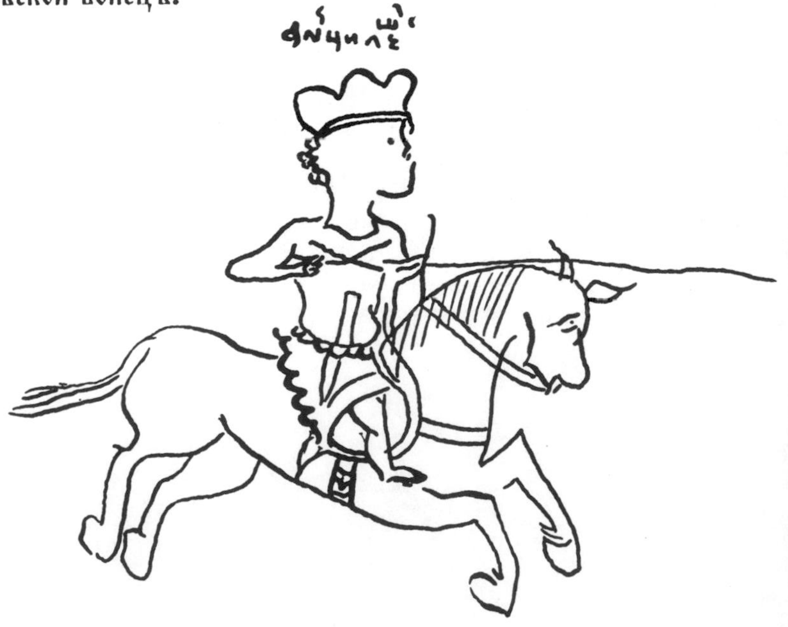

sent a message to his mother, Lady Thetis, saying: "O Lady Thetis, give me the same kind of weapons as you gave me before, for King Hector has killed my dear Patroclus, my milk brother; now I know, lady, that you are sad at the thought of my death, but whatever arms I shall find I shall go against King Hector and I shall fight with him and I shall risk my head beneath the walls of the Trojan city." And his mother was very sad, and she went to a certain mountain, to Vulcan the blacksmith, who had eighty seven little devils under him, who were teaching him. And Lady Thetis promised him much gold to make Achilles weapons like the ones he had made before. And he quickly made such weapons and sent them to Achilles. And King Hector hearing this, he sent a message to Achilles: "Know this: stay as clear of me as you can, for wherever I find you, know what I shall do to you!" And when the Emperors heard this they assigned twelve knights to guard Achilles. And King Hector came forth and caused much death in the Greek ranks."

A page from the Petris glagolitic Compendium

The Vision of Tundal

The Vision of Tundal *was written in the twelfth century, in Ireland. Probably composed originally in Latin, it is an early example of the guided tours through hell that were popular medieval precursors of Dante's tour of the* Inferno *in his* Divine Comedy.

Visio Tundali *was translated into many languages, an activity which was certainly facilitated by its inclusion in Vincent de Beauvais' widely-circulated* Speculum Historiae *(13th century). Among the Slavic languages, there are versions extant in Czech, Belo-Russian (from the Czech), and Serbo-Croatian. In Serbo-Croatian the* Vision *exists in both latinica and glagolitic manuscripts, with the latinica versions stemming from Italian adaptations, and the glagolitic from a Czech intermediary (see Stjepan Ivšić,* Starine, *41, 1948, 119-157 for more details concerning the provenance of the Serbo-Croatian examples of the Story.) A full critical edition of the Latin text is given in Wagner's* Visio Tugdali. Lateinisch und Altdeutsch *(Erlangen, 1882).*

Our selection is from the version given in the glagolitic Petrisov Zbornik *(1468), as transcribed and printed in* Pet stoljeća hrvatske književnosti, *I, 200-219. The language of the text is čakavian-ikavian, with an admixture of ekavisms of Church Slavonic origin.*

Najprija ovo reče: "Kada jure duša moja beše izašla is tela moga i videći telo mrtvo poče trepetati velikim strahom i strašiše se spominajući se na svoja pregrešen'ja i ne videše ča učiniti i vele se strašaše ne videći se ča domisliti ča bi ot sebe učinila. Bila bi se rada sopet v telo povratiti, ali nikakore ne moraše vniti jere imeše grozan strah oda vsih stran. I tako plačući se i cvileći i trepećući i tu pozrivši vide množastvo djavlov kako moćnu maglu k sebi gredući sa vseh stran. Ne da bi jih le samo mesto plno da vse ulice i vse strane biše jih plne. I tu obstupiše moju ubogu dušu i rekoše: „Vspojmo toj nečistoj duše skrbnu i tužnu pesan jere njej pristoji večna pogibel, zač je ta jure naša po nje zaslužen'ji i gotov je njoj večni oganj, kako jest jure od svetlosti odlučena vsake, a združena jest s večnimi v tamnost." I pristupiše k njej s veliku grozu i skrštahu svojimi zubi na nju i sami svoja lica derihu svojimi ognjenimi nohti i govorahu njoj: „O nečistivko zala, ovo su ti ljudi ke si sebi bila obljubila za prijatelje tvoje pri keh si tvoga Boga bil zabil. I zato se imaš š njimi va ognji paklenom mučiti i večno goren'je trpeti. Ti si bila delateljnica vsakoga zla i ljubiteljnica vseh stvari ke mi ljubimo. O duše okana, zač se sada ne gizdaš? zač sada ne greš na preljubodejstvo i ne ljubodeješ hodeći v tvojej velikoj gizde? Mnogije device posla po zle svetu i mnoge zakone žene v greh obrati i v nepočten'je postavi. O duše okana, kadi je sada tvoje

TUNDAL'S VISION

SYNOPSIS: Tundal is a free-living twelfth-century Irish nobleman, arrogant and hard on those around him. Once he visits a friend to collect a debt; when the friend confesses that he cannot repay the debt Tundal becomes enraged and has a stroke. Since his body is still warm his friend does not bury him, but allows him to lie in state. In the meantime his soul, accompanied by his guardian angel, takes a three-day guided tour of hell, purgatory, and paradise. When his soul finally returns to his body, Tundal awakes and describes for his friends what he has seen.

First of all he said this: "When my soul had already gone out of my body and it saw that the body was dead, it began to tremble with a great fear and it was frightened when it recalled its sins, and it was very frightened when there did not appear anything it could devise to help itself. It would have been happy to return again to its body, but in no way was it able to enter it, because it had a terrible fear of everything around it. And so weeping and wailing and trembling, it then looked and saw a multitude of devils, like a powerful cloud, moving toward it from all directions. Not only was the place itself full of them, but all the streets and the surrounding area was full of them. And now they encircled my poor soul and they said: "Let's sing a mournful and sad song for this unclean soul, because it deserves eternal ruin as its just reward, and the everlasting fire is ready for it, since it is already removed from every kind of light and it is allied with those who are eternally in the darkness." And they came toward it with much threatening and they gnashed their teeth at it, and they themselves tore at their own faces with their fiery fingernails, and they were saying to it: "O wicked, unclean one, these are the people whom you loved as friends, and with whom you forgot your God. And therefore you have to suffer with them in hell's fire and endure the eternal burning. You were the perpetrator of every sort of evil and the lover of all the things which we love. O miserable soul, why aren't you proud now? Why don't you go now to perform adultery, and why are you not fornicating, moving in your great pride? Many virgins you led astray, and many lawful wives you turned to sin and placed in dishonor. O miserable soul, where is your vainglorious boasting

hvaljen'je tašće slavno i tvoja vesel'ja sujetnaja? kadi su tvoji veliki smeh kadi jest sada tvoja velika sila i meč tvoj moćne ruke ku si ti mnozi ustrašil? zač tu jure očima tvojima ne moreš simo i tamo? i tu sada n postupiš gizdavo i ne govoriš prstom kažući, sada nimaš zalih i oholi pomišljen'ji v srci tvojem kako si običaj imel činiti va vsakoj zlobe nečistote."

I kada tako govorihu okolu njega pritečuće djavli, i ondi vid jednoga mlada detića lipa obrazom kako zvezda jutrnja. I poče na njeg gledati umiljeno duša Dundulova, nadejaše se ot njega niko utešen'j prijati kako ki ne vijaše ino nere djavle okol sebe. A to biše an'jel božj i njegove duše. Are vsaki človek ima pri sebi 2 an'jela, 1 božji a drug vražji. I kada se približi k njemu imenova ga njegovim imenem govore „Zdrav budi, Dundule! Ča tu činiš?"

ow, and your empty merriment? Where are your big laughs, and where ow is your great strength and the sword of your mighty arm, with which ou frightened so many? Why don't you move your eyes now, here and here? And here, now, you don't act proudly, and you don't point your nger while speaking; now you don't have wicked and arrogant thoughts n your heart as you were accustomed to doing, with all sorts of malice nd impurity."

And while the devils were talking in this way and running up nd around him, he then saw a young lad with a beautiful face, like a norning star. And Tundal's soul began to look at him ingratiatingly; t hoped to receive some comfort from him, since it could see nothing ut devils all around. And this was the angel of God and of his soul. Because every man has with him two angels, one from God and the other rom the Devil. And when he drew near to him he called his name, saying: "Hello, Tundal! What are you doing here?"

III

THE DALMATIAN RENAISSANCE AND BAROQUE

Dubrovnik

Dalmatian Lyric Poetry

Although the Italian Renaissance had little influence on the cultural life of most of the South Slavic area, it did evoke a strong burst of creativity on the Dalmatian coast, mainly within the Republic of Dubrovnik (see the note on Dubrovnik, preceding the section "Dubrovnik Treaties.") The prolific literary activity of the writers of Dubrovnik and neighboring islands such as Hvar, Brač, and Korčula, from the last part of the fifteenth century to the end of the seventeenth century, can be understood as another reflection of the same vitality that brought Dubrovnik to world prominence as a maritime power during this period.

Pride and self confidence, emanating from a recognition of Dubrovnik's economic and political importance, may help to explain the decision by the coastal writers to turn away from Italian and Latin, which had been the languages of culture and diplomacy in Dubrovnik for centuries, and to write in their native Slavic tongue. Dubrovnik's hostility toward Venice, in particular, may also have led her writers to be wary of cultural Italianization, even while recognizing the tremendous importance, as models, of Italian writers from Petrarch to Tasso and Ariosto. In a very real sense, then, the approximately two hundred years of Slavic Renaissance and Baroque writing on the Dalmatian Coast can be understood as a socio-political statement, as well as an early manifestation of Slavic cultural solidarity.

Poetry played a dominant role all during this period, with prose works occupying a minor and even inferior position, as Dragoljub Pavlović has pointed out in the introduction to his excellent anthology of Dubrovnik poetry (*Dubrovačka poezija*, 3rd ed., Beograd: Prosveta, 1963). The popularity of poetry, particularly lyric poetry, is not surprising in view of the

preeminent position assigned the poet by Renaissance literary doctrine, a well as the overwhelming importance of poetry in the oral literature c folklore of the South Slavs. Slavic folk poetry, by the way, provided th Dalmatian poets not only with a ready-made poetic vocabulary, but als with a store of traditional themes. The tie between folk poetry an Dalmatian Renaissance writing was established in the very beginning, b Šiško Menčetić (1457-1527) and Džore Držić (1461-1501), and was main tained right through the seventeenth century, by such excellent poets a Vladislav Menčetić (1617-1666) and Petar Kanavelović (1637-1719), fo example, in such poems as "Radonja" and "Stojna Pokojna."

It would be a mistake to exaggerate the Dalmatian dependence o Italian models, as Josip Torbarina may have done in his Italian Influenc on the Poets of the Ragusan Republic (London, 1931). Such an approac might obscure the fact that there steadily developed a native school o literature, beginning with the sometimes slavish Petrarchan imitations o Menčetić and Držić and proceeding to the far more complex and inde pendent Weltanschauung of Mavro Vetranović (1482-1576), with such dramatic change taking place in a period of less than fifty years. While th first two writers were mainly absorbed with writing love poetry, th prolific Benedictine monk Vetranović not only wrote such poetry, in hi early years, but he later engaged in social satire (as in his "Pjesanca: Aure Aetas") and political satire as well (see his allegory about Venetian rapacit "Vuk Ovci Priko Rijeke," as well as his appeal to the Christian kings o Europe "Pjesanca Gospodi Krstjanskoj"). Also indicative of Vetranović' profundity is his philosophical-autobiographical poem "Piligrin" (Th Pilgrim). And although as one proceeds from Vetranović to Dominko Zlatarić (1558-1613) and Ivan Gundulić (1589-1638) one does not find a dramatic a change in theme as one notes between Vetranović and his two precursors, still there is evidence of greater subtlety and refinement in Zlatarić and Gundulić, as well as a perfection in language that brings them closer to the modern literary language.

Not only is it possible to trace the development of an independen Dalmatian school of Renaissance and Baroque poetry, but it is also clea that the writers of this school were conscious of their participation in a collective effort of supreme importance. The Dalmatian writers knew wha they owed their predecessors and each other (see for example Antun Sasin's "U pohvalu pjesnika Dubrovačkijeh") and they defended each other's reputations at times when it was not politically wise (see Mavro Vetranović's "Pjesanca Marinu Držiću u Pomoć"). They also wrote highly poetic epistles to one another, as did Nikola Nalješković in his touching letter to Petar Hektorović of Hvar on their getting old ("Gospodinu Petru Hektoroviću Vlastelinu Hvarskomu - Nikola Stjepka Nalješković piše vrhu njih Starosti.") And most moving are their epitaphs and eulogies to com rades who have died, as next to love, death seems to have been a favorite lyrical theme, at a time when constant warfare and natural disaster were always a threat to wipe out family and friends.

Both Rafo Bogišić, in the introduction to volume 5 of Pet stoljeća hrvatske književnosti, *and Dragoljub Pavlović, in the introduction to his previously cited work, have pointed out that the Renaissance could not have taken root in Dubrovnik had it not been for the social and economic changes that took place as a result of the great prosperity that city enjoyed in the fifteenth and sixteenth centuries. Central to this social revolution was a change in the status of women, permitting women greater freedom, including the opportunity to attend theatrical productions; also important was the creation of a wealthy class of educated merchants and landowners, some of whom could afford to devote themselves to literary pursuits.*

The lyric poems presented below are not selected with any particular format in mind, but merely to give some idea of the number of poets involved, and the variety of themes. Most of these poems are excerpted from volumes 5 and 10 of Pet stoljeća hrvatske književnosti *(Rafo Bogišić editor). Those interested in knowing more about this literary period should read the introductions to both Bogišić's and Pavlović's books, cited above. More comprehensive treatment of the Dalmatian Renaissance and Baroque are given in M. Kombol's* Povijest hrvatske književnosti do preporoda *(Zagreb, 1945) and B. Vodnik's* Povijest hrvatske književnosti *(Zagreb, 1913). Special attention to the Italian influence on this literature is given in J. Torbarina's previously cited work, as well as in A. Cronia's* Il petrarchismo nel cinquecento serbo-croato. *(Bologna, 1948). Also of interest will be Vera Javarek's article on "Three Sixteenth-Century Dalmatian Poets," in the Slavonic and E. European Review (XLI, 96, London, 1962).*

BLAŽENA TI I SVA TVOJA LJEPOTA

Blaženi čas i hip najprvo kad sam ja
vidil tvoj obraz lip od koga slava sja.
Blažena sva mista kada te gdi vidih,
dni, noći, godišta koja te ja slidih.
Blažen čas i vrime najprvo kada čuh
ljeposti tve ime kojoj dah vas posluh.
Blažene boljezni ke patih noć i dan
cić tvoje ljubezni za koju gubljah san.
Blaženi jad i vaj ki stvorih dosade
želeći obraz taj sve moje dni mlade.
Blaženo vapinje kad ime tve zovih
i gorko trpinje u željah kad plovih.
Blažen trak od uze ljuvene u kojoj
stvorih plač i suze, želeći da sam tvoj.
Blažena ljepos tva, blažena tva mlados,
pokli se meni sva darova za rados.

BLESSED BE YOU AND ALL YOUR BEAUTY

Šiško Menčetić
(1457-1527)

Blessed be the hour and the moment
  when first I saw your lovely face, radiant in its glory.
Blessed be all the places where I saw you,
  the days, the nights, the years that I followed you.
Blessed be the hour and the season
  when first I heard your beautiful name, to which I gave full heed.
Blessed be the torments which I suffered night and day
  over my love for you, which kept me from sleep.
Blessed be the sorrow and the woe I have felt until now
  Wanting that face all my young days.
Blessed be the moaning when I called your name
  And the bitter suffering when I swam in desire.
Blessed be the bonds of love's prison
  in which I sobbed and cried, wishing to be yours.
Blessed be your beauty, blessed be your youth,
  Because they are given to me, for my happiness.

Francesco Petrarca
(1304-1374)

Benedetto sia 'l giorno, e 'l mese, et l'anno,
et la stagione, e 'l tempo, et l'ora, e 'l punto,
e 'l bel paese, e 'l loco ov'io fui giunto
da' duo begli occhi che legato m'ànno;

et benedetto il primo dolce affanno
ch'i' ebbi ad esser con Amor congiunto,
et l'arco, et le saette ond'i' fui punto,
et le piaghe che 'nfin al cor mi vanno.

Benedette le voci tante ch'io
chiamando il nome de mia donna ò sparte,
e i sospiri, et le lagrime, e 'l desio;

et benedette sian tutte le carte
ov'io fama l'acquisto, e 'l pensier mio,
ch'è sol di lei, sí ch'altra non v'à parte.

KROĆAHTA DIKLICE

Kroćahta diklice, ako ćeš slaviti,
ako ćeš tve lice da slove na sviti,
poteci sad hrlo, veće dni ne gubi,
ter mene za grlo uhvativ poljubi.
Zašto sam oni ja za koga na saj svit
od mnozih ime sja i cafti kako cvit;
zašto sam pisnivac i pjesni zač tvoru
od kojih jur vinčac ljuveni zadvoru.

TVOJA KOSA

Kad pustiš kosice, diklice gizdava,
u cvitku rozice ni vidit taj slava,
ter mi se sve vidi, tko na te pozire
da tebi zavidi a željom umire.

O SHY MAIDEN

Šiško Menčetić

O shy maiden, if you wish for glory,
  if you want the world to praise your face,
run quickly now, lose no more time,
  and take my throat and kiss me.
Because I am the one whose name in this world
  shines out among many and blooms like a flower;
because I am a poet and because I make poems
  with which to bestow love's crown.

YOUR HAIR

When you let down your hair, o beautiful maiden,
  Such glory won't be seen in the blossoming rose.
And it seems to me that whoever looks at you
  Either envies you or dies of desire.

DJEVOJKA JE PODRANILA

Djevojka je podranila, ružicu je brala;
   s bosilkom ju razbirala, trudna je zaspala.
Nad njom poju dva slavica, djevojku su zvala:
   "Ustan' gori, djevojčica, sanka ne zaspala.
Maglica se brijegom krade, sad je na te pala,
   cvitje hoće opaliti koje si nabrala;
još te hoće privariti, ako nis' dobrala
   za vjenačce drobnu ružu i cvitja ostala."
Djevojka se razbudila, slavicom se ozvala:
   "A vi, slavji lužanini, velika vam hvala,
koji me ste razbudili, jurve bih zaspala,
   razbiraje drobnu ružu i cvitja ostala.
Sinoć me je moja majka mladu hrabru dala,
   prid kojom sam vas večerak svezav ruke stala.
Žimi majka, žimi bratac, prije ga nijesam znala,
   niti mu sam rosnu travu prid konja metala,
razma sinoć. Mila majko, tebi budi hvala
   kâ si meni djevojčici mlada hrabra dala!"

VILA KA MNOM VLADA

Vila ka mnom vlada i mojim životom
   žestok mi trud zada ńe rajskom lipotom.
Ńe rajskom lipotom stravi me još toli,
   da vas vik i potom jur mnom se svak boli.
Jur mnom se svak boli, ar zgubih još dušu,
   toj vili pokoli odlučih da služu.
Odlučih da služu, mneći bit ńom blažen,
   a ne tač da tužu rańen i poražen.
Rańen i poražen u plaču još sahnem,
   ki će bit utažen jur kad ja izdahnem.
Jur kad ja izdahnem, nad mnom ću pisati:
   „Żeļah, da odahnem, tamnu smrt prijati.
Tamnu smrt prijati, ar velmi bi boļe
   i saj svit parjati a ne imat nevoļe.
A ne imat nevoļe ke ćutih cić vile
   jȁk jelin u poļe izrańen od strile."

A MAIDEN AROSE EARLY

Džore Držić
(1461-1501)

A maiden arose early, and she picked a rose;
  she chose sweet basil with it, and she fell fast asleep.
Above her sang two nightingales, calling to the maiden:
  "Get up, little maid, don't fall asleep.
A fog has stolen o'er the hill, it has fallen on you now,
  it wants to wither the flowers you gathered;
it wants to trick you, too, if you haven't picked
  the little rose and the other flowers for your wedding crown."
The maiden woke up, and she called to the nightingales:
  "Oh thank you, woodland nightingales, thank you very much,
If you hadn't woke me up, I would certainly have overslept,
  while picking a tiny rose and the other flowers.
Last night my mother gave me to a fine young man,
  all evening I stood before him, my arms folded over,
I swear by my mother, and also my brother, I didn't know him before now,
  nor had I placed dewy grass before his horse,
until last night. Mother dear, thanks be to you,
  for giving a maid like me her own young man.

THE VILA THAT RULES ME AND MY LIFE

The vila that rules me and my life
  has caused me great pain by her heavenly beauty.
By her heavenly beauty she has enchanted me so,
  That during this whole century, and later, everyone will pity me.
Everyone will pity me, because I have surrendered my soul,
  To that vila whom I chose to serve.
Whom I chose to serve, thinking I'd be blest,
  and not that I'd suffer, wounded and desolate.
Wounded and desolate, I wither in a sorrow,
  which will be assuaged only when I take my last breath.
Only when I take my last breath will they write above me:
  "I desired to rest, to accept dark death.
To accept dark death, for it was far better
  to depart this world and to have no more unhappiness.
To have no more the unhappiness I felt because of the vila,
  Like a stag in the field, wounded by an arrow."

ODILJAM SE

Odiljam se, moja vilo, Bog da nam bude u družbu;
  plač i suze i moju tužbu da bi znala, moja vilo!
  Odiljam se a ne vijem komu ostavljam ličce bilo.
Pokle ti je služba mila koju ti sam ja činio,
  a sad te sam ucvilio, ostaj zbogom, moja vilo!
  Odiljam se. . . .
Putovaje, uzdihaje i srdačcem svaki danak,
  a na oči moje sanak da t' ne priđe moja vilo!
  Odiljam se. . . .
Sila mi je putovati; oh, gorka je moja srjeća,
  od svijeh tuga mâ najveća, da bi znala, moja vilo!
  Odiljam se. . . .
Ne uzdam se u dni kratke da te viđu, srce moje,
  koje ostavljam da je tvoje; ostaj zbogom, moja vilo!
  Odiljam se. . . .
Ako drumak pomanjkaje ter te život moj ne vidi,
  srce moje ne slobodi; ostaj zbogom, moja vilo!
  Odiljam se. . . .
Neka srce ne zabludi da ne bude drugoj služit,
  a s tobom se ne razdružit; ostaj zbogom, moja vilo!
  Odiljam se. . . .
Ja ti dadoh vjeru moju do života da te služim,
  a po smrti da te združim; ostaj zbogom, moja vilo!
  Odiljam se. . . .
Govori se: pravi sluga i tko bude vjeran biti
  uvijek neće izgubiti, tko se bude potruditi.
Odiljam se, moja vilo. Oh, kako ja, moja vilo,
  odiljam se a ne vijem komu ostavljam ličce bilo.

"I AM DEPARTING"

Džore Držić

I am departing, my vila, and may God be with us both;
  if you could only know my weeping and tears and lamentation, o my vila!
  I am departing and I don't know to whom I leave the lovely little face.
You used to think I served you well,
  but now I have caused you pain, so farewell, my vila!
  I am departing. . . .
And while I'm travelling and my heart is sighing each day,
  let not sleep come to my eyes, o my vila!
  I am departing. . . .
I have to go; ah, bitter is my fortune,
  of all my sorrows this is the greatest, if you could know, o my vila!
  I am departing. . . .
I don't expect to see you soon, my heart,
  I am leaving you with her; farewell, o my vila!
  I am departing. . . .
If my road should run out, and in this life I see you not,
  don't set my heart free; farewell, o my vila!
  I am departing. . . .
May my heart not wander, may it not serve another,
  and may it not part company with you; farewell, o my vila!
  I am departing. . . .
I gave my word of honor to serve you for life,
  and to unite with you after death; farewell, o my vila!
  I am departing. . . .
They say: a true servant and one who will be faithful
  will never fail, if he will strive.
I am departing, o my vila. Ah, how I, my vila,
  am departing and I don't know to whom I leave the lovely little face.

PJESANCA ŠTURKU

Šturče, slatki razgovore,
  jeda te je koja vila
  u zelenci posred gore
  čemerikom opojila?
Ter nije čuti tvoje pjesni,
  da me tiho razgovori,
  od tužice i boljezni
  moje srce koje gori.
Zač ve zora bijela praska
  a Danica zove danak,
  i žuberi ptica svaka
  ostavivši noćni sanak;
samo pjesan nije čut tvoju
  mimo ptice sve ostale
  kê s Danicom rajsku poju
  ter nebesku Djevu hvale.
Dragi šturče i ljuveni,
  ako nijesu tuge koje
  u travici u zeleni
  obujmile srce tvoje,
pokomoli malo glave,
  pomoli se iz travice
  bez prikora i zabave
  od nebeske zgar Danice
Lje se čudim toj Danici,
  kako tebe s nebes zgara,
  gdi se tajiš u travici,
  ne kori te i ne kara?
Zašto bi se pristajalo
  da te kara, da te psuje
  meu stvorenje sve ostalo
  tvoje pjesni gdi ne čuje.
Tijem se bolim i tuguju
  u žalosti rad ljubavi,
  svake ptice gdi svud čuju
  biljišući po dubravi

"SONG TO A CRICKET"

Mavro Vetranović
(1482-1576)

O cricket, sweet enjoyment,
   has some vila
   amid the forest green
   given thee poison to drink?
So that one can't hear thy song,
   that gives me soft relief
   from the sadness and the melancholy
   which sear my heart.
Why, see, the white dawn is breaking
   and the Morning Star calls in the day,
   and every bird is warbling,
   leaving night's dream behind;
only thy song can't be heard
   beside all the other birds
   who with the Morning Star
   sing and praise the heavenly Virgin.
Dear beloved cricket,
   if it isn't that some sorrow
   in the grassy green
   has enveloped thy heart,
Show thy head a little,
   come show thyself from out the grass
   without reproach and commentary
   from the Morning Star above.
Only I'm surprised at the Morning Star,
   that from the heavens above
   it doesn't scold thee or chastize thee
   for hiding in the grass?
Because it would be proper
   to scold thee and to curse thee,
   when amongst all the rest of creation
   thy song can't be heard.
Thus I suffer and I sorrow
   from love's sadness,
   as I hear the birds everywhere
   thriving in the grove,

i pojući brijeme traju,
ter kraljici svijeh kraljica
u pjesance hvalu daju,
kâ je svjetlja ner Danica.
Tijem pridragi slatki šturče,
umoli se željnu meni,
nemoj takoj stati muče
u travici u zeleni.
Ti se ovdi u dubravi
u pjesance u medene
i proglasi i objavi
i sadruži trudna mene . . .

PISANCA U POMOĆ POETAM

Lončarom je gnjila dana
kada lonce pripravljaju,
da ručice pristavljaju
kako hoće sa svijeh strana;
a pengatur vrhu svega
ima volju i oblasti,
da ne štedi nijedne masti,
kako hoće da sve penga.
A poetam čes pogodi,
neka slijede mužu svoju,
da na volju pjesni poju,
kako hoće u slobodi.

and singing they pass the time,
    as to the queen of all queens
    they give praise in song,
    she who is more radiant than the Morning Star.
Thus dearest sweetest cricket,
    grant me my desire,
    don't stand silent so
    in the grassy green.
Here in the oak grove
    in song mellifluous
    proclaim thyself and make thy presence known,
    and be a friend to burdened me.

"A SONG IN SUPPORT OF POETS"

Potters are given potter's clay
    when they fix pots,
    so they can put on handles,
    as many as they wish;
and the painter above all
    has freedom and prerogative
    not to spare a single color,
    to paint everything as he wishes.
And to the poets' lot has fallen
    to heed their muse,
    to sing songs at will,
    in freedom as they wish.

GDI JE SAD RAZUM TVOJ

Gdi je sad razum tvoj, prilike komu nî,
  primudri starče moj u svemu pošteni? . . .
Plačeš sad, jer prika došla je po te smrt,
  kojojzi nije lika i kâ će vas svijet strt.
Nijesi li rekal ti da čovjek samohoć
  ima je iskati i željet dan i noć?
Tuga kâ svakako čovjeku prit ima
  strahom se nikako dočekat ne ima.
Tko dobra srca jes, slobodno boj slidi,
  a strašiv zgubi svijes, prije neg ga i vidi.
Zašto hoć' sada ti za život tvoj jedan
  dvije smrti prijati cvileći po vas dan?
jer dušu i tilo stojeć tač jadovan
  umaraš nemilo, jak da si sebe van.
Buduć jur od sviti sva mora pridobil
  i kad bi t' već priti u luku vrijeme bil,
hoć' jedra otvorit ter opet u more
  sa plavju tvojom it za slijedit tvê gore.
Budući boj dobil, od onijeh bježat hoć'
  kê si jur pridobil i vazel pod tvu moć.
Izidi mimo toj s pohvalom iz toga,
  prijatelju dragi moj, života tužnoga.
Vaskolik vijek si tvoj, šeset je jur ljeta,
  hrabreno tvoril boj s tugami od svijeta;
a sad kad od mrtvijeh jedan se mož' riti,
  bojiš se tuga tijeh da će te dobiti!
Ako si u vaju, ne jer ćeš s svijeta poć,
  negoli jer mladu domaću imaš oć,
ona kad bude tvê dijeljenje uznati,
  take su žene sve, malo će hajati . . .
Strah te je umriti, a plačeš život tvoj:
  razuman tvoriti opći li igdar toj?
Znaš, mnokrat život dug dovede čovjeka
  da je š njim smijeh i rug i prijekor do vijeka.
Da onda bude htil' na tebe smrt priti,
  mlađahan kad si bil i zelen na sviti,

"WHERE NOW IS YOUR REASON?"

Nikola Dimitrović
(1500?-1553)

Where now is your reason, of which there is no equal,
my most wise old man, honorable in all things? . . .
You are weeping now, because terrifying death has come for you,
against which there is no cure and which will wipe out everyone.
Wasn't it you who said that a man should voluntarily
seek it out and wish for it day and night? . . .
A sorrow which to man will come no matter what
should never be met with fear.
Who is of good heart follows the battle with equanimity,
but he who is afraid loses consciousness before he even sees it.
Why do you want now, for your one life
to receive two deaths, wailing the whole day through?
because in being so depressed you are killing both your soul and your body,
mercilessly, as though you were beside yourself.
Having mastered already all the seas of the world
now, when it is time to come into port,
you want to unfurl your sails and put out to sea again
with your ship, to pursue your grief.
Having won the battle, you want to flee from those
whom you have already conquered and taken under your power.
Go out, instead, with praise,
my dear friend, from this sad life.
All this life of yours, it's already sixty years,
you did bravely battle with the sorrows of the world;
and now when you can be called one of the dead,
you fear those sorrows will defeat you!
If your woe is not from leaving this world,
but because you leave a young wife behind,
she, when she finds out about your departure,
will be little concerned, for such are women. . . .
You're afraid to die, and yet you lament your life:
can anyone make sense of that?
You know, a long life often makes a man
the butt of laughter and ridicule and lasting reproach.
Now if Death had wanted to come to you
when you were young and green to the world,

rekô bih da imaš razlog tač plakati,
kî sada ne imaš nit ga mož' imati.
Nu ti kî sad se mož' pod zemljom mrtav rit,
bez srama žudiš još na svijetu poživit.
Eto se bez broja godišta navrši,
otkole sjen tvoja u ropstvu duh drži;
jure sve okove na nogah razdro jes,
a ti mu hoć' nove postavit u nesvijes.
U šeset godina života tko nije sit,
ni u šes stotina neće se nasitit . . .
Mož' li znat kade ja toliko bjeh bolan,
da nejmah pokoja ni javi ni u san,
ter mi ti ljuveni razgovor davaše,
kî srce u meni i život smiraše.
Vrh svega hti mi rit: ako se s' na saj svit
porodil za umrit, sada mreš za živit.
Koj bih ti svjȅt ini mogô dat sad bolji,
neg kî dâ ti meni u mojoj nevolji?
Kroz toj ga htij primit, kako sve tvoju stvar,
drugo ti neću rit: u družbu t' Višnji zgar.

would have said that you had reason so to weep,
  but now you have none, nor can you have any.
'et you who now could be said to be dead and under ground,
  shamelessly yearn to live a little longer in the world.
.ook at the numberless years that have been completed
  since your shadow first held your spirit slave;
lready you have shattered all the fetters on your feet,
  but in your delirium you want to take on new ones.
le who isn't content with sixty years
  will not be satisfied with six hundred. . . .
'erhaps you remember when I was so sick,
  I had no peace, neither awake nor sleeping,
nd you gave me loving conversation,
  which brought peace to my heart and life.
Aost of all you tried to tell me: if into this world
  you were born in order to die, now you are dying in order to live.
vhat better advice could I give you
  than what you gave me in my distress?
'herefore, receive it, as it were all your own,
  I'll say no more to you: may the God above be with you.

SUŽNJI

Iz daleka sužnji gremo
jeda bismo naprosili
čijem bismo se otkupili,
da u ropstvu ne umremo.
Iz daleka . . .
Bez broja je prošlo dana
da u ropstvu pribivimo;
a vi znate od sužana
kolika je žalos samo
da slobodu ne imamo,
što najdraže reć' moremo.
Iz daleka . . .
O gospodo plemenita,
pokli milos vaša slove
i bogastvo dokraj svita,
molimo vas, na nas ove
pogledajte vi robove,
gdi u gvozdijeh klopoćemo.
Iz daleka . . .
Ter vašega togaj blaga
molimo vas ne štedite,
vi gospodo naša draga,
neg nas tužnijeh otkupite,
ter za robe vi držite,
da se od vas ne krenemo.
Iz daleka . . .
A gospođe vi gizdave,
pokli slavnu milos vašu
vrh svih inih na svit prave,
viđ'te tužnu mlados našu,
ter ne bran'te stvar najdražu,
da se njome pomožemo.
Iz daleka . . .
Dobro znamo svaka od vas
milostiva velmi da je,
tijem pozrite srcem na nas,
pokli znate plata kâ je,

"SLAVES"

Nikola Nalješković
(1510-1587)

From afar we slaves are coming,
  so that we might beg
  what we might be ransomed with,
  lest we die in captivity.
    From afar. . . .
Days have passed without number,
  since we have been in bondage;
  and you know how great
  is the grief of prisoners
  only because we have no freedom,
  the dearest thing of all, as we can say.
    From afar. . . .
O noble lords,
  because your kindness and your riches
  are praised to the ends of the earth,
  we beg you to have a look
  at us slaves here,
  as we rattle in our chains.
    From afar. . . .
And of that treasure of yours
  we beg you not to spare,
  you our dear lords,
  but ransom us unfortunates
  and keep us as your slaves,
  so that we won't have to leave you.
    From afar. . . .
And you pretty ladies,
  because your splendid generosity
  surpasses all others in the world, they say,
  see our sorrowful youth,
  and don't refuse this most precious thing
  that will be a help to us.
    From afar. . . .
We know well that each of you
  is very kind indeed,
  so look at us with your hearts,
  because you know the recompense

za toj djelo kâ se daje,
prid oči ju vam dajemo.
Iz daleka . . .
Blago vaše jes veliko,
ter se neće ni poznati,
kad nam date njekoliko,
neće zatoj vam lipsati;
gospodari neće znati,
a spovidjet mi nećemo.
Iz daleka . . .
Toj li sluga kôj trjebuje,
naprijed samo pristupajte,
koga hoće da kupuje;
što smo blijedi ne gledajte,
nu nam malo mesa dajte,
opretiljet kako ćemo.
Iz daleka . . .
Rad togaj vas svijeh molimo,
počnite nas kupovati,
vam robovat er volimo
i kopati i orati,
i dan i noć rabotati,
a izvrsno toj umijemo.
Iz daleka . . .
Svaki od nas u ledini,
protrapiv ju kako on hoće,
lijep vinograd da t' učini,
da do ljeta rodi voće,
vjerujte nam kako hoće
gdi fatigat mi počnemo.
Iz daleka . . .
Ovi umije vunu presti,
ovi drugi umije tkati,
taj bječvice umije plesti,
tomuj mesa daj skuhati,
da ćeš prste ogrizati,
slas mu izrijet ne umijemo.
Iz daleka . . .
U vaše se zatoj ruke
milostive pridavamo,
moleći vas ove muke
čin'te da mi ne prijamo;
hotjejte nas kupit samo,
da se uz vas pritisnemo.
Iz daleka . . .

given for this deed,
before your eyes we give it to you.
From afar. . . .
Your wealth is great
so you won't even feel it,
when you give us a little
you won't miss it;
your masters won't know
and we won't tell.
From afar. . . .
If it's a servant you need
just step forward,
whoever wants to buy one;
pay no attention to our pale color,
just give us a little meat
and we'll fatten up some.
From afar. . . .
That's why we beg all of you,
do begin to buy us,
because we want to be your slaves
both to dig and to plow,
and to work day and night,
yes, we know how to do that quite well.
From afar. . . .
Each of us in virgin soil,
planting it the way he wants to,
will make you a fine vineyard
that will bear fruit before summer,
as much as you wish, believe us,
once we begin to work at it.
From afar. . . .
This one knows how to spin wool,
this other one knows how to weave,
that one is good at knitting socks;
give that one some meat to cook
and you'll lick your fingers afterwards,
we just can't tell you how good it is.
From afar. . . .
And so into your merciful hands
we give ourselves,
begging you to arrange it
so that we don't receive these torments;
only consent to buy us,
so that we may draw close to you.
From afar. . . .

MRNARICA

Na prozoru svome stoje
poglavica od Misine
reče slugam: "Sluge moje,
kažujte mi do istine,
koje su ono toli mila
velje plavi kako gora
bijela jedra priklopila
po pučini sinja mora?
Ter se diče i gizdaju,
ter se svijetli sinje more,
gdi korablje zlatne sjaju
kako sunce povrh gore.
I vidjet je svako jedro
po pučini gdi se bani,
kako kad je nebo vedro
ter Danica dzorom rani,
ali paun zlata krila
kada prospe i raširi,
ali vlase gorska vila,
tančac vodeć prid satiri.

. . . .

Zato svi mi rec'te sada,
tako da ste vazda zdravi,
tko njeguje, tko li vlada
toli krasne ove plavi.
Jeda Turke ali More
ona jidra zlamenuju,
da porobe naše dvore
pokraj mora i pljenjuju.

. . . .

Odgovor poglavice od Misine

Ne brini se, ne staraj se,
naš čestiti gospodine,
er ti ćemo dobre glase
kazovati do istine.

"THE FLEET"

Antun Sasin
(1524-1595)

At his window
Messina's ruler stands,
he says to his servants: "My servants,
tell me the truth,
whose is that multitude of ships
that covers a stretch of the open sea
like a beautiful forest of white sails?
Now they flaunt and preen themselves,
now the blue sea sparkles
where the golden ships glimmer
like the sun above the mountain top;
and it's something to watch
as each sail fills proudly along the open sea,
like the morning star at early dawn
when the sky is bright and clear,
or like the peacock, when it throws
and spreads its golden wings,
or the mountain vila her hair flings,
when dancing before satyrs.
. . . .
So tell me now all of you,
may you always be so sound,
who sponsors, who owns
such beautiful ships as these.
Is it Turks or is it Moors
those sails denote,
out to rob and plunder
our castles by the sea?
. . . .

The Answer To The Ruler Of Messina

Don't worry, and don't be anxious,
Your Excellency,
for it's truly good news
we are about to tell you.

Ni moreška ni turačka
ono nijesu jedra bijela,
neg su drijeva dubrovačka
hrla i brza kako strijela.
Trgovci su sve bogati,
ne gredu nas porobiti,
negli s nami trgovati
i tebi se pokloniti.
A plavi su toli mile,
po pučini kê se brode,
kako utve zlatokrile
po jedzeru bistre vode.
Mrnari su kako lavi,
hrabreni su i zamjerni,
plasi, hrli i gizdavi,
i krstjani pravovjerni.
Meju sobom se zovu bratja,
ter je ljubav tojli mila,
kako da je jedna majka
sve rodila i gojila.
Španjulim se bratski druže,
a Dubrovnik svi do glave
sa svijem srcem vjerno služe
i daju mu vječne slave.

. . . .

Kapetan je sveti Vlasi,
mrnaricu kî tu vlada,
po svem svijetu kâ se glasi
od istoka do zapada.
Tuj su pčele, tuj su ose,
tuj su zmaji, tuj su vuci,
koji zlatnu krunu nose
kad se morem biju s Turci.
Kako s Mori, kako s Turci
gdje se sretu i sastaju,
zazret neće nijednoj ruci
bijela jedra da kaljaju.

. . . .

Ter se more zakrvavi
rvući se tako s Turci,
kako kada u dubravi
zvjerenje se kolje s vuci,

Neither Moorish nor Turkish
are those sails of white,
no, they're ships from Dubrovnik,
swift and fast as an arrow.
Merchants rich are they all,
come not to rob us
but to trade with us
and to pay their respects to you.
And their ships are so appealing,
as they sail along the open sea,
like golden-winged wild ducks
over a lake of clear water.
Their sailors are like lions,
they're brave and matchless,
hot-tempered, quick, and handsome,
and true-believing Christians as well.
They call each other brothers,
and their love is so endearing,
as if one mother
had borne and raised them all.
With the Spaniards they are on brotherly footing,
and everyone, to the last man,
serves Dubrovnik faithfully with all their hearts,
and gives her everlasting praise.

. . . .

St. Blaise is their captain,
it is he who rules this navy,
famous throughout the world
from East to West.
Here are bees, here are wasps,
here are dragons, here are wolves,
who bear the golden crown as their emblem
when at sea they do battle with the Turks.
And be it Moors or be it Turks,
when they meet and come together,
they won't back away from any party
and strike their sails.

. . . .

And the sea becomes all bloody
from their fighting with the Turks,
as when in the oak grove
wild animals fight with wolves,

gdje se kolju, gdje se biju,
sijekući se i rvući,
a jednaga svi vapiju
jednijem glasom klikujući:
"Udri, brate, sijeci, brate,
udri svak tko može bolje,
neka Turci glavom plate
naše tuge i nevolje.
Bolje nam je smrt obrati
da se truda slobodimo,
neg se Turcim robi zvati,
okovani da vozimo."
A fortune kadli kure,
gdi se more plamom stvori,
počam s krme ter do bure,
pod skorupom drijevo nori,
pak se diči, pak se vija,
kad uzjaše vrhu vala,
kako soko kada zbija
u visini jato ždrala.
A mrnari nijesu lotri,
kako jeljen nego skaču,
okupani i svi mokri
gdi po toldi vali plâčū;
a djetići gologlavi
kom začuju naukijera,
navrat skaču po svoj plavi
kako da ih zla čes tjera.

. . . .

A kad sunce u zapad spravi,
ali zorom na Dijanu
na koljenijeh gologlavi
pjesan poju mnogo slavnu;
i u pjesni kû skladaju
Boga slave, Boga hvale,
gospodara salutaju
i mrnare sve ostale.

. . . .

To je sama mrnarica
kâ se pravo može rijeti
da je gospoja i kraljica
svijeh mrnara na sem svijeti.
I čestit se svak nahodi,
i čas mu je privelika
vjeran život tko provodi
pod bandijerom Dubrovnika.

here they fight with swords and there with fists,
slashing and fighting,
and all alike they shout,
crying out in one voice:
"Strike, brother, slash, brother,
strike as best you can,
let the Turks pay with their heads
for our sorrows and misfortunes.
Better to choose death,
and be free of torment,
than to be called Turkish slaves
and ride their ships in chains."
And when a storm blows up,
and the sea turns to flame,
first with stern, and then with prow,
the ship plunges beneath lathered waves,
then it dances and it hovers,
as it rides above the waves,
like a falcon when it drives
a flock of cranes on high.
And the sailors don't stand around,
but they run like stags,
all drenched and wet,
along the wave-washed deck;
and the lads bareheaded,
when they hear the helmsman call,
run back along the whole ship,
as though chased by some evil fate.

. . . .

And when the sun has headed westward,
or in the early dawn,
bareheaded and on their knees
they sing a most glorious song;
and in that song which they compose
they praise God and they thank Him,
and they salute their captain,
and all the other sailors as well.

. . . .

This is the same fleet
which can justly be called
the mistress and queen
of all the navies in the world.
And fortunate is he
and most great his honor,
who spends his life faithfully
beneath the flag of Dubrovnik.

MLAĐAHAT JOŠ NE IMAH NI ŠESNAES LJETA

Mlađahat još ne imah ni šesnaes ljeta
(ni) mukâ ne primah, želah trudan svjeta.

VILA JE MOMA TRI VJENAČCA

Vila je moma tri vjenačca; pelinak
bere, ružicu prosiple.
Jedan je vila od tratorka; pelinak
bere, ružicu prosiple.
Drugi je vila od bosioka; pelinak
bere, ružicu prosiple.
Tretji je vila od ružice; pelinak
bere, ružicu prosiple.
Koji je vila od tratorka; pelinak
bere, ružicu prosiple, –
taj mi (je) bracu darovala; pelinak
bere, ružicu prosiple.
Koji je vila od bosioka,
taj mi je sama pronosila; pelinak
bere, ružicu prosiple.
Koji je vila od ružice,
taj mi je hrabru darovala; pelinak
bere, ružicu prosiple.

A YOUNGSTER OF NOT YET SIXTEEN YEARS

Anonymous in Ranjina's Songbook

A youngster, I was not yet sixteen years,
I had no troubles, but I was burdened with earthly desires.

A VILA IS THE MAID OF THREE GARLANDS

A vila is the maid of three garlands; she gathers wormwood
and she strews roses.
One is the vila of the acanthus bush; she gathers wormwood
and she strews roses.
A second is the vila of sweet basil; she gathers wormwood
and she strews roses.
A third is the vila of the roses; she gathers wormwood
and she strews roses.
As for the vila of acanthus; she gathers wormwood
and she strews roses,–
That one she gave to her dear brother; she gathers wormwood
and she strews roses.
As for the vila of sweet basil,
that one she herself wore around; she gathers wormwood
and she strews roses.
As for the vila of the roses,
that one she gave to her betrothed; she gathers wormwood
and she strews roses.

JEDNOMU KÎ NIŠTO NE UČINI A TUĐE SVE HULI

Jadovni zleče moj,zavidos s kim bjesni,
za zle prem tolikoj ne scijeni mê pjesni.
Ak' u njih nî sada onijeh sve riči,
kîm staro njekada brijeme se tač diči:
"Svitlušto sunačce, rozice, diklice,
ljuveno srdačce, grimizna svilice,
zašto mê tač verna ostavi, moj venče,
krunice biserna, moj zlaćen prstenče? "
U ova vremena, moj hudi tamniče,
druga sad imena naše pjesni diče,
jer jȁk lis u cvitju tač nijedna na svit saj
u jednomu bitju ne trpi običaj.
Također i riči kime se jur njekad
stara svijes diči u scijeni nijesu sad.
I ove sad kê veće jesu, znaj, scijenjene
s vremenom bit neće od druzih primljene.
Razliki svit ovi kî trpi svoju čes,
sve vȅćī i nȍvī što godi na njem jes.
Tim ne kteć rug biti svijem spijevcom na svit saj
kad što hoć' huliti, prî dobro razmišljaj.

SAD GDI JE MRTVI DAN

Sad gdi je mrtvi dan, ovi t' svȉt daju moj,
gospȍđe češćita:
ktje dijelit za dušu tvê blago od svita
i meni vrhu svih taj dila satvori
milosna koga tvâ nemȉlōs umȍrī.
Molitav ne ištu, ni plama voštȅna,
nu onu milu slas od dobrȁ žūđȅna,
kâ moje žalosti
sve može svrnȕti u rajske radosti.
Tim mene uglȅdāj tač kao se dostȍjā,
ako ćeš da opêta oživȉt budu ja.

"TO ONE WHO HAS DONE NOTHING HIMSELF, BUT WHO CRITICIZES EVERYONE ELSE"

Dinko Ranjina (1536-1607)

O my poisonous enemy, you whom envy turns wild with rage,
don't count my poems quite so bad
if they don't have in them all those words
which were once the delight of bygone days:
"O radiant little sun, o little rose, o maiden,
o beloved little heart, o satiny silk,
why did you leave me so true, my crown,
o little crown of pearls, my golden ringlet?"
In these times, my evil bigot,
our poems give grace to other words,
for just as with the leaf of a flower, in this world no part
of any organism suffers routine.
So it is with words that once were the delight
of minds of yore, but now are out of fashion.
And know that those now in great esteem
will in time be unacceptable to others.
In this diverse world each thing is subject to its fate,
continually growing old and being renewed.
So if you don't want to be ridiculed by all the poets in the world,
when you want to condemn something, first think it over well.

"NOW WHEN IT IS ALL SOULS' DAY"

Now when it is All Souls' Day, I give you my advice,
o noble lady:
since you wish to part with your worldly treasure for some soul's sake,
why not start first with me,
a gentle soul slain by your ungentleness!
No prayers seek I, nor waxy flame,
but the sweet delight of quested good,
which my sorrows
all shall change to heavenly joy.
So look at me the way you should
if you want me to come back to life again.

U HVALU POKOJA I MIRNE PAMETI

Sad pokle snig kopni i trzan cvit plodi
  i sunce ljepše dni umrlim privodi,
  o polja, o luzi, k vami grem ošad toj
što drže jur druzi u scijeni velikoj.
  Neka ini u trudu provode sva lita,
da zlato stȅć budu i slavu od svita;
  jer moj duh uživa bez misli usnuti,
gdi slavic tih spiva svoj poraz minuti,
  upored ter s njime vil moju pripijevat,
da drago nje ime nauči gora zvat.
  Ne vidi puk ludi da ne ima nikada
dobra kâ on žudi, toj sreća čim vlada,
  ni čini carska vlas ni blaga zamirna
čestitijeh ovdi nas, neg istom svis mirna;
  jer nad čim sunce sja, sve da ima kî človik
a želi pokoja, njegov je tužan vik.

"IN PRAISE OF PEACE AND A QUIET MIND"

Dominko Zlatarić
(1558-1613)

Now as the snow is melting and the meadow is enriched with flowers
  and the sun sends better days for days gone by,
O fields, o groves, to you I go, leaving behind
  what others hold in high esteem.
Troubled let them spend their years,
  acquiring gold and world renown;
my spirit enjoys its carefree sleep,
  where the soft nightingale of past loss sings,
or joins me in praise of my vila,
  that the forest may learn to call her name.
The mad throng doesn't see that the wealth for which it yearns
  it never gets, since chance holds sway over all;
neither imperial power nor unlimited wealth
  can make us happy here, but only a peaceful conscience;
for no matter where the sun shines, if a man has everything
  but he longs for peace, his life is sorrowful.

U DRUGOJ ČIM STRANI

U drugoj čim strani prosvijetlja sad druge
drag pogled sunčani livade i luge,
i stupaj raskošni kud gre, lis i cvitje
pokrijeplja, jak u dni vesele prolitje;
ja grozni tvoreć cvil sva mjesta ophodim
gdje kûgod lijepe vil' spomenu nahodim.
I pravim u sebi: "Evo mâ razbluda
njekada ovdi bî i prođe ovuda;
ovdi se obrati i sjede u sjeni
i meni ne krati dat odvit žuđeni;
ovdi sve hitrija besjedeć ne prista;
ovdi se nasmija; vrh sebe ovdi sta."
Tako ja govorim,pak se sam zabudem,
a riječi nje zorim, uza nju i budem.
Viđu ju prida mnom (misal me tač vara),
gdi bitju mom tamnom svital dan otvara.
Ovako nemoćnik prid sobom gledat mni
njegovoj žeđi lik, vodu kê prid njim nî.

"SINCE IN OTHER PARTS"

Dominko Zlatarić

Since in other parts, in other vales and meadows
   the dear sunny gaze now casts its light,
and the luxuriant step, where it goes,
   refreshes leaf and flower, like spring in happy days;
feverishly lamenting, I visit all the places
   where I can find some reminder of the pretty vila.
And I say to myself: "Look, my delight
   once was here, and she passed this way;
here she turned and sat in the shade
   and she didn't refuse me the answer I longed for;
heres she wouldn't stop talking, wittier all the while,
   here she laughed; here she acted proud."
I go on in this way and I forget myself,
   now I hear her words, and I am beside her.
I see her before me (my mind deceives me so),
   as though a bright day were dawning for my darkened being.
Thus does an exhausted person think he sees before him
   the remedy for his thirst, the water that isn't there.

PRIDRAGI SINKO MOJ

«U smrt Šimuna sina svoga prvorođenoga koji živje godište i dva mjesec[a] i petnaes dana; umrije na tri setembra godišta 1592.»

Pridragi sinko moj, kî razlog ovo bî,
    da oči ovakoj zatvorim ja tebi,
    na mojoj što smrti od tebe prijat mnjah?
Evo mi umrije ti, a ja živ, jaoh!, ostah.
    Sunce svoj okoliš jednokrat obiđe
i mjesec još ne triš, ti k nami da priđe.
    Malo ti postoja, hrlo t' nas ostavi,
o diko sva moja i moja ljubavi!
    Ter brži od strile odletje u mal čas
i tvoje sve mile razblude skri od nas.
    Već nećeš ćaćka zvat da te u svoj kril primi,
ni njegov grlit vrat rukami drazimi.
    Prvo si veselje od srca moga bil;
jaoh! sad si dreselje i vječni plač i cvil.
    Koli se promini moja čes u kratko
i gorko učini ufanje prislatko!
    Ne bude sunce zać ni isteć vas moj vik
što sa mnom neće nać i oći plač velik;
    jer s tobom radosti umriješe sve meni,
i sa mnom svitlosti očiju mojijeh nî.

MY DEAREST SON

Dominko Zlatarić

"On The Death of Simon, His First-Born Son, Who Lived A Year And Two Months And Fifteen Days; He Died On The Third Of September, 1592."

My dearest son, what was the reason for this,
  that I should close your eyes thus for you,
  when I had thought that at my death you would be doing this for me?
So you died on me, and I, o woe! remained alive.
  The sun had made its circuit once
And the moon not yet three times, since you first came to us.
  You stayed too short a time, you left in too great a hurry,
O all my pride and my love!
  And swifter than an arrow you flew off in a little while
and hid all your dear charms from us.
  You won't be calling daddy to take you to his lap,
Nor hug his neck with dear arms.
  You were the first joy of my heart;
O woe! now you are sorrow, and eternal lament, and grief.
  How much my fortune has changed in a short time,
how much my fondest hopes have been made bitter!
  The sun will neither rise nor set all my days
without finding me and leaving me in great mourning;
  because with you died all joy for me,
and the light of my eyes is no longer.

NEMOJ, NEMOJ, MÂ LJUBICE

Nemoj, nemoj, mâ Ljubȉce,
u bistru viru virovȁti,
u kom rajsko tvoje lice
općiš često oglēdȁti.

Ere neće, vjeruj meni,
dugo vrijeme kazat tebi
medne usti, pram zlaćȁni
i dvije zore zgara s nebi.

Skoro, skoro promijenȉt će
vas tvoj ures i svu diku,
tebe istu tebi skrit će
da neć' poznat tvu priliku.

Bježi mlados, dni othȍdē
vele brže, vele plaše
neg' li istoga vira vode
i kâ se u njim sjena kaže.

Tijekom, tijekom lete ljeta,
sve pod suncem satira se,
i zasve dan dođe opeta,
naša doba ne vrate se.

Odori će bit i plijeni
od gusara, kȋ sve stira,
tvoj drag pogled, pram ljuveni,
slatke usti, lice od lira.

Tim se mlada ne oholi,
čim pogledaš sliku tvoju,
neg se smili na mê boli,
o ljubljeni moj pokoju!

"DO NOT, DO NOT, O MY BELOVED"

Ivan Bunić Vučić
(1591-1658)

Do not, do not, o my Beloved,
trust the limpid pool,
wherein your heavenly features
you are given oft to view.

For it won't, believe me,
Show you for long
honeyed lips, golden locks
and two eyes like dawns from heaven above.

Soon, soon, it will change
all your adornment and all your charms,
hiding you from yourself,
so you won't recognize your own reflection.

Youth flees, the days move on,
far more quickly, far more hastily
than the waters of that same pool
and the shadow that is shown in it.

Like a stream, like a stream the years fly by,
everything under the sun is wiped away,
and although day will again follow day,
our time will not return.

And plunder and booty
of the robber who ravishes all,
will be your dear look, your lovely locks,
sweet lips, lilied face.

So young woman be not proud,
as you look at your image there,
instead have mercy on my pains,
o my beloved solace!

STOJKA POKOJNA

Jutros sjela
    Stojna bijela
bješe vesela
    kon jezera,
gdje jučera
ovce dotjera,
    na cvijetice
vrh travice,
gdje pastjerice
    tance vode,
k kijem ishode
vile iz vode.
    I združene
razbluđene
pjesni ljuvene
    začinjaju
i uživaju
u slatkom raju.
    Ona mlada
buduć tada
svratila stada
    kitne grane
gdje ih brane
zrak' od sunčane,
    uze drag svoj
mir i pokoj
hvalit ovakoj:
    "Ubogoga
bitja moga
sreća je mnoga,
    kâ nathita
sva od svita
blaga čestita,
    jer se u njima
mir ne ima
ni pokoj prima,
    a u momu
ubogomu

"PEACEFUL STOJKA"

Petar Kanavelović
(1637-1719)

This morning sat down
  lovely Stojna
she was happy
  by the lake
where yesterday
she drove sheep,
  amid the flowers
o'er the grass,
where shepherdesses
  lead dances
to which vilas come
from out the water.
  And in unison
enchanting
love songs
  they compose
and enjoy
in sweet paradise.
  The young one
having then
turned her flocks
  where flowery branches
would protect them
from the sun's rays,
  began her dear
peace and quiet
thus to praise:
  "In my humble
way of life
there is much happiness,
  which surpasses
all the world's
noblest treasures,
  because in them
one can find
neither peace nor rest,
  but in my
humble

bitju ovomu
    sveđ se uživa
rados živa
i mir pribiva.
    U ovoj vodi
kâ ishodi
iz vrela odi
    ruke umivam,
pitje primam,
zrcalo imam.
    Na ovomu
zelenomu
dubu plodnomu
    meni hrana
raste izbrana
s nebesa dana.
    Sviona nije,
zlatna nije,
srebrna nije
    moja odjeća,
gdje inijem sreća
stoji najveća,
    jer njima krije
najvrlije
ćudi od zmije.
    Ruho moje
priprosto je,
ali bijelo je,
    jer ga bijeli
zrak veseli,
kî sunce dijeli,
    i ima sliku
svukoliku,
za moju diku,
    srca moga
pravednoga
pričistoga.
    U ovoj sjeni
i zeleni
vas je svijet meni,
    a u Dubravi
ovoj pravi
pokoj boravi.

(Odlomak)

way of life
  one always enjoys
real happiness
and peace resides.
  In this water
which comes out
of the spring here
  I wash my hands,
I get my drink,
I have a mirror.
  On this
green
fruitful oak tree
  grows for me
choice food
from heaven given.
  Neither of silk
nor of gold
nor of silver
  are my clothes,
wherein others find
their greatest pleasure,
  because with them they hide
the cruelest
viper natures.
  My clothing
is most simple,
but it is white,
  for it is bleached
by the joyful ray
which the sun imparts,
  and it gives a picture
complete
and praiseworthy,
  of my heart
righteous
and most pure.
  In this shade
and greenery
is all my world,
  and in this Oak Grove
true peace
resides. . . .

(Excerpt)

BRAVAC
ALITI CVILENJE PLANIČICE PASTIRICE U NJEGOVOJ SMRTI

. . .
Jaoh, što mi se ovo steče?
tko mi srce iskorijepi,
tko mi život, jaoh, posiječe,
kamo Bravac moj prilijepi?
dospio je; neka prije
i moj život, jaoh, dospije . . .

Na trpezu kad bih sjela
za pokrjepu dati tijelu,
ptičica bi doletjela
svud po platnu pršeć bijelu
i od svake bi piće htio
vazda kušat on svoj dio.

Kolikrat se tad mi zgodi,
što se čudim jošte ista,
scijenit da dаž na me hodi
a on proli perja čista:
dаž bi iz vode sipljo mili
s kvašenijem svojijem krili.

Većekrati u iglicu
kad bih htjela svilu udjesti
izmako bi s kljunkom žicu
ku bih htjela s rukom sresti
i uzalak bi učinio
neka bi me izmijenio.

Ali što ću za vaj gori
spomenivat igre mile
za me mnokrat ke on stvori
kad me na plač teži sile;
svaka od dobra izgubjena
nož je srca uspomena . . .

Čijem zlatom zlatno cvijeće
po tanahnom velu stvaram,
s kijem da se tužna veće,
za mu utjehu razgovaram,
i koga ruka da mâ srete
cvijet čineći, moj drag cvijete?

Antun Gledjević
(1656-1728)

"SPARROW" OR THE MOURNING OF A MOUNTAIN SHEPHERDESS AT HIS DEATH

. . .
O woe, what has heppened to me?
who has torn my heart out,
who has cut down my Life, o woe,
where has my most beautiful Sparrow gone?
he is done for; would that first
my life, o woe, were done . . .

When at table I would sit
to give my body nourishment
the little bird would fly in
and fluttering about the table cloth
he'd try to sample
a taste of every drink.

So many times did it happen then,
that I am still amazed -
I'd think that on me rain was falling
when it would be pouring from his pure feathers:
the dear would be raining water
with his moistened wings.

Oftentimes my needle
I'd try to thread with silken strand,
but he'd pull with his beak the thread away
that I'd be trying to work by hand,
and he'd make a little knot
as though to take my place.

But why should I make my woe worse
recalling those dear games
he played for me on many a time,
when it moves me to weep all the more;
every reminder of a good that is lost
is like a knife to the heart.

With whose gold will I gold flowers create
on gossamer veil,
with whom will I converse
for comfort when I am sad,
and whose hand will my hand meet
while making a flower, o my dear flower?

Gdje godi bih mê stupaje
iza truda obratila,
oko mene na sve kraje
prostiro bi brza krila.
Ako li bih gdjegod stala,
svuda bih ga uživala.

Nigda družbe mê ne pusti,
uživah ga da me uživa,
i moje su za har usti
uzdržale njega živa
iz kijeh hranu on sveđ prima
izmiješanu s cjelovima.

Zvijezda nebo, žala more,
gaji dubja, listja dubi,
polje trava, zvijeri gore,
suza ki vil hudu ljubi,
manje imaju neg celova
njemu daše usta ova.

On lijep, on drag, on onaki
dostoja cȅlōv dosta imati;
celivajuć čas ga svaki
još ga željah celivati
i da mi je moglo biti
sva se u celov obratiti . . .

Ljubih, ljubio me si,
bila ti sam vazda draga,
ti drag meni bio jesi,
dobar i blag, ja ti blaga,
i bile su naše svake
želje i misli sveđ jednake.

Što sam htjela, ti si htio,
što si htio, ja sam htjela,
u meni si ti živio
u tebi sam ja živila
od kada nas vez sastavi
čiste i prave od ljubavi.
. . .

(Odlomak)

Wherever my steps
at work would take me,
around me in all directions
he'd spread his swift wings.
And where I would stop
he would be there for my enjoyment.

He never left my company,
I took pleasure in his pleasure in me,
and my lips for their enjoyment
kept him alive,
wherefrom he always received his nourishment
mixed with kisses.

There are less stars in sky, beaches by sea,
oaks in groves, leaves on oaks,
blades of grass in fields, wild animals in forests,
tears for the love of an untrue vila,
than the kisses
these lips gave him.

He was handsome, he was dear, he was the kind
who deserved a lot of kisses;
kissing him every moment
I wanted to kiss him even more
and could I have turned completely into kisses
I would have.

I loved you, you loved me,
always dear was I to you,
as you were dear to me,
and good and kind; kind was I to you,
and our every thought and desire
were ever alike.
. . . .
What I wanted you wanted,
What you wanted I wanted,
you lived in me
and I in you
since we were first united
by the bond of pure true love.
. . . . .

(An excerpt)

Split

Marko Marulić (1450-1524), a native of Split, was the outstanding writer of Croatian humanism. Born of patrician parents, Marulić went to Latin school in Split and then studied at the University of Padua. *Judita*

Marulić was really a transitional writer, whose Latin writings reflect the strong traditional piety of medieval Christianity, plus the new learning of humanism. His De institutione bene vivendi per exempla sanctorum *(Venice, 1506) and* Evangelistarium *(Venice, 1516) brought him a European-wide audience, and several of his works were republished in cities like Venice, Florence, Basel, Cologne, Antwerp, and Paris. His* Evangelistarium *was published ten times, and* De Institutione *twelve times in the sixteenth and seventeenth centuries. Although he wrote more often in Latin than in his native tongue, Marulić was a patriot, proud of his Slavic ancestry. He translated into Latin the* Ljetopis Popa Dukljanina *(see our note accompanying that work), at the request of his friend Dmine Papalić, so that those who did not know Serbo-Croatian might be able to read it, and he wrote a letter to Pope Hadrian VI ("Epistola ad Adrianum VI"), warning the Pope about the Turkish threat to Europe and beseeching him to bring peace among the Christian rulers so that they might unite for a holy war against the Ottoman Empire.*

Marulić expressed his concern for the Turkish threat in his native language as well, in his "Molitva suprotiva Turkom" (Prayer against the Turks). This same concern underlies his major work in the Serbo-Croatian language, Judita, *which is closely based on the Biblical account of Judith's encounter with the oppressor of the Jews, Holofernes. First printed in Venice in 1521, this literary epic in six cantos was so popular, according to Marulić's biographer Franjo Božičević, that it was published three times in two years (1521, 1522, 1523).*

Marulić's native dialect is čakavian-ikavian, which accounts for such forms in his writing as smih (smeh), niki (neki), dila (dela), *etc.*

Oloferne stati na noge prejedva
  mogaše; jer jati koko mogahu dva,
  toliko sam on žva i obuja ga san.
  Vagav zatvaruć, zva inih da gredu van.

Idoše na svoj stan, sobom teturaje,
  jerbo ne jedan žban popiše spijaje:
  redom začinjaje, zdravicu obnose,
  jednu popijaje, a drugu donose.

Pojdoše zanose tud ovud nogami,
  sami se nadnose, kimljući glavami;
  u obraz jim plami a na nosu para,
  i na brade prami lašćaše se ckvara.

Trbuh kako žara nadmen odstojaše,
  rič, ku potopara, jazik prikošaše;
  sviste ne saznaše, ctakljahu jim oči,
  rugo njimi staše i smih se potoči;

jer niki o ploči udri sobom padše,
  niki se pomoči, niki kara svad se,
  niki držat rad se, druga uhitiše,
  ter i s drugom zad se uznak uzvrziše;

a niki rigniše, niki se gnušahu,
  a niki ležiše, niki na nj padahu;
  a druzih nošahu, stavit jih na odar:
  toko se saznahu, koko mrtav tovar.

Tko će imiti var ustegnuti grla,
  pogledaj ovi bar ter vi, je l' umrla
  tuj čast i doprla tamnost i grdinja,
  ka je oto svrzla da je vitez svinja.

JUDITH

/ The slaying of Holofernes by Judith. From Canto Five of *Judith.* /

Holofernes could barely stand on his feet,
For as much as two could take
He himself had eaten, and he was overcome by sleep.
Vagav, closing up, called the others to come outside.

They went to their quarters, tottering,
For they had emptied more than one mug, tossing them down:
They took turns singing and pouring out toasts,
As soon as they had drunk one down, someone brought another.

They set out, their legs sliding hither and yon,
They were leaning on one another, nodding their heads;
Their faces were all aflame, fumes came from their noses,
And grease glistened on the bristles of their beards.

Their bellies stood arrogantly out, like great pots,
They spoke in clipped, piercing speech;
They made no sense, and their eyes were glassy,
They disgraced themselves, amidst peels of laughter;

And some fell, hitting the floor,
Some were helping one another, some were calling each other names,
Some tried to hold themselves up by grabbing someone else,
And they both fell straight back together;

And some were throwing up, while others were getting nauseous,
And some were lying down, and others were falling on them;
And some were being carried and put to bed
As conscious as dead jackasses.

Whoever cares to stuff his throat,
Take a look at these people and see
Whether honor has died here, and darkness and arrogance have entered in,
To such an extent that a knight is a pig.

Sad vi kako linja Olofernja sila,
kako ju raščinja hot nečista dila. –
Postilja je bila na sridu komori,
mehka, čista, bila, s pisani zastori.

Na njoj se obori Oloferne unid,
zaspa većma gori nego morski medvid;
speći ga tako vid Judit, Abri svojoj
"Poj polako naprid," reče, "na vratih stoj!"

Ove dvi tad u toj ložnici ostale
s Olofernom, u njoj ne bihu zaspale;
poni od tej stale na vratoh Abra sta,
jesu l' straže pale, oslihovati ja.

I straže i ćeljad sva, ka biše okoli,
biše kako mrtva; svi bo na tom stoli
jiše kako voli, da još veće piše:
bditi ne bi koli, straže ne činiše.

Ki je nebes više i ki svaka more,
jur odlučil biše, puku da pomore. –
Judita zastore postilji razmače,
srce joj kopore, bliže se primače.

Ruku s rukom stače i k nebu podvignu,
na kolina klače i suzami rignu;
glasa ne izdvignu, da moli u sebi:
"Bože, daj da stignu, ča je godi tebi;

stvori milost meni, pokrip rabu tvoju,
strah mi vas odnemi, dvigni ruku moju,
da stvar svrši, koju misal moja plodi,
da se tebe boju puci ter narodi!

Sada, sada hodi, tvoj grad Jerosolim
od nevolj slobodi i vas puk tvoj, molim;
rasap daj oholim, ki se uzvišuju,
pokoj pošlji boljim, ki se ponižuju.

Ovo ča veruju po tebi ja moći,
koko potribuju, hoti mi pomoći,
u dne ter u noći tebi da hvalu dam,
jer u tvoje moći sad svršit to uzdam."

Now see how Holofernes' power fades away,
How it is undone by impure desire.
The bed was in the middle of the chamber,
Soft, clean, white, with decorated covers.

Holofernes tumbled onto it, prostrate,
He fell asleep, worse than some whale;
Seeing him thus asleep Judith said to her Abra:
"Go forward quietly, and stand at the doors."

These two then remained in that bedroom
With Holofernes, they did not fall asleep;
For Abra stood at the doors of those quarters
And began to listen, to make sure the guards had fallen asleep.

And the guards, and all the servants who were nearby
Were like the dead; for they all had eaten at the table
Like oxen; and they had drunk even more.
There was no one to stand watch, no one kept guard.

He who is above the skies and who can do everything,
Had already decided to help his people –
Judith pulled the covers of the bed aside,
Her heart was pounding as she moved closer.

She clasped her hands together and raised them to heaven,
She knelt down and her eyes filled with tears;
She didn't raise her voice, but she prayed to herself:
"Lord, grant that I may achieve what is dear to you;

"Be kind toward me, strengthen your servant,
Calm all my fears, move my arm
To accomplish the thing that my mind has planned,
So that peoples and nations may fear you!

"Come now, come and liberate from slavery
Your city of Jerusalem and all your people, I beg you;
Bring down the arrogant, who raise themselves on high,
Send peace to the better people, who humble themselves.

"With your help I believe I can do
Whatever I must; please help me,
And day and night I will give you thanks,
For I am trusting in your strength to finish this now."

To rekši dviže ram i na nogah postup,
ter muče bičag snam, ki višaše o stup,
podri ga, kičmu zdup Oloferna jednom,
a drugom rukom lup kla, skube objednom.

Hronu, strepi sobom, ležeći on uznak,
drhta ruka s nogom, vas se oslabi, pak
izdaše; ne bi jak; grkljanom siča krv:
tako t zgibe junak, tako spusti obrv.

aying this she raised her shoulders and got to her feet,
And silently taking the knife which hung from a post,
She drew it out, and seizing Holoferne's hair with one hand,
She struck him with the other, slaying him and pulling it out in one motion.

lis throat rattled, he shuddered, lying straight out,
An arm and a leg trembled together, he became completely weak,
He breathed his last; he was not powerful; the blood trickled down his throat.
Thus perished a hero, thus he lowered his eyebrows.

The Franciscan monastery in Dubrovnik

Dundo Maroje

*Marin Držič (1508?-1567) is the outstanding playwright of the Dalmatian Renaissance; his comedies, in the opinion of Mihovil Kombol, have never been equalled in Croatian literature (*Povijest hrvatske književnosti do preporoda, *Zagreb, 1945, 155).*

Born into a mercantile family which had a trading business that eventually went bankrupt, Držic struggled with poverty all his life, as did Molière, the French writer of comedies with whom he is often compared. In 1538 the Dubrovnik Senate awarded Držič a stipend, enabling him to travel to Sienna, Italy, to continue his studies. At the University of Sienna Marin Držič became very popular, being elected Vice Rector of the university by the student body in 1541. When Marin first arrived there Sienna was a city of intellectual ferment, where the craftsmen's guilds had literary societies at which they read and discussed the works of Petrarch, Boccaccio, and the Renaissance writers, and where new works were read, performed, and criticized. This atmosphere of free criticism eventually came to be regarded as dangerous, and all such open meetings were banned. In 1542 Marin Držić was arrested, along with some twenty-five players and spectators, for attending a play performance in a private home.

When Marin returned home, after several years in Sienna, it was to a life of economic need and social inferiority. He had come from a position of prestige in Sienna, where as Vice Rector he had welcomed the Pope and other dignitaries when they visited the city; in Dubrovnik he was just another impoverished cleric, eking out a living. Because of his recognized literary talent, Držić was sometimes commissioned by the Dubrovnik Senate and rich merchants to write plays for performance during the Carnival season. Držić's plays were of two types: pastoral

dramas, where stylized shepherds and shepherdesses and mythological characters such as Adonis and Cupid mixed with real Dalmatian peasants; and comedies, frequently based on the classical Latin plays of Plautus and Terrence, but focusing on contemporary Dubrovnik life.

Držić's best known pastorals are Tirena *(1548) and* Venera i Adon *(1550); his best known comedies, some of which are still played today, are* Novela od Stanca *(1551),* Dundo Maroje *(1550), and* Skup *(based on Plautus's* Aulularija, *as was Molière's* L'Avare). *Not all of Držić's works have survived; we know, for example, that he wrote a comedy* Pomet *(1547?), which preceded* Dundo Maroje, *and to which the latter play is linked.*

*Marin Držić is as important for his use of language as he is for his literary content. He was the first to write comedies in prose (*Dundo Maroje *and* Skup*), shunning the stylized poetic language that characterized his contemporaries and predecessors. His characters speak in the everyday language of Dubrovnik, and if they are peasants from the hinterlands they speak in the dialect of their region. Držić knew how to take maximum advantage of linguistic peculiarities to create a comic atmosphere.*

CHARACTERS

LONG NOSE, a magician (in the prologue)
UNCLE MAROJE
MARO MAROJEV, his son
BOKČILO, the tavern keeper, and servant of Uncle Maroje
POPIVA, Maro's servant
PERA, Maro's fiancée, dressed in a man's clothing
DŽIVO, Pera's first cousin
PERA'S NURSE
LAURA (MANDE KRKARKA), a courtesan
PETRUNJELA, Laura's maid
UGO THE GERMAN
POMET TRPEZA, Ugo's servant
TRIPČETA from Kotor
DŽIVULIN from Lopud
NIKO } young men of Dubrovnik
PIJERO }
VLAHO }
MAZIJA, the postman
PAVO from Novo Brdo, a friend of Uncle Maroje
GRUBIŠA, Pavo's son
GULISA, a Croat
SADI, a Jew
GIANPAULO OLIGIATI, a banker
LESSANDRO, a Roman Merchant
KAMILO, a native of Rome
A CAPTAIN
GUARDS
THREE ROMAN INNKEEPERS

DUNDO MAROJE

PROLOG

Plemeniti i dobrostivi skupe, puče stari i mudri, vidim er s ušima priklonitijema i s očima smagljivijemi stojite za čut i vidjet večeras kugodi lijepu stvar; i sumnim, ako se ne varam, da vi scijenite i želite vidjet kugodi izvrsnu stvar; a izvrsne stvari u ovizijeh stranah nijesu se dosle činile! Ni mi, koji se zovemo Pomet-družina, ako se i mogu činit, nijesmo toga umjetjeonstva da umijemo činit stvari dostojne od ovakoga toli lijepa i plemenita skupa. Ma ovo brijeme od poklada budući od starijch našijeh odlučeno na tance, igre i veselja, i videći se našoj družini od Pometa ne puštat proć poklade bez kojegodi feste ili lijepe ili grube, stavili se su za prikazat vam jednu komediju koja, ako i ne bude toliko dobra i lijepa, ali su ove žene lijepe koje ju će gledat, i vi dobri koji ju ćete slušat.

U njoj će bit jedna stvar koja scijenim da vam će draga bit, er će bit nova i stara,–nova er slijedi onu prvu komediju od Pometa, kako da je ona i ova sve jedna komedija, i u tu smo svojevoliju oto mi sami upali, –stara er ćete vidjet u njoj one iste prve prikazaoce, a to jes: Dundo Maroje, Pavo Novobrđanin, Pomet i ostali. I prva je prikazana u Dubrovniku, a ova će bit u Rimu, a vi ćete iz Dubrovnika gledat. Žene, para li vam ovo malo mirakulo Rim iz Dubrovnika gledat? Neka znate er Pomet-družina, kako ovo što je mučno umije dobro učinit, toliko bi bolje učinili drugu kugodi stvar koja je lašnja. I ako ne uzbude šena lijepa kako i prva, tužimo se na brijeme koje nam je arkitete odvelo; i ako komedija, od šta se ne varamo, ne uzbude vam toliko draga, ali vam će Dundo Maroje, Pomet, Grubiša i ostali drazi bit. I ne scijen'te da se je vele truda, ulja, knjige i ingvasta oko ove komedije stratilo: šes Pometnika u šcs dana ju su žđeli i sklopili. Mi ni vam obećavamo velike stvari, ni možemo: nismo tolici da možemo tolike stvari obećat i činit; kraci ljudi visoko ne dohitaju.

Ma oto vam ja brže i dotrudnih duzijem riječmi! U dvije riječi čujte argument od komedije „Dundo Maroje". Ako nijeste zaboravili kako mu biše ukradeni dukati i vraćeni s patom da se sinu spodesta od

UNCLE MAROJE

PROLOG

Noble and kind audience, aged and wise people, I see that you are standing with your ears cocked and your eyes all attention to hear and see something beautiful this evening; and I suspect, if I'm not mistaken, that you expect and wish to see something first class; but first class things have yet to be performed in these parts! And even if they could be performed, not even we, who call ourselves the Pomet Company, have the artistry to be able to do things worthy of such a beautiful and noble audience. But seeing that the carnival season was designated by our elders for dances, plays, and good times, and since our Pomet Company doesn't wish to let the carnival go by without some sort of performance, whether fair or foul, so they have prepared themselves to perform a comedy for you, which, even if it won't be so good and beautiful, still these women are beautiful who are going to see it, and you are good who are going to hear it.

In it there will be one thing which I expect will please you, for it will be both new and old—new, because its follows that first comedy about Pomet, so that that one and this are all one comedy, and here we ourselves have fallen into a kind of rut—old, because you will see in it those same first characters, and they are: Dundo Maroje, Pavo Novobrdjanin, Pomet and the others. Now the first play was set in Dubrovnik, but this one will be in Rome, and you will see it from Dubrovnik. Ladies, doesn't it seem a small miracle to see Rome from Dubrovnik? You also should know that the Pomet Company, which is able to do this difficult thing well, could do something easier much better. And if our scenery should not turn out as beautiful as in the first play, we must blame the times, which have taken our architects away; and if the comedy, as we have no doubt, should not please you as much, still you will like Dundo Maroje, Pomet, Grubiša and the others. And don't think that much work, lamp oil, paper, and ink have been spent on this comedy: six Pometniks worked on it and put it together in six days. We neither promise you great things, nor are we capable of them: we are not so great that we can promise and do great feats; short people don't reach very high.

But here now, I have already begun to tire you with this long-winded talk! Here, in a few words, is the plot of the comedy *Dundo Maroje*. Maybe you haven't forgotten how his ducats were stolen from

svega po smrti, po tomu znajte er su novi pat učinili da se sinu Maru za onada ne spodestava, ma da mu da pet tisuć dukata da otide u Jakin, a iz Jakina u Fjerencu za učinit svita i s tjezijem svitami pak da otide na Sofiju s patom, ako se dobro ponese i da mu s dobitkom dođe, da mu skrituru od spodestacijoni končas učini, i da ga oženi i da mu da vladat svijem ostalijem dinarmi. Ma prije neg vam ostalo izrečem, uzmite nauk od Pomet-družine večeras, i nigda ni sinu ni drugomu ne da'te dinare do ruke dokle mladića nijeste u vele stvari druzijeh provali, er je mlados po svojoj naravi nesvijesna i puna vjetra, i prignutija je na zlo neg na dobro; i pamet nje ne raširuje se dalje neg koliko joj se oči prostiru, i nju veće volje vladaju neg razlog. Da vam ne intravenja kako će i Dundu Maroju večeras intravenjat, koji, davši sinu Maru pet tisuć dukata u ruke, otpravi ga put Jakina, a on iz Jakina ne otide u Fjerencu neg u Rim s dukatmi, i tu spendža dukate. A Dundo Maroje čuvši toj, kako mahnit otide starac u Rim s Bokčilom, svojijem tovijernarom. Što će segvitat, komedija vam će sama rijet, koja će svršit u veselje. . . .

PRVI AT
PRVI PRIZOR

Dundo Maroje, Bokčilo Tovijernar, zatim Tripčeta iz Kotora, prvi i drugi oštijer.

MAROJE: Ajmeh, ajmeh, moja starosti, na što me si dovela, da se po svijetu tučem za dezvijanijem sinom, za haramijom, da iz morske pučine izvadim zlato, da iz jame beza dna izmem imanje! Pet tisuć dukata dah djetetu u ruke! Vuku dat u pohranu meso! Jaoh, valjalo bi mi dat dvaest i četiri konje na dan, na svaku uru svoga, za eror ki sam učinio.

BOKČILO: Bogme bi ti, gospodaru, valjao konjic i svaku uru svoj, i jedva bi se donio doma ako bi ga hranio kako i mene. Jaoh si ve meni, u koji ve ti čas pođoh iz Grada!

MAROJE: Bokčilo, jesam li ti rekao: ne davaj mi fastidija, ne pristaj mi tuzi! Ti se, pjanico, rugaš mnom.

BOKČILO: Tebi sam pjan, a tvoj tobolac najbolje zna kako stoji moj trbuh.

MAROJE: Nijesam li ti danaska dao po kutla vina popit?

him and returned to him, with the agreement that his son would inherit everything upon his death; you know that later they made a new agreement that his son Maro would not be made his heir for the time being, but that he would be given five thousand ducats to go to Ancona, and from Ancona to Florence, to buy textiles, and with those textiles he was to go to Sofia, with the understanding that if he behaved himself and if he made a profit, a will would then be made out in his favor, and he would be allowed to get married and Maroje would hand over the rest of his money under his control. But before I tell you the rest, take a lesson from the Pomet Company this evening, and never give your money to your son or to anyone else, until you have tested the young man in many other things, for youth is by nature without a conscience, and full of wind, and more inclined toward evil than toward good, and its mind reaches no further than the eye can see, and it is controlled more by willfulness than by reason. Let's hope that you won't experience what Dundo Maroje will experience this evening; he gave his son Maro five thousand ducats in hand, sent him off to Ancona, but he did not go from Ancona to Florence, instead he went to Rome with the ducats, and there he spends the ducats. And when Dundo Maroje heard about that, the old man went off like a madman to Rome, with Bokčilo, his tavern keeper. What follows after that will be told by the comedy itself, which has a happy ending . . . .

ACT ONE
SCENE ONE

Dundo Maroje, Bokčilo the tavern keeper, then Tripčeta from Kotor, and the first and second inn keeper.

MAROJE: O woe is me, woe is me, what has my old age brought me to, that I should be chasing around this world after a prodigal son, after a bandit, trying to extract my gold from the depths of the sea, to extricate my property from a bottomless pit! I handed five thousand ducats over to a child! Like giving meat to a wolf for safe keeping! Ouch! I ought to be put on the flogging horse twenty four times a day, one horse every hour, for making such a mistake.

BOKČILO: By golly, master, a good horse every hour, you'd barely make it home, if you fed him like you're feeding me. Woe is me, and woe the hour I set out from the City!

MAROJE: Bokčilo, haven't I already told you: don't be bothering me, don't add to my sorrow. You're giving me a hard time, you drunk!

BOKČILO: You think I'm drunk, but your wallet knows the condition of my stomach best of all.

MAROJE: Didn't I give you half a jug of wine to drink today?

BOKČILO: Jesi, sita me si napojio! Ovo, otkle sam iz Grada, nijesam se usrao, ni sam imao čim s tvojom hranom. Nađi ti one štono se iz Moreške zemlje donose kamilionte, kao li se zovu, koji se jajerom hrane; a vodi junake s sobom koji se jajerom ne pasu. Po kutla mi je vina dao! Jaoh si ve meni, jao!

MAROJE: Nevoljna mene, tužna mene! Veće sam ja otišao, veće mene pokri grob! Sin mi dukate uze, a ovi mi život uzimlje. Oči, što ne plačete? Ali ste doplakali? Ma zadosta je da srce za vas plače.

BOKČILO: Bog zna tko koga kolje i tko će prije umrijet. Duša mi othodi i od glada i od žeđe; tvojijem tugama hoćeš Bokčila hranit. Dukate plačeš, a dukati ti rđave u skrinji. Brižni ti dukati kad se ne umiješ njima hranit. Plače er mu je sin spendžao od svoga. Za česa su dukati neg da se pije i ije i trunpa?

MAROJE: Od svoga, pjanče, veliš, od svoga spendžao?! Ajme! ubode me, ajme!

BOKČILO: Ponta mu dođe, ubodoše ga, – rekoše mu istinu.

TRIPČETA: *Che ha questo pover omo?*

BOKČILO: *Misser,*ga boli: *fiol spenzuto denari, doglia!*

TRIPČETA: Po svetoga Tripuna, vi ste našijenci!

BOKČILO: *Misser,* bog te naučio! *De Ragusa?* I mi smo otuda.

TRIPČETA: Gospodine, što vam je? Vidim, ti si našjenac; *siate il ben vegnuo,* dobar si došao!

MAROJE: *Ben trovato, misser!* Vi ste našjenac? Drago mi je.

TRIPČETA: Ja sam od Kotora.

BOKČILO: Ah, da te bog pomože!

MAROJE: Susjed si naš! Susjede, prikloni obraz da mi se je s tobom pozdravit.

BOKČILO: Svoga mi, svoga, neka ti mi svoga, nije ti bez svoga! Koliko mišera srjetosmo, a nitko ne pristupi k nam neg sam našjenac, – svoj a k svojijem!

TRIPČETA: Ištom se obeselim kad čujem koga od našega jezika.

BOKČILO: Yes you did, you really filled me up! Look here, since I left the City I haven't taken a shit; I couldn't, the way you've been feeding me. Go find yourself some of those things they call chameleons, that they bring from Morocco, and they feed on air; but you brought a hero with you, who can't be kept happy on air. He gave me a half a jug of wine! Woe is me, woe!

MAROJE: Unhappy fate, sad fate! I'm done for, I'm already six feet under! My son took my ducats, and this one is taking my life. Eyes, why don't you cry? Haven't you any more crying left in you? But it's enough that my heart cries for you.

BOKČILO: God knows who is slaughtering whom, and who will die first. My soul is leaving my body because of the hunger and the thirst; you'd like to feed Bokčilo on your sorrows. You moan for your ducats, while your ducats rust in your coffers. Your ducats are miserable when you can't eat with them. He is crying because his son has spent some of his own inheritance. What good are ducats, except for drinking, eating, and having a good time?

MAROJE: Did you say he spent some of his own money, you drunk?! O woe, he has stabbed me, o woe!

BOKČILO: He's got the point, he's been stabbed,–because somebody told him the truth.

TRIPČETA: What is wrong with this poor man?

BOKČILO: He is ill, sir: his son has spent his money, a catastrophe!

TRIPČETA: By Saint Tripun, you're fellow countrymen!

BOKČILO: Sir, may God guide you! Are you from Dubrovnik? We're from there too.

TRIPČETA: What's wrong, sir? I can see that you're a fellow countryman; welcome, welcome!

MAROJE: Glad to meet you, sir! You're a countryman? The pleasure is mine.

TRIPČETA: I am from Kotor.

BOKČILO: Oh, may God help you!

MAROJE: You are our neighbor! Neighbor, lean your face this way, so we can exchange a brotherly kiss.

BOKČILO: Your own kind, your own kind, just give me your own kind, you can't get along without your own kind! We've met so many gentlemen, but no one came up to us, except one of our own countrymen,–one of our own came up to his own!

TRIPČETA: I too am overjoyed, when I hear someone speaking our language.

Hanibal Lucić

Hanibal Lucić was born in 1485, and died in 1553. A native of Hvar, an island off the Dalmatian Coast, he was strongly influenced by the Petrarchan-troubadour style of the Dubrovnik poets, especially by Djore Držić, and by the works of the "začinjavci," Dalmatian writers of religious poetry. There are also strong indications of folklore influence on his poetry. Robinja

Lucić's language is a blend of čakavian (Hvar dialect) and štokavian elements, the latter assimilated from the Dubrovnik writers. As he matured he became very critical of his earlier poetic attempts, and in 1519 he destroyed most of his poetry. After his death his illegitimate son Antun published his remaining poetry, including Robinja, *as* Skladanja izvarsnih pisan razlicih *(Venice, 1556). A second edition was published in 1585, again in Venice, under the title* Robinja.

Lucić's selection of the theme of liberation from Turkish captivity for his Carnival play Robinja *reflects the constant preoccupation of Dalmatian Renaissance writers with the Turkish threat; the Ottoman fleet and Turkish pirates sometimes raided and pillaged the towns along the coast, while carrying off captives to sell into slavery. Only Dubrovnik seemed to be impregnable, and Lucić's admiration for that city state is reflected not only in* Robinja *(which takes place in Dubrovnik), but also in his poem "U pohvalu grada Dubrovnika", where he writes:*

Pravda je temelj tvoj, razum je tva pića,
Tve stanje u pokoj počiva njih ćića.
Slobodan i vičan njima si, dobro znaj,
I od svih različan koji su tebe kraj.

Justice is thy foundation, reason thy drink,
Because of them your population remains at peace.
You are free and renowned for them, know it well,
And thus you differ from all your neighbors.

Interestingly, Lucić makes some of the same criticisms of Christian disunity in the face of the Ottoman threat that Marko Marulić made earlier, and that Njegoš will repeat three centuries later in Gorski vijenac. *Lucić deprecates the Christian rulers for their disunity and their treachery toward one another: "Jedan jih ne dajuć drugomu pomoći negli ga izdajuć." ("One of them not giving help to the other, but betraying him instead.")*

Robinja, *in adapted form, remained a popular Carnival play for more than 300 years, a good indication that its feeling and language were close to the people. As Marin Franičević writes in the* Pet Stoljeća *edition of the play (Vol. 7, Zagreb, 1968): "Robinja ...came from the people and it was returned to the people."*

ROBINJA

ANIBAL LUCIJ FRANCISKU PALADINIĆU POZDRAVLJENJE

Robinju ovuj moju pokazavši ja tebi ovih pokladnih minutih dan kako radi razgovora, velostvorni Paladiniću, očito si i ti pokazao da ti je ugodna bila kako i svaka moja kažeš da ti su. K tomu me si potaknuo da dopustim nadvor da izajde, veleći da mi sramotu neće učiniti; dopokon se si zahvalio da i dalje popeljavši ju biti joj hoćeš zapleće i straža. Ja dake, jere sudih da stvar u sebi (istom da bi načinom ne lihala) ne more nego s koristi biti ljudem (takove bo te pisni u pridnje vrime iznaštene biše, i općahu se puku prikaživati samo na konac da–razlike druzih kriposti i pomanjkanja slišajući i gledajući–svaki sam sebe i život svoj umiti bude bolje prociniti i srediti)....

OSOBE

DERENČIN
ROBINJA, kći banova
MATIJAŠ, Derenčinov sluga
GUSAR
MARA
PERA
ANICA
KNEZ dubrovački
VLASTELIN
Činjenje biva u Dubrovniku

GREETINGS!

When I showed you this Captive of mine for your enjoyment during these past Carnival days, most worthy Paladinić, you obviously enjoyed it, just as you say you have enjoyed everything of mine. You also urged me to publish it, claiming that it would not cause me any disgrace; finally, you promised to help it along, to be its support and protection. For that reason, I (likewise feeling that it was not lacking), decided that this piece could not help but be of benefit to people, (for such were these poems found to be in former days, when it was the custom to perform them for the common people, so that everyone, while hearing and seeing the various virtues and vices of others, might be better able to take stock of himself and bring order to his own life)....

CHARACTERS

DERENČIN
THE CAPTIVE, a ban's daughter
MATTHEW, Derenčin's servant
A PIRATE
MARA
PERA
ANICA
A DUBROVNIK PRINCE
A GENTLEMAN

The action takes place in Dubrovnik

ROBINJA

ISKLAD

Sa jedinim bratom banova kći mala
U stanu bogatom za ocem ostala.
Jedva za odaju prispila prem biše
Kad se zgoda da ju Turci zarobiše.
Ova jer kralju bî ugarskomu mila
Ne manje neg da bi prava mu kći bila,
Brez broja pineza i blaga on dati
Virom se obeza tko mu ju povrati.
Nu blago toj niko, ni pinez, ni zlato
Ne valja toliko, ni vridno bî na to;
Samo čudna sila ljuvena poraza
Od takova dila sluzi put ukaza,
Sluzi Derenčinu, netjaku banovu,
Ki mnogu gorčinu pritarpi za ovu
I moćno se muči i moćno oznoji
Za da ju izruči, za da ju posvoji.
A ne kako mladi vi kî ste pohitom
Od ljubavi radi stati se sa mitom,
Mnijući da reći dosta je samo toj
Uz prozor zarčeći: sunašce, ja sam tvoj.
Nije toj, nî tako: vridnu stvar doteći
Nije moć inako negli se poteći.
Zato molim milo, stanite svi muče,
Dokli se toj dilo ka svarsi dovuče.
Bit vam će s nauka vidiv ga u trudu,
Vidit pak da muka ne bi mu zaludu.
I vi dekle mlade, vi uši napnite
I što vam dim sade u sarce zapnite.
Bolje vam doteći služicu jest virna
Nego krug najveći zlata neizmirna.
Reče se ne mani: gusa me dostiže,
vojno me obrani, brajen me odbiže.
Da 'vo gre Derenčin s slugami odzgara,
Slište po kî način s njimi se zgovara.

THE CAPTIVE

PROLOGUE

With her only brother the ban's little daughter
Remained in a rich home after her father died.
She had barely reached a marriageable age
When it happened that the Turks captured her.
Because she was dear to the Hungarian king
No less than were she his own real daughter,
He vowed to give countless money and wealth
To whomever would bring her back to him.
But neither wealth nor money nor gold
Had such worth or value;
Only the amazing power of love's conquest
Could show her servant the way for such a feat,
Her servant Derenčin, the ban's nephew,
Who endured much anguish for her sake
And suffered mightily and mightily labored
To deliver her, to make her his own.
But not like you young men, who with lust for love
Are eager to get together with your prize,
Deeming it enough merely to say
While gazing up at her window: "Little Sun, I am yours."
That's not it, that's not the way: nothing worthwhile can be reached
Except through toil.
Therefore, I kindly beg you all to stand silently
Until this work reaches its finale.
It will be a lesson for you to see him labor
And to see that his torment was not in vain.
And you young maidens, you perk up your ears,
And what I tell you now–tuck away in your hearts.
Better for you to gain a servant who is faithful
Than the largest ring of immeasurable gold.
Not for nothing do they say: "A pirate caught up to me,
My husband defended me, my brother ran away."
But see, Derenčin is coming with his servants over there,
Hear him talking with them.

SKAZANJE PARVO

Derenčin, Sluga

DERENČIN

Mili druzi, i vèć nego druzi mili,
Sve strane, mogu reć, sa mnom ste shodili
Išćući gospoju po svitu dan i noć,
Vas svit bih za koju pridubal, da bi moć.
Evo srića nika i pomnja još vaša
Sada privelika na nju nas nanaša
Tako da približa višnjemu po sudu
Plaća i naliža vašemu jur trudu.
Vi znate da mito od kraljeve krune
Čeka me čestito i mire pripune,
A vam se rič ovo moja obezuje
(Makar da njegovo stanje mi daruje),
Sve ono što mi da, veći dil ja ću vam
Podati, tako da rečete: blȁgo nam!
Istom da rukama srića nas ophiti
Kâ bi reć da s nama združiti se hiti.
Jer oto ti zali kleti gusarine
Vide li ostali s nami su od cine.
I pinezi samo (toli su mogući)
Deri jih ovamo mogli su dovući,
U Dubrovnik koji viru štuje našu
I mirno pokoji s Turci na mejašu.
Sam nam Bog zaisto ruku je dal nato
Koji nas u misto dovede bogato,
gdi nam bî naparuč kakono na domu
I pomoć i naruč u dilu svakomu.
Zato se ja scinju srićan i blag dosti
I ne znam što činju od vele radosti
Ne zato jer dare imat ću od kralja:
Pineze, timare i blago kô valja,
Sebi samo vilu išću ja i prosim
Koje zlatu strilu u sarcu mom nosim,
A cinim od male cine i vridnosti
Stvari sve ostale pri njeje liposti.
Koju jer nablizu ovdika jur vidim,
Na nebo ja lizu ter se ne navidim.
S strane mi pak druge sarce se prijima
Tuga zacić tuge gospoja kû ima.
Ter kako na muci viseći se mučim,
Od zalih tih vuci dokli ju izručim.

ACT ONE

Derenčin, a Servant

DERENČIN

Dear friends, and more than dear friends,
 You've travelled with me everywhere, I'd say,
Throughout the world, night and day, looking for that lady
 For whose sake I would search the whole world, if I could.
And now a bit of good luck and your great pains as well
 Have brought us to her,
So that there approaches by higher decree
 The reward for your efforts, and your bounty.
You know that an award awaits me from the Crown
 Generous and overflowing with myrrh,
And I give you this my binding word
 (Even if he should give me his kingdom),
Of all he gives me I'll give you the greater part,
 So that you will say: "Lucky us!"
Just now fortune has embraced us in her arms,
 As if to say she seeks to become our friend.
For see, these cruel and cursed pirates
 Have struck a bargain with us.
Only money (such is its power)
 Could bring them this far,
To Dubrovnik which honors our word
 And remains calmly at peace with the Turks on its border.
God himself has had a hand
 In bringing us to this rich place
Where at our disposal as though at home
 Are help and aid for any venture.
That's why I consider myself most fortunate and blest
 And I don't know what I'm doing, so great is my joy,
And it's not because I'll have gifts from the king:
 Money, estates, and treasure in proper degree;
I seek and ask only for the vila
 Whose golden shaft I bear in my heart,
And all the rest I hold to be
 Of little value beside her beauty.
And because I see her now, here, close by
 I soar to the heavens, I can't see her enough.
On the other hand my heart is touched with sorrow
 Because of the sorrow which she has.
And I'll suffer as though hanging in torment
 Until I can free her from those cruel wolves.

A zatoj hodite, toj dobro počelo
    Pospihom vodite da dojde na čelo.
Dajte jim odbrojiv te jaspre kê smaže
    Neka jih posvojiv jure se utaže.
Stavite zatim red, na pazar da gredu,
    I moje na ogled sunašce da vedu,
Jak da ju prodali nisu ni cinili,
    Ni jaspre prijali ni me prî vidili.
A s drugu stran prima njim hoću ja izać
    I s vami mev njima totu se listo nać,
Jeda ju štogodi moja rič iskusi
    Prî nego slobodi svoje slast okusi.

And so go and bring with haste
    This good beginning to its rightful end.
Count them out the money for which they thirst,
    May they be weighted down with it as soon as they get it.
And then have them go to the market
    And let them bring my little Sun for my perusal
As though they hadn't sold her or set a price on her,
    Or accepted money or even seen me before.
I want to come toward them from the other direction,
    And only then will I come together with you and them,
So that I might test her a bit in speech
    Before she savors the sweetness of her freedom.

ROBIGNA

GOSPODINA

ANIBALA LVCIA

HARVASCHOGA VLASTELINA.

Con licenza de' Superiori, & Priuilegio.

Hvar

RIBANYE

I RIBARSCH

GOVARANY

CHESTVARI

XENE PO PETR

HECTOROVICHIV

HVARANINV.

IN VENETIA APPRESSO
GIOANFRANCESCO
CAMOTIO.

M. D. LXVIII.

.C. T.

The song "Kraljević Marko i brat mu Andrijaš" is a bugarštica, *a type of folk ballad sung in the Balkans until the eighteenth century. Unlike the folk epic song (*junačka pesma*), which has a fixed number of ten syllables per line, the* bugarštica *verse varies in length. Because its themes were invariably medieval, it was once commonly believed that the* bugarštica *was older than the* junačka pesma, *but such an opinion is not generally held by scholars today. For more on the* bugarštica, *see Benjamin Stolz's article: "On Two Serbo-Croatian Oral Epic Verses: The Bugarštica and the Deseterac," in* Poetic Theory/Poetic Practice. Papers of the Midwest Modern Language Association, no. 1, 1969. *A "bugarštica"*

Our text of the song comes from Petar Hektorović's (1487-1572) Ribanje i ribarsko prigovaranje (Fishing and Fishermen's Conversation), *as published in the critical edition of Ramiro Bujas (Zagreb: Jadranski Institut, JAZU, 1951). Hektorović's description of a three-day fishing trip in the Adriatic was written in the form of a dodecasyllabic rhymed letter to a friend. Completed in 1556, it was first published in Venice, in 1558.*

Ribanje *is sometimes referred to as a fishing eclogue, and although some scholars, such as Marin Franičević (*Pet stoljeća hrvatske književnosti, *VII, Zagreb, 1968) have noted the unlikelihood of the lofty thoughts expressed by Hektorović's plebeian companions, still one has to agree with Bujas that this is basically a realistic work, which attempts faithfully to reproduce the course and weather conditions, as well as the conversation of the trip. Bujas, in the introduction to his edition of* Ribanje, *mentions that he once tried to duplicate Hektorović's voyage, using the same type of equipment, under the same seasonal conditions; on the basis of that experience, he states: "From the data given us by Hektorović in* Ribanje *we can ascertain where he was located at every moment, we can even find the coves, which Hektorović doesn't name ... ." (Bujas, op. cit., p. 13).*

What makes this work noteworthy in the history of Yugoslav literature is not its fidelity as a sixteenth-century Dalmatian travellogue, but rather the fact that it contained the first published examples of Yugoslav folk songs. Hektorović implies that he is presenting these songs as they were sung to him by his two fishermen companions, and critical

opinion seems to agree that the words and music, as given by the autho are authentic.

The language of Hektorović and his companions is basically th čakavian spoken on the island of Hvar at that time. This accounts fc the abundance of ikavian forms in our song, such as: Vrime, plink lipo, dilila, razdilila, beside, nigda (negda *or* nekada *in standard SC), etc Also čakavian are the dual verb forms, such as* sta drugovala *instead o standard* su drugovali, *used when two persons are the subject of the verb One also finds such archaic features as the retention of "l" in such word as* dil *(standard SC* deo*) and* posal, *as well as archaic verb forms lik* dojdeš *for* dodješ. *Hektorović's spellings, such as* potarže, sardašce, ka vava, *have been retained in our text because such words are still pr nounced that way on Hvar. We have also kept such an example of no assimilation of consonants in clusters as* vasdakrat, *because of our co fidence that Hektorović was attempting to be consistent in his ortho graphy and to reproduce such words as they were being pronounced a the time. For more information on the relationship between Hektorović orthography and the dialect of his area, the interested reader shoul consult Aleksandar Mladenović's* Jezik Petra Hektorovića *(Novi Sad Matica srpska, 1968). For more information on Hektorović's life an works, the reader will find it useful to read the introductions to th volumes edited by Franičević and Bujas, cited above.*

APPRESSO GIO. FRANCESCO CAMOCCIO
DEL M. D LXVIII,

TRE HECTOROVICH ISTOMV GOSPODI-
NV MICHSCI PELEGRINOVICHIV.

Voti ſcagliu Chripoſtni i náredni Goſpodine Mi-ca, oni Sarbſchi nácin (oudi zlólu upiſán) Choyim Paſchoy i Nichola sfachi po ſebi bugarſcchiçu buga, I tochóye nácin od oné piſni I chlice Deuoycha: boyuſu obadua zayeduo pri piuali.

BVGARSCCHIÇA.

Chadamiſe radoſauc uoyeuoda od digliaſce,
Od ſuoyega grada diſnoga ſiuerina
Ceſtomiſe radoſaſ na ſiuerin obziraſce,
Teretomi ouacho bellu gradu beſiyaſce

KRALJEVIĆ MARKO I BRAT MU ANDRIJAŠ

Dva mi sta siromaha dugo vrime drugovala,
lipo ti sta drugovala i lipo se dragovala,
lipo plinke dilila i lipo se razdiljala,
i razdiliv se opet se sazivala.
Već mi nigda zarobiše tri junačke dobre konje
dva siromaha
tere sta dva konjica mnogo lipo razdilila.
O tretjega ne mogoše junaci se pogoditi,
negli su se razgnjivala i mnogo se sapsovala.
Ono to mi ne bihu, družino, dva siromaha,
da jedno mi biše vitez Marko Kraljeviću,
vitez Marko Kraljeviću i brajen mu Andrijašu,
mladi vitezi.
Tuj si Marko potarže svitlu sablju pozlaćenu
i udari Andrijaša brajena u sardašce.
On mi ranjen prionu za njegovu desnu ruku
tere knezu Marku po tihora besijaše:
Jeda mi te mogu, mili brate, umoliti,
nemoj to mi vaditi sabljice iz sardašca,
mili brajene,
dokle ti ne naručam do dvi i do tri beside.
Kada dojdeš, kneže Marko, k našoj majci junačkoj,
nemoj to joj, ja te molim, kriva dila učiniti,
i moj dil ćeš podati, kneže Marko, našoj majci,
zašto si ga nigdar veće od mene ne dočeka.
Ako li te bude mila majka uprašati,
viteže Marko:
Što mi ti je, sinko, sabljica sva karvava?,
nemoj to joj, mili brate, sve istinu kazovati
ni naju majku nikako zlovoljiti,
da reci to ovako našoj majci junačkoj:
Susrite me, mila majko, jedan tihi jelenčac,
koji mi se ne hti sa drumka ukloniti,
junačka majko,
ni on meni, mila majko, ni ja njemu.

KRALJEVIĆ MARKO AND HIS BROTHER ANDRIJAŠ

Two paupers were pals for a long time,
  They were good pals and very fond of one another,
  They divided their plunder fairly and they parted on good terms,
  And after they had parted they would summon one another again.
But once they captured three fine heroic horses,
                the two paupers,
And they divided two of the horses quite fairly.
On the third one they couldn't agree,
  Instead they became enraged and cursed one another roundly.
  Those were not two paupers, friends,
  For one was the knight Marko Kraljević,
The knight Marko Kraljević and his brother Andrijaš,
                the young knights.
Then Marko drew his bright golden sword
And struck his brother Andrijaš in the heart.
Wounded, he clung to his right arm
  And softly spoke to Prince Marko:
  May I make one request of you, dear brother?
Don't draw thc sword from my heart,
                dear brother,
  Until I leave two or three words with you.
When you go to our heroic mother, Prince Marko,
  Don't do her any wrong, I beg of you,
  And you will give my share to our mother, Prince Marko,
  Because she will never again receive anything from me.
If our dear mother should ask you,
                knight Marko:
  Why is your sword all bloody, son?
Don't tell her the whole truth, dear brother,
  Nor upset our mother in any way,
  But tell it this way to our heroic mother:
  I met a quiet little stag, dear mother,
Which didn't want to get off the road for me,
                heroic mother,
  Neither he for me, dear mother, nor I for him.

I tuj stavši potargoh moju sablju junačku
 i udarih tihoga jelenka u sardašce,
 i kada ja pogledah onoga tiha jelenka,
 gdi se htiše na drumku s dušicom razdiliti,
vide mi ga milo biše kako mojega brajena,
 tihoga jelenka,
 i da bi mi na povrate, ne bih ti ga zagubio.
I kada te jošće bude naju majka uprašati:
 Da gdi ti je, kneže Marko, tvoj brajen Andrijašu?,
 ne reci mi našoj majci istine po ništore;
 ostao je, reci, junak, mila majko, u tujoj zemlji,
iz koje se ne može od milin'ja odiliti
 Andrijašu;
 onde mi je obljubio jednu gizdavu devojku.
I odkle je junak tuj devojku obljubio,
 nikad veće nije pošal sa mnome vojevati,
 i sa mnome nije veće ni plinka razdilio.
 Ona t' mu je dala mnoga bil'ja nepoznana
i onoga vinca junaku od zabitja,
 gizdava devojka.
 Li uskori mu se hoćeš, mila majko, nadijati.
A kad na te napadu gusari u carnoj gori,
 nemoj to se prid njimi, mili brate, pripadnuti,
 da iz glasa poklikni brajena Andrijaša.
 Bud da me ćeš zaman, brate, pri potribi klikovati,
kada mi te začuju moje ime klikujući
 kleti gusari,
 taj čas će se od tebe junaci razbignuti,
kako su se vasdakrat, brajene, razbigovali,
 kada su te začuli moje ime klikovati;
 a neka da ti vidi tvoja ljubima družina,
 koji me si tvoga brata brez krivine zagubio!

And standing there I drew my heroic sword
  And I struck the quiet little stag in his little heart,
  And when I watched that quiet little stag,
  As it was about to part with its soul there on the road,
I was truly as sorry for him as for my own brother,
                the quiet little stag,
  And if I had it to do over again, I would not have killed him.
And when our mother will ask you further:
  But where, Prince Marko, is your brother Andrijaš?
  Don't tell our mother the truth for anything,
  Say: "the hero has remained in a foreign land, dear mother,
  Which he cannot leave, because of its charms,
                Andrijaš,
  He has fallen in love there with a pretty maiden.
And ever since the hero fell in love with that maiden,
  He has never again gone to war with me,
  Nor has he divided plunder with me again.
  She gave him many unknown herbs
And that wine of forgetfulness,
                the pretty maiden.
  But you can expect him soon, dear mother."
And when bandits attack you in the black forest,
  Don't cower before them, dear brother,
  But call out in a loud voice for your brother Andrijaš,
  Even though you will call for me in vain, in time of need.
When they hear you calling my name,
                the cursed bandits,
  At that moment the heroes will run away from you,
As they have always run away, brother,
  When they heard you call my name;
  And let your beloved band know
  Who killed me, your brother, without cause.

Pasc. Dua mista siromaha dugo urime drugouala.
Lipotista drugouala i lipose dragouála,
Lipo plinche dilila Ilipose razdigliala,
I razdilisse općtsé saziuala.
Vechmi nigda zarobisce tri yunacche dobre chognie,
Dua siromaha,
Teresta duá chogniça mnogo lipo razdilila.
Otretyega nemogosce yunáçise pogoditi,
Neglisuse razgniuala imnogose sapsouála,
Onotomi nebihu druxino dua siromaha,
Da yednomi bisce Vitez Marcho Chráglieuichiu.
Vitez Marcho Chráglieuichiu i brayenmu Andria:
Mladi Vitézi, (scu,
Tuysi Marcho potarxe sfitlu sabgliu pozláchienu.
Iudari Andriasca brayena u sardascçe,
Onmi ragnien prionu za gniegouu desnu rúchu,
Tere Chnezu Marchu potihora besiyásce,
Yedamite mogu mili brate umoliti.
Nemoytomi uaditi sabgliçé iz sardascça,
Mili brayene,
Dochleti nenarúcam do dni i do trí beside,
Chada doydesc Chnéxe Marcho chnascoy mayçi yuna:
Nemoytoyoy yáte molim chriua dilauciniti (choy,
Imoy dil chiesc podati Chnexe Marcho nascoy may:
Zasctosiga nigdar uechie od mene nedocecha. (çi,
Acholite bude mila maycha uprášcati,
Vitéxe Marcho,
Sctomitiye sincho sabgliça sfa charuáua.
Nemoytoyoy mili brate sfe istinu cházouati,
Ni nayu maychu nichacho zlouogliti,
Da reçito ouacho nascoy mayçi yunácchoy,
Susriteme mila maycho yedan tibi yelencaç.

Choyimise nehti sa drúmcha uchloniti,
Yunáccha Maycho,
Ni on meni mila maycho ni yá gniemu.
I tuy stafsci potargoh moyu sabgliu yunácchu,
I udarih tiboga yelencha u sardascçe,
I chada ya pogledah onoga tiha yelencha,
Gdise htiscc na drumchu sduscicom razdiliti,
V ide miga milo bisce chacho moyega brayena,
Tiboga yelencha,
.I dabimi napourate nebihtiga zagubio.
I chadate yoscchie bude nayu maycha uprascati,
Dagditiye Chnéxe Marcho tuoy brayen Andria:
Ne reçimi nascoy mayçi istiné po nisctóre, (scu,
Ostaoye reçi yunach mila maycho u túyoy zemgli.
Iz choyése nemoxe od milinya oddíliti,
Andriáscu,
Onde miye obgliubio yednu gizdauu deuóychu.
I odchleye yunach tuy deuoychu obgliubio,
Nichad uechie nie poscal samñome uoyeuati,
I samnóme nie uechie ni plíncha razdilio,
Onat muye dála mnoga bilya nepoznána.
I onoga ninça yunáchu od zábitya,
Gizdaua deuoycha,
Li uschorimuse hochiesc mila maycho nádiati.
Achad náte napádú gusari u çarnoy gori.
Nemoytose prid gnimi mili brate pripadnuti,
Da iz glása pochlichni brayena Andriasca,
Bud da mechiesc zamán brate pri potribi chlichouati.
Chada mite zacuyú moye ime chlichuyúchi,
Chléti gusári,
Taycas chiése od tebe yúnáçi razbignúti.
Chachosúse uasdachrát brayene razbigouali,
Chadasute zaculi moye ime chlichouati,
A ñecha dati uidi tuoya gliubima druxina,
Choyimcsi tuóga brata bréz chriuiné zagubio.

Gundulić

Ivan Gundulić (1589-1638) was perhaps the best of the seventeenth-century Croatian Baroque poets. Born and raised in Dubrovnik, and a member of its ruling oligarchy, Gundulić expressed in his works both the cultural orientation and the political interests of the ruling class.

Gundulić wrote in the period of the Jesuit-led Counterreformation, when the theme of repentance was fashionable in literature, as can be seen from the titles of two of his works: Pjesni pokorne kralja Davida (Penitential Psalms of King David, Rome, 1621) and Suze sina razmetnoga (Tears of the Prodigal Son, Venice, 1622), the latter written under the strong influence of Luigi Tansillo's Le Lacrime di San Pietro. In the opinion of Jakša Ravlić, Gundulić's Suze is "perhaps the most polished poetic work of old Croatian literature." (Pet stoljeća hrvatske književnosti, XII, 17.) Gundulić's Dubravka, a pastoral drama first played in 1628, is traditionally considered a hymn to the freedom of Dubrovnik, with the main character, Dubravka, representing the city of Dubrovnik; but Dubravka should also be understood as an apologia for the oligarchic system of government then prevailing in the city, as well as a thinly disguised criticism of Venice, Dubrovnik's chief rival on the Dalmatian Coast.

Ivan Gundulić began the writing of the epic poem Osman, which he intended to be his opus magnum, some time after the Polish victory over the Turks at Hotin (1621) and the death the following year of Osman II, the victim of a palace revolt. These two events were greeted with great enthusiasm by Christian Europe, and especially by the Balkan Slavs, who began to believe that their hour of deliverance was at hand. Perhaps the emotional atmosphere of the time helps to explain why Gundulić, who in writing his Osman was otherwise strongly influenced by Torkvatto Tasso's Jerusalem Delivered, failed to observe one of Tasso's chief rules concerning the writing of an epic, namely, that the theme should not concern events so recent that everyone knew the details.

Ivan Gundulić died before he could finish Osman, which was originally intended to have twenty cantos. Two of the cantos, fourteen and fifteen, were found to be missing from existing manuscripts, and it is not known whether Gundulić ever wrote them. The work was not published in the seventeenth or eighteenth centuries, but was circulated in manuscript form, evidently because the Dubrovnik authorities were sensitive to the possibility of arousing Turkish ire. Osman was finally completed by Ivan Mažuranić (1844), who did a masterful job of writing the missing cantos in the language and style of Gundulić, preparatory to its publication by Matica Hrvatska.

OSMAN

Ah, čijem si se zahvalila,
tašta ljudska oholasti?
Sve što više stereš krila,
sve ćeš paka niže pasti!

Vjekovite i bez svrhe
nije pod suncem krepke stvari,
a u visocijeh gora vrhe
najprije ognjeni trijes udari.

Bez pomoći višnje s nebi
svijeta je stavnos svijem bjeguća:
satiru se sama u sebi
silna carstva i moguća.

Kolo od sreće uokoli
vrteći se ne pristaje:
tko bi gori, eto je doli,
a tko doli, gori ustaje.

Sad vrh sablje kruna visi,
sad vrh krune sablja pada,
sad na carstvo rob se uzvisi,
a tko car bi, rob je sada.

Proz nesreće sreća iznosi,
iz krvi se kruna crpe,
a oni kijeh se boje mnozi,
strah od mnozijeh i oni trpe.

Od izdajstva i od zasjeda
ograđena je glava u cara,
a u čas se zgoda ugleda
od ke ne bi pametara.

OSMAN

Oh, why are you so boastful,
vain human pride?
The higher you stretch your wings,
the lower you'll fall again!

There is nothing so strong under the sun,
that it is eternal and without end,
and the fiery lightning bolt strikes first
amidst high mountain peaks.

Without heavenly intervention
everything is fleeting in this world:
strong and powerful empires
bear the seeds of their own destruction.

The wheel of fortune goes round and round,
it doesn't stop turning:
he who was on top is now on the bottom,
he who was on the bottom rises to the top.

Now the crown hangs o'er the sword,
now the sword falls o'er the crown,
now a slave is elevated to emperor,
and he who was emperor now is slave.

Happiness is gained through misfortunes
crowns are won in blood,
and those whom many fear,
have fear of many.

An emperor's head is surrounded
by treachery and intrigue,
and suddenly there is perceived
the opportunity for which there would be no recorder.

O djevice čiste i blage
ke vrh gore slavne i svete
slatkom vlasti pjesni drage
svijem pjevocim naričete,

narecite sad i meni
kako istočnom caru mladu
smrt vitezi nesmiljeni
daše u svom Carigradu.

Znam da bi se otprije htilo
da ja pjevam, vi kažete,
ko se on rodi srećno i milo
caru Ahmetu prvo dijete;

i po smrti oca svoga
s ke pomoći, s ke zasjede
vrh pristolja otmanskoga
Mustafa mu dundo sjede;

ko li se opet carsko misto
Mustafi ote, tere u slavi
na pristolje ono isto
sultan Osman car se stavi;

i on mlađahan kako paka,
željan starijeh slavu sresti,
podiže se na Poljaka
s mnogom silom, s malom česti.

Ali da tijem pjesni moje
sasma duge ne ishode,
samo objav'te smrti svoje
hude uzroke, tužne zgode!

Vladislave, poljačkoga
slavna kralja slavni sinu,
čim tva puni slava mnoga
svega svijeta veličinu,

na spjevanja ova obrati
veličanstvo vedra čela,
u kijeh ti ištem prikazati
nedobitna tvoja djela.

O pure and gentle maidens
who atop the glorious and holy mountain
recite dear songs with power sweet
to all poets,

tell me now, too,
how the merciless knights
killed the young sultan of the East
in his own Constantinople.

I know you would like
that first I sing, you say,
of his happy and pleasant birth,
as the first-born child of Sultan Ahmet;

and how after his father's death,
through whose help and through whose intrigue
his uncle Mustafa sat
on the Ottoman throne.

And again how the imperial seat
was taken from Mustafa, and Sultan Osman
was placed in glory
on that same imperial throne;

And again how he, a youngster,
desiring to taste his elders' glory,
rose against the Poles
with much force, but with little honor.

But lest my songs
turn out too long,
just tell about his death,
its evil causes, its sad circumstances!

Vladislav, glorious son
of a glorious Polish king,
your great glory
fills the earth's expanse,

Turn the majesty of your radiant brow
to these cantos,
in which I seek to portray
your unsurpassed deeds.

Kraljeviću plemeniti,
jur u smrti cara Osmana
svemogućom tvom dobiti
zamnjela je svaka strana.

Tim s me trublje da svit sliša
slavu tvoju svakčas veću,
ti sveđ djeluj djela viša,
a ja pjet ih pristat neću.

Jadna u srcu uspomena
caru Osmanu bješe ostala
da mu je vojska nebrojena
od poljačke ruke pala,

i da zemljom svom velikom
od tega se digla slava
glaseć carskijem dobitnikom
kraljevića Vladislava.

Ili putnik kopnom jaše,
il pomorac more brodi,
Vladislav se klikovaše
slavan carskoj pri nezgodi.

Gozbe časteć družba mila
i pastiri stada pase
strenitelja turskijeh sila
popijevahu u sve glase.

Jur na krilijeh od vjetara
glas po svemu svijetu prši
ko kraljević silna cara
kopja slomi, sablje skrši.

U vedrini nad oblacim
s istoka mu do zapada
sunce upisa zlatnim zracim
ime kojim slava vlada,

kažuć da on pri Nesteru
istočnoga razbi Zmaja,
leteć za njim u potjeru
sivi Oro do Dunaja.

Noble prince,
already all sides see
in your all-powerful victory
the cause of Sultan Osman's death.

Now the world will hear from my trumpet
of your ever-greater glory,
and if you should do even grander deeds,
I'll not cease to sing of them.

In Sultan Osman's heart remained
the woeful memory
that his innumerable army
had fallen at the Polish hand,

and that the glory of this deed
had spread throughout his great land,
proclaiming Prince Vladislav
the Sultan's victor.

Where a traveller rode o'er land,
where a seaman sailed o'er sea,
the news of Vladislav's glory was bruited,
as well as of the Sultan's woe.

Kind friends entertaining at banquets,
and shepherds grazing their flocks,
were singing in full voice
of the destroyer of the Turkish might.

Already on the wings of the wind
the news was borne throughout the world,
how the prince snapped the swords
and broke the lances of the powerful sultan.

In the clearing above the clouds
from east to west
in golden rays the sun has written
the name that glory rules,

telling how at the Dniester
he smashed the Dragon of the East,
flying after him as far as the Danube,
a grey eagle in pursuit.

IV

THE 18th CENTURY REVIVAL

Makarska

Born in Brist (Makarska) in 1704, Andrija Kačić-Miošić entered the Franciscan monastery of Zaostrog at an early age. Because of his intellectual ability he was later sent to Budapest, where he studied philosophy (1721-1726). Kačić-Miošić taught philosophy for nearly twenty years in Franciscan schools, finally returning to Zaostrog, where he spent the last decade of his life (1750-1760).

In 1752 Kačić published a book on the philosophy of Duns Scotus (Elementa peripatethica juxta mentem subtilissimi doctoris Johannis Duns Scoti, Venice), a work based largely on his own lectures. In 1756, Kačić published the first edition of his Razgovor ugodni naroda slovinskoga (A Pleasant Discourse About The Slavic People), which owed much, at least in its conception, to the work of a predecessor, the Franciscan Filip Grabovac (1697-1749), whose highly patriotic Cvit razgovora naroda i jezika iliričkoga aliti rvackoga (Venice, 1747) landed him in a Venetian jail, leading to his early death.

Like Grabovac, Kačić tells his history by enlivening his prose account with poems about famous battles and leaders. Most of his poems are original, and although they are written in a ten-syllable line they have elements, such as rhyme, which distinguish them from the true folk epic. Kačić was a gifted poet, and at one time his book was the most popular book in Croatia. Although a Franciscan monk, he was oecumenical in his approach, praising Orthodox and Catholic, Serb and Croat alike; his 1759 edition carries a picture of Saint Sava, with the inscription: "born 1169, son of the Serbian king Stefan Nemanja the Great, first Serbian Archbishop, established church administration and laid the foundations for national education. Died in 1237."

Andrija Kačić-Miošić's deep Slavic patriotism is also manifest in his third work, Korabljica (Venice, 1760), which purports to be a history of the world from the beginning until 1760. Heavily dependent on the Bible and the chronicle of Pavao Vitezović (1652-1713), Kačić reminds one of the Bulgarian Paisij (Istorija slavenobolgarskaja 1762), when he admonishes his readers not to be ashamed of their own language: "Nemoj se dakle stiditi u tvoj slavni jezik govoreći, kakono se ne stide Grci ni Latini govoreći u jezike njihove." ("Therefore, do not be ashamed to speak in your glorious language, just as the Greeks and the Latins are not ashamed to speak in their languages.") Kačić even ventures the opinion that our forebear Adam may have spoken Slavic, and he warns his readers not to tell the Italians that they are "šćavon" because schiavo means "slave" in Italian, but rather they should say: "Ja sam Dalmatin, Rvat, Bošnjak, oli Slovinac, jer smo od starine slavni a ne šćavi ni šćavoni rečeni." (I am a Dalmatian, Croatian, Bosnian, or Slovene, because we have been called 'slavni' (glorious) from olden times, and not 'šćavi' or 'šćavoni'.)

PISMA ČETVRTA VOJVODE JANKA I SV. IVANA KAPISTRANA KAKO RAZBIŠE CARA MEMEDA, SINA MURATOVA, POD BIOGRADOM NA 1456.

Divan čini Otmanović care,
po imenu Memede sultane,
u bijelu gradu Carigradu
koga biše skoro osvojio.
Gospodu je na divan sazvao,
sve poizbor paše i kadije:
Useina, velikog vezira,
mufti-odžu i janjičar-agu.
Car se šeta uz divan niz divan,
a gospoda podviv ruke stahu.
Svitlu krunu k vedru nebu baca
ter se care s krunom razgovara:
"Vira moja, svitla kruno moja,
oli ću te brzo izgubiti
oli carstvo moje raširiti,
što mi babo nije raširio."
Još se svojom sabljom razgovara:
"Ova sablja osvoji Carigrad
i pogubi grčkoga cesara,
od istočnih strana gospodara.
Osvojit će i Bosnu ponosnu,
više Bosne ravnu Ungariju,
Dalmaciju do sinjega mora,
Italiju do Rima biloga.
Osvetit ću starca babu moga,
po imenu Murata silnoga,
koji biše Biograd opsio,
ali njega uzeti ne može,
nego svoju svu izgubi vojsku
ter sramotan u Jedrenu dođe.
Da bi mene rodila Vlahinja,
a ne mlada kaduna Turkinja,

A FOURTH SONG ABOUT DUKE JANKO AND SAINT JOHN OF CAPISTRANO, HOW THEY ROUTED EMPEROR MEHMED, MURAT'S SON, BELOW BELGRADE IN 1456.

A council was held by the Ottoman Emperor,
The one called Sultan Mehmed,
In the white city of Constantinople
Which he had recently conquered.
He summoned his lords to the council,
All top pashas and judges:
The Grand Vezir Husein,
The Chief Priest, and the head of the Janissaries.
The Emperor walks up and down the council chamber,
While his lords, their arms folded, were standing.
The Emperor tosses his crown into the clear sky
And he converses with his crown:
"By my faith, shining crown of mine!
Either I shall quickly lose you,
Or I shall enlarge my kingdom,
Which my dad didn't enlarge."
He also conversed with his sword:
"This sword conquered Constantinople
And slew the Greek Emperor,
Ruler of the Eastern lands.
It will conquer proud Bosnia, too,
And beyond Bosnia level Hungary,
Dalmatia to the blue sea,
And Italy to white Rome.
I shall avenge my old dad,
Called Murat the Mighty,
Who laid siege to Belgrade
But couldn't take it;
Instead he lost his whole army,
And he arrived at Adrianopolis in shame.
May my mother have been a Christian
And not a young Turkish lady,

ako sada ne pogubim Janka
koji moga potira babajka
i isiče janjičare Turke
pod bijelim Biogradom gradom."
Još je Memed tiho besidio:
"Na noge se, paše i kadije,
brzo silnu vojsku sakupite,
mlade pišce i brze konjike;
šésēt hȉljād mojih janjičara,
a toliko i veće sejmena,
četrdeset tanenih galija,
sto i trijest tankih ormanica.
Otić ćemo uz Dunaj vodicu
do bijela grada Biograda,
brzo ćemo osvetiti njega
i svu ravnu zemlju Ungariju."
Kada paše njega razumiše,
silnu vojsku brzo sakupiše
ter odoše k ravnoj Ungariji
i prid njima Memed ponositi.
Al je malo vrime postajalo,
glas dopade kralju ungarskomu,
po imenu mladu Vladislavu,
u Požunu skoro okrunjenu:
"Zlo ga, kralju, igru zaigrao
i na glavu krunu postavio!
Eto na te Memed, care silni,
nit ćeš uteć ni odniti glave."
Kralj Vladislav mlado dite biše,
vojevati jošter ne znadiše,
nego moli vojevodu Janka
da kraljujc i za nj bojak bije.
Još Vladislav Janku besiđaše:
"Kaži pravo, desno krilo moje!
Smidemo li cara dočekati,
dočekati i š njim bojak biti?"
Veli njemu Sibinjanin Janko:
"Ovde ima fratar franceškane,
po imenu Ivo Kapistrane,
koji čini čudesa velika.
On će tebe svitovati lipo,
možemo li s Turcim bojak biti."
Kad je kralju riči razumio,
Ivanu je tiho besidio:

If now I don't slay Janko
Who chased my daddy
And cut down Turkish Janissaries
Beneath the white city of Belgrade."
Then Mehmed said softly:
"On your feet, pashas and judges!
Quickly gather a mighty army:
Young infantry and swift cavalry,
Sixty thousand of my Janissaries,
And as many and more of my crack guardsmen,
Forty sleek galleys,
And one hundred thirty warships.
We'll set off up the Danube's waters
To the white city of Belgrade,
We'll avenge it quickly
And all the level land of Hungary."
When the pashas understood their orders,
They quickly gathered a mighty army
And they set off for level Hungary
With proud Mehmed at their head.
When a small time had passed,
The news reached the Hungarian king,
Young Vladislav by name,
Crowned recently in Požun:
"You played the game badly, King,
Placing a crown on your head!
Look, Mehmed the mighty Emperor is after you,
You'll not escape, nor save your head."
King Vladislav was a young child,
He still didn't know how to wage war,
Instead he asked Duke Janko
To rule and do battle for him.
Vladislav also said to Janko:
"Tell me the truth, right wing of mine!
Do we dare to wait for the Emperor,
To wait for him and do battle with him?"
Janko Sibinjanin said to him:
"There's a Franciscan brother here,
By the name of John Capistrano,
Who performs great miracles.
He'll advise you well,
Whether we can do battle with the Turks."
When the king grasped these words,
He softly spoke to John:

"Slugo božja, Ivo Kapistrane,
kaži pravo, tako bio zdravo!
Smidemo li cara dočekati
i na njega skladno udariti?"
Ali mu je svetac besidio:
"Ne brini se, svitla kruno moja,
ja ću poći s Turcim bojak biti,
za Isusa moju krv proliti.
Janko ima dvajest hiljād vojske,
malo manje ja ću sakupiti,
križ Isusov na nje postaviti,
zvati će se od sada Madžari
božja vojska imenom križari."
To govori, na noge se skače
ter otiđe priko Ungarije,
mnogo hiljād sakupi junaka,
sve čobana i mladih težaka.
Sastade se s vojevodom Jankom
ter je njemu tiho besidio:
"Potribno je, Sibinjanin Janko,
da načinjaš od boja đemije,
brze šajke, tanene galije,
koje mogu s Turcim bojak biti
na Dunaju, studenoj vodici,
blizu bila grada Biograda,
jer će Dunaj vodu zapričiti
turske šajke, tanene galije,
ter će nami pute zatvoriti,
da ne damo pomoć Biogradu.
Zavest ćemo niz Dunaj vodicu,
razbit ćemo turske ormanice
i dat ćemo pomoć Biogradu
na sramotu cara silenoga."
Kad je njega Janko razumio,
Ivana je lipo poslušao.
Od Budima šajke dojedriše,
iznova se mnoge sagradiše:
sto i šeset malih i velikih,
koje mogu s Turcim bojak biti,
među njima Jankova đemija,
strahovita kano sultanija.
Maleno je vrime postajalo,
glas dopade vojevodi Janku:
"Đenerale od vojske ungarske,
turska vojska pod Biograd dođe!

"Servant of God, John Capistrano,
Tell the truth, for heaven's sake!
Do we dare to wait for the Emperor
And to attack him together?"
But the saint said to him:
"Don't be afraid, illustrious majesty,
I'll go do battle with the Turks,
I'll shed my blood for Jesus.
Janko has twenty thousand soldiers,
I'll gather nearly the same,
I'll put the cross of Jesus on them,
From now on the Hungarians will be called
God's army, the Crusaders by name."
Saying this he jumped to his feet,
And he set out through Hungary;
He raised many thousands of warriors,
All of them peasants and young farm hands.
He got together with Duke Janko
And he softly said to him:
"It's necessary, Janko Sibinjanin,
For you to build some warships,
Fleet flat-bottomed boats and sleek galleys,
That can do battle with the Turks
On the Danube's cold waters,
Near the white city of Belgrade;
For the Danube's waters will be blockaded
By the Turkish flat boats and sleek galleys,
And they'll shut us off,
So we won't be able to help Belgrade.
We'll sail down the Danube's waters,
We'll smash the Turkish warships
And we'll give aid to Belgrade,
To the shame of the mighty Emperor."
When Janko understood his orders
He did his bidding well;
Flat boats came sailing down from Buda,
Many of them newly built.
One hundred and sixty, small and large,
That could do battle with the Turks,
Among them Janko's warship,
As terrifying as the Sultan's wife.
A short time passed,
Word came to Duke Janko:
"General of the Hungarian armies!
The Turkish army is arriving below Belgrade!

Opside ga sa četiri strane:
od istoka Turci janjičari,
od zapada crni Arnauti,
od Dunaja tanene galije,
a od Save ohole balije.
Dunaj vodu šajke zatvoriše,
verugam se teškim izvezaše,
Biograd je u nevolji teškoj,
ne može mu dobra pomoć doći."
Kad je Janko glase razumio,
ormanice biše oružao;
na nje meće ognjene topove
i oružje što je od potribe.
Sveti Ive slavnu misu reče,
kad je reče, na kolina kleče:
blagosivlje vojevodu Janka
i njegovu sablju madžarkinju.
Pak se skače na noge viteške,
uze barjak u desnicu ruku,
na barjaku ime Isusovo,
ter prid vojskom k Biogradu pođe.
Zavezoše šajke ormanice,
a niz Dunaj, vodicu studenu,
i prid njima vojevoda Janko
u velikoj od boja đemiji.
Kadali se blizu sastadoše
bojne šajke turske i ungarske,
potrese se Dunaj, voda hladna,
od onizih bojnih lumbarada.
Evo, brate, boja žestokoga,
na Dunaju ognja paklenoga!
Stoji jauk ranjenih delija,
lomljavina tanenih galija.
A kadli se lipo sastadoše
ormanice turske i ungarske,
ne pucaju puške ni topovi,
već zvekeću sablje i kadare.
Sikoše se pô bijela danka
na Dunaju dvi ognjene vojske;
Dunaj hladni vas krvav bijaše,
u njega se krvca salivaše.
Biše Janku srića pristupila,
jer potopi dvadeset galija
i osvoji mnogo ormanica,
dvajest hiljad pogubi Turaka.

They are besieging it from four sides:
  Turkish Janissaries from the East,
  Black Albanians from the West,
  Sleek galleys from the Danube,
  And arrogant Bosnians from the Sava.
The flat boats have closed off the Danube,
  They are chained together with heavy chains,
  Belgrade is in heavy straights,
  No help can get through to her."
When Janko heard the news
  He armed his warships;
  He put fiery cannon on them
  And the necessary arms.
Saint John said a glorious mass.
  When he had said it he knelt on his knees;
  He blessed Duke Janko
  And his sword, the Hungarian maiden.
Then he jumped to his knightly feet,
  He took a banner in his right hand,
  On the banner the name of Jesus.
  And he set out for Belgrade at the head of the army.
The flat boats set sail
  Down the Danube's cold waters.
  And at their head was Duke Janko
  In a big warship.
And when they drew near to each other,
  The Turkish and Hungarian flat boats,
  The Danube's cold waters shook
  From those war cannon.
There's a fierce battle for you, brother,
  Hell's fire on the Danube!
  The screaming of wounded warriors all around,
  And the fleet galleys' din.
And when they locked neatly in battle,
  The Turkish and Hungarian warships,
  They weren't shooting muskets and cannon,
  Instead they were rattling sabres and daggers.
They slashed at each other half a day,
  The two fiery armies on the Danube;
  The cold Danube was all bloody,
  Their blood poured into it.
Good fortune was on Janko's side,
  For he sunk twenty galleys
  And he captured many warships,
  Killing twenty thousand Turks.

Dok se Janko s Turcim prigonjaše,
sveti Ivo na kolinim kleči,
k vedru nebu ruke uzdizaše
ter za Janka moli brez pristanka.
Moli Ivo i domoli Boga:
razbi Janko na Dunaju Turke,
zdravo dođe u Biograd s vojskom
na sramotu cara silenoga.
Kad to vidi Otmanović care,
poče biti s topovim Biograd,
vas se bili grade tresijaše
od topova turskih i ungarskih.
A kadali probiše bedene
i široke laze otvoriše,
prokušaše sriću od mejdana,
udariše Turci sa svih strana.
Dočeka ih na oružju Janko,
Turke siče nemilo i jako:
koliko ih na grad udaraše,
on'liko ih strmoglav padaše.
Ali Turci nigda ne pristaju,
juriš čine, lagum potkapaju,
teško oni viču i alaču,
listve nose, na bedene skaču.
Kano soko Janko prilićaše
ter po poli Turke prisicaše;
bedeni su s glavam okićeni
i svi s turskom krvju poliveni.
Te žalosti car Memed gledaše,
bradu guli, suze prolivaše;
kruto ječi, jedva izgovara,
s janjičarim ter se razgovara:
"Dico moja, Turci janjičari,
sve uzdanje cara čestitoga!
Kako sjutra zorica zabili,
na Biograd snažno udarite.
Ako nami Bog i srića dade,
ter Biograd sjutra, osvojite,
isicite malo i veliko,
a Janka mi živa uhvatite
i papaza fra Ivana fratra:
mučit ću ih godinu danaka,
jer su meni puno dodijali
i svu rusu bradu ogulili."

While Janko was driving the Turks back
  Saint John was kneeling on his knees;
  To the clear sky he raised his hands
  And he prayed for Janko without cease.
John prayed and God heard his prayer,
  Janko routed the Turks on the Danube.
  He arrived safely in Belgrade with his army
  To the shame of the mighty Emperor.
When the Ottoman Emperor saw this
  He began to pound Belgrade with his cannon.
  The white city completely shook
  From the Turkish and Hungarian cannon.
And when they had pierced the ramparts
  And had opened wide paths,
  They tried their luck in battle;
  The Turks attacked from all sides.
Janko greeted them with weapons,
  Cutting down Turks mercilessly and resolutely:
  As many as attacked the fortress,
  The same number fell headlong down.
But the Turks never stop trying,
  They charge, they mine the walls,
  They loudly scream and shout "Allah,"
  Carrying daggers they jump onto the ramparts.
Janko flew about like a falcon,
  Cutting the Turks in half;
  The ramparts were adorned with heads
  And all awash in Turkish blood.
These sad things Emperor Mehmed was watching,
  He was plucking out his beard, he was shedding tears;
  He moaned deeply, he could barely speak,
  And then he talked with his Janissaries:
"My children, Turkish Janissaries,
  The only hope of an honorable Emperor!
  Tomorrow, as soon as the dawn turns light,
  Attack Belgrade in force.
If God and good fortune should grant
  That tomorrow you capture Belgrade,
  Cut down the big and the small,
  But take Janko alive for me
And that priest, Brother John the friar;
  I'll torture them for a full year,
  Because they have caused me much pain
  And have plucked out all my blonde beard."

Kadali je zora zabilila,
sa svih strana udariše Turci:
prisloniše skale uz bedene,
s golim sabljam skaču na zidove.
Mili Bože, tuge i žalosti!
Da je komu pogledati bilo
di se brani malo i veliko,
slipo, hromo, staro i bolesno!
Janka niko poznat ne mogaše,
vas u krvi ogreznuo biše,
bihu mu se umorile ruke
prisicajuć janjičare Turke.
Ali ko će sili odoliti,
ko l' isići svu vojsku carevu!
Prve šance Turci osvojiše
ter barjake na nje postaviše.
Na zidove druge udariše,
na silu ih, pobre, osvojiše,
mrtvi Turci za skale služahu,
u grad živi priko njih skakahu.
Cvili Janko kano zmija ljuta:
"Pogibosmo, Ivo Kapistrane!"
Lipo ga je svetac slobodio:
"Ne plaši se, đenerale Janko!
Branimo se do mrkloga mraka,
pak ćeš vidit čudo od Turaka!
Kako žarko opočine sunce,
sažeć ćemo bakovite junce."
Kadli poče misu govoriti,
za građane Bogu uzdisati,
zgodiše se velika čudesa:
leti strila ozgar od nebesa,
na otar je prid Ivana pala.
Lipa dara, našem Bogu hvala!
Sveti Ivan uze je u ruke,
na njoj štije: "Dobit ćete Turke".
Ovo pismo svi građani štiše
ter jedino Bogu zahvališe.
Sablje oštre, gorke suze taru, –
jao sada Otmanović caru!
Kako žarko opočinu sunce,
sve se skoči, malo i veliko,
nose grede, daske opakljene,
sijeno, slamu, goru svakojaku.

When the dawn turned light
  The Turks attacked from all sides:
  They leaned ladders against the ramparts,
  With naked sabres they jumped onto the walls.
Dear God, such sorrow and pain!
  If anyone could have seen
  How they fought back, the big and the small,
  The blind, the crippled, the old and infirm!
No one could recognize Janko,
  He had become completely covered with blood,
  His arms had grown weary
  Cutting down Turkish Janissaries.
But who can resist force?
  Who could cut down the Emperor's whole army!
  The Turks captured the first trenches
  And set their banners on them.
They attacked the second set of walls,
  They took them by force, brother;
  Using dead Turks as ladders
  The living jumped over them into the city.
Janko wailed like an angry snake:
  "We're done for, John Capistrano!"
  The saint calmed him nicely:
  "Don't be afraid, General Janko!"
We'll defend ourselves until the murky darkness
  And then you'll see a miracle happen to the Turks.
  When the hot sun goes down
  We'll roast ourselves some copper bulls."
When he began to say mass
  And to sigh to God for the city's dwellers,
  Some great miracles took place:
  An arrow flew down from heaven,
Landing on the altar in front of John.
  A beautiful present, thanks be to God!
  Saint John took it into his hands,
  He read on it: "You'll defeat the Turks."
All the citizens read the letter
  And as one they gave praise to God.
  They sharpen their swords, rub away their bitter tears,
  Woe now to the Ottoman Emperor!
When the hot sun went down
  Everyone jumped up, big and small,
  They carried beams and boards smeared with pitch,
  Hay, straw, and all kinds of fuel.

Užegoše, na Turke baciše,
vojnici ih straga zatekoše:
koji Turčin od vatre bižaše,
on od sablje uteć ne mogaše;
koji, pobre, od sablje bižahu,
oni živi u vatru skakahu.
Sve izgori, niko ne uteče,
kano miši izgorili ječe.
Posli toga juriš učiniše
na tobdžije i na kumbardžije
ter oteše carevo oružje,
ognjenite šibe i lumbarde.
Sjajni misec pomrčao biše
od crnoga praha i olova.
Što god Tūrāk oko grada biše,
sve Ungarci pod mač okrenuše.
Kadali je danak osvanuo,
govorio Ive Kapistrane:
"Ko je godir srca junačkoga,
neka sada nasliduje mene!
Dunaj ćemo vodu pribroditi
i na carev dundar udariti."
To je čuo vojevoda Janko
ter je svojoj govorio vojsci:
"Ko se nađe od sve vojske moje,
da pribrodi Dunaj, vodu hladnu,
i udari jurišem na Turke
mojom sabljom odsić ću mu glavu.
Zadosta je našega junaštva
koje noćas jesmo učinili;
neka Turci s mirom doma iđu,
ne dajimo sriću za nesriću"
Sva je vojska Janka poslušala,
ali ne kti Ivan Kapistrane
ni njegovi križari junaci
nego Dunaj vodu pribrodiše.
Pet hiljada, ni manje ni više,
svega glasa "Jezus!" zavikaše
ter udriše jedino na Turke,
na vas tabor cara silenoga.
Za šest uri s Turcim bojak biše,
od praha se ništa ne viđaše
od topova ništa ne čujaše:
Turci zovu sveca Muhameda,
a kršćani ime Isusovo.

They set fire to it, they threw it on the Turks;
  The soldiers caught them from behind:
  When some Turk would flee from the fire
  He couldn't escape the sword.
Those who ran from the sword, brother,
  They jumped alive into the fire.
  They all burned up, no one escaped,
  Moaning like burning mice.
After that they made a charge
  Against the gunners and the mortar men,
  And they carried off the Emperor's arms,
  His rockets and his mortars.
The bright moon had darkened over
  From the black powder and the lead.
  Whatever Turks were near the town
  All were put to the sword by the Hungarians.
When the day turned light
  John Capistrano spoke:
  "Whoever is of heroic heart,
  Let him follow me now!
We'll ford the Danube's waters
  And attack the Emperor's rear guard."
  Duke Janko heard this,
  And he said to his army:
"If anyone from all my army
  Fords the Danube's cold waters
  And attacks the Turks on the run,
  I'll cut off his head with my sword.
We showed enough heroism
  In what we did last night;
  Let the Turks go home in peace,
  Let's not trade good luck for bad!"
The whole army obeyed Janko
  But John Capistrano didn't want to,
  Nor did his crusader heroes,
  Instead they forded the Danube's waters.
Five thousand, no more nor less,
  Shouted "Jesus" in full voice
  And struck as one against the Turks,
  Against the whole camp of the mighty Emperor.
Six hours they did battle with the Turks.
  Because of the gunpowder nothing could be seen,
  And because of the cannon nothing could be heard:
  The Turks call out to their saint Mohammed
  And the Christians call the name of Jesus.

Ali ko će s Bogom bojak biti,
ko l' božiju vojsku pridobiti?
Pogiboše Turci janjičari
al ih siku božiji križari.
Oteše im aznu i zairu
čadorove i alaj-barjake,
sve oružje, ognjene topove,
tambalase, bubnje i svirale.
Tu gospoda mnoga izgiboše,
sve poizbor age i spahije,
mlađah vezir s agom janjičarskim,
ine vojske ni broja se ne zna.
Al uteče Memed, care silni,
uđe ranjen, vesela mu majka!
Ovo uvik nek se pripovida,
kako Ivan Turke pridobiva!

But who will do battle with God,
  Who can defeat God's army?
  The Turkish Janissaries perished,
  Cut down by God's crusaders.
They captured their treasure and their provisions,
  Their tents and their ceremonial banners,
  All their weapons, their fiery cannon,
  Their kettle drums, bass drums, and flutes.
Many lords perished there,
  All top agas and spahijas,
  A young vezir and the head of the Janissaries;
  Of the other troops not even the number is known.
But Mehmed, the mighty Emperor, escaped;
  He left wounded, may his mother be joyful!
  May this story always be told,
  How John defeated the Turks.

Slavonia

Matija Antun Reljković (1732-1798) belongs, together with Kačić-Miošić, Stefan Rajić, Dositej Obradović and others, to that generation of Serbs and Croats of the second half of the eighteenth century who were inspired by the tenets of the European Age of Enlightenment to work for the education of their people in their own language. Satyr

Reljković was from the village of Svinjar, in Slavonia, a rich farming area in the northeastern part of today's Yugoslavia. His Bosnian ancestors had moved to this depopulated area after the failure of the second Turkish siege of Vienna in 1683. The Reljkovići were a military family, serving the Austrian Imperial Army on the Vojna Granica (Military Frontier) that separated the Austro-Hungarian Empire from the Ottoman-held lands. When Matija was nine years of age, his widower father Captain Stipa Reljković, placed him in a Franciscan monastery (in 1741), while he went off to war. In the monastery, and later in Hungary, Matija received the typical classical education of the day, which concentrated heavily on languages and the classics. By the age of sixteen he was in the army, serving as a simple private; later, in papers recommending him for promotion to sergeant, he was praised for knowing five languages: Illyrian (Serbo-Croatian), French, German, Latin, and Hungarian.

Reljković fought for nearly forty years in the Imperial Army, retiring as captain. He seems to have participated in every major war of the Austrian forces during that period, including the Seven Years War, from 1756 to 1763 (known in America as "The French and Indian War"). During that war Reljković was taken prisoner, and for a time was held at Frankfurt-On-Oder, where he was allowed to make ample use of the public library. In 1762, while in Dresden, Reljković published the first edition of his Satir. *So successful was* Satir *that it was published three more times during Reljković's lifetime. It was "translated" into the "Slaveno-Serbian" literary language then being used by Serbs (a mixture of spoken Serbian and Russian), by Stefan Rajić, a schoolmaster in Osijek, who published it twice in cyrillic (in 1793 and 1807).*

Reljković wrote in the ikavian subdialect common to many parts of Slavonia, and stemming perhaps from the Bosnian origin of much of the population. His orthography featured combinations of letters (cz= č), instead of the single letters with diacritical marks common to the latinica alphabet since Gaj's time (see our notes to Mažuranić's Smrt Smail-Age Ćengića*).*

In addition to Satir, *Reljković also published a grammar (*Nova Slavonska i Nimaczka Gramatika, *Zagreb, 1767, 552 pages), published twice more in 1774 and 1789; a manual on sheep raising* Ovczarnica, *a translation of a German manual by Venceslav Ivan Paul; a book on natural law,* Postanak naravne pravice *(Osijek, 1794), a translation of a Latin school book:* Institutio elementorum iuris naturalis in usum gymnasiorum et scholarum grammaticarum per regnum Hungariae et provincias eidem adnexas; Nek je svashta, *a collection of anecdotes and stories about heroic deeds taken from various sources (Osijek, 1795; subsequently published twice more); a translation of Aesop's Fables* (Ezopove fabule), *not published during his lifetime; and a translation of Pilpaj's fables* (Pilpajeve fabule i Nauk politiczan i moralski), *also not published during Reljković's lifetime, but published together with the preceding work in the collected works of Reljković,* Djela M.A. Reljkovića, *Vinkovci, 1875.*

RELJKOVIĆ'S COAT OF ARMS

SATIR ILITI DIVJI ČOVIK

Dunđerin niki na jednoj crkvi lip načini toran, kojega kada dovršio, sajde na zemļu i metnuvši ruku na čelo poče ga od sviju strana promatrati, ovako u sebi govoreći: „Sada neka dojde tko mu drago, ne će na ovomu tornu nikakve mahane naći."

Dvoje dice, koja na crkvenoj ulici jedno drugom prah u oči sipajući igrau se, motreći dunđerina okolo torna obiodećega, jedno reče: Što ovaj okolo torna gledajući u ńega obihodi? Vaļada mu je toran grbav." Još ovo i ne svrši svoje govoreńe, a drugo povika: „Na kjivo tojan! Na kjivo tojan!"

Dunđerin pogleda u dicu pak opet u toran i vidi, da nije ni od kud na krivo, ali za izvaditi ńima iz glave tu zlu misao, upita ńih: „Je li dico, na krivo toran?" Rekoše: „Jest." „Ej dobro", slidi dunđerin, „mi ćemo ńega sada popraviti."

On uzamši klupko kanafa, peńe se po svojih skelah gori na toran, pak svezavši jedan kraj za križ, baci klupko na zemļu ńima govoreći: „Uzmite to uže pak vucite onamo na pravac, od kuda je toran grbav, a ja ću ga ramenom poduprti, i kada bude dosta, onda mi kažite."

Dica vuku za kanaf, a dunđerin, poduprvši ramenom toran, steńe, kako da bi mu težko bilo, pak pita ńih: „Je l' dobro?" Oni rekoše: „De još malo." Drugi put uprvši, reče: „Hoću l' još?" Rekoše: „Dobro je." Dunđerin upita: „Je l' dobro?" Odgovoriše: „Jest."

Tada on, otrgavši kanaf od križa, sajde na zemļu veseleći se, što je tako lako izpravio toran, a dica povikaše: „Mi nacinismo tojan! Mi nacinismo tojan!" Ele dunđerin ńima odgovori: „Volim, da ste ga i vi načinili, nego da je grbav."

Stioče slavonski! Ja znam, da ti jedva čekaš znati, u što nišani ovaj dunđerin, ovo dvoje dice i ovaj ńiov toran, ali budi ustrpļiv, dok ja kažem.

Poslidńeg prajskog rata, koji poče godine 1756., a svrši 1763., i koji za ono sedam godina, što se proteže, ne drugo

SATYR OR THE WILD MAN

A certain carpenter built a beautiful steeple on a church and when he had finished it he descended to the ground, and placing his hand on his forehead he began to examine the steeple from all sides, while saying to himself: "Now, let anyone come who wants to, they won't find any defects in this steeple."

Two children were playing on the church street, pouring dirt into each other's eyes, when one of them observed the carpenter walking around the steeple and said: "Why is that guy walking around the steeple and looking at it? Probably his steeple is bent. This lad had not finished his speech, when the other one shouted out: "The teeple is cwooked! The teeple is cwooked!"

The carpenter looked at the children and then once more at the steeple, and he saw that it wasn't crooked anywhere; but in order to remove that wicked idea from their heads he asked them: "Is the steeple crooked, children?" They said: "Yes." "Well, good," continued the carpenter, "We'll straighten it out right now."

Picking up a coil of rope he climbed up his scaffolding to the steeple, and after tying one end to the cross he threw the coil to the ground saying to them: "Take that rope and pull it from the direction in which the steeple is bent, and I'll push against it with my shoulder, and when it's enough just tell me."

The children pulled on the rope and the carpenter pushed against the steeple with his shoulder, groaning as though it were hard for him, and he asked them: "Is it all right?" They said: "C'mon, a little more!" Pushing against it a second time he said: "Shall I push it some more?" They said: "That's good." The carpenter asked: "Is it good?" And they answered: "Yes, it is."

Then pulling the rope from the cross he descended to the ground, delighted that he had straightened out the steeple so easily; and the children shouted: "We built the teeple! We built the teeple!" And the carpenter answered them: "I would rather that you built it than it be bent."

Slavonian reader! I know that you can hardly wait to hear what is the point behind this story of the carpenter, these two children, and this steeple of theirs; but be patient, and I'll tell you.

The last Prussian War, which began in the year 1756 and ended in 1763, during the seven years that it lasted was nothing else but a school,

nego jedna skula, osobito za mlade ļude bijaše, ukaza bo se prilika prohoditi bodjavad vilaete, zemļe i gradove onima, koji to želeći prez velikog troška drugačije ne bi mogli učiniti.

I kako ļudi običaju reći, da u vojski svačta ima, tako i ondi događa se: niki tekoše blago, niki izgubiše i ono svoje, niki pak pokraj svoje dužnosti motriše lipe zemļe, jake gradove, plemenite varoše, lipo uređena sela i obštine. Motriše uredbu, ńiovu službu Božju, ńiov posao u poļu, vladańe u domu, timareńe marve, prohod rukotvorja, – jednom ričju, motriše sve ono, što je nedokučeni uzdržiteļ zemaļskoga klupka i sviju stvari umrlomu čoviku za ńegovu potribitu hranu, branu i odiću ostavio.

Ovako indi motreći sva kolika, komu ne bi na pamet pala ńegova ista otačbina, tko ne bi na vagu metnuo svoj isti vilaet i prama drugima procinio, kakvi je i kakvi bi mogao biti, da se najprije ukloni s puta drvje i kameńe, o koje se ļudi do sada potipaše, to jest da se uklone s puta pridsude i zli običaji, koji odavna od nekrštenika ostavļeni i duboko ukoreńeni ovakvi plemenit vilaet obagavili i naružili jesu?

* * * * * * * *

Bivši i ja u rečenom prošastom prajskom ratu s ostalima, ni prvi ni poslidńi, ni najboļi ni najgorji, nego u polak, i kako poradi vlastitog dobitka nisam išao, tako se nisam za dobitkom ni žestio, nego dužnost moju, koliko je od moje strane moguće bilo, činio i obsluživao. Zadovoļan dakle s onime, što imam, ja se naslađiva u promatrańu lipše uređenih vilaeta, nego je moja otačbina Slavonija, pak mi žao bijaše, što sam privaren, misleći prije toga, da nejma urednijeg vilaeta od ńe, jerbo ja drugih još nisam bio vidio.

Promišļavajući na ovaj način, kada se svrši rat, ako doživim, šta bi ja mojoj otačbini iz tuđih zemaļa donio, čim bi joj se barem za to udobrio, što me ima i što sam se u ńezinom krilu odgojio, šta li bi ja mojim domorodcem kakono pazara poklonio, evo pade mi na pamet, da jim dovedem Satira, to jest da jim kńižicu jednu pod ovim imenom sastavim i u verše složim, jerbo su i onako domorodci moji svi pivači i od naravi pjesnici, sva svoja junački učińena dila u pisma pivaju i u uspomeni drže.

Ista dica za marvom hodeći iznenada verše prave pivajući:

Dobro mi je i boļem se nadam,
u čem hodim, u tomu i spavam,

especially for young people; for it presented them with the opportunity to travel through countries, lands, and cities free of charge, something which they could not have done, except at great expense.

Now people are accustomed to saying that in the army all sorts of things happen, and so it happened then too that some acquired wealth, some lost even their own, and some, besides doing their duty, got to see beautiful lands, powerful cities, noble towns, and beautifully organized villages and communities; they observed their administration, their home life, their cattle raising, and their manufacturing; in a word, they observed everything that the incomprehensible protector of the earth's globe and of all things has left to mortal man for his needed nourishment, protection, and clothing.

While observing all sorts of things in this way, who would not have had his own fatherland cross his mind? Who would not have placed his own homeland on the scales and compared it to other lands, the way it is now and the way it could be, if one could first clear away the dead wood and the rocks against which people have been stumbling up to now, that is: if one could clear away the prejudices and evil customs left behind by the unbaptized ones long ago, which became deeply rooted, and which have crippled and disfigured this noble homeland.

* * * * * * * *

I, too, was in the said Prussian War with the others, being neither first nor last, neither best nor worst, but somewhere in between; and since I didn't go to war for my own personal gain I therefore didn't strive for gain, but rather I did my duty and served as well as I could. Satisfied thus with what I had, I enjoyed myself in the observation of more beautifully organized places than my motherland Slavonija, but I didn't regret that I had been mistaken formerly in thinking that there was no better organized country than she, since I hadn't yet seen any others.

I was reflecting in this manner about what I–if I survived–would bring my motherland from foreign lands after the war was over, something that would make her happy that she had me and that I had been raised in her lap, something I could give my fellow countrymen as a kind of gift from the market: –and lo, there came to my mind the idea that I might bring them *Satyr*, that is, that I might put together a little book for them with this name, and that I might write it in verse form, since my countrymen are all singers and poets by nature anyway: they sing songs about all their heroically-performed deeds, thus preserving their memory.

Our own children, while minding the cattle, suddenly sing real verses:

> I have it good and I hope for better,
> What I walk in I also sleep in, etc.

i tako dałe. Ova će, reko, kńižica baš zato ńima po ćudi biti, jerbo je kakono na pisme razdilita i u verše složena.

Toga istoga uzroka radi godine 1761, u Saksoniji napisa rečenog Satira i u stolńem gradu Dresden pritiskati dado, u kojemu sva kolika onako, kako se onda nahodiše, popisana bijau, premda sada mlogo drugačija vide se.

Ali što misliš, štioče, kako se primi ovaj Satir, došavši u Slavoniju? Od hiładu i pet stotina kńižica ne osta meni u dvi godine ni jedna, kojom bi jednu imati želećega prijateła poslužit mogao. Međuto i od hiładu i pet stotina štioca ne najdoše se nego samo dvojica, kojima ovaj Satir čińaše se na krivo, kano dici dunđerinov toran. Evo sam ga dakle za ńiovu łubav popravio, i srićan ja, ako oni poviču: „Mi načinismo Satira", jer volim, da su ga i oni načinili, nego da vilaet ostane onako grbav.

* * * * * * * *

Slavonac, sikući u šumi drva, namiri se na jednoga Satira, s kojim učinivši prijatełstvo, da će odsele zajedno hoditi i pajdašiti se, čovik zovnu Satira, da s ńime ruča, koji, dok čovik zgotovi jegek, pripovidi ńemu u verše lipotu od Slavonije i ukaza ńezino prvašńe i sadašńe stańe, donese prid očci Slavoncu ńegove falinge i ukaza način, kako bi ńe iste popraviti mogao.

Satir u verše Slavoncu

Slavonije, zemło plemenita,
vele ti si lipo uzorita,
nakićena zelenim gorama,
obałana četirim vodama.
Na priliku zemałskoga raja
rike teku sa četiri kraja:
od istoka Dunaj voda pliva,
od zapada studena Ilova,
od ponoći Drava voda miče,
kod Almàša u Dunaj utiče,
a od podne Sava voda teče
i u Dunaj o Biograd češe,
a ti ležiš posrid ovih vodâ
kano jedna zelena livada.
Bog je tebe lipo namirio
i svakakvim plodom nadilio
i dao ti svakakvog imańa
kako onoj zemłi obećańâ,
da ti rodi vino i pšenica,
kom se hràni i junak i ptica.

For that reason this little book will be just their style, I said, since it is divided, as it were, into songs and it is written in verse form.

And for this same reason, in Saxony in the year 1761, I wrote the said *Satyr* and had it printed in the capital city of Dresden; everything in it [*Satyr*–trans.] is described as it was then, even though it appears to be much different now.

But what do you think, reader? How was this *Satyr* received when it arrived in Slavonija? After two years, out of fifteen hundred copies there wasn't a single book left for me to offer a friend who might want one. And of the fifteen hundred readers only two could be found to whom *Satyr* appeared crooked, like the carpenter's steeple to the children. For their sake, then, I have straightened it out, and I shall be fortunate if they shout: "We built the *Satyr*," because I would rather that they built it than that our homeland remained bent that way.

A Slavonian, cutting wood in the forest, comes upon a Satyr with whom he makes friends, with the idea that from then on they would go places and pal around together; the man invited the Satyr to have dinner with him, and while the man was preparing dinner the Satyr described for him in poetry the beauty of Slavonija and he indicated her original and her present condition; he brought before the Slavonian's eyes his defects, and he showed him how he might correct the same.

The Satyr Sings in Verses to the Slavonian

Slavonija, o noble land,
You are very beautifully formed,
Adorned with green hills,
And bordered by four waters,
As in an earthly paradise
Your rivers flow from four corners:
From the East the Danube's waters flow,
From the West the cold Ilova;
From the North the Drava's waters move,
Flowing into the Danube by Almaš,
And from the South the Sava's waters flow
Touching the Danube at Belgrade,
And you lie midst these waters
Like a green meadow.
God took handsome care of you
And bestowed on you every kind of fruit
And he gave you all sorts of wealth
As he did to that promised land,
So you might have wine and wheat,
With which to nourish hero and bird.

Al ti zalud sva druga lipota,
kad ti fali najlipša dobrota,
baš dobrota skule i nauci,
koje slide svi koliki puci.

But all other beauty is in vain,
When you lack the most beautiful virtue,
The very virtue of schooling and the sciences,
Which all nations study.

The Life and Adventures

*Serbian culture began to take on new life toward the end of the eighteenth century, after nearly three and one-half centuries of stagnation. A prime-mover in the Serbian cultural rebirth was Dositej Obradović (1742-1811), of whom Vojislav Djurić writes: "There are two epochs in the history of Serbian culture: the old one–from Saint Sava to Dositej, and the new one–from Dositej to the present day. Sava is the first Serbian man of letters, Dositej is the first Serbian modern man of Letters." (*Srpska književnost u sto knjiga, *X, 7).*

*As his autobiography (*Život i priključenija, *Life and Adventures,*

Leipzig, 1783) demonstrates, Dositej was uniquely prepared to lead Serbia toward a cultural revival. Orphaned at the age of ten, he was educated in a monastery (Hopovo), and for a time he was so devoted to the Lives *of the saints that his main and sole ambition was to live the ascetic life and become a saint himself. By the age of sixteen he had become a monk and deacon, but his love for learning and the gradual loss of his fervor led him to leave the monastery within two years, in 1760. Thus began a life of wandering and study at places like Mount Athos, Smyrna, Vienna, Leipzig, Paris, and London. Dositej's physical travels were an intellectual jouney as well; he moved from the fantastic* Lives *of the saints to the writings of the Greek church reformers of the eighteenth century, from the philosophy of Leibnitz and Wolff to the* Ethics *of Soave, from the pronouncements of the French "philosophes" to the pamphlets and articles of the English free-thinkers. And throughout this period of more than forty years, Dositej was continually absorbing the new culture of the Age of Enlightenment and transmitting it to his Serbian countrymen, through his works, which were largely translations or adaptations.*

Inspired by the spirit of "Josephinism", the enlightened despotism which prevailed in Austria during the reign of Joseph II (1780-1790), Dositej sought the largest possible audience among his countrymen; he wrote in what closely approximated his spoken language (which included some Russianisms), and not in the "mish-mash" of spoken Serbian and Russian Slavonic that was then popular with Serbian writers. In his "Letter to Haralampije," which was published together with his Život *and which functioned as Dositej's manifesto on the Serbian literary language, he wrote: "When learned men write their thoughts in the common language of the whole nation, then enlightenment and ... learning are not restricted to persons who understand the old literary language.... . I know that some one may reply that if we begin to write in the common language, the old language will be neglected and will gradually disappear. I answer: 'What profit do we have from a language which, if you take our people overall, not one person in ten thousand understands correctly." Dositej paved the way for Vuk Karadžić, who thirty years later set forth the principles for a thorough and consistent reform of the Serbian literary language.*

In addition to his Život i priključenija, *Dositej Obradović's most important works were:* Sovjeti zdravago razuma... *(The Counsels of Common Sense, Leipzig, 1784);* Ezopove...basne *(Aesop's ...Fables, Leipzig, 1788; this book also contains the second part of Dositej's* Life*);* Pjesna na vzjatie Belgrada *(Song on the Deliverance of Belgrade, Vienna, 1789);* Sobranie raznyh nravoučitelnyh veščej v polzu i uveselenie *(Collection of Various Morally-Instructive Articles for Profit and Amusement, Vienna, 1793);* Etika *(Ethics, Venice, 1803; a fairly close translation of Soave's* Instituzioni di etica*); and* Bukvica *(The Little Alphabet Book), Dositej's first work, circulated in manuscript form, and published posthumously in Vienna in 1830.*

Dositej Obradović

ЖИВОТ И ПРИКЉУЧЕНИЈА ДИМИТРИЈА ОБРАДОВИЋА, НАРЕЧЕНОГА У КАЛУЂЕРСТВУ ДОСИТЕЈА, ЊИМ ИСТИМ СПИСАТ И ИЗДАТ.

Приклад других народа даје ми дрзновеније. Наћи ће се довољно оструомних и правосудних лица између браће моје који ће познати чији сам ја интерес и ползу пишући желио и искао. Ако ли што гди буде погрешено, учени ће људи после мене исправити и мени ће человекољубно као чловеку простити. Мени је довољно утјешенија дајући приклад ученим мојега народа да српски почињу на штампу што добро издавати. Штета да толики многочислени народ остаје без књига на свом језику у време у које наука близу нас сија како небесно сунце. ...

* * *

Љубими предраги друже!

Ево ме већ, фала богу, у одавно чувеној и задуго пожељеној Инглитери, у граду Доверу. По Францији ходећи и пролазећи чињаше ми се на неки начин и земља и људи познати, јер језик њихов знађах и са сваким могах говорити, а овде–нигде ни слова! Старо и младо, жена и дете, све ти то инглески говори, нити им можеш разабрати шта ти људи мисле, шта ли хоће. Гледам жене и девојке: лепа су то створења да ништа лепшега на свету нити је могуће видити ни помислити. Хиљаду очију да сам имао, и за хиљаду година не бих их се могао нагледати. Колико их више гледаш, толико ти се лепше чине. Хоћеш ли да си читав, иди својим путем, нити их гледај, јер ако диже очи и погледа, већ не оде даље; ту ћеш остати до века. Та и по другим земљама има лепота, али су свуда по вишој части лепе поносите, пак како их човек види да се горде и чудеса о себи мисле, не мари за њих– нек иду својим путем. Ал' ево чуда овде, гди рекао би да оне нити маре, нити мисле, нити знаду да су прекрасне, него гледају на свакога с таковим природним и простосердечним очима, а у исто време с отвореним пријатељским и благохотним лицем, баш као да га одавно познају.

Сад нека представи и вообрази себи, ко може, како је мени морало бити кад сам се међу оваковим божијим прекрасним створе-

THE LIFE AND ADVENTURES OF DIMITRIJE OBRADOVIĆ, CALLED IN MONASTIC LIFE DOSITEJ WRITTEN OUT AND PUBLISHED BY HIM

The example of other nations gives me courage. There will be enough clever and fairminded individuals among my brothers who will recognize whose interest and benefit I have desired and sought in my writing. If there should be an error here or there learned people will correct it after me, and they will pardon me charitably, as a fellow human being. Setting an example for the learned people of my nation, so that they may begin to publish something good in Serbian, is comfort enough for me. It's a pity that such a populous nation should remain without books in its own language at a time when, close by, science is shining like a sun in the heavens. ...

* * *

Beloved, dearest friend!

Here I am already, thank God, in the long famed and long wished-for England, in the city of Dover. While I was touring and travelling through France, both the country and the people seemed familiar to me somehow, because I knew their language and could talk with everyone, but here—not a word anywhere! Old and young, woman and child, all of them speak English; nor can you figure out what these people are thinking, or what they want. I look at the women and the girls: they are such beautiful creatures that it is impossible to see or to imagine anything more beautiful in the world. Were I to have a thousand eyes and a thousand years I wouldn't be able to see enough of them. The more you look at them the more beautiful they seem to you. If you want to remain of sound mind, keep moving and don't even look at them, because if you raise your eyes and take a look you'll go no further; you'll remain here forever. Of course there is beauty in other countries, too, but beautiful women everywhere are mostly proud, and once a man sees they are proud and think marvellous things about themselves he doesn't pay attention to them—let them go their way! But what a wonderful thing it is here, where I would say they neither care, nor think, nor know that they are beautiful, and they look at everyone with such natural and artless eyes, and at the same time with an open, friendly, and kindly face, as if they had known you for a long time.

Now just imagine and picture, if you can, how I must have felt

њем нашао, не могући с њима ни речи проговорити. Милостиви, благи боже, мишљах у себи, тешко ли су ти људи сагрешили били кад си им толике и тако различне језике дао! То ти је њима њихов торо̂њ донео и пре времена на небо пењање, као да им је мало земље било да по њојзи ходе. А кад се већ здраво на оне прве исрдим људе, онда топрв почнем се сам на себе срдити, гди толики живише и живу и данас без инглеског језика и књига, а мени се не може живити, ако не сазнам шта мисле ови људи, како живу, шта ли се и у њиховим находи књигама. Хоћеш Инглитеру? Ево ти је; ајде сад говори с људма.

Душа человеческа има ово у себи добро својство: како је о чем нибуд оскорбљена, она природно брже-боље тражи способно средство како ће себе утешити. Из овога зар узрока и мени дођу на памет неки лепи латински стихови, но нипошто не памтим ни гди сам их читао нити ко је њихов списатељ; доста–они мене утеше. Ово су:

Non quisquam fruitur veris odoribus,
Hyblaeos latebris nec spoliat favos,
Si fronti caveat, si timeat rubos;
Armat spina rosas, mella tegunt apes.

Нико не ужива пролећне мирисе,
Из хиблејских пећина не извлачи сате,
Ако чело чува и боји се купине;
Вооружава трн ружицу, мед бране пчеле.

О неваљало малодушије, помислим у себи. Ако не знам инглески, а ја сам баш онде гди ваља за научити. Многоцене вешти не купују се за малу цену.

Један млад свештеник, римокатолик из Ирландије, који се је у Францији учио, сад иђаше натраг у своје отечество и пут му бијаше на Лондон; с овим пођем у друштво. Пред вече остановимо се у древњејшем Инглитере, на предивном високом положенију граду, зовомом Канторбери, за преноћити овде. Имали смо пре ноћи два часа времена за обићи велика зданија архиепископије и великолепну старинску церков....

Како ми је пак било сутрадан с високих места на ужасне величине непрегледатог пространства красњејши и славњејши на свету град Лондои гледајући, о овом не знам ни речи рећи. Свештеник Ирландез и ја имали смо прво седалиште у великом инглеском интову; но полазећи из Канторбера, дао сам моје место другом, а пошао сам сести на покров интова (и ту се на лепом времену комодно седи) за моћи боље свуда гледати. И сам сам се себи крстио и чудио у какав ме је блажен час мила мати моја зачела. Гди сам ја ово сад? Ко ли сам ја? Чињаше ми се као да сам се изнова у некакав нови свет родио. Необично представљаше ми се постигнути јесам ли ја онај исти који пре неколико дана с мојим комшијом, Ником Путиним, из Баната све

when I found myself in the midst of such beautiful, divine creatures, and I unable to utter even a word to them! "Merciful, sweet God," I thought to myself, "those people must have sinned mightily against you, for you to have given them so many and such different languages. That's what their tower brought them, and their climbing to heaven before their time, as if there were too little earth for them to walk around on." And after I had fully vented my anger at those first people–only then did I begin to get angry at myself, because so many people have lived and are living today, too, without the English language and English books, but I can't live if I don't learn what these people are thinking, how they live, and what is to be found in their books. So it's England you want? Well, here she is; now go and speak with the people.

The human spirit has this good quality: when it has been hurt by something, it naturally seeks, as quickly as possible, a suitable form of consolation. This is exactly why there came to my mind some beautiful Latin verses, but for the life of me I can't remember where I read them or who their author is; enough–they console me. Here they are:

> No one enjoys the scents of Spring,
> Nor extracts the honeycomb from Hyblaean caves,
> If he guards his forehead and fears the bramblebush;
> The thorn arms the rose, bees guard the honey.

"O wretched cowardice," I thought to myself. "Even though I don't know English, I am just where one should be in order to learn it. Things of value are not purchased at a low price."

A young priest, a Roman Catholic from Ireland who had been studying in France, was now returning to his fatherland, and his route was via London; I set out together with him. Toward evening we stopped to spend the night in the most ancient part of England, at a city called Canterbury, situated in a most wonderful, high location. We had two hours before nightfall in which to tour the large buildings of the archbishop's see and the magnificent ancient church....

I am incapable of saying even a word about how I felt the next day, looking from high places at the awesome dimensions of the vast expanse of London, the most beautiful and most famous city in the world. The Irish priest and I had the front seat in the large English coach; but as we were setting out from Canterbury I gave my seat to somebody else, and I went to sit on the roof of the coach (when the weather is good one can sit comfortably there, too), so that I might have a better view in all directions. And I crossed myself and I wondered at what lucky hour my mother must have conceived me. Where am I now? Who am I? It seemed strange for me to realize that I was the same person who some days before had walked with my neighbor Nika Putin from the Banat,

покрај Бегеја у Срем, а одавде у црвени ајдучки опанци с Атанасијем покрај Дунава у Хорватску у великој итошти иђах? Сад на покрову таквог интова, у који за улести ваља се пењати по мердевинам, седим као неки римски диктатор, и победивши љуту скудост и суровог мучитеља убожество, аки у победоносном триумфу улазим у славнији и лепши град, него је икада Рим био, вмењајући себе тако благополучна зато што га видим и у њега улазим, аки би сав мој био прекрасни Лондон.

Љубими мој, ласно је предвидити да сарданапалскаго духа и мудрованија љубитељи и почитатељи, који све блаженство у наслажденију гортана и у пријатном и изобилном преспољенију црева полажу и који по теготи кесе и злата цену душе и достоинство ума мере и цене; такови ће се без сумњенија овом мојем хваљењу и дичењу не само као детињском и простачком него као безумном посмејавати. Но, с друге стране, они који познају небесно и божествено благородство словесне и разумне душе, који умеду распознати несравњено отличије бесмертнога и вечнога богатства разума, срца и нарава од привременога и земнога; они (били Инглези били други) који списанија Адизонова, Свифтова, Попе и овима подобних без свакога сравњенија више него сва зданија Лондона града почитују и цене, заисто нећe се посмејати, но весма ће похвалити и даће ми право. Ево овоме просто и осјазатељно доказатељство, које и слеп, ако не видити, а он опипати може. ... Ко је био икада већи и богатији од царева персијских, македонских и римских? Ко се је већма у сласти ваљао од Сарданапала, Криса и различних других султана, хана и сатрапа? Пак гди је то све сад? Нигда. Нестало, пропало и ишчезло да му ни трага нема, како год ластавици која кроз воздух лети. А списанија просвештених науком умова? Нећу ни Омирова ни Аристотелова спомињати, зашто њихових имаде одвећ много, него само неколико стихова Симонидових, Фоцилидових, Солонових и Менандрових, којих је врло мало, али су свету полезнији и народу овихречених људи славнији него све оних више поменутих сласти, богатства и сујетне помпе. ...

Свештеник Ирландез учини ми љубов и позна ме с једним магистром деце, Инглезом, који умеђаше којекако францески. С овим се погодим да ми даје лекције, квартир и храну за три гинеје на месец; то чини око двадесет и пет форинти. Купити нужне књиге, и за то се хоће неколико. Кад учиним мој еспап, нађем да имам трошити за три месеца.

Плаше ме да је изговарање инглеског језика весма мучно, а њега разумјеније за једнога ко зна немецки и францускИ, при том и

all along the Begaj River into Srem, and from there, in red haiduk sandals, had gone in great haste with Atanasije along the Danube into Croatia. Now, on the roof of a coach that one enters only by climbing a ladder, I was sitting like some Roman dictator, and having overcome harsh want and poverty, that fierce tormenter, as in victorious triumph I was entering a more glorious and beautiful city than Rome had ever been, thinking myself so fortunate because I was seeing and entering beautiful London as though it were all mine.

My dear friend, it is easy to foresee that the devotees and admirers of the spirit and philosophizing of Sardanapalus, who see all bliss in delights of the palate and in the pleasant and bountiful cramming of the intestines, and who measure and evaluate the worth of a soul and the dignity of a mind by the weight of the purse and of gold,—that such people will undoubtedly laugh at this boasting and pride of mine, not only as something childish and simpleminded, but as something crazy. But on the other hand, those who recognize the heavenly and divine nobility of the educated and rational spirit, who know how to distinguish the incomparable difference between the immortal and eternal riches of reason, heart, and morals, and what is temporary and earthly—those people (whether they be Englishmen or others) who respect and value the writings of Addison, Swift, Pope and the like incomparably more highly than all the buildings of London town, truly will not laugh at me, but will praise me fully and will agree with me. Here is a simple and tangible example, which even the blind man can feel, even though he cannot see it. ... Who was ever greater and richer than the Persian, Macedonian, and Roman emperors? Who ever lolled in delights greater than those of Sardanapalus, Croesus and various other sultans, khans, and satraps? And where is all that now? Nowhere; it has gone, vanished, and disappeared, so that there isn't even a trace of it—like the swallow that flies through the air. But what about the writings of minds enlightened by learning? I won't even mention those of Homer and Aristotle, because we have many of their writings, but let me mention only some of the verses of Simonides, Phocylides, Solon, and Menander, of which there are very few, and yet they are more beneficial to the world and bring more glory to the nation of these writers than all the delights, riches, and vain pomp of the above mentioned men. ...

The Irish priest was kind enough to introduce me to a teacher of children, an Englishman who knew a bit of French. I arranged with this man to give me lessons, lodging, and board for three guineas a month; that amounts to about twenty-five florins. To buy the necesarry books would also require a few guineas. When I totalled everything up I found that I had enough money for three months.

People were frightening me by saying that English pronunciation would be a total torment, but that understanding it would be quite easy

латински, да је весма ласно. Што бог да, мислим, кад је мени разумјеније језика готово, његовом изговору преодолећу ја, ако ће он бити седамдесетоглавна хидра. А кад ли ме почну учити, чисто ми се кожа узме јежити и длаке на мени узгору дизати. Загазио сам, ајде напред! Трудољубије у друштву с постојанством многом послу дође на крај. Ови се узао не да пресећи као Гордијев. Сам Александер овде да дође, морао би га размршивати; мач његов не би му ништа помогао. И да сам самога учитеља имао, о једном сату на дан ништа не бих учинио; но велико добро за ме што сам поваздан у кући за сваку реч и по много реди за исту реч имао кога питати. Старица, мати учитељева, жена његова, сестра, брат, снаха и ко би год у кућу из комшилука дошао, сви су то били моји предраги и мили учитељи, и желим им срдечно благополучан од бога живот. Љубезно су ме и радо настављали и учили, и често би се отимали ко ће ми што боље и лакше казати. ...

По обеду запитају ме да им прави узрок откријем зашто, будући таков љубитељ њихова језика, тако скоро из Англије полазим. С оваковим људма чистосердечну не бити, ово би точно светотатство било. „Који ћете правији узрок од овога"–одговорим–„него, прво, што нејмам новаца, а друго, ни од кога на свету није ми вексела чекати." „Ако је то само"–рече ми мистер Ливи–„није нужда да одлазиш: ја ћу ти сваки дан по ручку лекције давати, а ручати и вечерати можеш с нами."

По неколико дана нађу ми и квартир баш у свом комшилуку. Ово је доказатељство онога што сам повише рекао, да јединствено за недостатак трошка получио сам познанство ових неописане доброте људи. ...

Одлазио бих у дом мојега господина Ливи сваки дан у десети или једанаести час пред подне, и с помоћу и наставленијем његове пречестне супруге читао бих изговора ради, а потом преводио бих коју Езопову басну с греческога језика на инглески. И она би сваки дан по један сат што гречески читала, који језик она и муж њен весма љубљаху. И тако би се проводило време до обеда, то јест до два часа по полудне. Затим до саме вечере господин Ливи (кад не би куд за делом својим изишао) би ме учио. ...

На неколико недеља затим дође из Харвича госпође Ливи сестра, мистрис Телар, и брат њејзин, м[исте]р Кок, на посештеније. Већ после тога сваки дан бивале су како у њиховом дому тако и код других њихових пријатеља части и весеља и прохођања по најлепши мести града и наоколо, куда сам и ја почти свуда морао ходити. Ово би ме неколико чинило дангубити, но с друге стране било ми је мило и полезно, дајући ми начин боље познати љубведостојњејша свој-

for one who already knew German and French, as well as Latin. "May God grant that it be so," I thought; "since understanding the language is already a sure thing, I shall conquer its pronunciation, though it be a seventy-headed hydra." But when they began to teach me, my skin simply began to break out in goose pimples, and my hair began to stand on end. I had taken the first step, so forward march! This knot can't be cut like the Gordian knot. If Alexander the Great himself were to come here, he would have to unravel it; his sword wouldn't help him a bit. And if I had had only the teacher for one hour a day I wouldn't have accomplished a thing; but it was a great boon for me that all day I had someone in the house whom I could ask about many words, and many times about the same word. The old mother of the teacher, his wife, sister, brother, sister-in-law, and whoever in the neighborhood would drop in,–all were my dearest and kindest teachers, and I sincerely wish that God will grant them a happy life. They kindly and gladly instructed and taught me, and often they would compete to see who could give me the better and simpler explanations. ...

After dinner they asked me to disclose to them the real reason why I, who loved their language so much, was leaving England so soon. Not to have been frank with such people would have been a simple sacrilege. "What reason could be more real than this," I answered: "first of all I haven't any money, and secondly, there's no one in the world from whom I could expect a bank draft." "If that's all there's to it," said Mr. Livie–"there's no need for you to leave: I shall give you lessons every day after dinner, and you can have dinner and supper with us."

After a few days they found me lodging right in their neighborhood. This is proof of what I said a little earlier, that solely because of lack of funds I made the acquaintance of these indescribably good people. ...

I used to visit the home of Mr. Livie every day at ten or eleven a.m., and with the help and instruction of his most honorable wife I would read for pronunciation practice, and then I would translate one of Aesop's fables from Greek into English. And for an hour every day she would read something in Greek, a language which she and her husband loved entirely. And that is how the time was spent until dinner, that is, until two o'clock in the afternoon. From then until supper Mr. Livie would teach me (unless he had to go somewhere on business). ...

A few weeks later Mrs. Livie's sister, Mrs. Taylor, and her brother, Mr. Coke, came from Harwich for a visit. From then on there were parties and good times every day, both in their home and at the homes of their friends, as well as excursions to the most beautiful places in the city and its suburbs, and I almost always had to go along. I lost some time as a result of this, but on the other hand, it was pleasant and profitable for me, because it gave me the opportunity to become better acquainted

ства и непреухиштрена но проста и чистосердечна опхожденија Инглезов. И кромје ових гостију, мој пријатељ господин Ливи свакога фторника частио би неке своје пријатеље од учених људи, а свакога петка бивали би у довољном содружеству на части у господина Гулјелма Фордајц, медика и златнога руна кавалера, којему је краљ ово достоинство дао за његову отменост у медическом знању. Ови достојњејши господин б'јаше срдечни пријатељ мојега благодјетеља Ливи, и како ме чрез њега позна, постане и мој особити патрон, наложивши својему љубимому, док год будем у Лондону, да ми даје на његов конат што ми год буде од потребе за књиге или за хаљине и за прочи ситни трошак.

Све ово благородно великодушије и вечнога воспоминанија достојну доброту Инглезов не бих могао искусити и познати, да се нисам у потреби нашао. Од мене је сад зависило, да сам хотео за живота остати у Инглитери, зашто, како ја радо лекције предајем, како бих језик места совершено постигао, могао бих весма лепо ту живити. Човек од колевке до гроба мора имати каковунибуд поглавиту жељу која њим совершено влада. Дете ни за што тако не мари као за игру, јуноша жели науку или другу коју забаву–како се ко на што да и окрене. Добро за онога ко изберe то што је честно, похвално и полезно. Моја је жеља у ово време сва у том состојала се да јошт који лист на мојем матерњем језику издам. Сам сам по себи судио како би мени у мојеј младости не токмо полезно но и мило било што паметно на мојем познатом дијалекту читати. Како бих ја благодаран био ономе од рода мојега који се је за то постарао, и што је сам с довољним трудом и позадуго времена постигао, то исто уму и души мојеј без труда и у кратко време приподаје! Ово исто, дакле, што бих ја о другима мислио и чувствовао, то ћеду, природно, други о мени. Какововo ласкатељно предслућивање! Какова слатка бесмертнаго живота надежда! Збогом, дакле, нек остане не само Лондон и Париз него које му драго на свету место, гди ја ову моју верховњејшу жељу исполнити не бих могао. Зато, како и друга три месеца прођу, познам изговор језика инглескога и видим себе у состојанију да могу и сам о себи у напредак напредовати, јавим мојим пријатељем и благодјетељем да морам поћи. Бог сам зна како ми је жао било ове преслатке људе оставити! Већ сам ту рекао да ћу се одсад крепко чувати да се с ником живим тако не пријатељим кад се морам растати и жалити што с њима нисам до гроба.

Господин Гулијелм Фордајц наложи мистер Ливи да ми купи књига лепих, и да се извести колико се хоће трошка по мору до Хамбурга и одавде до Лајпсика, и да ми то да. Један трактат на латинском

with the most amiable qualities of the English. And in addition to these guests, my friend Mr. Livie would give a party every Tuesday for some of his friends in the scholarly community, and every Friday we would be in pleasant company at parties at the home of Mr. William Fordyce, a physician and Knight of the Golden Fleece, to whom the king had awarded this honor in recognition of his eminence in medical science. This most worthy gentleman was a close friend of my benfactor, Mr. Livie, and after he had got to know me through him he became my special patron, instructing his dear friend to give me, on his account, whatever I needed for books or clothes or other minor expenses while I was in London.

All this noble magnanimity and kindness of the English, worthy of eternal remembrance, I should not have been able to experience and know had I not found myself in need. Now it depended on me whether I wanted to remain in England for life, since I would have been able to live quite nicely there, once I had completely learned the language and could give lessons, which I enjoy doing. From the cradle to the grave a man should have some principal desire which completely rules him. A child cares for nothing as much as he does for play, a young man desires learning or some other entertainment—everyone turns to something. Happy the one who chooses something honorable, praiseworthy, and useful. At that time my only desire was to publish one or two pages more in my mother tongue. On the basis of my own experience I had come to the opinion that it would have been not only useful but pleasant in my youth to have read something intelligent in my own familiar dialect. How grateful I should have been to that member of my nation who had endeavored to do that, and who had managed to impart to my mind and soul, quickly and without effort, that same knowledge which he himself had acquired through much labor and over a long period of time! It is natural, therefore, that what I should have thought and felt about others, others will think and feel about me. What a flattering thing to look forward to! What a sweet hope for immortality! Farewell, then, not only to London and Paris, but to any other place in the world where I could not realize this supreme desire of mine. When the second three-month period had passed, therefore, and I had learned the pronunciation of the English language and felt able to make further progress on my own, I notified my friends and benefactors that I must go. God himself only knows how sorry I was to leave these very sweet people! Indeed it was then that I said that henceforth I should strongly guard against becoming such close friends with any living being, since I would have to part with them and would regret that I could not be with them to the grave.

Mr. William Fordyce instructed Mr. Livie to buy me some beautiful books and to find out what it would cost to go by sea to Hamburg, and from there to Leipzig, and to give me that amount. He also gave me as a special and lasting remembrance a treatise in Latin, entitled "Fragmenta

језику, зовоми „Fragmenta hirurgica et medica”, у којему он своје својствене важњејше опите описује, и који је у моје време ту на штампу издао, за особито и всегдашње воспоминаније даде ми. У овој књижици овако се обојица потпишу:

Dositheo Obradovics, Serbiano, viro linguis variis erudito, sanctissimis moribus morato, Anglis, apud quos per sex menses diversatus est, perquam dilecto, Fragmenta haecce, parvulum quidem at amoris sincerissimi et amicitiae pignus, libentissime merito obtulerunt.

Londoni,
VIII. kal. junii MDCCLXXXV

Gulielmus Fordyce
Joannes Livie

Chirurgica et Medica," in which he describes his most important experiments, and which he had had published during my stay there. They both signed this book as follows:

Dositheo Obradovics, Serbiano, viro linguis variis erudito, sanctissimis moribus morato, Anglis, apud quos per sex menses diversatus est, perquam dilecto, Fragmenta haecce, parvulum quidem at amoris sincerissimi et amicitiae pignus, libentissime merito obtulerunt.

Londoni,
VIII. kal. junii MDCCLXXXV

Gulielmus Fordyce
Joannes Livie

V

REVOLUTION AND ROMANTICISM

Old Serbia

The Serbian Governing Council

In publishing his Miloš Obrenović *(1828) Vuk Karadžić stated in the Foreword: "In writing this book I never lost sight of the* truth, *which is the most important thing in history, nor of* posterity, *for which history is written."*

Vuk firmly believed that the eye-witnesses of the First Serbian Uprising (1804-1813) should record what they saw for history, and he strongly feared the kinds of misstatements and misinterpretations being made about Serbia and the Balkans by foreign writers such as D. N. Bantiš-Kamenskij, in his Putešestvije v Moldaviju, Valaxiju i Serbiju *(Moscow, 1810). Vuk was aware that Europe knew very little about Serbia, and he felt it necessary to acquaint foreign readers with the background of the Serbian struggle for independence if the Serbs were ever to attract outside support in maintaining their freedom.*

Vuk's account of the operations of the Serbian Governing Council was not published until 1860, in Vienna. In his Foreword the aged Vuk, who had experienced not only Serbia's struggle for independence but also his own long struggle for the acceptance of his new simplified alphabet and orthography, marvels at the fact that 2357 Serbs had subscribed to his book in advance. He took this to signify that not only were Serbs interested in their own history, but that literacy was no longer rare among them.

Our text is from Vuk's Sabrana dela, *XVI (Beograd:Prosveta, 1964, 49-96).*

„ПРАВИТЕЛСТВУЮЩІИ СОВѢТЪ СЕРБСКІИ" ЗА ВРЕМЕНА КАРА-ЂОРЂИЈЕВА или ОТИМАЊЕ ОНДАШЊИЈЕХ ВЕЛИКАША ОКО ВЛАСТИ

написао
ВУК СТЕФ. КАРАЏИЋ

Кад један од прве Руске господе запита Српске посланике /прота Матију Ненадовића, Јована Протића и Петра Чардаклију/ у Петербургу на свршетку године 1804., ко им је старјешина у Србији, прото Ненадовић одговори, да немају никаквога једног старјешине, него да нахије имају своје старјешине, које се између себе договарају и савјетују. На то им рекне онај Руски господин, да ваља да поставе „совѣтъ" састављен од људи из свију нахија, који ће народом и земљом управљати и заповиједати свијем старјешинама. Ово проту Ненадовићу и Јовану Протићу буде врло по вољи, јер су знали, да Јаков Ненадовић, протов стриц, и Миленко Стојковић, који је Јована Протића одредио на овај пут, никако не би ради да им Кара-Ђорђије заповиједа.

Кад се ови посланици Српски године 1805. врате у Србију, прото Ненадовић и Божо Грујовић, којега су посланици из Русије довели са собом, навале једнако око Јакова да се постави совјет, које и Јакову буде по вољи. И тако оне исте године, пошто освоје Карановац и Ужичани им се предаду и плате уцјену, Јаков позове Кара-Ђорђија да дође о Великој госпођи у манастир Боговађу, да се о томе разговоре и договоре. Но Кара-Ђорђије не хтједне отићи у Боговађу, него он дозове Јакова у нахију Биоградску у село Борак, и ондје се сазову и остале знатније поглавице, те уреде, да свака нахија изабере по једнога поштена и паметна човјека, па ти сви људи да се састану на једно мјесто, да суде и пресуђују све веће распре и тужбе земаљске, и ето тако постане у Србији совјет, који се у почетку највише звао *синод* или *скупштина*; а на печату /на коме су били грбови Србије — под круном крст и четири оцила — и Тривалије — под круном свињска глава са стријелом забоденом у чело — који су на сриједи свезани један за други и између њих расте крин; одозго огријало сунце и луче своје спустило до круна, а доље испод грбова „1804"/ био је натпис: *„правителствующій совѣтъ сербскій"*. Совјет се овај најприје намјести у манастиру Вољавчи, у нахији Рудничкој, но будући да ондје

THE SERBIAN GOVERNING COUNCIL DURING THE TIME OF KARADJORDJE
or
THE STRUGGLE FOR POWER AMONG THE LEADERS OF THAT TIME

VUK STEFANOVIĆ KARADŽIĆ

When one of the leading members of the Russian aristocracy asked the Serbian emissaries (Prota Matija Nenadović, Jovan Protić and Petar Čardaklija) in Petersburg, at the end of 1804, who was their leader in Serbia, Prota Nenadović answered that they didn't have any single leader, but that the districts had their own leaders, who discussed things among themselves and consulted one another. On hearing this, that Russian gentleman said that they should form a "council" composed of people from all the districts, which would govern the people and the country, and would give orders to all the leaders. This pleased Prota Nenadović and Jovan Protić, because they knew that Jakov Nenadović, the Prota's uncle, and Milenko Stojković, who had chosen Jovan Protić for this trip, would in no way like to have Karadjordje give them orders.

When these Serbian emissaries returned to Serbia in 1805 Prota Nenadović and Božo Grujović, whom they had brought with them from Russia, continually urged Jakov to form a council, an idea which Jakov liked too. And so that very same year, after they had captured Karanovac and after the natives of Užica had surrendered to them and paid a ransom, Jakov invited Karadjordje to come to Bogovadja Monastery on the day of the Assumption of the Blessed Virgin, so that they could talk about this matter and come to some agreement. But Karadjordje didn't want to go to Bogovadja, and instead he summoned Jakov to the village of Borak, in the Belgrade district, and other influential leaders were also convened there, and they ordered that each district should select one honorable and intelligent man, and that all these men should convene in one place, in order to hear cases and to pass judgment on all important national disputes and complaints, and that's how there came to be a council in Serbia, which in the beginning was most often called a synod or assembly; and on its seal (on which were the coats of arms of Serbia—a cross and four pieces of flint steel under a crown—and of Trivalija—a pig's head with an arrow stuck in its forehead under a crown—which were linked to one another through the center, and between them grew a lily; from above a rising sun sent its rays down to the crowns, while

у пустињи нити су имали совјетници шта јести, нити је ко долазио да се суди, за то се премјести у манастир Боговађу а оданде послије некога времена у Смедерево. Први су совјетници постали она троица, што су били у Русији, то јест: прото Ненадовић, који је био као и предсједник, од нахије Ваљевске, и Јован Протић, од нахије Пожаревачке, и Божо Грујовић као секретар или писар; а послије је дошао Вукоман из нахије Јагодинске, Аврам Лукић из нахије Пожешке, Младен Миловановић из нахије Крагујевачке, Јанко Ђурђевић из нахије Смедеревске и Милија Здравковић из нахије Ћупријске.

Српске поглавице пристану и поставе совјет, али управо нијесу знале, шта ће то да буде; него су Јаков и Катић, и други гдјекој већи, мислили, да совјетом мало зауздају власт Кара-Ђорђијеву, а Кара-Ђорђије мислио је, да њиме плаши Јакова и Катића, и друге, који би му се противили; а сви су мислили да ће совјет само којекаке ситнице судити, па и то онако, како они хоће, а остало све да они сами уређују и заповиједају по својој вољи; Божо пак и прото Ненадовић мислили су, да совјет буде највећа власт у земљи, и да свима поглавицама заповиједа у свачему, као што свједочи и натпис на печату: „*Правителствующій* совѣтъ", јер *правительствовать* у Руском језику значи: „Имѣть правительственную, или верховную власть".

Тако је совјет у Вољавчи и у Боговађи за она неколика мјесеца само судио, ако му је ко на суд дошао; али сад намјестивши се у Смедереву и уредивши своју канцеларију, стане се мијешати и у земаљске уредбе и старати се мало по мало да власт себи присвоји. Тога ради Божо и прото Ненадовић и Биоградски владика Леонтије /који је у почетку године 1805. изишавши из Биограда остао међу Србима, и у Смедереву се помијешао међу совјетнике/ наговоре којекако Кара-Ђорђија и остале поглавице, да се сад опет у Смедереву сазове скупштина, да се совјет потврди и призна за највећу власт у земљи. Кад се та скупштина састане и у совјетној канцеларији каже се управо, шта се хоће, онда Кара-Ђорђије, видећи да му се гледа власт из руку да узме, изиђе на поље, па са својијем момцима, којијех је било више него у свију осталијех поглавица, опколи ону кућицу гдје је совјет био, и промоливши кроз прозоре пушке у канцеларију, повиче: „На поље, курве, по души вас ....! Лако је у врућој соби уређивати и заповиједати; него да вас видим сјутра у пољу, кад Турци ударе". Катић истина проговори: „Бог с тобом, Ђорђије, шта је теби?

under the coats of arms was "1804" and the inscription "Serbian Governing Council"). This Council was first situated in the Monastery of Voljavča, in the Rudnik district, but in that wilderness the councillors neither had anything to eat nor did anyone come there to stand trial, and for that reason it was moved to the monastery of Bogovadja, and after some time it was moved from there to Smederevo. The first councillors were the three men who had been in Russia, namely: Prota Nenadović, who served as its chairman, from the district of Valjevo, Jovan Protić, from the district of Požarevac, and Božo Grujović, its secretary or scribe; and later there came Vukoman from the district of Jagodin, Avram Lukić from the district of Požega, Mladen Milovanović from Kragujevac district, Janko Djurdjević from Smederevo district, and Milija Zdravković from the district of Ćuprija.

The Serbian leaders agreed to establish a council, but they didn't really know what it would be like; rather, Jakov [Nenadović–trans.] and Katić, and other influential men thought that they might use the Council to curb Karadjordje's power, and Karadjordje thought that he might use it to frighten Jakov and Katić, as well as others who might oppose him; and they all thought that the Council would judge only some minor matters or other, and in the way they wanted it to judge them, and that they would take care of everything else and would give orders as they saw fit; Božo and Prota Nenadović, however, thought that the Council would be the supreme power in the country, and that it would give commands to all the leaders on everything, as is evidenced by the inscription on the seal: "Pravitel'stvujuščii Sovět," because *pravitel'stvovat'* in Russian means: "to have the governing or supreme power."

Thus during the several months the council was in Voljavča and Bogovadja it only tried cases when someone came to court for trial; but now, when it had established itself in Smederevo and had set up its own office, it began to get involved in national laws and to endeavor, little by little, to take over the power for itself. With this in mind, Božo and Prota Nenadović and Bishop Leontije (who at the beginning of 1805 had left Belgrade and stayed with the Serbs, and in Smederevo had got mixed up with the councillors) somehow persuaded Karadjordje and the other leaders that now again in Smederevo there should be convened a national assembly, so that the council might be confirmed and recognized as the supreme power in the land. When the assembly convened, and they were told in the Council office just what exactly was desired of them, it was then that Karadjordje, realizing that they wanted to take the power out of his hands, went outside and surrounded the Council's little house with his soldiers, who outnumbered those of all the other leaders, and after they had stuck their guns through the windows of the office he shouted: "Outside, you whores; .... your souls! It's easy to run things and give orders from a warm room, but let's see you tomorrow on the battlefield when the Turks attack." True, Katić did say:

Нијеси ти полудио; ходи унутра;" Јаков, ваљада бојећи се од своје нахије тако далеко ићи и с Кара-Ђорђијем се у граду затјецати, није ту био ни дошао, а совјетници и друге мање и страшивије поглавице оборе очи преда се; и тако се овај разговор прекине: Кара-Ђорђије и све остале поглавице остану као и дотле, а совјет и непотврђен за највећу власт стане се све више и више мијешати у различне уредбе земаљске. Да би се боље видјело како је совјет Српски онда заповиједао, и како се називао и потписивао, вриједно је овдје додати једно његово писмо, писано у самом почетку његова уређивања Петру Добрињцу. Ево га од слова до слова:

Благопоченородный Г Бинбаша Петре
Здравствȣите!

Вашима мољцима, кои сȣ дошли на заповесть Господар Ђорђа ȣ скȣпщинȣ поради Скела Пожаревачкїи за Васъ, — даемо ово Писмо, и Вамъ Являмо, да е овай Совѣтъ народный Заключио, да се нїедна скела, никоме не прода; него да овай Синодъ Свꙋда на све скеле свое люде метне; Тако Мы не дамо ниедномȣ поглаварȣ скеле державати, да се народъ не бȣни; како што сȣ почели были, — И тако смо већъ метнȣли на Забрежскȣ, и Грочанскȣ скелȣ наше люде; а на дрȣге спремамо. — Зато Вамъ отписȣемо да ће скȣпщина ова и Пожаревачке скеле державати, као и дрȣге, — и Вы више немойтесе ништа ȣ скеле мешати, и рȣке извадите — а Нашь ће човекъ тамо скоро поставлѣнъ быти

Съ тимъ Васъ любезно поздравлямо.
Ȣ Смедеревȣ 15° Декем. 1805.

Протоерей Матѳей Ненадовичъ,
(м. п.) Председатель Совѣта съ целимъ Синодомъ.

Вы сте войвода, — маните се такови послова, и скела, — веће добро воинике Ваше гледайте, и уређуйте.

Поглавице су до сад једнако народу говориле, да се они не бију с царем Турскијем, него, по заповијести царској, с дахијама и с крџалијама; али сад /у почетку године 1807./, убивши царева везира и искрстивши Турске жене и дјецу по Биограду и по Шапцу, то се више није могло говорити ни вјеровати, него кметови навале на поглавице:

"God be with you, Djordje, what's the matter with you? You haven't gone crazy; come on inside." Jakov had not even come there, probably because he was afraid to go so far from his district and to meet with Karadjordje in the town; and the councillors, and other lesser and more fearful leaders, lowered their eyes and gave in; and so this discussion was broken off: Karadjordje and all the other leaders remained as they had been before, and the Council, even though unconfirmed as supreme power, began more and more to involve itself in various national statutes. It is worthwhile to include here one of the Council's letters, written to Petar Dobrinjac at the very beginning of its administration, so that one might see how the Council governed, and what it called and signed itself. Here it is, word for word:

> Honorably born Mr. Major Petar, Greetings!
>
> We are giving this letter to your soldiers who have come to the council at the order of Gospodar Djordje in order to get the Požarevac ferry for you; and we inform you that this national Council has decided not to sell any ferries to anyone, but rather to put its own people on all the ferries everywhere; so we aren't giving a single leader a ferry to maintain, so that the people won't be stirred up, as they had begun to be–and so we have already placed our people on the Zabrežje and Grocka ferries; and we are getting ready to do the same with the others.– Therefore, our answer to you is that this council will keep the Požarevac ferry, as well as the others – and don't you have anything more to do with the ferries, and keep your hands off them–and our man will soon be appointed there.
>
> With kind greetings to you.
> In Smederevo, December 15, 1805.
>
> Archpriest Matija Nenadović,
> Chairman of the Council, and the
> whole Council.

Up to now the leaders had told the people that they were not fighting against the Turkish Sultan, but rather they were fighting at the Sultan's command against the Janissary rebels and irregulars; not now (in the beginning of 1807), when they had killed a vezir of the Sultan and had baptized Turkish women and children in and around Belgrade and Šabac, this could no longer be said nor believed, but instead the local

„Ми се сами не можемо борити с царством Турскијем, него нам дај-те цара, који ће нас се примити, и коме ћемо се ми за скут ухватити." За то се старјешине договоре, и одреде Петра Чардаклију, и Аврама Лукића, совјетника нахије Пожешке, и совјетскога писара Јеремију Гагића, те их пошаљу у Карабогданску, у Руски главни квартир, да се договоре с Русима за помоћ, која ће се Србима давати, и да ишту једнога Рускога министра, да га доведу у Србију, једно да се народ увјери, да су се Руси заиста примили Србије, а друго, да их којешта поучава и да се с њим о свачему могу договарати. Посланици ови дошавши у Јаш нађу ондје дејствитељнога статског совјетника Константина Константиновића Родофиникина /којега су Срби назвали и звали *Родофиником*, као што ћу и ја у напредак овдје писати/ родом Грка, с којијем се Чардаклија још из Петербурга познавао. Дознавши Родофиник да посланици ови хоће да ишту једнога Рускога министра у Србију, он им се стане нудити и наметати да ишту управо њега. И тако они, или изнајприје и не знајући да је Родофиник Грк или не мислећи како се Срби и Грци рђаво слажу, замоле се фелдмаршалу да им даде Родофиника да га воде у Србију, и фелдмаршал им га да. Пошто посланици сврше своје послове и стану се спремати натраг, даду им се на дар три прстена с драгијем камењем и неколико стотина дуката на пут. Прстење друкчије нијесу могли подијелити, него њима тројици свакоме по један; али од дуката Аврам и Чардаклија, као господари, узму себи више, а Гагићу, као писару своме, даду мање, на које Гагићу буде жао, и расрди се. По том Чардаклија и Аврам заостану још неко вријеме у Јашу чекајући док се Родофиник спреми, а Гагића пошаљу напријед у Србију, да каже како и они иду, и однесе нешто новаца, што су Руси Србима дали. Кад Гагић дође у Србију, он, срдит на Аврама и на Чардаклију што су оне дукате по њега криво подијелили, каже Кара-Ђорђију, да Аврам и Чардаклија воде Грка, и да је он говорио, да га не воде, него да ишту кака правога Руса, па они нијесу хтјели да га послушају. Кара-Ђорђије се на то врло расрди, и одмах пошаље књигу Авраму и Чардаклији, да Грка ни по што не воде, већ нека ишту какога правог Руса: „За што", вели, „знате, да ни с овијем, што су међу нама, не можемо никако на крај да изиђемо." Књига ова Кара-Ђорђијева срете Аврама и Чардаклију у Каравлашкој, но њима се учини сад срамота враћати се натраг и искати другога министра, за то Родофинику и не кажу управо, шта Кара-Ђорђије пише, него га доведу у Србију. Кара-Ђорђију је већ Гагић био

officials were pressing the leaders: "We can't fight the Turkish Empire alone; instead, give us a Tsar who will take our part, one whose skirts we can cling to." This is why the leaders made an agreement and chose Petar Čardaklija and Avram Lukić, councillor from the district of Požega, and council secretary Jeremija Gagić, and sent them to Karabogdanska, to the main Russian encampment, so that they might strike an agreement with the Russians on the aid which would be given the Serbs, and so that they might ask for a Russian minister to bring back with them to Serbia, first so that the people would believe that the Russians had really taken Serbia's side, and secondly so that he might teach them a thing or two and they might discuss everything with him. When they had arrived in Jaşi the emissaries found there a real Councillor of State, Konstantin Konstantinovič Rodofinikin (whom the Serbs named and called Rodofinik, which is how I will write his name from here on), a Greek by birth, whom Čardaklija had got to know in Petersburg. When Rodofinik learned that these emissaries wanted to request a Russian minister for Serbia he began to offer himself and to insist that they ask for none other than him. And so, either because in the beginning they didn't even know that Rodofinik was a Greek, or because they didn't consider how poorly Serbs and Greeks got along, they asked the Field Marshal to give them Rodofinik so that they might take him along to Serbia, and the Field Marshal gave him to them. After the emissaries had finished their business and had begun to get ready to go back, they were given as presents three rings with precious stones, plus several hundred ducats for the journey. Now they couldn't divide the rings in any way except to give the three of them one ring each, but when it came to the ducats, Avram and Čardaklija, as big shots, took more for themselves and gave less to Gagić, as their secretary, which made Gagić feel bad and infuriated him. After that Čardaklija and Avram stayed a bit longer in Jaşi, while they waited for Rodofinik to get ready, but they sent Gagić ahead into Serbia, to announce that they were coming and to bring some money that the Russians had given the Serbs. When Gagić arrived in Serbia, angered at Čardaklija and Avram because, in his opinion, they had divided those ducats unfairly, he told Karadjordje that Avram and Čardaklija were bringing a Greek, and that he had told them not to bring him and to ask for a real Russian, but they didn't want to listen to his advice. Karadjordje got very angry at this, and he immediately sent a letter to Avram and Čardaklija, telling them by no means to bring a Greek, but to ask for a real Russian instead: "Because," he said, "you know that we can't get along at all with those who are amongst us." This letter of Karadjordje caught Avram and Čardaklija in Karavlaška but it seemed a disgrace to them now to turn back and request another minister, so they didn't tell Rodofinik just what Karadjordje wrote, but instead they brought him along into Serbia. Gagić had already filled Karadjordje's head with the idea that

напунио главу, да је Родофиник Грк какогод и остали Грци; а још на већу несрећу доведе Родофиник са собом некаква Грка, као тумача, који је био обучен као што се носе Цариградски Грци и Каравлашки и Карабогдански бољари, па га пошаље Кара-Ђорђију, да му јави, да је он дошао и да га пита, кад је вријеме да дође к њему. Кара-Ђорђије угледавши овога Родофиникова тумача у оној великој Цариградској тантули и у црвенијем шалварама и жутијем мествама и папучама, одмах му све оно дође на памет, што му је Гагић казивао за Родофиника, па рече: „Та ми оваке гонимо између себе." Но при свему томе Срби приме Родофиника, као Руског „ђенерала", врло лијепо, и даду му Кучук-Алијну кућу /једну од најљепшијех и највећијех у Биограду/ да у њој сједи, и одреде му стражу пред кућу, и уреде, да му се даје и набавља све што му треба; и видећи да се и он њима врло пријатељски показује, стану се с њим договарати, као с Рускијем министром, надајући се, да ће он, као Руски човјек, бити друкчији од осталијех Грка. Но то пријатељство њихово, ни од једне ни од друге стране, није могло дуго трајати; за што Родофиник, који, будући родом чак из Родоса, може бити да није ни знао, како Грци и Срби између себе живе, стане све Грке Биоградске око себе призивати, каоноти људе од свога народа и језика, а особито се стане дружити с митрополитом Биоградскијем Леонтијем, за којега су Срби већ били увјерени да воли Турцима него њима. Леонтије пак, који досад није могао Србе Турцима да покори и од Руса да одврати, прибјегне сад к Родофинику и стане му казивати, како Срби мрзе на све Грке, и на њега самога, и да су то људи простаци и варвари, с којима се ништа учинити не може, и да није њега било међу њима, они би одавно пропали.........

Rodofinik was a Greek like the rest of the Greeks; and to make things worse, Rodofinik had brought along some Greek as an interpreter, dressed like the Constantinople Greeks and the Karavlaška and Karabogdanska boyars, and he sent him to Karadjordje to announce that he had arrived and to ask him when he would like to see him. Karadjordje, taking one look at Rodofinik's interpreter in his great Constantinople tantula, red pantaloons, and yellow spats and slippers, immediately remembered all that Gagić had said about Rodofinik and he said: "Well, this is just the type of person we have been driving out." But in spite of everything the Serbs received Rodofinik very nicely, as a Russian "general", and they gave him Kučuk-Alija's house (one of the most beautiful and largest in Belgrade) so that he might live there, and they assigned him a guard for the front of his house, and they ordered that he be given and provided with everything he needed; and seeing that he behaved in a very friendly manner toward them they began to discuss things with him, as with a Russian minister, hoping that he, as a Russian subject, would be different from the other Greeks. But that friendship of theirs could not last long, because Rodofinik, being from Rhodes by birth, perhaps didn't even know how Greeks and Serbs got along, and he began to gather around him all the Belgrade Greeks, since they were people of his nation and language, and he became especially friendly with the Metropolitan of Belgrade, Leontije, of whom the Serbs were already convinced that he preferred the Turks to them. And Leontije, who up to now had been unable to subject the Serbs to the Turks and to turn them away from the Russians, ran to Rodofinik and began to tell him how the Serbs hated all Greeks, including himself, and that they were crude people and barbarians with whom one could do nothing, and that if he had not been among them they would have collapsed long ago.............. Vuk Karadžić

Ајдук Вељко Петровић

Ајдук Вељко Петровић, војвода крајински и комендат неготински, родио се око године 1780. у Црној ријеци, у селу Леновцима. Кад Пасманџијине крџалије, тукући се с војском биоградском, попале и поарају Леновце (који се потом прозову Негалица), као и млога друга села наоколо, Вељко, као дијете од десетак-петнаест година, остави оца и мајку и браћу, и отиде у Видин те се најми у некака Турчина да му чува овце, или управо да послужује друге чобане; а послије некога времена дође у Пожаревац и онђе се најми у војводе да му готови јело. Пошто и ту проведе неко вријеме, задоцни се на Васкрсеније играјући с момчадма у колу, те своме господару не зготови на вријеме вечере, зато га господар поћера да бије, а он утече и отиде у *ајдуке* к Станоју Главашу, с којима оно љето (1803. године) проведе. Кад пред зиму ајдуци отиду по јатацима, њега Главаш намјести у нахији смедеревској у селу Дубони код некаква човека као да му чува овце. И тако на јатаку, као најамлик чувајући овце, ожени се у том селу, ушавши у кућу некаквој удовици, рођаци или посестрими Станоја Главаша, која није знала да је он ајдук, него је мислила да је прави најамлик. Кад се у почетку 1804. године почне дизати буна на даије, он се једно вече обуче тајно код свога бившег газде у ајдучке аљине и припаше оружје, па онако накићен дође к жени у кућу, а жена кад га види, стане се бусати рукама у прси: „Куку мене, међер сам ја пошла за ајдука!“ Но он је утјеши и запријети јој да не казује ником ништа, па отиде да тражи друштво. Кад се већ буна почне, он се изнајприје држао са Станојем Главашем, а послије се прилијепи Ђуши Вулићевићу, као поглавици наије смедеревске, и тако је уза њ' га ишао и војевао готово двије године; а кад Ђуша (1805. године) погине у Смедереву, он остане код његова брата Вујице; но утом је већ и сам био стекао неколико момака и начинио се као буљубашица. Те зиме, између ма-

THE LIFE OF HAJDUK-VELJKO PETROVIĆ

by Vuk Stefanović Karadžić

Hajduk Veljko Petrović, Military Commander of Krajina and Commendant of Negotin, was born about the year 1780, at Crna Rijeka, in the village of Lenovci. When the *krdžali* of Pasman Oglu, fighting against the Belgrade army, set fire to and ravaged Lenovci (which after that was nicknamed Negalica), as they did to many other villages in the area, Veljko, as a child of ten to fifteen years, left his father and mother and brothers and went to Vidin, where he hired on with some Turk to watch his sheep, or more accurately, to help the other shepherds; and after some time he came to Požarevac, and there he went to work for a military commander, to cook his food. After he had spent some time there, too, he was late one Easter Day because he had been dancing the kolo with the young fellows, and he didn't cook his master's dinner on time, and for this his master chased after him to beat him, but Veljko fled and went off to join the hajduks under Stanoje Glavaš, with whom he spent that summer of 1803. Just before winter, when the hajduks departed for their aeries, Glavaš found a place for him in the Smederevo district, in the village of Dubona, with some man whose sheep he was supposed to watch. And thus in his aerie, as a hired man watching over sheep, he got married in that village, entering the house of some widow, a relative or blood sister of Stanoje Glavaš, who didn't know that he was a hajduk but who thought that he was a real hired man. At the beginning of 1804, when the uprising was beginning against the *dayis,* he secretly got dressed in his hajduk clothes one evening at his former master's house and he strapped on his weapons, and all dressed up like that he went home to his wife; but when his wife caught sight of him she began to beat her breast, saying: "Woe is me; so I've married a hajduk!" But he comforted her and he warned her not to tell anyone anything, and he went out to find company. When the uprising had already begun he stayed first with Stanoje Glavaš and later he attached himself to Djuša Vuličević, who was the leader of the district of Smederevo, and so he went with him and he fought for almost two years; and when Djuša (in the year 1805) perished at Smederevo he remained with Djuša's brother, Vujica; but in

лога и великог Божића, дође са своја неколика момка пијан у Смедерево, те оплијени некаке Турке који су се били предали Србима; зато га Срби позову на суд, но он не смједне доћи, него побјегне опет у ајдуке, и тако се са својим момцима крио и веркао којекуда по Крајини, док негђе кад су се Срби спремали да дочекају Турке, изиђе с подоста момака те се преда Црном Ђорђију, и тако му се опрости све.

У почетку 1807. године, пошто Срби завладају Биоградом, Вељко се стане молити српском Совјету да му даду допуштање да пређе из параћинске наије на Криви Вир, да побуни Црну ријеку или мали Тимок и да отме од Турака, за који посао он није искао никакве друге помоћи до један барјак, и отворено писмо да сваки човек од бегунаца или дошљака из онога краја, који хоће, може слободно с њима поћи на тај посао. Понајвише ондашњи совјетника српски нити су знали што је Криви Вир, ни Црна ријека, нити су тије имена прије чули до од њега; зато су га изнајприје све разбијали, а кад им он досади молећи се сваки дан, онда рече Младен, који је као најстарији био у Совјету: „Ајде, море, кад је тако навалио да га пошљемо, па ако да бог те што отме, добро, распространићемо земљу нашу; ако ли погине и пропадне, ми му нијесмо криви, видиш да неће да мирује, него ће отићи и без допуштења." И тако му даду барјак и отворено писмо, у коме га наименују буљубашом, и допусте му да може сваки од дошљака из онога краја, који оће, поћи с њим слободно; и даду му још неколике стотине гроша новца и мало џебане. Вељко сад с тим барјаком и с писмом скупи готово 100 којекаки бјегунаца и беећара из онога краја, па удари с њима управо преко Кривога Вира, и дође у село Подгорац, те онђе опколи некака бега у кули. Истина да с бегом није било више до десетак-петнаест душа, али је кула била тврда, зато му дању нијесу могли ништа учинити; а кад буде увече, Вељко нађе у селу неколико буради и каца, па и напуни сламом и сијеном и, приваљавши под кулу запали, те тако упали кулу. Кад кула стане горети, бег се преда. Ту Вељко нађе код бега у ћемеру 800 дуката, и још некаке двојице трговаца, који су били пошли да купе говеда, па се ту застали, пуне двије зобнице бијели

addition he himself had already gathered together several soldiers and was passing himself off as a mini-*buljubaša*. That winter, between January 1st and January 6th, he came into Smederevo drunk, with several of his soldiers, and he robbed some Turks who had already surrendered to the Serbs; for this the Serbs summoned him to court, but he didn't dare come; instead he again fled to the hajduks and so he and his soldiers hid and climbed here and there through the Krajina, until once when the Serbs were getting ready to meet the Turks in battle he came out of hiding with a fair amount of soldiers and surrendered to Black George and so everything was forgiven him.

At the beginning of 1807, after the Serbs had taken over Belgrade, Veljko began to beg the Serbian Governing Council to give him permission to cross from the District of Paraćin into Krivi Vir, to stir up Crna Rijeka or Mali Timok and to seize them from the Turks, for which task he sought no help other than a banner and an open letter stating that every fugitive or newcomer from that area who wished to could freely go with him on that mission. Most of the Serbian councillors of that period neither knew what Krivi Vir was, nor Crna Rijeka, nor had they even heard those names before hearing them from him; for this reason, from the very beginning they were continually turning him down, but when he had thoroughly annoyed them with his daily requests to go, Mladen, who was senior man in the Council, said: "Come on then, let's send him, since he's been after us so much; and if God grants that he capture something – good, we'll enlarge our nation; if he perishes and fails it won't be our fault; can't you see that he won't quiet down, and that he'll go off even without our permission." And so they gave him a banner and an open letter appointing him a *buljubaša* [captain] and granting him his request that every newcomer from that region could freely go there with him if he wished; and they also gave him a few hundred grosh in money, and a little ammunition. With that banner and letter Veljko now gathered together nearly one hundred fugitives and single men from that region, and with them he struck out straight across Krivi Vir and he arrived in the village of Podgorac, and there he surrounded some beg in his fortified tower. True, there were no more than ten or fifteen men with the beg, but the tower was strong, and for that reason they could do nothing to it by day; but when it was evening Veljko found several barrels and vats in the village, filled them with straw and hay, and rolling them up to the tower he set fire to them, thus setting fire to the tower. When the tower began to burn the beg surrendered. Then Veljko found in the

новаца; осим тога поузима од Турака све оружје; а од аљина што буде у Турака боље, оно помијењају (Вељко и бег, а његови момци и остали Турци) за своје горе; тако Вељко узме и бегова ата себи, а њему даде свога коња, па га сјутрадан са свима Турцима лијепо испрати у Турску. Потом Вељко искупи све своје момке у параду, па им ону једну торбу бијели новаца подијели свима једнако; тако им раздијели и оружје бегови момака; а што су узели од бега и од она два трговца неколико пари лијепи пиштоља и ножева, од оније он најбоље избере за себе, а остале испоклања знатнијим момцима, говорећи једноме: „На, ти си мој бимбаша"; другоме: „Ти си мој буљубаша"; трећему: „Ти си мој барјактар" итд. Па онда ону другу торбу новаца запечати и по своме бимбаши пошаље Совјету, и пише му како је њему бог дао те је задобио, и од добитка својега шаље по *своме бимбаши* дијел у народну касу. Кад бимбаша те новце с писмом донесе и преда Совјету, совјетници нијесу знали или ће се прије чудити како Вељко тако одма доби толике новце и њима посла, или откуд њему бимбаша кад је он тек буљубаша! Најпослије дозову бимбашу унутра па га запитају: „Ко си ти?' А он одговори: „Ја сам бимбаша господара Вељка." — „А кад си ти бимбаша, шта је Вељко?" — „Он је, вели, господар." Да су господар и бимбаша искали што од Совјета, могло би бити и више разговора, али будући да су давали, тако Совјет прими торбу новаца драговољно и благодари и бимбаши и господару.

Кад пређу Руси 1810. године у Крајину, отиде и он са својим момцима преда њи, и то је цијело љето с њима рабро војевао око Дунава и Тимока, и за раброст своју добио златну колајну; а под јесен је водио руску војску на Варварин, ђе се у оној славној битки ранио у лијеву руку, и потом у шаци мало остао сакат (нити је могао прста добро скупити ни исправити). Тога љета добије негђе од Турака врло лијепу сабљу, оковану сребром и златом и искићену камењем, па је преко ондашњега поглавара руске војске пошаље фелдмаршалу Каменскоме на дар, но он му је врати натраг, изговарајући се да он није вриједан такву сабљу носити, него нека је носи онај јунак који је од Турака задобио; и пошаље му 200 дуката на дар.

beg's money belt eight hundred ducats, and he also found two feed bags full of silver with two merchants who had set out to buy some cattle and had stopped there; in addition he took all their weapons from the Turks; and they exchanged their bad clothes for the Turks' better clothes (Veljko with the beg, and his soldiers with the other Turks); and in the same manner Veljko took the beg's horse for himself and gave him his horse, and the following day he gave him and all the Turks a good send-off for Turkey. Then Veljko got all his soldiers together in formation and he divided one bag of silver equally among them all; and in the same manner he divided up the weapons of the beg's men; and since they had seized several pairs of fine pistols and knives from the beg and those two merchants, he picked the best for himself and gave the rest as gifts to the more outstanding soldiers, saying to one: "Here, you are my *bimbaša* [major] to another: "You are my *buljubaša*," and to a third: "You are my *barjaktar* [standard bearer] etc." Then he sealed the other bag of money and sent it via his *bimbaša* to the Governing Council, and he wrote to them that God had granted him victory and that he was sending part of his spoils via his *bimbaša* for the national treasury. When his *bimbaša* brought that money and the letter, and handed them over to the Council, the councillors didn't know whether to be astonished first because he had got so much money so fast and had sent it to them, or because he could have a major when he himself was only a captain. Finally, they called the *bimbaša* inside and asked him: "Who are you?" And he answered: "I am the *bimbaša of gospodar* [lord] Veljiko."—"Since you are a *bimbaša*, what is Veljko?"—"He is," says he, "a *gospodar*." Had the *gospodar* and the *bimbaša* asked for something from the Council there might have been further conversation, but seeing that they were giving something the Council graciously accepted the bag of money and thanked both the bimbaša and the gospodar.

* * * * * * * *

When in 1810 the Russians crossed into the Krajina, he went ahead of them with his soldiers, and so he fought bravely with them all that summer near the Danube and the Timok, and he received a gold medallion for his bravery; and towards fall he led the Russian army to Varvarin, where during that glorious battle he was wounded in the left arm and from then on his hand was a little crippled (he could neither make a good fist, nor could he straighten his fingers out all the way). That summer he won from the Turks somewhere a very beautiful sword, forged in silver and gold and encrusted with precious stones, and he sent it as a gift to Field Marshal Kamenskij via the then commander of the Russian army, but Marshal Kamenskij sent it back to him, saying that he was not worthy to wear such a sword, but let that hero wear it who won it from the Turks; and he sent him two hundred ducats as a gift.

* * * * * * * *

Кад се војска турска прикупи у Видин, онда се дигну неколике иљаде турски коњаника, те пређу преко Тимока само да виде како је; но Вељко и дочека око Буковаче и срећно и узбије натраг. Потом трећи дан удари сва сила турска, с топовима и са свом оправом, те пређе преко Тимока. Он, истина, с оно своје војске што је могао извести из шанчева изиђе опет пред Турке и са неисказаном раброшћу удари да би и опет узбио; но шта је он са своји 3—400 коњика и с толико влашки солдата у равну пољу могао учинити турској војсци од 15—16.000? С једном се војском тукао, а двије су три обилазиле да му зађу с леђа; и тако он уступи и измичући се пред Турцима дође у Неготин. Ту ноћ изиђе опет из Неготина те удари на Турке; но Турци се одрже. И тако је послије неколико дана сваки дан изилазио у поље и са неисказаном раброшћу тукао се с Турцима, но Турци се утврде и пограде шанчеве око Неготина. Турцима дође у помоћ Рецеп из Адакале и каравлашки кнез Караџа и сам велики везир Рушић-паша; а у њега и од оно мало војске што је имао изгину и изране се најбољи јунаци. Турци су се сваку ноћ кроз земљу ближе прикучивали к српским шанчевима и најпослије су се тако близу били прикучили да су се батинама пустимичке могли тући. Ту већ сад другога боја није било осим са шанчева из топова и из кумбара и из пушака. Турци све куле неготинске топовима и кумбарама развале и оборе, и сама она највећа кула ђе је он сједио падне, и он сиђе у подрум. Најпослије му нестане џебане, особито танета и топовски и пушчани, зато покупи сва калајна кандила и кашике и тањире, те растопи на пушчана танета; а у топове је, кад су негђе Турци чинили јуриш, метао најпослије и талијере.

Још из почетка, како је виђео да му џебане нестаје, писао је Совјету у Биоград да му пошаљу џабане; и кривио и што заранције нијесу то уредили и више му џебане послали; и најпослије пријетио им, говорећи: „Ако бог да те ову рану преболим која је сад на мени (тј. ако изиђе жив из Неготина), оћемо се на зиму питати како се држи царевина.“ Из Биограда пошаљу му одма (по ономе истом пријатељу који му је говорио да се не зат-

When the Turkish army had gathered at Vidin, at that time several thousand Turkish cavalry began to move out, and they crossed the Timok just to see what the situation was; but Veljko met them near Bukovča, and he successfully drove them back. Then on the third day the whole Turkish force attacked, with cannon and full equipment, and it crossed the Timok. True, he and those soldiers whom he could spare from the trenches went out again against the Turks, and with indescribable heroism he attacked and drove them back again; but what could he do with his three or four hundred cavalry and with the same number of *vlah* soldiers, on a level field, against a Turkish army of fifteen or sixteen thousand? While he fought with one army, two or three other armies were moving around him in order to come at him from behind; so he gave ground, and slipping out ahead of the Turks he arrived in Negotin. That night he went out again from Negotin and he attacked the Turks; but the Turks held their positions. And so after a few days he went out into the field every day and with indescribable bravery he did battle with the Turks, but the Turks fortified their positions and built trenches around Negotin. Redžep from Adakala, and the Karavlaška knez Karadža, and the Grand Vezir himself, Rušić Pasha, came to the Turkish aid, while the best of his fighters, from that small number of soldiers which he had, either perished or were wounded. Each night the Turks came through the ground, closer to the Serbian trenches, and finally they had got so close that they could easily have fought with fruit poles. Now there was no other way to fight except from the trenches, with cannon, and mortar, and rifles. The Turks had demolished and flattened all the fortified towers of Negotin with cannon and mortar, and when the largest tower fell, where he had based himself, he went down into the cellar. Finally he ran out of ammunition, especially shells for cannon and rifles, so he collected all the tin icon lamps and spoons and plates, and he melted them down into rifle bullets; and in the end, when the Turks made a charge, he would put *thalers* in the cannon.

From the very beginning, when he saw that he was going to run out of ammunition, he was writing to the Council in Belgrade to send him ammunition, and he was blaming them for not having arranged earlier to send him more ammunition; and finally he threatened them, saying: "If God grants that I should recover from this wound that I have on me now (i.e., if he gets out of Negotin alive), this winter we'll be asking how the empire is holding up." They immediately sent him from Belgrade (via that same friend who had told him not to hole up

вора у Неготин) једну лађу топовски танета и нареде да се барута и пушчане џебане узме из Пореча и да му како пошље ако буде могуће; но то све за њега стигне доцкан у Пореч, а ни осталима се не могне унијети у Неготин. Такођер је писао и Младену да му се пошље помоћ, као што је било уговорено; но Младен, уздајући се у Вељково јунаштво, мислио је да Неготин неће тако ласно пропасти, а што ће се Вељко мало више намучити, није марио, него је још говорио: „Кад је мир, њему се пјесма пјева и по 10 музиканта за ручком свирају: нек се држи сад." И тако одгађајући од данас до сјутра, не пошље му помоћи.

Сад већ како су се Турци тако прикучили, и није се више могло излазити на поље да се с њима бије, он је и дан и ноћ одао по шанчевима и људе слободио и уређивао да чувају добро. Тако једно јутро (први дана мјесеца августа) изиђе у један мали шанац, и на табљама стане нарећивати и казивати како ће се нешто заградити и поправити што су турски топови били развалили; а турски га тобџија загледа, па потегне из топа, те га удари испријека кросред плећа и тако га прекине и разнесе да ништа више није могао рећи до „Држ—", и с том половином ријечи падне мртав на земљу. Како он тако падне, момци његови, који су онђе били око њега, одма узму некакве траве, што је за коње била донешена и онђе се десила, те га покрију да га људи не виде; и тако је до мрака ту лежао мртав, а увече га брат његов Милутин с момцима узме те га изнесе из шанца и сарани код цркве. Залуду су тако смрт његову крили: војска сва још онај дан позна да Вељка нема међу њима; и изнајприје једни стану говорити да се ранио па лежи, а други да је прошао кроз Турке и отишао по индат; а мало послије сви дознаду да је погинуо. Док је он са својим момцима сваки час по шанчевима пролазио, нико није смио показати да се поплашио и слутити на зло, него је сваки морао бити слободан и весео, ако му се и неће; а како њега нестане, војска одма повиче да се више не може држати у Неготину, него да се мора бјежати макар како. И тако Срби пети дан послије његове смрти оставе Неготин и побјегну у Пореч. Потом одма сав онај крај, а мало послије и сва Србија, позна да Вељка нема.

in Negotin) a boat load of artillery shells, and they ordered that lead and rifle ammunition be taken from Poreč and sent to him somehow, if possible; but all that arrived in Poreč too late for him, nor could it be brought into Negotin for the others. He also wrote Mladen to send him help, as had been agreed; but Mladen, trusting in Veljko's heroism, thought that Negotin would not fall so easily, and he didn't mind causing Veljko a little more pain, and instead he said: "When all is quiet he has songs sung, and he has ten musicians playing at his dinner: now let him hold!" And so, putting it off from one day to the next, he didn't send him any help.

Now when the Turks had already drawn so close that it was no longer possible to go out on the field to do battle with them, he went from trench to trench, day and night, and he encouraged his men and he arranged them so they could guard their positions well. Thus one morning (in the first days of August) he went out into a small trench and standing on a gun carriage he began to give orders and to explain how something that the Turkish cannon had knocked down should be built up and repaired; but a Turkish artillery man spotted him and fired his cannon, and he hit him from the side, right through the shoulders, and it stopped him short and blew him apart, so that he could say nothing more than "hold", and with that half a word he fell to the ground, dead. As soon as he fell, his men who were near him immediately took some grass which had been brought in for the horses and happened to be there, and they covered him up so that people wouldn't see him; and so he lay there until dark, and in the evening his brother Milutin and some soldiers took him and carried him out of the trench, and they buried him at a church. In vain did they conceal his death in this way: the whole army found out that very same day that Veljko was not among them; and at first some began to say that he was wounded and was lying down, and others were saying that he had crossed through the Turkish lines and had gone off to get help; and a little later everyone found out that he had perished. While he had been continually walking through the trenches with his men no one dared to show that he was afraid or even to hint that things weren't going well; instead everyone had to be optimistic and cheerful, even if he didn't feel that way; but when he disappeared the army immediately began to shout that it could no longer hold out in Negotin and that it had to flee as best it could. And so on the fifth day after his death the Serbs left Negotin and they fled to Poreč. Then at once that whole region, and a little later all of Serbia, learned that Veljko was no longer.

A village on the Croatian Primorje

Smail Aga Čengić

Ivan Mažuranić was a participant in the Croatian Illyrian Movement (1830-1848), whose original goal was a common literary language, orthography, and literature for all South Slavs. Eventually, the movement became political as well as literary, and almost exclusively a Croatian phenomenon. Illyrianism drew its roots from the Croatian cultural past, but it also reflected the widespread upsurge of nationalism throughout Europe.

In 1830, when the movement began, the primary goal of the Illyrians was the development of a national literary language and its use within the Croatian educational system; at that time the spoken language was not taught in a single Croatian grammar school or gymnasium. It was not until 1835 that Antun Mažuranić, Ivan's brother, was permitted to teach the vernacular language in Zagreb.

Perhaps the most decisive step taken by the Illyrians, in the area of language, was their adoption of the štokavian dialect as the basis for the Illyrian literary language, instead of the kajkavian dialect spoken by the majority of the Illyrian leaders. By adopting štokavian the Illyrians extended their range to include the štokavian speakers of Bosnia and southern Dalmatia, and they also emphasized their ties with the writers of the Dalmatian Renaissance. The literary vehicle of the Illyrian Move-

ment was Danica, *the periodical begun in 1835 by Ljudevit Gaj, who was also a leader in the reform of the Croatian orthography. Gaj's new alphabet (often called "gajica") opted for diacritical marks (č) over the combinations of letters that had been used in the past (ch).*

Ivan Mažuranić (1814-1890) was born on the Croatian Primorje, in Novi, a čakavian-speaking region. He grew up steeped in the poetry of Kačić-Miošić and in the folk poetry of his region. Mažuranić was a practicing lawyer. In 1848 he entered Croatian political life, when the Austrian government, frightened by the Hungarian Revolution that year, sought Croatian support by allowing commoners to participate in politics for the first time. Mažuranić played a skillful role in Croatian political life for several decades. In 1861 he was named Croatian Court Chancellor, and in 1873 he was named Ban (governor), the first Croatian Ban to come from the common people. Mažuranić believed, as did the Slovene Jernej Kopitar, that if the Croats and other Slavic nationalities in the Austro-Hungarian Empire worked together within the Empire, their very numbers would eventually give them control of the government.

Besides his legal training, Ivan Mažuranić had a broad background in classical (Greek and Latin) literature, Dalmatian Renaissance literature, and modern European literature. He read Italian, German, English, and Russian works in the original, and was known to be an admirer of both Byron and Pushkin. Between 1835 and 1848 Mažuranić published lyric poetry in Gaj's Danica. *In 1842, together with Jakov Užarević, he published a* German-Illyrian Dictionary. *In 1844, at the request of the cultural society Matica Ilirska, which was preparing the first publication of Ivan Gundulić's* Osman *(see our note to Gundulić's work), Mažuranić wrote the missing fourteenth and fifteenth cantos for Gundulić's poem. According to Antun Barac, "the average reader could not distinguish between Gundulić's cantos" and those of Mažuranić (Antun Barac,* Hrvatska književnost od preporoda do stvaranja Jugoslavije, *I:* književnost ilirizma. *Zagreb, 1964, 217).*

But the literary work which earned for Mažuranić a lasting place in Croatian literature was his Smrt Smail-age Čengića, *a synthesis of all the influences which helped to form Mažuranić culturally, including the classical, the Dalmatian Renaissance, and modern European Romantic literature.* Smrt Smail-Age *is based on an actual event, the ambush and killing of the Hercegovinian Moslem leader Čengić, who was a scourge to the Christian Slavs living within his domain, and who had killed many Christians, including the nephew of Njegoš, the Prince Bishop of Montenegro (see the note on Njegoš), who laid the plans for Smail-Aga's death.*

Mažuranić's poem provided the Illyrian Movement with a chef d'oeuvre which was not only unimpeachable in its literary qualities, but which also embodied the highest ideals of the Illyrians, including their hatred of oppression and their conviction that the Christian Slavs would avenge themselves on their Moslem oppressors in the end.

Ivan Mažuranić

SMRT SMAIL-AGE ČENGIĆA

Agovanje

Sluge zove Smail-aga,
Usred Stolca kule svoje,
A u zemlji hercegovoj:
"Ajte amo, sluge moje,
Brđane mi izvedite,
Štono sam ih zarobio robjem
Na Morači, vodi hladnoj.
Još Duraka starca k tome,
Što me hrđa svjetovaše
Da ih pustim domu svome,
Jer su, reče, vlašad ljuta;
Oni će mi odmazditi
Mojom glavom vlaške glave:
Kô da strepi mrki vuče
S planinskoga gladna miša."

Hitre sluge poslušaše,
Izvedoše tamničare.
Na noguh im teške negve,
A na rukuh lisičine.
Kad ih vidje silan aga,
On namaknu gojne vole
I dželate ljute rise,
Ter ih turskijem darivao darom:
Svakom momku ostar kolac daje,
Kome kolac, kome li konopac,
Kome britku palu namjenjuje.
"Ajte, krsti, dijeliti dare,
Štono sam vi Turčin pripravio,
Vam i vašijem Brdam kamenijem:
Vi bo kako, sva će Brda tako."

Turčin reče, al mrijeti
Za Hristovu vjeru svetu
Teško nije, tko se za nju bije.

THE DEATH OF SMAIL AGA ČENGIĆ

The Aga's Rule

Smail Aga calls his servants
Amidst his fortress of Stolac,
And in the land of Hercegovina:
"Come here, my servants,
Bring me out the Montenegrins
That I took prisoner
At the cold waters of the Morača.
And old Durak, too;
He advised me, the scoundrel,
To let them go home.
Because, said he, the Vlahs are fierce;
They'll make me pay–
My head for the Vlah heads:
As if the dark wolf should tremble
Because of a hungry mountain mouse."

The quick-footed servants did his will;
They led out the prisoners.
Heavy shackles on their feet,
Fetters on their arms.
When the mighty aga saw them,
He called for well-fed oxen
And executioners, the fierce lynxes;
Then he bestowed on them a Turkish gift:
To each young man he gives a sharp stake,
To some a stake, to some a noose,
To some he assigns a sharp sword.
"Go ahead, Crosses, share the gifts
Which I, a Turk, have prepared for you,
For you and your rocky Montenegro:
What you get, all of Montenegro will get."

Spoke the Turk, but to die
For Christ's holy faith
Isn't difficult for those who fight for it.

Krcnu kolac nekoliko puta,
Zviznu pala nekoliko puta,
Zadrktaše ta vješala tanka,
Al ne pisnu Crnogorčad mlada,
Niti pisnu, niti zubi škrinu.
Proz poljanu mrka krvca teknu:
Niti pisnu, niti zubi škrinu.
Poljana se napuni tjelesa:
Niti pisnu, niti zubi škrinu.
Već tko zovnu Boga velikoga,
Tko lijepo ime Isusovo,
Ter se lasno rastadoše s suncem,
Zatočnici mrijet naviknuti.

Rijekom krvca poljem teče;
Turad bulji skrstiv ruke.
Tko je mlađi, rado gleda
Na lipovu krstu muke,
A tko starij', muke iste
Sam na sebi s vlaške ruke
Već unaprijed od strâ ćuti.

Ljutit aga mrko gleda,
Gdje se silom divit mora,
Silan arslan gorskom mišu.
Tko si junak, osvetit se ne mo'š
Na junaku dotle dok ne preda.
Smaknu Ture toliko junaka,
Posmica ih, srca ne iskali,
Što bez straha svi su pred njim pali.

Boj se onoga, tko je vikô
Bez golema mrijet jada!

Videć aga krepost taku,
Zazebe ga na dnu srca,
Kô ledenijem ratom leden
Šiljak dušu da mu dirnu.

Od tuge li za junaci,
Što ih silan zaman strati?
Turčin tuge za krstove neima.
Od straha li, jer se glavi boji?
Silan aga to sam sebi taji.

The stake crackled several times,
The sword whistled several times,
That slender gallows trembled,
But the young Montenegrins made no sound,
Made no sound, nor gnashed their teeth.
Their dark blood flowed across the meadow:
They made no sound, nor gnashed their teeth.
The meadow filled with their bodies:
They made no sound, nor gnashed their teeth.
Instead, some called out to the great God,
Others called the beautiful name of Jesus,
And lightheartedly they parted with the sun,
Champions for whom death is nothing new.

Blood flows like a river through the field;
The Turks, arms folded, gaping stand.
The younger ones gladly watch
The linden cross of torment;
But the older ones, from fear,
Already anticipate the same torture
When they fall into Vlah hands.

The angry aga darkly watches there,
And against his will the powerful lion
Must admire the mountain mouse.
No hero gets any satisfaction
Until his opponent gives up.
The Turk had finished off so many heroes,
He killed them, but he did not appease his anger,
Because all fell fearlessly before him.

Fear the one who has grown accustomed
To dying without much fuss!

In the face of such strength the aga felt
A sudden chill in the depths of his heart,
As though a cold lance's frozen tip
Had touched his soul.

Is it sorrow for the heroes
The mighty one has killed in vain?
A Turk has no sorrow for Crosses.
Or is it fear, is he afraid for his head?
The mighty aga keeps that to himself.

Zar ne vidiš kako radi
Hrabar junak uspreć zimu
Što mu s one piknje male
Po svem tijelu mrazne valja vale?

Gledaj glavu put nebesa
Gdje se oholo hrabra diže;
Gledaj čelo jasno, i oko,
Kako bistro pod njim sijeva;
Gledaj krepki stas gdje svoju
Znajuć snagu ravno stoji;
Pak mi kaži: ima l' koja
Tudijer straha i najmanja sjena?

A pak slušaj kako junak zbori
I strašljivce kako ostro kori:
"Vaj, Durače, starče stari,
Kuda 'š sade, kamo li ćeš?
Sad gdje smakoh gorske miše?
Il u goru? Brđani su tamo;
Il u ravno? na ravno će sići:
Il ćeš živjet da izgubiš glavu?
Najbolje je bježat pod oblake.
Mišad grize, ali po tlih gmiže;
Sam sur oro pod nebo se diže.
Penjite ga na vješala tanka,
Neka znade što mu strah valjade.
A Turčina ako još imade
Gdjegod koga ter se vlaha boji,
Popet ću ga nebu pod oblake,
Tu nek plijen vranom vranu stoji."

Mukom muče ropske sluge,
Mukom muče, plijen svoj grabe.
"Aman, aman!" starac pišti,
I Novica sin mu zaman
"Aman, aman!" suzan vrišti.

Stoji aga, gorsko zvijere,
Gvozden stupac, kamen tvrdi,
Dokle dahnu, rukom mahnu,
Starac Durak skoro izdahnu.
"Medet, medet! . . ." dželat ljuti
Već mu i grlo dotle sputi.
Durak huknu, sve zamuknu.

Can't you see how the brave hero
Tries to resist the wintry cold
That from that small point
Sends waves of frost throughout his body?

Look at the head, the brave head,
Arrogantly raised in heaven's direction;
Look at the clear forehead and the eye
That brightly flashes beneath it;
Look at the strong physique,
Upright, conscious of its power;
Then tell me: do you see there
Even the faintest shadow of fear?

And listen, too, to the hero talking,
As he sharply scolds the faint of heart:
"Too bad, Durak, old timer,
Where will you go now, where will you go,
Now that I have knocked off the mountain mice?
To the mountains? The Montenegrins are there;
To the plains? They'll come down to the plains;
Or will you live, only to lose your head?
It's best to flee beneath the clouds.
The mice bite, but they crawl on the ground;
The grey eagle alone rises beneath the sky.
So raise him up on the slender gallows,
Let him know what his fear is worth.
And if there be any other Turk, anywhere,
Who fears the Vlahs,
I'll lift him skyward, beneath the clouds,
Let him stand there, prey to the black raven."

The slavish servants are deeply silent,
Deeply silent as they seize their prey.
"Mercy, mercy! " the old man wheezes,
And Novica, his son,
Vainly sobs: "Mercy, mercy!"

The aga stands, a mountain beast,
An iron pillar, a hard rock.
Before they took one breath he had waved his hand,
Old man Durak will soon breathe his last.
"Mercy, mercy! . . ." The fierce executioner
Already has bound his throat.
Durak gasped, and became completely silent.

Noćnik

Sunce zađe, a mjesec izađe.
Tko se vere uz klance niz klance
Ter se krade k onoj Gori Crnoj?
Obnoć grede, a obdan počiva,
Junak negda, sad ne junak više,
No trst kojoj svaki hlad kidiše.
Šušne l' gdjegod pokraj puta guja,
Il rujeva ispod grma zeče,
Tad on, negda ljući guje ljute,
Malne zeca plašljiviji kleca.
Misli jadan da je gorski vuče,
Il još gori brđanski hajduče,
Ter se boji gdje će poginuti,
A ne stiže što mu srce muti.
Skupo drži svoju rusu glavu;
Nit je zlatna, nit je pozlaćena:
Vidi mu se, mrijet mu se neće,
A jest nešto što ga naprijed kreće.

Je li hajduk, il uhoda turska,
Što uhodi sviloruna krda,
Il volova stada vitoroga?
Nit je hajduk, nit uhoda turska,
Već Novica, Čengića kavazu:
Bijesan Turčin, krvnik Gore Crne,
Koga znade i staro i mlado,
I ne bi ga pronijele vile,
A kamoli noge na junaku
Crnom Gorom na bijelu danu.

Ob rame je diljku objesio,
Ljut jatagan o pojasu reži
I kraj njega do dva samokresa.
Gujsko gnijezdo strukom prikrilio,
Lak opanak na noge pritegô,
A gô rakčin na junačku glavu;
Od saruka ni spomena neima.
Bez saruka eto Turčin iđe;
Vidi mu se, ginut mu se neće,
A jest nešto što ga naprijed kreće.

The Night Person

Ivan Mažuranić

The sun set, and the moon appeared.
Who climbs up and down ravines,
And steals toward that Montenegro?
He goes by night and he rests by day,
A hero once, a hero no longer,
But a reed that every shadow scares to death.
If a snake rustles somewhere along the road,
Or a little rabbit under a sumac bush,
Then he, once fiercer than the fierce snake,
Staggers, nearly as frightened as the rabbit.
The poor wretch thinks it's a mountain wolf,
Or even worse, a Montenegrin haiduk,
And he's afraid that he'll perish
Without attaining what troubles his heart.
He values his blonde head highly;
Though it's neither of gold, nor gilded over:
You can tell he doesn't want to die,
There's something that keeps driving him onward.

Is it a haiduk, or some Turkish spy,
Scouting out the silk-maned flocks,
Or the curl-horn oxen herds?
It's neither a haiduk nor a Turkish spy,
Instead it's Novica, Čengić's bodyguard:
A mad-dog Turk, the mortal enemy of Montenegro,
Known to young and old,
And not even the vilas could have carried him,
Never mind his hero's feet,
Through Montenegro in broad daylight.

Over his shoulder he has slung a rifle,
From his belt snarls a fierce dagger,
And two pistols beside it.
He has hidden this vipers' nest beneath a peasant cloak,
Pulled light peasant slippers onto his feet,
And a bare skull cap on his hero's head,
But there's no sign at all of a turban.
So, the Turk goes without a turban;
You can tell he doesn't want to perish,
There's something that keeps driving him onward.

Pomno junak Cuce prevalio,
Još Bjelice ratoborne k tome,
Ter se maša kršnijeh Ćeklića.
Njih se maša, a Bogu se moli
Da mu dade i njih prevaliti
Ni čuvenu, ni gdje ugledanu;
Vidi mu se, mrijet mu se neće,
A jest nešto što ga naprijed kreće.

Drugi pijetli u polju cetinjskom
A Novica u polje cetinjsko;
Treći pijetli u mjestu Cetinju,
A Novica pade na Cetinje.

Tudijer straži božju pomoć zove:
"Božja pomoć, cetinjski stražaru!"
Ljepše njemu straža prihvatila:
"Dobra kob ti, neznana delijo!
Otkuda si, od koje li strane?
Koja li te sreća nanijela,
Ter si junak rano podranio? "

Mudar Turčin, za nevolju mu je,
Mudar Turčin mudro odgovara:
"Kad me pitaš, kazat ću ti pravo:
Ja sam junak od Morače hladne,
Od Tusine sela malenoga,
Ispod gore glasna Durmitora.
Nosim troje na srdašcu jade:
Jedni su mi na srdašcu jadi,
Što ni Čengić smaknu Moračane;
Drugi su mi na srdašcu jadi,
Što mi Čengić pogubio baba;
A treći mi na srdašcu jadi,
Što 'e još više: da još krvnik diše.
Već tako ti Boga velikoga,
Pusti mene tvome gospodaru,
Gospodaru i mome i tvome,
Ne bi li mi izliječio jade."

Mudrije mu odvratila straža:
"Skin' oružje, neznana delijo,
Pa nos' glavu kuda tebi drago."
Uprav Turčin dvoru na kapiju,
A pošljednja iz vidika zvijezda:
Bješe zvijezda age Čengijića.

Carefully the hero passed through the Cuce,
And the warlike Bjelice as well;
Then he is making his way through the rugged Ćeklići.
He is making his way through them, and praying to God
To let him pass through them, too,
Unheard and unseen.
You can tell that he doesn't want to die,
There's something that keeps driving him onward.

The second cock crows on Cetinje field
And Novica is in the Cetinje field;
The third cock crows in the town of Cetinje,
And Novica has reached Cetinje.

He calls a greeting to the sentry there:
"God's help to you, sentry of Cetinje!"
The sentry came back to him better yet:
"Good fortune to you, unknown hero!
Where are you from, from what part?
What luck brought you, a hero,
To get up so early?"

The Turk is wise, though at a loss,
The Turk is wise, wisely does he answer:
"Since you ask, I'll tell you the truth:
I am a hero from the cold Morača,
From Tusına, a little village
Beneath famed Mount Durmitor.
I bear three sorrows in my heart:
The first sorrow in my heart
Is that Čengić killed off our people from the Morača;
The second sorrow in my heart
Is that Čengić killed my father;
And the third sorrow in my heart,
And greater yet: is that the assassin still breathes.
And so by God almighty,
Let me go to your lord,
To your lord and mine,
To see if he might not cure me of my sorrows."

The sentry answered him more wisely still:
"Remove your weapons, unknown hero,
Then carry your head wherever you like."
The Turk went straight to the gates of the palace,
And the last star passed from view:
It was the star of Aga Čengić.

(an excerpt)

Petar II Njegoš

The Mountain Wreath

Petar II Petrović Njegoš (1813-1851) was both a poet and a ruler. Prince Bishop of Montenegro from 1830 to 1851 Njegoš devoted most of his adult life to uniting the loosely-linked Montenegrin tribes, and to imposing his own autocratic rule over them. He was convinced that only through a strong and united state could the Montenegrins resist the constant threat of Turkish conquest.

Njegoš's poetry reflects both concern for Montenegrin freedom and philosophical speculation about the nature of life. Raised in the heroic epic tradition, from an early age Njegoš began to compose his own poems about contemporary events. These poems were composed "na narodnju" (in the folk style), and one of the earliest was his "Nova pjesma crnogorska o vojni Rusah i Turakah početoj u 1828 god." ("A New Montenegrin Song About the War Between the Russians and the Turks Begun in 1828"). In writing such poems Njegoš was really continuing the tradition of his immediate predecessor Bishop Petar I, whose poetry he later included in his Ogledalo Srpsko (Serbian Looking Glass, 1845).

Njegoš's development as a poet is usually considered to have had three stages: a "narodni" or folk period, when he composed epic poems on the oral folk model; a neo-classical period, when he translated Homer and Milton, and wrote odes dedicated to the ruling house of Russia, to European statesmen such as Metternich, and to God; and finally, a romantic period which combined the preceding folk and neo-classical elements with a new philosophy of freedom, and with lyrical reflection. Njegoš's three most important works date from this period: Luča Mikrokozma (Ray of the Microcosm, Beograd, 1845), Lažni Car Šćepan Mali (The Tsar Pretender Little Stefan, Trieste, 1851), and Gorski Vijenac (The Mountain Wreath, Vienna 1847).

Njegoš's Gorski Vijenac, an epic poem in dramatic form, is his best known work. Written in the deseterac (ten-syllable verse) of the oral folk epic, Gorski Vijenac represents the final stage of an opus that can be traced back to Njegoš's first attempt at a literary epic on the theme of the Montenegrin struggle for survival against the Turks, Glas Kamenštaka. When the Austrian censors in Vienna prohibited the publication there of Glas (evidently because of its anti-Turkish theme), Njegoš reworked the poem as Svobodijada (1835), a neo-classical type of poem, modelled after the Serbianka of his teacher, Sima Milutinović Sarajlija, and written in eight-syllable lines (osmerac). It is fortunate that Njegoš had the experience of writing Svobodijada, because although it was never published in his lifetime—still its eight-syllable line did force him to develop the compression of poetry and meaning to which Gorski Vijenac owes so much of its power.

ГОРСКИ ВИЈЕНАЦ

ПОСВЕТА
ПРАХУ ОЦА СРБИЈЕ

Нек се овај вијек горди над свијема вјековима,
он ће ера бити страшна људскијема кољенима!
У њ се осам близанацах у један мах изњихаше
из колевке Белонине и на земљи показаше:
Наполеон, Карло, Блихер, кнез Велинктон и Суворов,
Карађорђе, бич тирјанах, и Шварценберг и Кутузов.
Ареи је, страва земна, славом бојном њих опио
и земљу им за попришће, да се боре, назначио.
Из грмена великога лафу изаћ трудно није:
у великим народима генију се пњ'ездо вије;
овде му је поготову материјал к славном дјелу
и тријумфа дични в'јенац, да му краси главу смјелу.
Ал' хероју тополскоме, Карађорђу бесмртноме,
све препоне на пут бјеху, к циљу доспје великоме:
диже народ, крсти земљу, а варварске ланце сруши,
из мртвијех Ср̏ба дозва, дуну живот српској души.
Ево тајна бесмртника: даде Србу сталне груди,
од витештва одвикнута, у њим, лафска срца буди.
Фараона источнога пред Ђорђем се мрзну силе,
Ђорђем су се српске мишце са витештвом опојиле!
Од Ђорђа се Стамбол тресе, крвожедни отац куге,
сабљом му се Турци куну – клетве у њих нема друге.
***

Зна Душана родит Српка, зна дојити Обилиће;
ал хероје кâ Пожарске, дивотнике и племиће,
гле, Српкиње сада рађу! Благородством Српство дише!
Бјежи, грдна клетво, с рода – завјет Срби испунише!

/У Бечу на Ново љето 1847. года.

THE MOUNTAIN WREATH

DEDICATION
TO THE DUST OF THE FATHER OF SERBIA

May this age pride itself above all ages,
It will be an awesome era for mankind's generations!
In it eight twins all at once shot up
From Bellona's cradle, and showed themselves on earth:
Napoleon, Karl, Blücher, Prince Wellington and Suvorov,
Karadjordje, the scourge of tyrants, and Schwartzenberg and Kutuzov.
Ares, earth's dread, made them drunk with martial glory
And assigned them the earth as a battleground, so they could fight.
From a large bush a lion comes easily forth:
In large nations the genius's nest is woven;
Here, especially, is the material for glorious deed
And the illustrious wreath of triumph to adorn his bold head.
But, for the hero from Topola, the immortal Karadjordje,
All obstacles were in the way, yet he reached his great goal:
He made the people rise up, christened the land, and crushed the barbarians' chains,
He called the Serbs back from the dead, he breathed life into the Serbian soul.
Here's the secret of that immortal man: he gave the Serbs chests of steel,
He awoke in them their lion's hearts, grown away from chivalry.
The Eastern Pharaoh's forces froze before George,
George made Serbian muscles drunk with chivalry!
Istanbul, bloodthirsty father of the plague, quaked because of George,
The Turks take oaths by his sword – they have no other oath.
* * *
A Serbian woman could give birth to a Dušan, could nurse an Obilić;
But see, it's heroes like the Požarskijs, men of grandeur and nobility,
That Serbian women now give birth to! Serbdom breathes of nobility!
Flee, awful curse, from our people – the Serbs have fulfilled their destiny!

In Vienna, on New Year's Day, 1847.

СКУПШТИНА УОЧИ ТРОЈИЧИНА ДНЕ НА ЛОВЋЕНУ

Глухо доба ноћи, свак спава.

ВЛАДИКА ДАНИЛО
/сам собом/

Виђи врага су седам биљиших,
су два мача а су двије круне,
праунука Туркова с кораном;
за њим јата проклетога кота,
да опусте земљу свуколику,
кâ скакавац што поља опусти!
Француского да не би бријега,
аравијско море све потопи!
Сан паклени окруни Османа,
дарова му луну кâ јабуку.
Злога госта Европи Оркана!
Византија сада није друго
но прћија младе Теодоре:
звијезда је црне судбе над њом.
Палеолог позива Мурата
да закопа Грке са Србима.
Своју мисли Бранковић с Герлуком!
Мухамеде, то је за Герлуку!
Сјем Азије, ђе им је гњијездо,
вражје племе позоба народе;
дан и народ како ћуку тица:
Мурат Српску, а Бајазит Босну,
Мурат Епир, а Мухамед Грчку,
два Селима Ципар и Африку,
сваки нешто, не остаде ништа!
Страшило је слушат што се ради!
Мален свијет за адова жвала,
ни најест га, камоли прејести!
Јанко брани Владислава мртва;
што га брани, кад га не одбрани?
Скендербег је срца Обилића,
ал' умрије тужним изгнаником. –
А ја што ћу, али са киме ћу?
мало руках, малена и снага,
једна сламка међу вихорове,

AN ASSEMBLY ON THE EVE OF TRINITY SUNDAY ON MOUNT LOVĆEN

Petar Njegoš

It is the still time of night, everyone is sleeping.

BISHOP DANILO
(to himself)

See the devil with seven mantles,
With two swords and with two crowns,
The great-grandson of Turk with the Koran;
Behind him swarms from his accursed bitch,
To devastate the whole earth,
Like a grasshopper that lays waste the fields!
If it weren't for France's dike
The Arabian Sea would have flooded all!
An infernal dream gave Osman the crown,
Gifted him with the moon, like an apple.
Orkhan, Europe's evil guest!
Byzantium now is nothing more
Than the dowry of young Teodora:
The star of a dark fate is over it.
Paleologus called in Murat
To bury the Greeks as well as the Serbs.
Branković and Gerluka think they'll get theirs!
Mohammed, that took care of Gerluka!
Besides Asia, where is their nest,
The devil's tribe swallowed nations;
A nation a day, like a bird to the forest owl:
Murat Serbia, and Bajazit Bosnia,
Murat Epirus, and Mohammed Greece,
The two Selims Cyprus and Africa,
Each takes something, nothing remains!
It's a horror to listen to what is happening.
The world is too small for hell's maw,
You can't feed it enough, never mind overfeed it!
Janko defends the dead Vladislav;
Why defend him when he can't protect him?
Skenderbeg had the heart of an Obilić,
But he died a forlorn exile.
And I, what shall I do, and with whom shall I do it?
Few hands and little strength,
A wisp of straw amidst the gale,

сирак тужни без нигђе никога!
Моје племе сном мртвијем спава,
суза моја нема родитеља,
нада мном је небо затворено,
не прима ми плача ни молитве;
у ад ми се свијет претворио,
а сви људи паклени духови.
Црни дане, а црна судбино!
О кукавно Српство угашено,
зла наджвјех твоја сваколика,
а с најгорим хоћу да се борим!
Да, кад главу раздробиш тијелу,
у мучењу издишу чланови.
Куго људска, да те бог убије!
али ти је мало пô свијета
те си својом злошћу отровала,
но си отров адске своје душе
и на овај камен избљувала?
Мала ли је жертва сва Србија
од Дунава до мора сињега?
На трон сједиш неправо узети,
поносиш се скиптром крвавијем;
хулиш бога с светога олтара,
мунар дуби на крст раздробљени!
Али сјенку што му шће тровати
те је у збјег собом унијеше
међу горе за вјечну утјеху
и за спомен рода јуначкога?
Већ је у крв она прекупата
стопут твоју, а стотину нашу!
Виђи посла цара опакога,
кога ђаво о свачему учи:
„Црну Гору покорит не могу
ма никако да је сасвим моја;
с њима треба овако радити...”
па им поче демонски месија
лажне вјере пружат посластице.
Бог вас клео, погани изроди,
што ће турска вјера међу нама?
Куда ћете с клетвом прађедовском?
су чим ћете изаћ пред Милоша
и пред друге српске витезове,
који живе доклен сунца грије? –
***

A sad orphan with no one to turn to!
My tribe sleeps the sleep of the dead,
My tear has no parent,
Heaven is closed above me,
It doesn't receive my lament or my prayer;
The world has turned into a hell for me,
And all men are hellish spirits.
Black day and black fate!
O Serbdom sad and suppressed,
I have lived through all your evils,
And now I shall struggle with the worst one!
Yes, when you sever the head from the body,
The limbs die off in torment.
Plague of mankind, may God strike you dead!
Is half the world too little for you
To have poisoned with your malice,
Did the venom of your infernal soul
Have to be spewed out on this rock, too?
Is all of Serbia too small a victim,
From the Danube to the blue sea?
You sit on a throne unjustly taken,
You lord it with your bloody sceptre;
You blaspheme God from the holy altar,
Your minaret rises from a shattered cross!
But why do you want to poison its shadow
Which they carried with them to refuge
Amongst these mountains, for eternal solace
And as a memorial to a heroic people?
It has already been drenched in blood,
A hundred times in yours, and a hundred in ours!
See the method of that evil emperor
Whom the devil instructs in all things:
"In no way can I humble Montenegro
So that she'll be mine completely;
Here's what we'll have to do with them. . . ."
And the devil's messiah then began
To offer them the delicacies of a false faith.
May God curse you, you unclean monsters,
What do we need the Turkish faith for?
Where will you go with your ancestors' curse on you?
With what will you go before Miloš
And before the other Serbian knights,
Who will live as long as the sun gives warmth?
* * *

Вук Мићуновић лежи близу владике;
притајио се као да спава,
али све чује дивно.

ВУК МИЋУНОВИЋ

Не, владико, ако бога знадеш!
каква те је спопала несрећа
тено кукаш као кукавица
и топиш се у српске несреће?
Да ли ово светковање није
на кому си сабра̂ Црногорце
да чистимо земљу од некрсти?
***

Без момчади ове те су овђе
шест путах је јошт овлико дома;
њина сила, то је твоја сила.
Докле Турци све њих савладају,
многе ће се буле оцрнити;
борби нашој краја бити неће
до истраге турске али наше. –
На̂да нема право ни у кога
до у бога и у своје руке;
надање се наше закопало
на Косово у једну гробницу.
У добру је лако добро бити,
на муци се познају јунаци!
***

СКУПШТИНА О МАЛОМ ГОСПОЂИНУ ДНЕ НА ЦЕТИЊУ: ПОД ВИДОМ ДА МИРЕ НЕКЕ ГЛАВЕ

Главари су се макли на страну,
а народ коло води.

КОЛО

Бог се драги на Србе разљути
за њихова смртна сагрешења.

Vuk Mičunović is lying near the Bishop; he has pretended to be sleeping, but he hears everything quite well.

VUK MIČUNOVIĆ

No, Bishop, for God's sake!
What kind of misfortune has happened to you
That you should wail like a cuckoo bird
And wallow in Serbian woes?
Isn't the purpose of this holy celebration,
At which you have gathered Montenegrins,
To rid the land of the unchristian?
* * *
Not counting these lads who are here
There are six times as many like them at home;
Their strength is your strength.
Before the Turks will overcome all of them,
Many a Turkish woman will be wearing black.
Our struggle will have no end,
Until either the Turks are wiped out or us.
We can't really hope in anyone else
Except in God and our own hands;
Our hope was buried
At Kosovo in a common grave.
In good times it's easy to be good,
In times of trouble you can tell the heroes.
* * *

ASSEMBLY ON THE FEAST OF THE NATIVITY OF MARY AT CETINJE UNDER THE PRETEXT OF MAKING PEACE AMONG SOME LEADERS

The Leaders Have Moved to the Side,
And the People Are Dancing a Kolo.

KOLO

Our dear God got furious at the Serbs
Because of their mortal sins.

Наши цари закон погазише,
почеше се крвнички гонити,
један другом вадит очи живе;
забацише владу и државу,
за правило лудост изабраше.
Невјерне им слуге постадоше
и царском се крвљу окупаше.
***

О проклета косовска вечеро,
куд та срећа да грдне главаре
све потрова и траг им утрије,
сâм да Милош оста на сриједи
са његова оба побратима,
те би Србин данас Србом био!
Бранковићу, погано кољено,
тако ли се служи отачаству,
тако ли се цијени поштење? —
О Милоше, ко ти не завиди?
Ти си жертва благородног чувства,
воинствени геније свемогући,
гром стравични те круне раздраба!
Величаство витешке ти душе
надмашује бесмртне подвиге
дивне Спарте и великог Рима;
сва витештва њина блистателна
твоја горда мишца помрачује.
Шта Леонид оће и Сцевола
кад Обилић стане на поприште?
Ова мишца једнијем ударом
престол сруши а тартар уздрма.
Паде Милош, чудо витезовах,
жертвом на трон бича свијетскога.
Гордо лежи велики војвода
под кључевма крви благородне,
кâ малопред што гордо иђаше,
страшном мишљу прсих надутијех,
кроз дивјачне тмуше азијатске,
гутајућ их ватреним очима;
кâ малопред што гордо иђаше
к светом гробу бесмртног живота,
презирући људско ништавило
и плетење безумне скупштине. —
***

Our rulers trampled the law,
They began to persecute one another cruelly,
One putting out the eyes of the other;
They neglected the government and state,
And they made folly the rule.
Their servants became disloyal to them
And they bathed in royal blood.
* * *
O cursed Kosovo supper,
If only fortune had poisoned all those leaders
And wiped away their traces,
If only Miloš himself had remained in the center
With both his blood brothers,
Then today a Serb would be a Serb!
Branković, you filthy breed,
Is that how one serves the fatherland,
Is that how one values self respect?
O Miloš, who doesn't envy you?
You are the victim of a noble feeling,
An all powerful military genius,
A dreadful thunder that smashes crowns!
The greatness of your knightly soul
Surpasses the immortal feats
Of wonderful Sparta and great Rome;
All their brilliant chivalric deeds
Are overshadowed by your proud muscles.
What can Leonidas do, and Scaevola
When Obilić stands on the field of battle?
These muscles with one blow
Destroyed a throne and shook hell.
Miloš fell, a marvel among knights,
A sacrifice on the throne of the scourge of the world.
Proudly lies the great war leader
Under pools of noble blood,
He who a while before proudly made his way,
His breast swelling with an awesome plan,
Through the savage Asiatic hordes,
Devouring them with his fiery eyes;
He who a while before proudly made his way
To a holy grave of immortal life,
Scorning human nothingness
And the intrigue of an insane assembly.
* * *

ВЛАДИКА
/чита писмо од ријечи до ријечи/

„Селим везир, роб роба свечева,
слуга брата сунца свијетскога,
а посланик од све земље цара.
На знање ви, главари с владиком:
Цар од царах мене је спремио
да облазим земљу свуколику,
да уредбу видим како стоји;
да се вуци не преједу меса,
да овчица која не занесе
своје руно у грм покрај пута,
да пострижем што је предугачко,
да одлијем ђе је препунано;
да прегледам у младежи зубе
да се ружа у трн не изгуби,
да не гине бисер у буниште,
и да раји узду попритегнем,
е је раја кâ остала марва.
Па сам чуо и за ваше горе;
породица света пророкова
зна јунаштву праведну цијену.
Лажу људи што за лафа кажу
да се миша и најмање боји.
Хајте к мени под мојим шатором,
ти, владико, и главни сердари,
само да сте цару на бјељегу,
за примити од мене дарове,
па живите као досле што сте.
Јаки зуби и тврд орах сломе;
добра сабља топуз иза врата,
а камоли главу од купуса.
Шта би било одучити трске
да не чине поклон пред орканом?
Ко потоке може уставити
да к сињему мору не хитају?
Ко изиде испод дивне сјенке
пророкова страшнога барјака,
сунце ће га спржит као муња.
Песницом се нȁда не растеже!
Миш у тикви – што је него сужањ?

(He reads the letter word for word)

"Selim Vezir, slave of the prophet's slave,
Servant of the brother of the world's sun,
And emissary of the Emperor of all the earth.
For your information, leaders and Bishop:
The Emperor of Emperors has sent me
To go throughout the whole land,
To see how things are being run;
So that the wolves don't eat too much meat,
And some sheep doesn't carry away its fleece
Into a bush along the roadside;
To trim what has grown too long,
To skim off what is brimming over;
To examine the teeth of the young people
Lest some rose get lost among the thorn,
Or a pearl perish in the dung heap,
And to tighten a bit the reins on the raya,
Because the raya is like the rest of the cattle.
Now I've heard of your mountains, too;
The Prophet's holy family
Knows the true value of heroism.
People lie who say about the lion
That he fears the mouse even in the least.
Come visit me in my tent,
You, Bishop, and the chief serdars,
Just so you'll be on the Emperor's list,
And to receive gifts from me,
And then go on living as you have up to now.
Strong teeth crack even the hard nut,
And a good sword – a mace at the handle,
Never mind a cabbage head.
What would happen if you trained the reeds
Not to bow before the hurricane?
Who can hold back the streams
From rushing toward the blue sea?
He who comes out from under the wondrous shade
Of the prophet's awesome banner,
The sun will roast like lightning.
A bare fist can't pull apart steel!
A mouse in a pumpkin – what is he but a prisoner?

Узду глодат – да се ломе зуби!
Небо нема без грома цијену;
у фукаре очи од сплачине.
Пучина је стока једна грдна –
добре душе кад јој ребра пучу.
Тѐшко земљи куда прође војска!
***

ВЛАДИКО ДАНИЛО
/отпишује/

„Од владике и свијех главарах
Селим-паши отпоздрав на писмо.
Тврд је орах воћка чудновата,
не сломи га, ал' зубе поломи!
Није вино пошто прије бјеше,
није свијет оно што мишљасте;
барјактару дариват Европу –
грехота је о том и мислити!
Веља крушка у грло западне.
Крв је људска ра́на наопака,
на нос вам је почела скакати;
препунисте мјешину гријеха!
Пуче колан свечевој кобили;
Леополдов храбри војевода,
Собијевски, војвода савојски
саломише демону рогове.
У ћитапу не пише једнако
за два брата једноимењака;
пред Бечом је Бурак посрнуо,
обрнуше кола низа страну.
Не требује царство нељудима,
нâко да се пред свијетом руже.
Дивљу памет а ћуд отровану
дивљи вепар има, а не човјек.
Коме закон лежи у топузу,
трагови му смрде нечовјеством.
Ја се сјећам што си рећи хтио.
„Трагови су многи до пећине" –
за горске се госте не приправља';

Gnaw the reins and you'll break your teeth!
Heaven has no value without thunder;
Scoundrels have eyes of swill.
The common people are a rotten cattle –
They are good when you crack their ribs.
Woe to the land where the army passes through!
* * *

BISHOP DANILO

(He writes off an answer.)

"From the Bishop and all the leaders
To Selim Pasha, in reply to his letter.
The hard nut is a wondrous fruit,
You can't crack it, but it'll crack your teeth!
Wine isn't going for the same price it used to,
Nor is the world what you used to think it was.
Give Europe to the Turkish standard bearer –
It's a sin to even think about it!
A great pear has got stuck in your throat.
Blood is an evil food for humans,
It has begun to come out your nose;
You have become glutted with crimes!
The girth on the prophet's horse has snapped;
Leopold's brave Duke,
And Sobieski, the Duke of Savoy,
Have smashed the demon's horns.
In the books they don't write the same
About the two brothers with the same name;
Burak stumbled before Vienna,
Upsetting your carriage.
Inhuman people need no kingdom
To scandalize the world in this way.
A savage mind and a poisoned nature
Has the wild boar, not man.
He whose law lies in the mace,
His tracks stink of inhumanity.
I understand what you wanted to say.
"There are many tracks to the lion's den" –
Don't expect any mountain guests;

у њих сада друге мисли нема
до што о̏стре̑ зубе за сусједе,
да чувају стадо од звјеради.
Тијесна су врата уљанику;
за међеда скована сјекира.
Јошт имате земље и овацах,
па харајте и коже гулите.
У вас стење на свакоју страну,
зло под горим, као добро под злом.
Спуштавах се ја на ваше уже,
умало се уже не претрже;
отада смо виши пријатељи,
у главу ми памет ућерасте".

They have no other thought right now
Than to sharpen their teeth for their neighbors,
And to guard their flock from the wild beasts.
Narrow are the gates to the bee hive,
And the axe has been forged for the bear.
You have other land and sheep,
So go pillage and tear off their hides.
In your land there is groaning on all sides,
There is bad under worse, just as there is good under bad.
I once got myself in your clutches,
I nearly had them tighten too much on me.
Since then we have been better friends,
You knocked some sense into my head.

(An Excerpt)

VI

FOLKLORE

A Bogomil cemetery

Ever since the nineteenth century, with the beginning of scholarly interest in the collecting of folklore, the Balkans have been recognized as an area rich in folklore. The geographical position of the Balkan peninsula, as a land bridge between Europe and Asia, may possibly explain some of the variety and wealth of its folklore, but the crucial factor in the preservation and continued renewal of such lore until modern times was the illiteracy of much of the population. For specialists generally agree that an oral folk tradition remains vital where illiteracy prevails.

It would be difficult, if not impossible, to speak of separate Croatian and Serbian folklore traditions. As Maja Boškovic-Stulli writes: "Serbo-Croatian folklore is an indivisible entity, forged not only by common themes, subjects, images, forms of expression . . . but also by the same language." (Narodne pripovijetke. Zagreb: Matica Hrvatska, 1963, 9-10.) Serbo-Croatian folklore may be classified according to three main genres: tales (pripovetke), which are always in prose; lyric songs (lirske or ženske pesme), and epic songs (epske or junačke pesme). There are other forms of folklore, such as puzzles, riddles, and proverbs, which do not fit any of the above categories; these are sometimes grouped in a nondescript category called "kraće vrste" ("shorter forms"; for a standard discussion of the typology of Serbo-Croatian folklore it will be useful to consult Vido Latković's Narodna književnost. Belgrade: Naučna knjiga, 1967).

Now the various folklore genres have not been found to be uniformly distributed throughout the Serbian and Croatian areas; the oral epic tradition, for example, has been concentrated in the Dinaric Mountain Range of Montenegro, Bosnia, and Hercegovina, at least from the fifteenth century on. Other folk genres, believed by some to be more ancient, such as the ritual rainmaking songs (dodolske pesme) and yuletide songs (koledske pesme) were to be found until recent times throughout the Serbian and Croatian lands.

The following three poems: "The Fall of the Serbian Empire," "The Maid of Kosovo," and "The Death of the Mother of the Jugovići" all concern the battle of Kosovo or its aftermath. First published by Vuk Stefanović Karadžić in Volume II of his Srpske narodne pesme (Serbian Folk Songs), these poems were generally believed to be remnants of a

Serbian cycle about the battle of Kosovo, one similar to the French songs about Charlemagne's times, and the German Niebelunglied. But there have been a few Serbian scholars who have doubted the antiquity and/or the native roots of the Kosovo "cycle." Nikola Banašević once proposed to trace their origin to the French "chansons de geste," which he claimed had made their way into the Balkans via Venice and the Adriatic Coast (see his "Le cycle de Kosovo et les chansons de geste," in Revue des Études Slaves, *VI, 1926, 224-244). And Svetozar Matić saw the Kosovo poems as relatively recent compositions, products of a nationalistic "epic" that developed in Srem in the eighteenth century, in the vicinity of the monasteries of Fruška Gora (see his* Naš narodni ep i naš stih. *Novi Sad: Matica Srpska, 1964).*

Whether they date from Kosovo times or not, these beautiful songs are inspired with deep religious feeling and with compassion for those who were left at home after the battle, defenseless and hopeless. Although composed in the standard Serbo-Croatian heroic epic line of ten syllables, with obligatory caesura after the fourth syllable, they are lyrical in content and should be classified as ballads rather than epic poems. For a classic example of the oral epic, the reader should examine the poem "Kraljević Marko and Mina of Kostur" which appears later in this section.

For a scholarly discussion of the composition of the oral epic one might first begin with Albert B. Lord's The Singer of Tales *(originally published as* Harvard Studies in Comparative Literature, *24, and republished by Atheneum in 1968 and later). Also of interest will be Tomo Maretić's* Naša narodna epika *(*Our Folk Epic*; republished by Nolit, Belgrade, in 1966). For a discussion of the antiquity of the Serbo-Croatian epic it will be useful to consult Roman Jakobson's "Studies in Comparative Slavic Metrics" (*Oxford Slavonic Papers, *3, 1952), as well as Maretić's* Kosovski junaci i dogadjaji u narodnoj epici *(*Kosovo Heroes and Events in Folk Epic*; Zagreb, 1889). Lord's recent article "The Effect of the Turkish Conquest on Balkan Epic Tradition" (in* Aspects of the Balkans: Continuity and Change, *Henrik Birnbaum and Speros Vryonis, Editors. Mouton: The Hague, 1972, 298-318) will also be of interest in this regard.*

Guslar

ПРОПАСТ ЦАРСТВА СРПСКОГА

Полетио соко тица сива
Од светиње од Јерусалима,
И он носи тицу ластавицу.

То не био соко тица сива,
Веће био светитељ Илија;
Он не носи тице ластавице,
Веће књигу од Богородице,
Однесе је цару на Косово,
Спусти књигу цару на колено,
Сама књига цару беседила:
„Царе Лазо, честито колено!
„Коме ћеш се приволети царству?
„Или волиш царству небескоме,
„Или волиш царству земаљскоме?
„Ако волиш царству земаљскоме,
„Седлај коње, притежи колане,
„Витезови сабље припасујте,
„Па у Турке јуриш учините,
„Сва ће Турска изгинути војска;
„Ако л' волиш царству небескоме,
„А ти сакрој на Косову цркву,
„Не води јој темељ од мермера,
„Већ од чисте свиле и скерлета,
„Па причести и нареди војску;
„Сва ће твоја изгинути војска,
„Ти ћеш, кнеже, шњоме погинути."
А кад царе саслушао речи,
Мисли царе мисли свакојаке:
„Мили Боже, што ћу и како ћу?
„Коме ћу се приволети царству?
„Да или ћу царству небескоме?
„Да или ћу царству земаљскоме?
„Ако ћу се приволети царству,
„Приволети царству земаљскоме,
„Земаљско је за малено царство,
„А небеско у век и до века."

THE FALL OF THE SERBIAN EMPIRE

A falcon took off, a grey bird,
From a holy place, from Jerusalem,
And it carried a lark.

That was not a falcon, a grey bird,
But it was the holy man, Elijah
He wasn't carrying a lark,
But a letter from the Mother of God;
He brought it to the Tsar at Kosovo,
And he dropped the letter on the Tsar's knee;
The letter itself spoke to the Tsar:
"O Tsar Lazar, noble lineage,
Which empire will you choose?
Do you want the heavenly kingdom,
Or do you want an earthly kingdom?
If you want an earthly kingdom,
Saddle your horses, tighten your saddle girths,
Let your knights strap on their swords,
And make an attack against the Turks:
The whole Turkish army will perish;
If you want the heavenly kingdom,
Then build a church at Kosovo,
Don't make its foundation of marble,
But of pure silk and scarlet,
Then give your army communion, and give them their orders;
Your whole army will perish,
And you, Prince, will die with them."
Now when the Tsar had listened to these words,
He thought all kinds of thoughts:
"Dear God, what am I to do?
Which kingdom shall I choose?
Will it be the heavenly kingdom?
Or will it be an earthly kingdom?
If I choose a kingdom,
Choose a kingdom on earth,
An earthly kingdom is only for a short time,
But the heavenly one is eternal, and forever."

Цар воледе царству небескоме,
А него ли царству земаљскоме,
Па сакроји на Косову цркву,
Не води јој темељ од мермера,
Већ од чисте свиле и скерлета,
Па дозива Српског патриара
И дванаест велики владика,
Те причести и нареди војску.
Истом кнеже наредио војску,
На Косову ударише Турци.
Маче војску Богдан Јуже стари
С девет сина девет Југовића,
Како девет сиви соколова,
У свакої је девет иљад' војске,
А у Југа дванаест иљада,
Па се бише и секоше с Турци;
Седам паша бише и убише,
Кад осмога бити започеше,
Ал' погибе Богдан Јуже стари,
И изгибе девет Југовића,
Како девет сиви соколова,
И њиова сва изгибе војска.
Макош' војску три Мрњавчевића:
Бан Угљеша и војвода Гојко
И са њима Вукашине краље,
У свакога триест иљад' војске,
Па се бише и секоше с Турци:
Осам паша бише и убише,
Деветога бити започеше,
Погибоше два Мрњавчевића,
Бан Угљеша и војвода Гојко,
Вукашин је грдни рана доп'о,
Њега Турци с коњма прегазише;
И њиова сва изгибе војска.
Маче војску Ерцеже Степане,
У Ерцега млога силна војска,
Млога војска, шездесет иљада,
Те се бише и секоше с Турци:
Девет паша бише и убише,
Десетога бити започеше,
Ал' погибе Ерцеже Степане,
И његова сва изгибе војска.
Маче војску Српски кнез Лазаре,

The Tsar wanted the heavenly kingdom,
Rather than the earthly one,
So he built a church at Kosovo.
He didn't make its foundation of marble,
But of pure silk and scarlet;
Then he summoned the Serbian patriarch,
And twelve great bishops,
And he gave the army communion, and he gave them their orders.
The prince had barely given the army its orders,
When the Turks attacked Kosovo.
Old Jug Bogdan moved his army forward,
With his nine sons, the nine Jugovići,
Like nine grey falcons,
Each with nine thousand soldiers,
And Jug with twelve thousand.
Then they fought and clashed with the Turks,
Seven pashas they defeated and killed,
When they began to defeat an eighth,
Old Jug Bogdan perished,
And the nine Jugovići died,
Like nine grey falcons,
And all their army perished too.
The three Mrnjavčevići moved their army forward,
Ban Uglješa and Vojvoda Gojko,
And with them King Vukašin, –
Each with thirty thousand soldiers;
Then they fought and clashed with the Turks:
Eight pashas they defeated and killed,
When they began to defeat a ninth,
The two Mrnjavčevići perished,
Ban Uglješa and Vojvoda Gojko;
Vukašin received some horrible wounds,
The Turks trampled him with their horses,
And all their army perished.

Herceg Stepan moved his army forward,
The Herceg has many mighty soldiers,
Many soldiers, sixty thousand,
Then they fought and clashed with the Turks:
Nine pashas they defeated and killed,
When they began to defeat a tenth,
Herceg Stepan perished,
And all his army perished too.
The Serbian prince Lazar moved his army forward,

У Лазе је силни Србаљ био,
Седамдесет и седам иљада,
Па разгрне по Косову Турке,
Не даду се ни гледати Турком,
Да камо ли бојак бити с Турци;
Тад би Лаза надвладао Турке,
Бог убио Вука Бранковића!
Он издаде таста на Косову;
Тада Лазу надвладаше Турци,
И погибе Српски кнез Лазаре,
И његова сва изгибе војска,
Седамдесет и седам иљада;
Све је свето и честито било
И миломе Богу приступачно.

Laza has a powerful lot of Serbs,
Seventy seven thousand;
And they chased the Turks across Kosovo,
The Turks couldn't get a look at them,
Never mind do battle with them:
Then Laza would have overwhelmed the Turks,
May God strike Vuk Branković dead!
He betrayed his father-in-law at Kosovo:
Then the Turks overwhelmed Laza,
And the Serbian prince Lazar perished,
And all his army perished, too,
Seventy seven thousand.

All was holy and honorable,
And according to God's plan.

КОСОВКА ДЈЕВОЈКА

Уранила Косовка девојка,
Уранила рано у недељу,
У недељу прије јарка сунца,
Засукала бијеле рукаве,
Засукала до бели лаката,
На плећима носи леба бела,
У рукама два кондира златна,
У једноме лађане водице,
У другоме руменога вина;
Она иде на Косово равно,
Па се шеће по разбоју млада,
По разбоју честитога кнеза,
Те преврће по крви јунаке;
Ког јунака у животу нађе,
Умива га лађаном водицом,
Причешћује вином црвенијем
И залаже лебом бијелијем.
Намера је намерила била
На јунака Орловића Павла,
На кнежева млада барјактара,
И њега је нашла у животу,
Десна му је рука осечена
И лијева нога до колена,
Вита су му ребра изломљена,
Виде му се џигерице беле;
Измиче га из те млоге крвце,
Умива га лађаном водицом,
Причешћује вином црвенијем
И залаже лебом бијелијем;
Кад јунаку срце заиграло,
Проговара Орловићу Павле:
„Сестро драга, Косовко девојко!
„Која ти је голема невоља,
„Те преврћеш по крви јунаке?
„Кога тражиш по разбоју млада?
„Или брата, или братучеда?
„Ал' по греку стара родитеља?"

THE MAID OF KOSOVO

The maid of Kosovo arose early,
Arose early on Sunday,
On Sunday before the sun got hot;
She rolled up her white sleeves,
Rolled them up to her white elbows,
On her shoulders she carries white bread,
In her hands two pitchers of gold,
In one cold water,
In the other red wine.
Then she goes to Kosovo Plain,
And the young maid walks through the battlefield,
Through the battlefield of the noble prince,
And she turns the heroes over in their blood.
What hero she finds alive
She washes with cold water,
Gives him red wine for communion,
And feeds him white bread.
Fortune led her
To the hero Pavle Orlović,
To the prince's young standard bearer,
And she found him alive.
His right arm had been severed,
As well as his left leg to the knee,
His lower ribs had been crushed,
Showing his white liver;
She moved him out of all that blood,
Washed him with cold water,
Gave him red wine for communion,
And fed him white bread.
When his hero's heart began to beat,
Pavle Orlović spoke out:
"Dear sister, maid of Kosovo,
What is your great misfortune,
That you should be turning heroes over in their blood?
Whom are you seeking on the battlefield, young maiden:
Is it your brother, or your cousin,
Or is it your own old father?

Проговара Косовка девојка:
„Драги брато, делијо незнана!
„Ја од рода никога не тражим:
„Нити брата, нити братучеда,
„Ни по греку стара родитеља;
„Мож' ли знати, делијо незнана,
„Кад кнез Лаза причешћива војску
„Код прекрасне Самодреже цркве
„Три недеље тридест калуђера?
„Сва се српска причестила војска,
„Најпослије три војводе бојне:
„Једно јесте Милошу војвода,
„А друго је Косанчић Иване,
„А треће је Топлица Милане;
„Ја се онде деси на вратима,
„Кад се шета војвода Милошу,
„Красан јунак на овоме свету,
„Сабља му се по калдрми вуче,
„Свилен калпак, оковано перје,
„На јунаку коласта аздија,
„Око врата свилена марама,
„Обазре се и погледа на ме,
„С' себе скиде коласту аздију,
„С' себе скиде, па је мени даде:
„ „На, девојко, коласту аздију,
„ „По чему ћеш мене споменути,
„ „По аздији по имену моме:
„ „Ево т' идем погинути, душо,
„ „У табору честитога кнеза;
„ „Моли Бога, драга душо моја,
„ „Да ти с' здраво из табора вратим,
„ „А и тебе добра срећа нађе,
„ „Узећу те за Милана мога,
„ „За Милана Богом побратима,
„ „Кој' је мене Богом побратио,
„ „Вишњим Богом и светим Јованом;
„ „Ја ћу теби кум венчани бити." "
„За њим иде Косанчић Иване,
„Красан јунак на овоме свету,
„Сабља му се по калдрми вуче,
„Свилен калпак, оковано перје,
„На јунаку коласта аздија,
„Око врата свилена марама,
„На руци му бурма позлаћена,

The maid of Kosovo spoke out:
"Dear brother, unknown hero,
I am not seeking any of my kin:
Neither brother, nor cousin,
Nor my own old father.
Perhaps you know, unknown hero,
How Prince Laza gave communion to the army
At the beautiful church of Samodreža,
For three weeks, with thirty monks?
The whole Serbian army took communion,
And last of all, the three battle commanders:
One was vojvoda Miloš,
A second was Ivan Kosančić,
A third was Milan Toplica.
I happened to be at my gate
When Vojvoda Miloš walked by,
The most handsome hero in this world,
His sword touched the ground,
The hero wore a silk hat topped with feathers,
And a colorful tunic with circular designs.
Around his neck he had a silk neckerchief.
He gazed around and he looked at me;
He took off his tunic,
He took it off and he gave it to me:
"Here, maiden, take my tunic,
You'll remember me by this,
By my tunic, and by my name:
Well, love, I must go to die
In the camp of the noble prince;
Pray to God, dear love of mine,
That I'll return healthy from the camp,
And good fortune will find you, too;
I'll take you for my Milan,
For Milan, my blood brother in God,
Who has sworn blood brotherhood to me,
By the God above, and by Saint John;
I'll be your wedding witness."
After him came Ivan Kosančić,
The most handsome hero in this world,
His sword touched the ground;
The hero wore a silk hat topped with feathers,
And a colorful tunic with circular designs.
Around his neck he had a silk neckerchief,
And on his hand a gold engagement ring;

„Обазре се и погледа на ме,
„С руке скиде бурму позлаћену,
„С руке скиде, па је мени даде:
„ „На, девојко, бурму позлаћену,
„ „По чему ћеш мене споменути,
„ „А по бурми по имену моме:
„ „Ево т' идем погинути, душо,
„ „У табору честитога кнеза;
„ „Моли Бога, моја душо драга,
„ „Да ти с' здраво из табора вратим,
„ „А и тебе добра срећа нађе,
„ „Узећу те за Милана мога,
„ „За Милана Богом побратима,
„ „Кој' је мене Богом побратио,
„ „Вишњим Богом и светим Јованом;
„ „Ја ћу теби ручни девер бити." "
„За њим иде Топлица Милане,
„Красан јунак на овоме свету,
„Сабља му се по калдрми вуче,
„Свилен калпак, оковано перје,
„На јунаку коласта аздија,
„Око врата свилена марама,
„На руци му копрена од злата,
„Обазре се и погледа на ме,
„С руке скиде копрену од злата,
„С руке скиде, па је мени даде:
„ „На, девојко, копрену од злата,
„ „По чему ћеш мене споменути,
„ „По копрени по имену моме:
„ „Ево т' идем погинути, душо,
„ „У табору честитога кнеза;
„ „Моли Бога, моја душо драга,
„ „Да ти с' здраво из табора вратим,
„ „Тебе, душо, добра срећа нађе,
„ „Узећу те за верну љубовцу." "
„И одоше три војводе бојне.
„Њи ја данас по разбоју тражим."
Ал' беседи Орловићу Павле:
„Сестро драга, Косовко девојко!
„Видиш, душо, она копља бојна
„Понајвиша а и понајгушћа,
„Онде ј' пала крвца од јунака
„Та доброме коњу до стремена,
„До стремена и до узенђије,

He gazed around and he looked at me,
And from his hand he removed the gold ring,
He removed it from his hand and he gave it to me:
"Here, maiden, take this gold ring,
You'll remember me by this,
By the ring, and by my name:
Well, love, I must go to die
In the camp of the noble prince;
Pray to God, dear love of mine,
That I'll return healthy from the camp;
And good fortune will find you, too;
I'll take you for my Milan,
For Milan, my blood brother in God,
Who has sworn blood brotherhood to me,
By the God above, and by Saint John;
I'll give you away at the wedding."
After him came Milan Toplica:
The most handsome hero in this world,
His sword touched the ground;
The hero wore a silk hat topped with feathers,
And a colorful tunic with circular designs.
Around his neck he had a silk neckerchief,
And on his hand a gold veil;
He gazed around and he looked at me,
And from his hand he removed the gold veil,
He removed it from his hand, and he gave it to me:
"Here, maiden, take this gold veil,
You'll remember me by this,
By the veil, and by my name:
Well, love, I must go to die
In the camp of the noble prince;
Pray to God, dear love of mine,
That I'll return healthy from the camp,
And good fortune will find you, too;
I'll take you for my faithful wife."
And the three battle commanders went away.
It's them I seek on the battlefield today."
Then Pavle Orlović spoke:
"Dear sister, maid of Kosovo,
Can you see, love, those war lances,
The tallest and thickest of all?
There heroic blood was shed,
Right up to the stirrups of a good horse,
Right up to the stirrups, right up to the foot rests,

„А јунаку до свилена паса,
„Онде су ти сва три погинула,
„Већ ти иди двору бијеломе,
„Не крвави скута и рукава."
Кад девојка саслушала речи,
Проли сузе низ бијело лице,
Она оде свом бијелу двору
Кукајући из бијела грла:
„Јао јадна! уде ти сам среће!
„Да се, јадна, за зелен бор ватим,
„И он би се зелен осушио."

And up to a hero's silk belt.
All three of them died there!
So go home to your white manor,
Don't bloody your skirt and your sleeves."
When the maiden had listened to these words,
She shed tears down her white face,
And she went home to her white manor
Wailing from her white throat:
"Woe, poor wretch, my luck is bad!
If I, poor wretch, were to take hold of a green pine,
It would dry up, though green.

СМРТ МАЈКЕ ЈУГОВИЋА

Мили Боже, чуда великога!
Кад се слеже на Косово војска,
У тој војсци девет Југовића
И десети стар Јуже Богдане;
Бога моли Југовића мајка,
Да јој Бог да очи соколове
И бијела крила лабудова,
Да одлети над Косово равно,
И да види девет Југовића
И десетог стар-Југа Богдана.
Што молила Бога домолила:
Бог јој дао очи соколове
И бијела крила лабудова,
Она лети над Косово равно,
Мртви нађе девет Југовића
И десетог стар-Југа Богдана,
И више њи девет бојни копља,
На копљима девет соколова,
Око копља девет добри коња,
А поред њи девет љути лава,
Тад' завришта девет добри коња,
И залаја девет љути лава,
А закликта девет соколова;
И ту мајка тврда срца била,
Да од срца сузе не пустила,
Већ узима девет добри коња,
И узима девет љути лава,
И узима девет соколова,
Пак се врати двору бијеломе.
Далеко је снае угледале,
Мало ближе пред њу ишетале,
Закукало девет удовица,
Заплакало девет сиротица,
Завриштало девет добри коња,
Залајало девет љути лава,

THE DEATH OF THE MOTHER OF THE JUGOVIĆI

Dear God, what a great sight!
When the army gathered at Kosovo,
In that army the nine Jugović brothers
And the tenth, old Jug Bogdan;
The mother of the Jugovići asks God
To give her the eyes of a falcon,
And a swan's white wings,
That she might fly over Kosovo Plain
And see the nine Jugovići,
And the tenth, old Jug Bogdan.
What she asked for, God granted:
God gave her the eyes of a falcon
And a swan's white wings;
She flew over Kosovo Plain,
Found the nine Jugovići dead,
As well as the tenth, old Jug Bogdan,
And above them nine battle lances,
On the lances nine falcons,
Around the lances nine good horses,
And beside them nine wild lions.
Then whinnied the nine good horses,
And roared the nine wild lions,
And shrieked the nine falcons;
Here, too, the mother kept a hardened heart,
Her heart held back the tears,
Instead, she took the nine good horses,
And she took the nine wild lions,
And she took the nine falcons,
Then she went back to her white manor.
From afar her daughters-in-law caught sight of her,
They walked out a bit closer toward her,
The nine widows began to wail,
The nine orphans began to sob,
The nine good horses began to whinny,
The nine wild lions began to roar,

Закликтало девет соколова;
И ту мајка тврда срца била,
Да од срца сузе не пустила.
Кад је било ноћи у по ноћи,
Ал' завришта Дамјанов зеленко;
Пита мајка Дамјанове љубе:
„Снао моја, љубо Дамјанова!
„Што нам вришти Дамјанов зеленко?
„Ал' је гладан шенице бјелице,
„Али жедан воде са Звечана?"
Проговара љуба Дамјанова:
„Свекрвице, мајко Дамјанова!
„Нит' је гладан шенице бјелице,
„Нити жедан воде са Звечана,
„Већ је њега Дамјан научио
„До по ноћи ситну зоб зобати,
„Од по ноћи на друм путовати;
„Пак он жали свога господара
„Што га није на себи донијо."
И ту мајка тврда срца била,
Да од срца сузе не пустила.
Кад у јутру данак освануо,
Али лете два врана гаврана,
Крвава им крила до рамена,
На кљунове б'јела пјена тргла;
Они носе руку од јунака
И на руци бурма позлаћена,
Бацају је у криоце мајци;
Узе руку Југовића мајка,
Окретала, превртала с њоме,
Па дозивље љубу Дамјанову:
„Снао моја, љубо Дамјанова!
„Би л' познала, чија ј' ово рука?"
Проговара љуба Дамјанова:
„Свекрвице, мајко Дамјанова!
„Ово ј' рука нашега Дамјана,
„Јера бурму ја познајем, мајко,
„Бурма са мном на вјенчању била."
Узе мајка руку Дамјанову,
Окретала, превртала с њоме,
Пак је руци тијо бесједила:
„Моја руко, зелена јабуко!
„Гдје си расла, гдје л' си устргнута!
„А расла си на криоцу моме,

The nine falcons began to shriek
Here, too, the mother kept a hardened heart,
Her heart held back the tears.
When it was night, at midnight,
Why, Damjan's dapple began to whinny;
The mother asked Damjan's wife:
"My daughter-in-law, wife of Damjan!
Why is Damjan's dapple whinnying?
Is it hungry for some white wheat,
Or is it thirsty for some water from the Zvečan?"
Spoke out the wife of Damjan:
"Mother-in-law, mother of Damjan!
He's not hungry for some white wheat,
Nor is he thirsty for water from the Zvečan,
But Damjan taught him
To munch fine oats until midnight,
And after midnight to go for a ride on the road;
So he mourns for his master,
Because he hasn't brought him back home."
Here, too, the mother kept a hardened heart,
And her heart held back the tears.
When in the morning the day grew light,
Why, there flew two black ravens,
Their wings bloody to their shoulders,
White foam gushing to their beaks;
They carry the arm of a hero,
And on the arm is a gold engagement ring,
They throw it into the mother's lap.
The mother of the Jugovići took the arm,
Turned it around and around, and then over and over,
Then she called to Damjan's wife:
"My daughter-in-law, wife of Damjan!
Would you know whose arm this is?"
Spoke out the wife of Damjan:
"Mother-in-law, mother of Damjan!
This is the arm of our Damjan,
Because I recognize the ring, mother,
I had the ring with me at our wedding."
The mother took the arm of Damjan,
Turned it around and around, and then over and over,
Then she spoke to the arm softly:
"My arm, green apple!
Where did you grow, where were you torn off!
Why, you grew on my lap,

„Устргнута на Косову равном!"
Надула се Југовића мајка,
Надула се, па се и распаде
За својије девет Југовића
И десетим стар-Југом Богданом.

And you were torn off at Kosovo Plain!"
Swelled the heart of the mother of the Jugovići,
Swelled, and then burst,
For her nine Jugovići,
And for the tenth, old Jug Bogdan.

If one were asked to choose the outstanding figure of the Serbian cultural revival in the nineteenth century the first and only name to come to mind would be that of Vuk Stefanović Karadžić (1787-1864), whom Miodrag Pavlović has called "the cultural ideologist of the Serbian nation." (Miodrag Pavlović, Istorija srpske književnosti, *I,* Romantizam, *Beograd: Nolit, 1968).* *Marko Kraljević*

Born in the village of Tršić, in backward Turkish-held Serbia, Vuk followed a road to renown that was lined with obstacles, of which the greatest was not *the Austrian police, who reported his activities to their chief Sedlnicky, and through him to Metternich, but rather it was his own countrymen, including the Serbian Orthodox hierarchy, the Serbian bourgeoisie in Austro-Hungary, and Prince Miloš Obrenović himself,*

who hindered the publication of his works and prevented the introduction in Serbia of his language reforms.

*Grammarian, linguist, lexicographer, collector of folklore, and historian of the first Serbian Uprising (1804-1813) in which he took part, Vuk Karadžić's activities seem to have touched almost all aspects of Serbian cultural life in the first half of the nineteenth century. Under the tutelage of the brilliant Slovene, Jernej Kopitar, Slavic Censor and librarian in Vienna, Vuk prepared and published the first Serbian grammar based on the spoken language of the peasantry (*Pismenica serbskoga jezika po govoru prostoga naroda napisana, *Vienna, 1814). Also with Kopitar's encouragement, Vuk published his first book of Serbian folk songs (*Mala prostonarodnja slaveno-serbska pjesmarica, *Vienna, 1814). In 1818 Vuk's* Srpski rječnik *was printed, which included more than 27,000 words, almost all of them taken from the spoken language. The inclusion in his* Rječnik *of particularly vulgar words and sometimes racy definitions earned Vuk the undying enmity of Metropolitan Stefan Stratimirović, head of the Serbian Orthodox Church in Austro-Hungary, whose name was listed in the book as a subscriber. Until his death in 1836, Stratimirović actively opposed many of Vuk's efforts in the Serbian cultural sphere, continually stirring up the Serbian intelligentsia and merchant class in Austro-Hungary against the impoverished and beleaguered cultural revolutionary.*

*But Vuk's work in the field of folklore had brought him the support of some renowned Europeans, including Jakob Grimm and Goethe, and he was awarded membership in several learned societies, including those of Göttingen, Petersburg, Krakow, Tübingen, and Moscow. Goethe translated some Serbian folk poems for his journal, and Grimm wrote more than once in high praise of Serbian folk poetry. Teresa Von Jakob (pen-name Talvj), who had helped Goethe with his translations, published a two-volume German translation of the songs (*Volkslieder der Serben, *Halle, 1825-1826) and John Bowring came out with an English translation based on Talvj (*Serbian Popular Poetry, *London, 1827). Vuk's European fame encouraged him to collect and publish more folk songs, and between 1823 and 1833 he issued four volumes (the Leipzig edition) of songs, both epic ("junačke pesme") and lyric ("ženske pesme"). He also published a volume of proverbs (*Srpske narodne poslovice, *Cetinje, 1836), and a book of folktales (*Srpske narodne pripovijetke, *Vienna, 1853).*

*Vuk was also important both as a translator (*Novi Zavjet, *the* New Testament, *1847) and historian. He had intended to write a history of contemporary Serbia in two volumes, but Prince Miloš Obrenović prevented him from publishing the first volume, which eventually formed the basis for Leopold Ranke's work* Die serbische Revolution *(Hamburg, 1829). Vuk did manage to publish a monograph on the life of Miloš (*Miloš Obrenović, knjaz Serbii, *Buda, 1828) and several biographical sketches which are gems of Serbian prose, including that of Hajduk Veljko, which is included in this book.*

Vuk Stefanović Karadžić

МАРКО КРАЉЕВИЋ И МИНА ОД КОСТУРА

Сједе Марко с мајком вечерати
Сува љеба и црвена вина;
Али Марку три књиге дођоше:
Једна књига од Стамбола града,
Од онога цара Појазета;
Друга књига од Будима града,
Од онога краља Будимскога;
Трећа књига од Сибиња града,
Од војводе Сибињанин-Јанка.
Која књига од Стамбола града,
Цар га у њој на војску позива,
На арапску љуту покрајину;
Која књига од Будима града,
Краљ га у њој у сватове зове,
У сватове на кумство вјенчано,
Да га вјенча с госпођом краљицом;
Која књига од Сибиња града,
Јанко у њој на кумство зазива,
Да му крсти два нејака сина.
Марко пита своју стару мајку:
„Сјетуј мене, моја стара мајко,
„Куда ми је сад ићи најпрече:
„Ил' ћу ићи на цареву војску,
„Ил' ћу ићи краљу у сватове,
„Да га вјенчам с госпођом краљицом;
„Ил' ћу ићи Сибињанин-Јанку,
„Да му крстим два нејака сина?"
Вели мајка Краљевићу Марку:
„О мој синко, Краљевићу Марко!
„У свате се иде на весеље,
„На кумство се иде по закону,
„На војску се иде од невоље:
„Иди, синко, на цареву војску;
„И Бог ће нам, синко, опростити,
„А Турци нам не ће разумјети."
То је Марко послушао мајку,
Па се спреми на цареву војску,

MARKO KRALJEVIĆ AND MINA FROM KOSTUR

Marko had just sat down with his mother to a supper
Of dry bread and red wine,
When three letters arrived for Marko:
One letter was from Istanbul town,
From that Sultan Bajazit;
A second letter was from Buda town,
From that Hungarian king;
A third letter was from Sibinj town,
From Duke Janko Sibinjanin.
In the letter from Istanbul town
The Sultan summons him to the army,
To the wild Arabian region;
In the letter from Buda town
The King invites him to a wedding,
To a wedding, as a wedding witness,
To crown him and Madame Queen;
In the letter from Sibinj town
Janko invites him to be a kum,
To christen his two frail sons for him.
Marko asks his old mother:
"Give me your advice, my old mother,
Where is it most urgent for me to go now:
Shall I go to the Sultan's army,
Or shall I go to the King's wedding,
To crown him and Madame Queen;
Or shall I go to Janko Sibinjanin
To christen his two frail sons for him?"
Says his mother to Kraljević Marko:
"Oh, my son, Kraljević Marko,
One goes to a wedding for a good time,
One goes to a Christening to keep God's law,
One goes to the army because one has to:
Go, son, to the Sultan's army;
And God will forgive us, son,
But the Turks will never understand."
Marko then heeded his mother's advice
And he made ready for the Sultan's army,

С' собом води слугу Голубана;
На походу мајци наручује:
,,Чу ли мене, моја стара мајко!
,,Граду врата рано затворајте,
,,А у јутру доцкан отворајте;
,,Јера сам ти, мајко, у завади
,,С проклетијем Мином од Костура,
,,Па се бојим, моја стара мајко,
,,Да ми б'јеле не похара дворе."
Оде Марко на цареву војску
Са својијем слугом Голубаном.
Кад су били на трећем конаку,
Сједи Марко вечер' вечерати,
Голубан му рујно вино служи:
Узе чашу Краљевићу Марко,
Чашу узе, у сан се занесе,
И испусти чашу на трпезу,
Чаша паде, вино се не просу;
Буди њега слуга Голубане:
,,Господару, Краљевићу Марко!
,,И досад си на војску ишао,
,,Ал' нијеси тако дријемао,
,,Ни из руке чашу испуштао!"
А Марко се трже иза санка,
Па говори слуги Голубану:
,,Голубане, моја вјерна слуго!
,,Мало тренух, чудан санак усних,
,,Чудан санак а у чудан часак,
,,Ђе се прамен магле запођеде
,,Од Костура града бијелога,
,,Пак се сави около Прилипа,
,,У тој магли Мина од Костура,
,,Он похара моје б'јеле дворе,
,,Све похара и огњем попали,
,,Стару мајку с коњма пригазио,
,,Зароби ми моју вјерну љубу,
,,Одведе ми коње из арова,
,,И однесе из ризнице благо."
Вели њему слуга Голубане:
,,А не бој се, Краљевићу Марко!
,,Добар јунак добар сан уснио:
,,Сан је лажа, а Бог је истина."
Кад дођоше граду Цариграду,
Диже царе силовиту војску,

Taking with him his servant Goluban.
On setting out, he instructs his mother:
"Listen to me, my old mother,
Shut the gates to the city early,
And in the morning open them late;
Because I am on bad terms, mother,
With that cursed Mina from Kostur,
And I am afraid, my old mother,
That he will ransack my white castle."
Marko went off to the Sultan's army
With his servant Goluban.
When they had reached the third day's stopping place,
Marko sat down to eat dinner,
And Goluban served him red wine:
Kraljević Marko took a glass,
He took a glass, fell into a deep sleep,
And let the glass fall to the table;
The glass fell, but the wine didn't spill.
His servant Goluban wakes him up:
"Lord Kraljević Marko!
You have gone to the army before now,
But you never dozed off like that,
Nor did you let the glass fall from your hand!"
And Marko rouses himself from his sleep,
And he says to his servant Goluban:
"Goluban, my faithful servant!
I dozed off a little and I had a strange dream,
A strange dream and at a strange time:
A patch of fog arose
From Kostur, the white city,
And it curled around Prilep;
In that fog was Mina from Kostur,
He ransacked my white castle,
He ransacked everything and put the castle to the torch,
He trampled my old mother with horses,
He abducted my faithful wife,
Led away my horses from their stables,
And carried off my treasure from the treasury."
His servant Goluban says to him:
"Now don't you worry, Kraljević Marko;
A good hero has dreamed a good dream;
Dreams are lies, but God is truth."
When they arrived at the town Istanbul,
The Sultan raised a powerful army,

Отидоше преко мора сињег
На арапску љуту покрајину,
Те узимљу по мору градове,
Четрдесет и четири града;
Кад дођоше под Кара-Окана,
Окан бише три године дана,
Окан бише, узет' не могоше;
Марко с'јече Арапске јунаке,
Па све главе пред цара износи,
А цар Марку бакшише поклања.
То Турцима врло мучно било,
Па говоре цару честитоме:
„Господине, царе Појазете!
„Марко није јунак николико,
„Веће мртве одсијеца главе
„И пред тебе на бакшиш доноси."
То зачуо Краљевићу Марко,
Па се моли цару честитоме:
„Господине, царе поочиме!
„Мене јесте сутра крсно име,
„Крсно име лијеп данак Ђурђев;
„Већ ме пусти, царе поочиме,
„Да прославим моје крсно име
„По закону и по обичају;
„И дај мене побра Алил-агу,
„Да се с миром понапијем вина."
Од ина се цару не могаше,
Веће посла Краљевића Марка,
Да он слави своје крсно име,
И даде му побра Алил-агу.
Оде Марко у гору зелену
Подалеко од војске цареве,
Па разапе бијела шатора,
Под њим сједе пити мрко вино
Са својијем побром Алил-агом.
Кад у јутру јутро освануло,
Одмах позна стража од Арапа,
Да у војсци не имаде Марка,
Па повика стража од Арапа:
„Сад навали, љута Арапијо!
„Нема оног страшнога јунака
„На шарену коњу великоме."
Тад' навали љута Арапија,
Оде цару триест хиљад' војске.

And they set off across the blue sea
To the wild Arabian region,
And they took cities along the coast,
Forty four cities;
When they arrived before Kara-Okan
They pounded Okan for three full years,
They pounded Okan, but they couldn't take it;
Marko cuts down Arab heroes,
Then he brings their heads to the Sultan
And the Sultan gives bakshish to Marko.
This was hard for the Turks to take,
So they said to the honorable Sultan:
"Lord Sultan Bajazit!
Marko is no kind of hero,
Why he cuts the heads off dead men
And brings them to you for bakshish."
Kraljević Marko got wind of this,
And he beseeched the honorable Sultan:
"Lord Sultan foster-father,
Tomorrow is my family's saint's day,
Our saint's day, the beautiful day of Saint George;
So let me go, Sultan foster-father,
To celebrate my saint's day
By our religion and by our custom;
And give me my blood brother, Alil Aga,
That I may do a little heavy drinking, in peace."
The Sultan had no choice,
But to send Kraljević Marko off
To celebrate his saint's day,
And he gave him his blood brother, Alil Aga.
Marko went into the green forest,
Some distance from the Sultan's army,
Then he pitched his white tent,
And he sat beneath it to drink dark wine
With his blood brother, Alil Aga.
When in the morning it grew light,
At once the Arab lookout realized
That Marko was not with the army,
So the Arab lookout shouted out:
"Attack now, fierce Arabs!
They haven't got that terrifying hero
On the big piebald horse."
Then the fierce Arabs attacked,
And the Sultan lost thirty thousand soldiers.

Онда царе Марку књигу пише:
„Брже ходи, мој посинко Марко!
„Пропаде ми триест хиљад' војске."
Али Марко цару одговара:
„Када брже, царе поочиме!
„Још се нисам вина напојио,
„А камо ли у славу устао!"
Кад је друго јутро освануло,
Опет виче стража од Арапа:
„Навалите, љута Арапијо!
„Нема оног страшнога јунака
„На шарену коњу великоме."
А Арапи јуриш учинише,
Оде цару шесет хиљад' војске.
Опет царе Марку књигу пише:
„Ходи брже, мој посинко Марко!
„Пропаде ми шесет хиљад' војске."
Али Марко цару одговара:
„Чекај мало, царе поочиме,
„Још се нисам добро почастио
„С кумовима и с пријатељима."
Кад је треће јутро освануло,
Опет виче стража од Арапа:
„Навалите, љута Арапијо!
„Нема оног доброга јунака
„На шарену коњу великоме."
А Арапи јуриш учинише,
Оде цару сто хиљада војске.
Онда царе Марку књигу пише:
„Брже да си, мој посинко Марко!
„Брже да си, мој по Богу синко!
„Арапи ми шатор оборише."
Онда Марко усједе на Шарца,
Пак он оде у цареву војску;
Кад у јутру бијел дан освану
И двије се ударише војске,
Опази га стража од Арапа,
Пак повика из грла бијела:
„Сад уступи, љута Арапијо!
„Ето оног страшнога јунака
„На шарену коњу великоме."
Онда Марко уд'ри међ' Арапе,
На три стране војску рашћерао:
Једну војску сабљом исјекао,

Here the Sultan wrote a letter to Marko:
"Come faster, my foster-son Marko!
I've lost thirty thousand soldiers."
But Marko answered the Sultan:
"What's the hurry, Sultan foster-father!
I still haven't drunk my fill of wine,
Never mind standing in praise of Saint George.
When a second morning dawned,
Again the Arab lookout shouted out:
"Attack, fierce Arabs!
They haven't got that terrifying hero
On the big piebald horse."
The Arabs made an attack,
And the sultan lost sixty thousand soldiers.
Again the Sultan wrote a letter to Marko:
"Come quickly, my foster-son Marko!
I've just lost sixty thousand soldiers."
But Marko answered the Sultan:
"Wait a while, Sultan foster-father!
I haven't finished entertaining
My kums and my friends."
When a third morning dawned,
Again the Arab lookout shouted out:
"Attack, fierce Arabs!
They haven't got that good hero
On the big piebald horse."
The Arabs made an attack,
And the Sultan lost 100,000 soldiers.
Now the Sultan wrote a letter to Marko:
"Faster, will you, my foster-son Marko!
Faster, will you, my godson!
The Arabs have knocked my tent down."
Then Marko mounted Šarac,
And he rode off to the Sultan's army.
When on the morrow the bright day dawned,
And the two armies clashed,
The Arab lookout spotted him,
And he shouted from his white throat:
"Now retreat, fierce Arabs!
There's that terrifying hero
On the big piebald horse."
Then Marko struck among the Arabs
Scattering their army in three directions:
One army he cut down with his sword,

Другу војску Шарцем погазио,
Трећу војску пред цара догнао;
Ал' се Марко љуто изранио:
Седамдесет рана допануо,
Седамдесет рана од Арапа;
Пак он цару паде преко крила,
Пита њега царе господине:
„Мој посинко, Краљевићу Марко!
„Јесу ли ти ране од самрти?
„Можеш ли ми, синко, пребољети,
„Да ти тражим мелем и ећиме?"
Вели њему Краљевићу Марко:
„Господине, царе поочиме!
„Нијесу ми ране од самрти,
„Чини ми се, могу пребољети."
Цар се маши руком у џепове,
Те му даје хиљаду дуката,
Да он иде грдне ране видат',
За њим посла двије вјерне слуге,
Да гледају, да не умре Марко;
Али Марко не тражи ећима,
Већ он иде из крчме у крчму,
Те он тражи, ђе је боље вино.
Тек се Марко вина понапио,
И грдне му ране зарастоше;
Али њему ситна књига дође,
Да су њему двори похарани:
Похарани, огњем попаљени,
Стара мајка с коњма прегажена
И вјерна му љуба заробљена;
Тад' протужи Краљевићу Марко
Уз кољено цару поочиму:
„Господине, царе поочиме!
„Б'јели су ми двори похарани,
„Вјерна ми је љуба заробљена,
„Стара мајка с коњма прегажена,
„Из ризнице однешено благо,
„Однијо га Мина од Костура."
Њега тјеши царе господине:
„Не бој ми се, мој посинко Марко!
„Ако су ти двори изгорели,
„Љепше ћу ти дворе начинити
„Поред мојих, кô и моји што су;
„Ако ти је благо однешено,

A second army he stamped with Šarac,
And a third army he drove before the Sultan.
But Marko was severely wounded:
He had received seventy wounds,
Seventy wounds from the Arabs;
And he fell across the lap of the Sultan;
The Lord Sultan asks him:
"My foster-son, Kraljević Marko,
Are your wounds mortal?
Can you recover, my son?
Shall I get ointment and doctors for you?"
Kraljević Marko says to him:
"Lord Sultan foster-father:
My wounds are not mortal,
It seems to me that I can recover."
The Sultan puts his hand in his pockets,
And he gives him one thousand ducats
To go look after his terrible wounds;
He sent two faithful servants after him,
To see to it that Marko didn't die;
But Marko doesn't look for doctors,
Instead he goes from tavern to tavern
Looking for the best wine.
Marko had just drunk his fill of wine,
And his terrible wounds had just healed,
When a small letter arrived for him,
Saying that his castle has been ransacked,
Ransacked and put to the torch,
His old mother has been trampled with horses,
And his faithful wife has been carried off.
Then Kraljević Marko complained
At the knee of his Sultan foster-father:
"Lord Sultan foster-father!
My white castle has been ransacked,
My faithful wife has been carried off,
My old mother trampled with horses,
And my treasure has been taken from my treasury;
Mina from Kostur has taken it."
The Lord Sultan consoles him:
"Don't worry about it, foster-son Marko!
If your castle has burned down
I'll build you a more beautiful castle,
Next to mine, and just like mine;
If your treasure has been taken away

„Да т' учиним агом харачлијнским,
„Пак ћеш више блага сакупити;
„Ако ти је љуба одведена,
„Бољом ћу те љубом оженити."
Ал' говори Краљевичу Марко:
„Фала тебе, царе поочиме!
„Кад ти станеш мене дворе градит',
„Мене хоће сиротиња клети:
„ „Гле курвића Краљевића Марка!
„ „Они су му двори изгорели,
„ „А ови му пусти останули!" "
„Да м' учиниш агом харачлијнским,
„Ја харача покупит' не могу
„Док не свежем ништа и убога,
„Па ће мене сиротиња клети:
„ „ Гле курвића Краљевића Марка!
„ „Оно му је благо однешено,
„ „А ово му остануло пусто!" "
„А што ћеш ме женит' другом љубом,
„Кад је моја љуба у животу?
„Већ дај мене триста јаничара,
„Покуј њима криве косијере,
„И дај њима лагане мотике,
„Ја ћу ићи бијелу Костуру
„Не би л' своју повратио љубу."
Цар му даде триста јаничара,
Покова им криве косијере,
И даде им лагане мотике.
Јаничаре сјетовао Марко:
„Браћо моја, триста јаничара!
„Ви идите бијелу Костуру,
„Кад дођете ка Костуру граду,
„Вама ће се Грци радовати:
„ „Благо нама, ево нам аргата!
„ „Ефтино ће радит' винограде." "
„Ви немојте, браћо моја драга,
„Већ падните под Костуром градом,
„Пијте вино и бистру ракију,
„Докле и ја у Костур не дођем."
Отидоше триста јаничара,
Отидоше бијелу Костуру,
Марко оде Светој гори славној,
Причести се и исповједи се,
Јер је многу крвцу учинио;

Let me make you a tax-collecting aga,
So you can collect more treasure than before;
If your wife has been carried off
I'll marry you to a better wife."
But Kraljević Marko answers:
"Thank you, Sultan foster-father!
When you start building me a castle
The poor will curse me:
'Look at that whoreson, Kraljević Marko!
His castle burned down on him,
And may this one remain empty on him!"
If you make me a tax-collecting aga,
I won't be able to collect the taxes
Until I tie up the poor and the destitute,
And the poor will curse me:
"Look at that whoreson, Kraljević Marko!
That treasure of his was taken,
And may this one remain useless to him!"
And why should you marry me to another wife,
When my wife is still alive?
Give me, instead, three hundred janissaries,
Forge curved scythes for them,
And give them light picks,
And I will go to white Kostur
To see if I can get back my wife."
The Sultan gave him three hundred janissaries,
He forged curved scythes for them,
And he gave them light picks.
Marko instructed the janissaries:
"Brothers of mine, you three hundred janissaries!
You go to white Kostur,
And when you come toward Kostur town
The Greeks will be happy to see you:
"Lucky us, here's some day labor!
They'll work our vineyards for us cheap."
But don't you do it, my dear brothers,
Head for Kostur town instead,
And drink wine and clear brandy
Until I, too, come to Kostur."
Off went the three hundred janissaries,
Off they went to white Kostur;
Marko went to the glorious Holy Mountain,
He took communion and he went to confession,
For he had spilled much blood.

Па обуче рухо калуђерско,
Пусти црну браду до појаса,
А на главу капу камилавку;
Па се баци Шарцу на рамена,
Оде право бијелу Костуру.
Када дође Мини од Костура,
Ал' он сједи, рујно пије вино,
А Маркова служи му га љуба;
Пита њега Мина од Костура:
„Ој Бога ти, црни калуђере!
„Откуд тебе тај шарени коњиц?"
Вели њему Краљевићу Марко:
„Ој Бога ми, Мина господару!
„Ја сам био у царевој војсци
„На арапској љутој покрајини,
„Тамо бјеше једна будалина
„По имену Краљевићу Марко,
„И он тамо јесте погинуо:
„И ја њега јесам саранио
„По закону и по обичају,
„Дадоше ми коња од подушја."
Кад то зачу Мина од Костура,
Од радости на ноге скочио,
Па говори Краљевићу Марку:
„Бе аферим, црни калуђере!
„Ево има девет годин' дана
„Како чекам ја такове гласе:
„Маркове сам похарао дворе,
„Похарао, огњем попалио,
„Вјерну сам му љубу заробио,
„Још је за се нијесам вјенчао;
„Све сам чек'о, док погине Марко,
„А сад ћеш ме ти вјенчати с њоме."
Узе књигу Краљевићу Марко,
Књигу узе, те Мину вјенчава,
Да са киме, већ са својом љубом!
Па сједоше рујно пити вино,
Вино пити и веселити се,
Ал' говори Мина од Костура:
„Чујеш, Јело, и срце и душо!
„До сад си се Марковица звала,
„А од сад си Минина госпођа;
„Иди, душо, у ризнице доње,
„Те донеси три купе дуката,

Then he put on a monk's clothes,
Let his black beard fall down to his waist,
And on his head he threw a priest's hat
Then he jumped on the shoulders of Šarac
And headed straight for white Kostur.
When he arrived at Mina from Kostur's,
Why Mina was sitting down, drinking red wine,
And Marko's wife was serving him.
Mina from Kostur asks him:
"Hey, by your God, black monk!
Where did you get that piebald horse?"
Says Kraljević Marko to him:
"Hey, by my God, Lord Mina!
I was in the Sultan's army
In the wild Arabian region,
There was a big fool there
By the name of Kraljević Marko,
And he died there;
And I buried him
By our religion and by our custom;
They gave me his horse for praying for his soul."
When Mina from Kostur heard that
He jumped to his feet with joy,
And he said to Kraljević Marko:
"Well, bravo, black monk!
Here it's nine full years
That I've been waiting for news like that:
I ransacked Marko's castle,
Ransacked it and put it to the torch,
I carried off his faithful wife
But I haven't married her yet;
I've been waiting and waiting for Marko to die,
And now you will marry us."
Kraljević Marko took out his prayer book,
He took out his prayer book and he married Mina,
And to whom else but to his own wife!
Then they sat down to drink red wine,
To drink wine and to have a good time,
But Mina from Kostur spoke up:
"Listen, Jela, my heart and my soul!
Up to now they've called you Marko's wife,
But from now on you're to be Mina's lady;
Go, my soul, to the vaults below,
And bring up three goblets of ducats,

„Да дарујем црна калуђера."
Оде Јела у ризнице доње,
Те донесе три купе дуката,
Не носи их од Минина блага,
Већ их носи од Маркова блага;
И донесе сабљу зарђалу,
Па је даје црном калуђеру:
„На ти и то, црни калуђере,
„Од подушја Краљевићу Марку."
Узе сабљу Краљевићу Марко,
Сабљу узе, па је загледује,
Па говори Мини од Костура:
„Господару, Мина од Костура!
„Јел' слободно на весељу твоме
„Поиграти ситно калуђерски?"
Вели њему Мина од Костура:
„Јест слободно, црни калуђере,
„Јест слободно, за што не би било?"
Скочи Марко на ноге лагане,
Обрну се и два и три пута,
Сав се чардак из темеља тресе;
Па потрже сабљу зарђалу,
Ману сабљом с десна на лијево,
Те он Мини одсијече главу,
Па повика из грла бијела:
„Сад навал'те, моја аргатијо!
„Нема вама Мине од Костура."
Навалише триста јаничара
У дворове Мине од Костура,
Бијеле му дворе похараше,
Похараше, огњем попалише;
Марко узе своју вјерну љубу
И Минино он покупи благо,
Па отиде бијелу Прилипу
Пјевајући и поп'јевајући.

So that I may make a gift to the black monk!"
Jela went to the vaults below,
And she brought up three goblets of ducats,
But she didn't take them from Mina's treasure,
She took them from Marko's treasure instead.
She also brought up a rusty sword,
And she gave it to the black monk.
"You might as well take this, too, black monk,
For some prayers for the soul of Kraljević Marko!"
Kraljević Marko took the sword,
He took the sword and he looked it over,
And he said to Mina from Kostur:
"Lord Mina from Kostur!
Is it all right at your party
To dance a little monk's dance?"
Mina from Kostur says to him:
"It's all right, black monk,
It's all right, why wouldn't it be?"
Marko jumped to his light feet,
And he turned around two times and then three times;
The whole upper story shook from its foundation.
Then Marko drew the rusty sword,
He waved the sword from right to left,
And he cut off Mina's head.
Then he shouted from his white throat:
"Now attack, my day laborers!
Mina from Kostur is no more."
In rushed the three hundred janissaries,
Into the castle of Mina from Kostur,
They ransacked his white castle,
Ransacked it, and put it to the torch.
Marko took his faithful wife
And he gathered up Mina's treasure,
Then he set off for white Prilep,
Singing and chanting.

A Turkish Fortress in Dalmatia

Hasan Aga's Wife

The "Hasanaginica" ("Hasan Aga's Wife") is a folk ballad written in the ten-syllable heroic epic line. It first came to the attention of West Europeans when it was published by the abbot Alberto Fortis, in his two-volume *Viaggio in Dalmazia* (A Voyage In Dalmatia, Venice, 1774). Fortis gave the song both in Serbo-Croatian and in Italian translation. The *Viaggio* was translated into English in 1778 (republished by Arno Press in 1971), and into German, by Werthes (1775). It was Werthes's translation that Goethe used in preparing his own rendition of the poem, "Klaggesang von der edlen Frauen des Asan Aga," published by Johann Herder in the first volume of his *Volkslieder* (1778). Sir Walter Scott also did a translation of the poem, very free and fanciful, based on Goethe. It was, fortunately, never published (see D. H. Low, *Slavonic Review*, III, Dec. 1924, for more on this).

The translation of the "Hasanaginica" into Italian, German, and English came at a time when all over Europe there was a growing interest in folklore, nurtured by the works of MacPherson, the brothers Grimm, and Herder. It is no surprise, then, that the highly-cultured Slovene, Jernej Kopitar, who first met Vuk Karadžić in Vienna in 1813, quickly persuaded his new disciple of the high value attached to folklore within cultured European circles. Vuk's first publication *Mala prostonarodnja slaveno-serbska pjesmarica* included the "Hasanaginica," taken from Fortis's book. Now Fortis's version was probably copied from an ikavian text and altered to suit the style of language then prevailing in Dubrovnik; it contains a mixture of predominantly jekavian and some ikavian forms, as well as some misspellings. Vuk modified the poem, using jekavian forms throughout and changing some words; he even added a line of his own. We have decided to print Vuk's version, minus the added line, as given in Volume 3 of his *Srpske narodne pjesme* (Serbian Folksongs). Vuk's poem has the advantage, at least, of modern orthography and internal consistency. We have also included, for comparative purposes, a facsimile of the poem as published by Fortis in 1774.

Those interested in reading other poems about Hasan Aga and his wife may consult Gerhard Geseman's publication of the *Erlangenski rukopis* (SKA, *Zbornik za istoriju, jezik, i književnost srpskoga naroda, prvo odeljenje*, knj. XII, 1925). Also of interest will be a recent issue of Život (XXIII, 5, Sarajevo, 1974), which is devoted exclusively to the "Hasanaginica."

ХАСАНАГИНИЦА

Шта се б'јели у гори зеленој?
Ал' је снијег, ал' су лабудови?
Да је снијег, већ би окопнио,
Лабудови већ би полетјели;
Нит' је снијег, нит' су лабудови,
Него шатор аге Хасан-аге,
Он болује од љутијех рана,
Облази га мати и сестрица,
А љубовца од стида не могла.
Кад ли му је ранам' боље било,
Он поручи вјерној љуби својој:
„Не чекај ме у двору б'јелому,
„Ни у двору, ни у роду мому."
Кад кадуна р'јечи разумјела,
Још је јадна у тој мисли стала
Јека стаде коња око двора;
Тад' побјеже Хасанагиница,
Да врат ломи куле низ пенџере;
За њом трче дв'је ћере дјевојке:
„Врати нам се, мила мајко наша!
„Није ово бабо Хасан-ага,
„„Већ даица Пинторовић беже."
И врати се Хасанагиница,
Тер се вјеша брату око врата:
„Да мој брате, велике срамоте!
„Гдје ме шаље од петеро дјеце!"
Беже мучи, ништа не говори,
Већ се маша у џепе свионе,
И вади јој књигу опрошћења,
Да узимље потпуно вјенчање.
Да гре с њиме мајци у натраге.
Кад кадуна књигу проучила,
Два је сина у чело љубила,
А дв'је ћере у румена лица,
А с малахним у бешици синком
Од'јелит' се никако не могла,
Већ је братац за руке узео

HASAN AGA'S WIFE

What gleams white in the green forest?
Is it snow, or is it swans?
If it were snow it would have melted by now;
And swans would have already taken to flight.
No, it is neither snow nor is it swans,
But the tent of Aga Hasan Aga.
He is suffering from terrible wounds.
His mother visits him, and his sister;
But his wife could not, because of modesty.
When his wounds began to heal
He sent word to his faithful wife:
"Don't wait for me in the white manor,
Neither in the manor nor amidst my family."
When the lady understood these words
The poor one was still pondering them
When hoofbeats resounded near the manor:
Hasan Aga's wife started to run
At breakneck speed beneath the windows of the tower;
After her ran her two maiden daughters:
"Come back, dear mother of ours;
That isn't daddy Hasan Aga,
It's Uncle Pintorović Beg."
And Hasan Aga's wife came back.
Then she hung her arms around her brother's neck.
"Yes, my brother, it's a great disgrace
For him to send me away from my five children!"
The beg is silent, he says nothing.
Instead he reaches into his silken pockets
And he takes out a certificate of annulment for her,
Requesting full payment of the divorce penalty
And stating that she is going with him, back to her mother.
When the lady had examined the document
She kissed her two sons on the forehead
And her two daughters on their rosy faces;
But with her tiny little son in the cradle
She could not part in any way.
Instead her brother had to take her by the arms,

И једва је с' синком раставио,
Тер је меће к себи на коњица,
С њоме греде двору бијеломy.
У роду је мало вр'јеме стала,
Мало вр'јеме, ни недјељу дана,
Добра када и од рода добра,
Добру каду просе са свих страна,
А највише имоски кадија.
Кадуна се брату своме моли:
„Ај тако те не желила, брацо!
„ Немој мене дават' ни за кога,
„Да не пуца јадно срце моје
„Гледајући сиротице своје."
Али беже ништа не хајаше,
Већ њу даје имоском кадији.
Још кадуна брату се моћаше
Да напише листак б'јеле књиге,
Да је шаље имоском кадији:
„Дјевојка те л'јепо поздрављаше
„А у књизи л'јепо те мољаше:
„Кад покупиш господу сватове,
„Дуг покривач носи на дјевојку,
„Када буде аги мимо двора,
„Да не види сиротице своје."
Кад кадији б'јела књига дође,
Господу је свате покупио,
Свате купи, греде по дјевојку.
Добро свати дошли до дјевојке,
И здраво се повратили с њоме;
А кад били аги мимо двора,
Дв'је је ћерце с пенџера гледаху,
А два сина пред њу исхођаху.
Тере својој мајци говораху;
„Сврати нам се, мила мајко наша!
„Да ми тебе ужинати дамо."
Кад то чула Хасанагиница,
Старјешини свата говорила:
„Богом брате, свата старјешина!
„Устави ми коње уза двора,
„Да дарујем сиротице моје."
Уставише коње уза двора.
Своју дјецу л'јепо даровала:
Сваком сину ноже позлаћене,
Свакој ћери чоху до пољане;

And he barely separated her from her little son.
Then he set her in front of him on his horse
And he went with her to the white manor.
She stayed only a short time with her family,
A short time, not a full week.
A good lady and from a good family
She was sought after from all sides,
And especially by the Imoski judge.
The lady implored her brother:
"Oh, dear brother, for the sake of our mother,
Don't give me in marriage to anyone,
Lest my poor heart should break
At the sight of my orphans."
But the beg didn't mind at all,
And he gave her to the Imoski judge.
The lady implored her brother a second time,
To write a letter for her, on a white sheet of paper,
And to send it to the Imoski judge.
"The bride sends you her greetings
And in her letter she kindly asks
That when you assemble the wedding party,
You bring a long veil for the bride;
So that when she will be opposite the aga's manor
She won't be able to see her orphans."
When the white letter reached the judge
He assembled the wedding party.
He assembled the wedding party and he went for the bride.
The party arrived at the bride's place in fine fettle
And they started their return trip in good spirits.
But when they were opposite the aga's manor
Her two daughters were watching her from a window,
And her two sons came out to her.
And they said to their mother:
"Come visit us, dear mother of ours,
So we can give you something to eat."
When Hasan Aga's wife heard this
She said to the leader of the wedding party:
"Brother in God, leader of the wedding party,
Stop my horses by the manor
So that I may give gifts to my orphans."
They stopped her horses by the manor.
She gave fine gifts to her children.
To each little son gilded knives,
To each daughter a homespun dress to the ground;

А маломе у бешици синку,
Њему шаље у бошчи хаљине.
А то гледа јунак Хасан-ага,
Пак дозивље до два сина своја:
„Ход'те амо, сиротице моје!
„Кад се неће смиловати на вас
„Мајка ваша срца каменога."
Кад то чула Хасанагиница,
Б'јелим лицем у земљу уд'рила
Упут се је с душом раставила,
Од жалости гледајућ' сироте.

But to the little son in the cradle,
To him she sends clothes wrapped in a bundle.
Now the hero Hasan Aga sees all this
And he calls to his two sons:
"Come here, my orphans,
Since she won't have pity on you,
Your mother of the stone heart."
When Hasan Aga's wife heard that
Her white face struck the ground;
At that moment she parted with her soul
From the sorrow of looking at her orphans.

VIAGGIO
IN
DALMAZIA

DELL'

ABATE ALBERTO FORTIS.

... Modò exuſtione, modò eluvione terrarum diuturnitati rerum intercedit occaſus.
MACROB. *in Somn. Scip. L.* 2. *c.* 10.

VOLUME PRIMO.

IN VENEZIA.
PRESSO ALVISE MILOCCO, ALL' APOLLINE.

MDCCLXXIV.

DE' COSTUMI

XALOSTNA PJESANZA

PLEMENITE

ASAN-AGHINIZE.

SCto se bjeli u gorje zelenoj?
Al-su snjezi, al-su Labutove?
Da-su snjezi vech-bi okopnuli;
Labutove vech-bi poletjeli.
Ni-su snjezi, nit-su Labutove;
Nego sciator Aghie Asan-Aghe.
On bolu-je u ranami gliutimi.
Oblaziga mater, i sestriza;
A Gliubovza od stida ne mogla.
Kad li-mu-je ranam' boglie bilo,
Ter poruça vjernoi Gliubi svojoj:
Ne çekai-me u dvoru bjelomu,
Ni u dvoru, ni u rodu momu.
Kad Kaduna rjeci razumjela,
Josc-je jadna u toj misli stala.
Jeka stade kogna oko dvora:
I pobjexe Asan-Aghiniza
Da vrât lomi kule niz penxere.
Za gnom terçu dve chiere djevoike:
Vrati-nam-se, mila majko nascia;
Ni-je ovo babo Asan-Ago,

Vech

Vech daixa Pintorovich Bexe.
I vrâtiſe Aſân Aghiniza,
Ter ſe vjeſcia bratu oko vrâta.
Da! moj brate, velike ſramote!
Gdi-me ſaglie od petero dize!
Bexe muçi: ne govori niſta.
Vech-ſe mâſcia u xepe ſvione,
I vadi-gnoj Kgnigu oproſchienja,
Da uzimglie podpunno viençanje,
Da gre s' gnime majci u zatraghe.
Kad Kaduna Kgnigu prouçila,
Dva-je sîna u çelo gliubila,
A due chiere u rumena liza:
A s' malahnim u beſicje ſinkom
Odjeliti . . . nikako ne mogla.
Vech-je brataz za ruke uzeo,
I jedva-je ſinkom raztavio:
Ter-je mechie K' ſebi na Kogniza,
S' gnome grede u dvoru bjelomu.
U rodu-je malo vrjeme ſtâla,
Malo vrjeme, ne nedjegliu dana,
Dobra Kado, i od roda dobra,
Dobru Kadu proſe ſa ſvî ſtrana;
Da majvechie Imoski Kadia.
Kaduna-ſe bratu ſvomu moli:
Aj, tako te ne xelila, bratzo!
Ne moi mene davat za nikoga,
Da ne puza jadno ſerze moje
Gledajuchi ſirotize ſvoje.
Ali Bexe ne hajaſce niſta,
Vech-gnu daje Imoſkomu Kadii.
Joſc Kaduna bratu-ſe mogliaſce,
Da gnoj piſce liſtak bjele Knighe,
Da-je ſaglie Imoſkomu Kadii.

„ Dje-

„ Djevoika te ljepo pozdravgliasce,
„ A u Kgnizi ljepo te mogliasce,
„ Kad pokupisc Gospodu Svatove
„ Dugh podkliuvaz nosi na djevojku;
„ Kadà bude Aghi mimo dvora,
„ Neg-ne vidî sirotize svoje. "
Kad Kadii bjela Kgniga doge
Gospodu-je Svate pokupio.
Svate kuppi grede po djevoiku.
Dobro Svati dosli do djevoike,
I zdravo-se povratili s' gnome.
A kad bili Aghi mimo dvora,
Dve-je chierze s' penxere gledaju,
A dva sîna prid-gnu izhogiaju,
Tere svojoî majçi govoriaju.
Vrati-nam-se, mila majko nascia,
Da mi tebe uxinati damo.
Kad to çula Asan-Aghiniza,
Stariscini Svatov govorila:
Bogom, brate Svatov Stariscina,
Ustavimi Kogne uza dvora,
Da davujem sirotize moje.
Ustavise Kogne uza dvora.
Svoju dizu ljepo darovala.
Svakom' sinku nozve pozlachene,
Svakoj chieri çohu da pogliane;
A malomu u besicje sinku
Gnemu saglie uboske hagline.

A

A to gleda Junak Aſan-Ago;
Ter dozivglie do dva sîna ſvoja:
Hodte amo, ſirotize moje,
Kad-ſe nechie milovati na vas
Majko vaſcia, ſerza argiaſkoga.
Kad to çula Aſan Aghiniza,
Bjelim liçem u zemgliu udarila;
U pût-ſe-je s' duſcjom raztavila
Od xaloſti gledajuch ſirota

Non eſſendo i varj caratteri uſati in Dalmazia molto comunemente noti, credo prezzo dell'opera il traſcrivere queſti quattro verſi ne' tre principali, cioè nel Glagolitico, o Geronimiano de' libri Liturgici, nel Cirilliano de' documenti antichi, e nel corſivo Cirilliano de' Morlacchi, che molto ſomiglia al corſivo de' Ruſſi, ſe alcune ſue note particolari ſe n'eccettuino.

[illegible] ?
[illegible] ?
[illegible] ;
[illegible] .

Што се бѣли въ горѣ зеленой?
Аль су снѣзи аль су лабутове?
Да су снѣзи вещбы шкопнули;
Лабутове вещбы полетѣли.

Il corſivo de' Morlacchi è men bene ortografato, ma mantiene più la verità della loro qualunque ſiaſi pronunzia, da cui nel teſto io mi ſono un pò allontanato.

[illegible]
[illegible]
[illegible]
[illegible]

Il Serviano majuſcolo de' Calogeri; e il corſivo uſato nell'interiore della Boſna, ch'è quaſi arabizzato, ſono anch'eſſi curioſi; ma ſarebbe di noja il riferirli.

The Turkish bridge at Višegrad

"The Building of Scutari" is a ballad, written in the ten-syllable heroic line. In spite of the stark beauty of this song, the German poet Goethe declared that he was repulsed by the cruelty of its theme.

Scutari

The Bridge at Višegrad

*"The Building of Scutari" may be grouped, both in theme and structure, with other Balkan building songs, including the Moslem song "The Building of the Bridge at Višegrad," a translation of which appears in this anthology. Vuk Karadžić identified "The Building of Scutari" with the oldest Serbo-Croatian folk songs, those stemming from a pre-Christian era. William J. Entwistle (*European Balladry, *Oxford, 1939) states categorically that "The Building of Scutari" is "borrowed from the Greek 'Bridge of Arta'," a Cappadocian ballad about a bridge that will not stand up until the master builder's wife is enclosed in it alive (op. cit., 309 and 326).*

In these building songs there seems to be at work a primitive intuition that man-made structures, such as castles and bridges, eventually take on a living quality of their own, and that one way to hasten the assumption of such a quality is to immure a living person within the foundation of the structure.

ЗИДАЊЕ СКАДРА

Град градила три брата рођена,
До три брата три Мрљавчевића:
Једно бјеше Вукашине краље,
Друго бјеше Угљеша војвода,
Треће бјеше Мрљавчевић Гојко;
Град градили Скадар на Бојани,
Град градили три године дана,
Три године са триста мајстора,
Не могоше темељ подигнути,
А камо ли саградити града:
Што мајстори за дан га саграде,
То све вила за ноћ обаљује.
Кад настала година четврта,
Тада виче са планине вила:
,,Не мучи се, Вукашине краље,
,,Не мучи се и не харчи блага;
,,Не мо'ш, краље, темељ подигнути,
,,А камо ли саградити града,
,,Док не нађеш два слична имена,
,,Док не нађеш Стоју и Стојана,
,,А обоје брата и сестрицу,
,,Да зазидеш кули у темеља,
,,Тако ће се темељ обдржати,
,,И тако ћеш саградити града."
Кад то зачу Вукашине краље,
Он дозива слугу Десимира:
,,Десимире, моје чедо драго,
,,До сад си ми био вјерна слуга,
,,А од саде моје чедо драго
,,Ватај, сине коње у интове,
,,И понеси шест товара блага,
,,Иди, сине, преко б'јела св'јета,
,,Те ти тражи два слична имена,
,,Тражи, сине, Стоју и Стојана,
,,А обоје брата и сестрицу;
,,Ја ли отми, ја л' за благо купи,
,,Доведи их Скадру на Бојану,

THE BUILDING OF SCUTARI

Three brothers were building a city,
Three brothers, the three Mrljavčevići:
One was King Vukašin,
Another was Duke Uglješa,
The third one was Gojko Mrljavčević;
They were building the city of Scutari on the Bojana,
They were building the city for three full years,
For three years with three hundred masons;
They couldn't lay the foundation,
Never mind finish building the city:
What the masons would build in a day
The vila would level in a night!
When the fourth year had begun
The vila then cried out from the mountain:
"Don't trouble yourself, King Vukašin,
Don't trouble yourself and don't waste your treasure!
You can't lay the foundation, King,
Never mind finish building the city,
Until you find two of similar name,
Until you find Stoja and Stojan,
The two of them brother and sister,
And wall them up in the foundation of the tower:
That way the foundation will hold up,
And that way you will finish building the city."
When King Vukašin heard that
He called in his servant Desimir:
"Desimir, my dear child!
Up to now you have been my faithful servant,
But from now on you will be my dear child;
Hitch some horses to a carriage, son,
And take along six loads of treasure,
Go the wide world over, son,
And look for two of similar name,
Look for Stoja and Stojan, son,
The two of them brother and sister;
Either kidnap them, or buy them with treasure,
And bring them to Scutari on the Bojana,

„Да зиђемо кули у темеља,
„Не би л' нам се темељ обдржао,
„И не би ли саградили града."
Кад то зачу слуга Десимире,
Он увати коње у интове,
И понесе шест товара блага,
Оде слуга преко б'јела св'јета,
Оде тражит' два слична имена;
Тражи слуга Стоју и Стојана,
Тражи слуга три године дана,
Ал' не нађе два слична имена;
Ал' не нађе Стоје и Стојана,
Па се врну Скадру на Бојану,
Даде краљу коње и интове,
И даде му шест товара блага:
„Ето, краље, коњи и интови,
„И ето ти шест товара блага,
„Ја не нађох два слична имена,
„Ја не нађох Стоје и Стојана."
Кад то зачу Вукашине краљу,
Он подвикну Рада неимара,
Раде викну три стотин мајстора,
Гради краље Скадар на Бојани,
Краље гради, вила обаљује,
Не да вила темељ подигнути,
А камо ли саградити града;
Па дозивље из планине вила:
„Море, чу ли? Вукашине краљу!
„Не мучи се и не харчи блага,
„Не мо'ш, краље, темељ подигнути,
„А камо ли саградити града;
„Но ето сте три брата рођена,
„У свакога има вјерна љуба,
„Чија сјутра на Бојану дође
„И донесе мајсторима ручак,
„Зиђите је кули у темеља,
„Тако ће се темељ обдржати,
„Тако ћете саградити града."
Кад то зачу Вукашине краљу,
Он дозива два брата рођена:
„Чујете ли, моја браћо драга!
„Ето вила са планине виче,
„Није вајде, што харчимо благо,
„Не да вила темељ подигнути,

So we can wall them up in the foundation of the tower;
Let's see if the foundation won't hold up for us,
Let's see if we can't finish building the city."
When the servant Desimir heard this
He hitched some horses to a carriage,
And he took along six loads of treasure.
The servant travelled the wide world over,
He went looking for two of similar name.
The servant was looking for Stoja and Stojan,
The servant was looking for three full years,
But he didn't find two of similar name,
He didn't find Stoja and Stojan,
So he returned to Scutari on the Bojana,
Gave the king back his horses and carriage,
And gave him back his six loads of treasure:
"Here are your horses and carriage, King,
And here are your six loads of treasure:
I couldn't find two of similar name,
I couldn't find Stoja and Stojan."
When King Vukašin heard this
He summoned Rade the Mason,
Rade called his three hundred masons:
The king builds Scutari on the Bojana,
The king builds and the vila knocks it down,
The vila won't let him lay the foundation,
Never mind finish building the city!
Then the vila calls down from the mountain:
"Didn't you hear me, King Vukašin,
Don't trouble yourself and don't waste your treasure!
You can't lay the foundation, King,
Never mind finish building the city!
But look now, you are three brothers,
Each of you has a faithful wife:
Whoever's wife comes tomorrow to the Bojana
And brings the masons their lunch,
Wall her up in the foundation of the tower,
That way the foundation will hold up,
That way you will finish building the city."
When King Vukašin heard that,
He called in his two brothers:
"Listen, my dear brothers,
The vila has cried out from the mountain
That it's useless for us to waste our treasure,
She won't let us lay the foundation,

„А камо ли саградити града;
„Још говори са планине вила:
„Ев' ми јесмо три брата рођена,
„У свакога има вјерна љуба,
„Чија сјутра на Бојану дође
„И донесе мајсторима ручак,
„Да ј'у темељ кули узидамо,
„Тако ће се темељ обдржати,
„Тако ћемо саградити града.
„Но јел', браћо, Божја вјера тврда,
„Да ни један љуби не докаже,
„Већ на срећу да им оставимо,
„Која сјутра на Бојану дође?"
И ту Божју вјеру зададоше,
Да ни један љуби не докаже.
У том их је ноћца застанула,
Отидоше у бијеле дворе,
Вечераше господску вечеру,
Оде сваки с љубом у ложницу.
Ал' да видиш чуда великога!
Краљ Вукашин вјеру погазио,
Те он први својој љуби каза:
„Да се чуваш, моја вјерна љубо!
„Немој сјутра на Бојану доћи
„Ни донијет' ручак мајсторима,
„Јер ћеш своју изгубити главу,
„Зидаће те кули у темеља."
И Угљеша вјеру погазио,
И он каза својој вјерној љуби:
„Не превар' се, вјерна моја љубо!
„Немој сјутра на Бојану доћи
„Ни донијет' мајсторима ручак,
„Јера хоћеш млада погинути,
„Зидаће те кули у темеља."
Млади Гојко вјеру не погази,
И он својој љуби не доказа.
Кад у јутру јутро осванули,
Поранише три Мрљавчевића,
Отидоше на град на Бојану.
Земан дође да се носи ручак,
А редак је госпођи краљици,
Она оде својој јетрвици,
Јетрвици, љуби Угљешиној:
„Чу ли мене, моја јетрвице!

Never mind finish building the city!
The vila also says from the mountain:
Look now, we are three brothers,
Each of us has a faithful wife:
Whoever's wife comes tomorrow to the Bojana
And brings the masons their lunch,
Let's wall her up in the foundation of the tower:
That way the foundation will hold up,
That way we will finish building the city.
But shall we take a firm and sacred oath, brothers,
That no one will warn his wife,
Instead we'll leave it to chance
Which one comes tomorrow to the Bojana?"
And then they took a sacred oath
That no one would warn his wife.
Here night came on them.
They went off to their white manors,
And they ate a princely dinner.
Each went with his wife to the bed chamber.
But what a strange thing happened then!
King Vukašin broke his word
And he was the first to tell his wife:
"Watch out, my true love;
Don't come tomorrow to the Bojana
And don't bring the masons their lunch,
Because you will lose your head if you do,
They'll wall you up in the foundation of the tower."
Uglješa broke his word, too;
He too told his faithful wife:
"Don't be fooled, my true love:
Don't come tomorrow to the Bojana
And don't bring the masons their lunch,
Because you will die young if you do,
They'll wall you up in the foundation of the tower."
Young Gojko didn't break his word
And he didn't warn his wife.
The next morning, when it grew light,
The three Mrljavčevići arose early,
And they went off to the city on the Bojana.
It came time for lunch to be brought in,
And it was Madame Queen's turn.
She went to her sister-in-law,
To her sister-in-law, the wife of Uglješa:
"Listen, my sister-in-law,

„Нешто ме је забољела глава,
„Тебе здравље! преболет' не могу;
„Но понеси мајсторима ручак."
Говорила љуба Угљешина:
„О јетрво, госпођо краљице!
„Нешто мене забољела рука,
„Тебе здравље! преболет' не могу,
„Већ ти збори млађој јетрвици."
Она оде млађој јетрвици:
„Јетрвице, млада Гојковице!
„Нешто ме је забољела глава,
„Тебе здравље! преболет' не могу;
„Но понеси мајсторима ручак."
Ал' говори Гојковица млада:
„Чу ли, нано, госпођо краљице!
„Ја сам рада тебе послушати,
„Но ми лудо чедо некупато,
„А бијело платно неиспрато."
Вели њојзи госпођа краљица:
„Иди," каже, „моја јетрвице,
„Те однеси мајсторима ручак,
„Ја ћу твоје изапрати платно,
„А јетрва чедо окупати."
Нема шта ће Гојковица млада,
Већ понесе мајсторима ручак.
Кад је била на воду Бојану,
Угледа је Мрљавчевић Гојко,
Јунаку се срце ражалило,
Жао му је љубе вијернице,
Жао му је чеда у кол'јевци,
Ђе остаде од мјесеца дана,
Па од лица сузе просипаше;
Угледа га танана невјеста,
Кротко ходи, док до њега пријђе,
Кротко ходи, тихо бесјеђаше:
„Што је тебе, добри господару!
„Те ти рониш сузе од образа?"
Ал' говори Мрљавчевић Гојко:
„Зло је, моја вијернице љубо!
„Имао сам од злата јабуку,
„Па ми данас паде у Бојану,
„Те је жалим, прегорет' не могу."
Не сјећа се танана невјеста,
Но бесједи своме господару:

I have a bit of a headache,
Good health to you!–I'm not getting any better;
So you take the masons their lunch."
Spoke the wife of Uglješa:
"O sister-in-law, Madame Queen,
I have a bit of an arm ache,
Good health to you!–I'm not getting any better;
Speak to our younger sister-in-law, instead."
She went to their younger sister-in-law:
"Sister-in-law, young wife of Gojko,
I have a bit of a headache,
Good health to you!–I'm not getting any better;
So you take the masons their lunch."
But spoke the young wife of Gojko:
"Listen, Nana, Madame Queen,
I would be happy to obey you,
Only my little baby needs a bath,
And my white linen has to be washed."
Madame Queen says to her:
"Go," says she, "my sister-in-law,
And take the masons their lunch,
I will wash your linen,
And our sister-in-law will bathe your child."
There was nothing left for the young wife of Gojko
But to bring the masons their lunch.
When she was at the Bojana's waters,
Gojko Mrljavčević caught sight of her,
The hero's heart grew very sad,
He was sorry for his wife, his true love,
He was sorry for the babe in the cradle,
Only one month old,
And his face was wet with tears;
The slender bride caught sight of him,
Meekly she walked, until she drew near to him,
Meekly she walked, and softly she spoke:
"What is the matter, good lord,
Why is your face wet with tears?"
Spoke now Gojko Mrljavčević:
"It's awful, my own true love!
I had an apple made of gold,
But today it fell into the Bojana,
So I mourn it, and I can't get over my grief."
The slender bride doesn't catch wise,
And she says to her lord:

„Моли Бога ти за твоје здравље,
„А салићеш и бољу јабуку."
Тад' јунаку грђе жао било,
Па на страну одвратио главу,
Не шће више ни гледати љубу;
А дођоше два Мрљавчевића,
Два ђевера Гојковице младе,
Узеше је за бијеле руке,
Поведоше у град да уграде,
Подвикнуше Рада неимара,
Раде викну до триста мајстора;
Ал' се смије танана невјеста,
Она мисли, да је шале ради.
Туришe је у град уграђиват',
Оборише до триста мајстора,
Оборише дрвље и камење,
Узидаше дори до кољена,
Још се смије танана невјеста,
Још се нада, да је шале ради.
Оборише до триста мајстора,
Оборише дрвље и камење,
Узидаше дори до појаса,
Тад' отежа дрвље и камење,
Онда виђе, шта је јадну нађе,
Љуто писну, како љута гуја,
Па замоли два мила ђевера:
„Не дајте ме, ако Бога знате!
„Узидати младу и зелену."
То се моли, ал' јој не помаже;
Јер ђевери у њу и не гледе.
Тад' се прође срама и зазора,
Паке моли свога господара:
„Не дај мене, добри господару!
„Да ме младу у град узидају,
„Но ти прати мојој старој мајци,
„Моја мајка има доста блага,
„Нек ти купи роба ил' робињу,
„Те зидајте кули у темеља."
То се моли, но јој не помаже,
А кад виђе танана невјеста,
Да јој више молба не помаже,
Тад' се моли Раду неимару:
„Богом брате, Раде неимаре!
„Остави ми прозор на дојкама,

"Be grateful to God for your health,
And you will cast an even better apple."
Here the hero became sadder still,
And he turned his head away,
He didn't want even to look at his wife any longer.
But the other two Mrljavčevići came over,
The two brothers-in-law of the young wife of Gojko,
They took her by her white arms
And they led her into the city, to wall her in,
They summoned Rade the Mason,
And Rade called his three hundred masons;
But the slender bride is laughing,
She thinks that it's just a joke.
They pushed her into the city, to wall her in:
The three hundred masons hewed away,
They hewed wood and stone,
They walled her right up to the knees.
The slender bride is laughing still,
She still hopes that it's just a joke.
The three hundred masons hewed away,
They hewed wood and stone,
They walled her right up to the waist.
Now the wood and stone weighed heavy on her,
Now the poor woman saw what was coming.
She hissed angrily, like an angry snake,
And she begged her two dear brothers-in-law:
"For God's sake, don't hand me over
To be walled up so young and green!"
She begs, but it doesn't help her,
For the brothers-in-law don't even look at her.
Then she cares no longer about shame and disgrace,
And she asks her lord:
"Don't hand me over, good lord,
To be walled up so young in the city!
But send someone to my old mother:
My mother has sufficient treasure,
Let her buy a male or a female slave for you,
And you wall it up in the foundation of the tower."
She begs, but it doesn't help her.
And when the slender bride saw
That further begging would not help her,
She entreated Rade the Mason:
"Brother in God, Rade the Mason,
Leave me an opening for my breasts,

„Истури ми моје б'јеле дојке,
„Каде дође мој нејаки Јово,
„Каде дође, да подоји дојке."
То је Раде за братство примио,
Остави јој прозор на дојкама,
Па јој дојке у поље истури,
Каде дође нејаки Јоване,
Каде дође, да подоји дојке.
Опет кужна Рада дозивала:
„Богом брате, Раде неимаре!
„Остави ми прозор на очима,
„Да ја гледам ка бијелу двору,
„Кад ће мене Јова доносити
„И ка двору опет односити."
И то Раде за братство примио,
Остави јој прозор на очима,
Те да гледа ка бијелу двору,
Каде ће јој Јова доносити
И ка двору опет односити.
И тако је у град уградише,
Па доносе чедо у кол'јевци,
Те га доји за нећељу дана,
По нећељи изгубила гласа;
Ал' ђетету онђе иде рана,
Дојише га за годину дана.
Како таде, тако и остаде,
Да и данас онђе иде рана
Зарад' чуда, и зарад' лијека,
Која жена не има млијека.

And pull out my white breasts for me
When my frail Jovo comes,
When he comes to nurse at my breast!"
This Rade agreed to, for brotherhood's sake,
He left her an opening for her breasts,
And he pulled her breasts outside
When the frail Jovan came,
When he came to nurse at her breast.
Once more the afflicted one called to Rade:
"Brother-in-God, Rade the Mason,
Leave me an opening for my eyes:
That I may look toward the white manor
When they bring Jovo to me
And when they take him home again.
This Rade also agreed to, for brotherhood's sake,
He left her an opening for her eyes:
That she might look toward the white manor
When they were bringing Jovo to her,
And when they were taking him home again.
And so they walled her into the city.
They brought the baby in his cradle
And she nursed him for a week;
After a week she lost her voice.
But the child's nourishment was still coming there:
She nursed him for a full year.
And so it has remained to this day,
Even today nourishment comes from that spot:
As a miracle, and as a medicine
For the woman who is without milk.

ZIDANJE ĆUPRIJE U VIŠEGRADU

Mehmed paša tri cara dvorio,
Pa tri kule izdvorio blaga,
Pa on sio misli premišljati,
Kud će tol'ko blago dijevati:
Al će blago davat sirotinji,
Al će blago u Drinu sipati,
Al će gradit po Bosni haire.
Sve mislio na jedno smislio:
„Hoću gradit po Bosni haire,
Najnaprijed na Drini ćupriju."
Pa on gradi knjigu na koljenu,
Pa je posla Mitru neimaru,
Šta j' u knjizi paša načinio?
„Oj čuješ li, Mitre neimare,
Hrani konja od Mitrova dana,
Od Mitrova do Đurđeva dana.
Kad ti, Mitre, Đurđev danak dođe,
A ti hajde gradu Višegradu,
Da sagradiš na Drini ćupriju,
Ti povedi do trista majstora
I hiljadu djece irgatina,
Što će studen kamen dohićati."
A kad viđe Mitre neimare
On je njemu drugu učinio:
„O bora mi, Soko Mehmed paša,
Koliko je polje višegradsko,
Da je tovar do tovara blaga,
Još na tovar po tri kese blaga,
Još i uz to tvojeg haznadara,
Što će brojit nebrojeno blago,
Jedva bi se gradila ćuprija." –
A kad knjiga Soko paši dođe,
I kad viđe Soko Mehmed paša,
Kad vidio što mu knjiga kaže,
On je opet drugu načinio:
„Koliko je polje višegradsko,
Biće tovar do tovara blaga,

THE BUILDING OF THE BRIDGE AT VIŠEGRAD

Mehmed Pasha served three sultans,
And he earned three castles full of treasure,
Then he sat down and began to ponder
What he would do with all that treasure:
Either he could give the treasure to the poor,
Or he could pour the treasure into the Drina,
Or he could build charitable works throughout Bosnia.
The more he thought the more he came to the same idea:
"I shall build charitable works throughout Bosnia,
And first of all a bridge over the Drina."
So he put together a letter on his knee,
And he sent it to Mitar the builder;
What did the Pasha say in his letter?
"Hey, listen, Mitar the builder,
Feed your horse from St. Demetrius's Day,
From St. Demetrius's to St. George's Day.
And Mitar, when St. George's Day arrives,
You go to Višegrad town
To build a bridge over the Drina;
Take along three hundred masons
And a thousand young day laborers
To haul the fresh-cut stone."
But when Mitar the builder read this,
He wrote another letter back to him:
"Oh, by my wrinkles, Mehmed Pasha Sokolović,
As big as the Višegrad field is,
If it were filled with load after load of treasure,
And on each load there were three bags of treasure,
And if your treasurer, along with all that,
Were to count out countless treasure,
The bridge would barely be built."–
Now when the letter reached Pasha Sokolović,
And when Mehmed Pasha read it,
When he read what the letter was saying,
He wrote back a second letter:
"As big as the Višegrad field is,
There'll be load after load of treasure,

Još na tovar po tri kese blaga,
I evo ti Muja haznadara,
Što će brojit nebrojeno blago;
Veće hajde gradu Višegradu,
Da se gradi na Drini ćuprija."
Kad to viđe Mitre neimare,
Pa mu dođe danak Đurđev danak,
On uzima do trista majstora
I hiljadu djece irgatina,
Pa uzjaha vranca debeloga,
Pa eto ga gradu Višegradu.
Natjerao vranca debeloga
Da okuša je l' kolika Drina,
More li se graditi ćuprija.
Taman vranac na sred vode dođe,
Pa se dalje ni maknuti neće:
Mitar bije čizmom i mamuzom,
A konj mu se ni maknut ne more;
Mitar bije trostrukom kandžijom,
A konj mu se ni maknut ne more,
Sve to gleda Soko Mehmed paša,
Pa povika Mitra neimara:
„Na ti Mitre moju hamajliju."
Pa mu baci svoju hamajliju,
Uhvati je Mitre neimare,
Pa objesi konju oko vrata,
Istom vranac na suho iskoči,
I iznese bjelogorku vilu,
Rusa joj se kosa obavila
Vrancu konju oko prvih nogu.
Htjela ona da utopi Mitra
I njegova vranca debeloga,
Pa je vranac na suho iznio.
Kad to viđe Mitre neimare,
On poteže sablju od pojasa,
Da on njojzi odsiječe glavu,
A ona ga Bogom pobratila:
„Bogom brate, Mitre neimare,
Pusti mene u Butkove st'jene
Kad ti staneš graditi ćupriju,
Ja ću tebi na jardumu biti."
To je Mitar za Boga hajao.
Pustio je u Butkove st'jene,
Pa on stade graditi ćupriju.

And on each load three bags of treasure,
And you can have Mujo, my treasurer,
To count out countless treasure;
Now go to Višegrad town
So the bridge will be built over the Drina."
When Mitar the builder read this,
And the day arrived, St. George's Day,
He took three hundred masons
And a thousand day laborers,
And he mounted his stout black horse,
And in no time he was nearing Višegrad town.
He spurred his stout black horse on,
To see how big the Drina was,
And whether a bridge could be built over it.
The dark horse reached the middle of the water,
But it wouldn't move any further:
Mitar kicked him with boot and spur,
But his horse couldn't move at all;
Mitar beat him with his triple-ply whip,
But his horse couldn't move at all;
Mehmed Pasha Sokolović took all this in,
And then he called to Mitar the builder:
"Here Mitar, take my amulet."
And he threw him his amulet;
Mitar the builder caught it
And he hung it around the horse's neck,
The black horse barely jumped out onto dry land,
Carrying with him a vila of the forest;
Her blonde hair was entwined
Around the black horse's front quarters.
She had wanted to drown Mitar
And his stout black horse,
But the horse had carried her out to dry land.
When Mitar the builder saw this
He drew his sword from his belt
So he could cut off her head,
But she appealed to him in God's name:
"Brother in God, Mitar the builder,
Let me go to Butkov Cliffs,
And when you begin to build the bridge
I'll be a help to you."
For God's sake Mitar heeded her plea.
He let her go to Butkov Cliffs
And he began to build the bridge.

Gradio je sedam godinica.
Što je Mitar u dan načinio,
Ono nešto noćom batalilo.
Dok povika Soko Mehmed paša:
„Kam' ti, Mitre, tvoja posestrima,
Što t' je rekla na jardumu biti,
Kad ti staneš graditi ćupriju?"
Kad to začu Mitre neimare,
On povika svoju posestrimu:
– Ona mu se ozgo odazvala. –
„Sad ti meni na jardumu budi."
A veli mu vila sa stijene:
„Bogom brate, Mitre neimare!
Ne mogu ti na jardumu biti,
Ne dadu mi moje sestrenice,
Već pošetaj niz polje zeleno,
Te uhvati Stoju i Ostoju,
Te uzidaj u ćupriju kulu.
Staće tebi na Drini ćuprija."
Kad to čuo Mitre neimare,
On pošeta niz polje zeleno,
Te uhvati Stoju i Ostoju,
Te uzida u ćupriju kulu;
Stade njemu na Drini ćuprija.
Svršili je devete godine.
Dođe Drina mutna i pomamna,
Pomoli se vitka omorika,
Te udari u ćupriju kulu,
Te zanjiha na Drini ćuprijom;
Prepade se Soko Mehmed paša,
Oboriće na Drini ćupriju.
Dok povika Mitre neimare:
„O bora mi, Soko Mehmed paša,
Ti nijesi Drine darovao;
Već nasiplji na ćupriju blago,
Pa ti uzmi srebrenu lopatu.
Pa ti daruj tu premutnu Drinu."
Šćadijaše Mitre neimare,
Da okuša Soko Mehmed pašu,
Žali l' paša to toliko blago,
Što je tol'ko potrošio blago.
Kad to čuo Soko Mehmed paša,
On donese nekoliko blaga,
Pa nasiplje na ćupriju blago.

He was building it for seven years.
Whatever Mitar did by day
Was undone by night.
Until Mehmed Pasha Sokolović shouted to him:
"Hey, Mitar, where is your blood sister,
Who said she'd be a help to you
When you began to build the bridge?"
When Mitar the builder heard this
He shouted to his blood sister:
(She answered him from above.)
"Now be a help to me!"
But the Vila spoke from the cliffs:
"Brother in God, Mitar the builder!
I can't be a help to you,
My sisters won't let me,
But you go for a walk down the green field,
And seize Stoja and Ostoja,
And wall them up in a pillar of the bridge.
Then the bridge over the Drina will stand up for you."
When Mitar the builder heard this
He went for a walk down the green field
And he seized Stoja and Ostoja,
And he walled them up in a pillar of the bridge;
The bridge over the Drina stood up for him.
They finished it in the ninth year.
Then came the Drina, troubled and in a frenzy,
A slender pine tree heaved into view
And it lashed against a pillar of the bridge,
And it made the bridge over the Drina begin to sway;
Mehmed Pasha Sokolović became frightened
That it would topple the bridge over the Drina.
Then Mitar the builder shouted to him:
"Oh, by my wrinkles, Mehmed Pasha Sokolović,
You didn't give a gift to the Drina;
So pour some treasure onto the bridge,
Then you take a silver shovel
And you give your gift to the much-troubled Drina."
Mitar the builder was trying
To test Mehmed Pasha Sokolović,
To see whether the Pasha regretted all the treasure,
All the treasure he had already spent.
When Mehmed Pasha heard this
He brought several loads of treasure
And he poured the treasure out on the bridge.

Pa on uze srebrenu lopatu,
Pa on tura na četiri strane,
On darova tu premutnu Drinu.
A kad vide Mitre neimare,
Gdje on tura, hič ne žali blaga,
Onda veli Mitre neimare:
„Dosta već je, Soko Mehmed paša,
Nasadi mi bradvu naopako,
Pa me spusti na tanke tenefe,
Da siječem vitku omoriku."
Kad to čuo Soko Mehmed paša.
Svojom rukom bradvu nasadio,
Pa ga spusti na tanke tenefe.
Mitar s'ječe vitku omoriku,
Iz omore krvca udarila,
Iz omore nešto progovara:
„Osta danas na Drini ćuprija,
Osta danas, osta dovijeka."
I paša je đumruk postavio,
Na pješaka dva b'jela dinara,
Na konjika četiri dinara;
A ko nema četiri dinara,
Skidaju mu sa konja pokrovce.
Dok evo ti jednog kiridžije,
Pa zapjeva preko Okolišta:
„Oj čuješ li, Soko Mehmed paša,
Jesi čudan hair načinio,
Al' si nešto malo okvario,
Što si na njoj đumruk postavio." –
Kad to čuo Soko Mehmed paša,
On dobavi onog kiridžiju.
„Deder more, zapjevaj mi pjesmu.
Zapjevaj mi pjesmu otojčinu!"
On ne smije pjesme zapjevati,
On se boji da ga ne pos'ječe.
Opet njemu paša govorio:
„De zapjevaj pjesmu otojičnu."
A zapjeva oni kiridžija:
„Oj čuješ li, Soko Mehmed paša,
Jesi čudan hair načinio,
Načinio na Drini ćupriju,
Al si malo, paša, okvario.
Što si na njoj đumruk postavio,
Na pješaka dva b'jela dinara,

Then he took a silver shovel,
And he shovelled in four directions,
Making his gift to the much troubled Drina.
And when Mitar the builder saw this,
How he shovelled, not regretting the treasure at all,
Then said Mitar the builder:
"That's already plenty, Mehmed Pasha Sokolović,
Stick my adze behind my back,
And lower me on slender ropes,
So I can cut up the slender pine tree."
When Mehmed Pasha Sokolović heard this,
With his own hand he stuck the adze in place,
And he lowered him down on slender ropes.
Mitar cut up the slender pine tree,
And from the pine tree there spurted blood,
And from the pine tree something spoke out:
"Today the bridge over the Drina stood fast,
Stood fast today, stood fast forever."
And the Pasha set a toll,
Two silver dinars for each man on foot,
Four dinars for the man on horseback;
And whoever didn't have the four dinars,
They took the blanket from his horse instead.
Until along came a certain teamster,
And he began to sing through Okolište
"Hey listen, Mehmed Pasha Sokolović,
You've done a wonderful work of charity,
But you spoiled it a little, Pasha,
When you put a toll on it."–
When Mehmed Pasha Sokolović heard this,
He got hold of that teamster.
"Come on now, sing me the song.
Sing me that one song."
He didn't dare to sing the song,
He was afraid he would lose his head.
Again the Pasha said to him:
"Come on, sing me that one song."
And the teamster began to sing:
"Hey listen, Mehmed Pasha Sokolović,
You've done a wonderful work of charity,
You built a bridge over the Drina,
But you spoiled it a little, Pasha,
When you put a toll on it:
Two silver dinars for the man on foot,

Na konjika četiri dinara;
A ko nema četiri dinara,
Skidaju mu sa konja pokrovce."
Kad to čuo Soko Mehmed paša,
On je pravo đumruk oborio.

And four dinars for the man on horseback;
And whoever doesn't have the four dinars,
They take the blanket from his horse instead."
When Mehmed Pasha Sokolović heard that,
He straightaway removed the toll.

A Folktale

The folk tale is an oral prose form common at one time to many nations of Indo-European origin; a large number of the themes of such tales seem to spring from a common Indo-European store of myths.

Vuk Karadžić was the most important collector of Serbian and Croatian folk tales, publishing his first volume of tales Narodne srpske pripovijetke *in 1821, not long after the brothers Grimm had issued their first two collections of German folk tales (*Kinder Und Haus Märchen, *1812 and 1815). In 1853 Vuk published a more complete collection,* Srpske narodne pripovijetke. *Although Vuk was heavily dependent on Vuk Vrčević and others, in his folk tale collecting, still his work provided the basis for all future collections of Serbo-Croatian folk tales.*

ЧАРДАК НИ НА НЕБУ НИ НА ЗЕМЉИ

Био један цар, па имао три сина и једну кћер, коју је у кафез хранио и чувао као очи у глави. Кад ђевојка одрасте, једно вече замоли се оцу своме да јој допусти да изиђе са браћом мало пред двор у шетњу, и отац јој допусти. Али тек што изиђе пред двор, у један мах долети из неба змај, шчепа ђевојку између браће и однесе је у облаке. Браћа отрче брже боље к оцу и кажу му шта је било, и реку да би они радо своју сестру потражили. Отац им допусти да иду да је траже, да им свакоме по коња и остало што треба за пут, и тако они отиду. По дугоме путовању наиђу на један чардак, који нити је на небу ни на земљи. Дошавши онђе, помисле да неће у ономе чардаку бити њихова сестра, па се одмах стану договарати како би се уњ попели, и послије дугога промишљавања и договора, договоре се да један од њих свога коња закоље, и од коже коњске да окроје опуту, па притврдивши један крај од ње за стријелу, да пусте одоздо стријелу из лука да се добро за чардак прихвати, како би се уз њу пети могли. Млађа два брата реку најстаријему да он свога коња закоље, али он не шћедне па ни средњи не шћедне, онда најмлађи закоље свога, од коже његове окроји опуту, један крај од ње веже за стријелу, пак је пусти из лука у чардак. Кад дође да се пење уз опуту, опет најстарији и средњи не шћедну се пети, него се попне најмлађи. Попевши се горе, стане ићи из једне собе у другу, и тако наиђе на једну собу у којој види своју сестру ђе сједи а змај јој метнуо главу на крило па спава а она га бишће. Она кад види брата својега, уплаши се и почне га тихо молити да бјежи док се није змај пробудио, али он не шћедне, већ узме буздован, па размахне њиме и удари змаја у главу, а змај иза сна маши се руком на оно мјесто ђе га је он ударио па рече ђевојци: „Баш овђе ме нешто уједе." Кад он то рекне, а царев га син још једном удари у главу, а змај опет рече ђевојци: „Опет ме нешто овђе уједе." Кад он и трећи пут замахне да га удари, онда му сестра руком покаже да га удари у живот, и он га удари онамо, и како га удари, змај остане на мјесту мртав, а царева

THE HOUSE NEITHER IN THE SKY NOR ON LAND

There was a certain emperor, and he had three sons and one daughter whom he kept in a cage and guarded like the eyes in his head. When the girl grew up she begged her father one evening to allow her to go out for a walk with her brothers in front of the castle, and her father let her go. But no sooner had she gone out in front of the castle when all at once a dragon swooped down from the sky, snatched up the girl from amidst her brothers, and carried her off into the clouds. The brothers ran to their father as fast as they could and told him what had happened, and they said they would be glad to go search for their sister. Their father allowed them to go look for her and he gave them each a horse and whatever else they needed for the trip, and so they set out. After a long journey they came upon a house which was neither in the sky nor on land. When they reached it they wondered whether their sister might be in that house, and they immediately began to discuss how they might climb up into it; and after lengthy deliberation and discussion they agreed that one of them would slaughter his horse, and from the hide of the horse they would fashion a strap and then they would attach one end of the strap to an arrow and shoot it with a bow from down below so that it would get a good hold on the house, so that they could climb up it. The younger two brothers told their eldest brother that he should slaughter his horse, but he didn't want to, nor did the middle one, so the youngest brother slaughtered his, fashioned a strap from its hide, tied one end of it to an arrow, and shot it into the house with a bow. When it came time for them to climb up the strap, again the eldest and middle brother didn't want to climb, and so the youngest brother climbed up it. When he had finished climbing he began to go from room to room, and so he came upon a room in which he saw his sister sitting, and a dragon had put his head in her lap and was sleeping while she was picking his lice for him. She became frightened when she saw her brother, and she quietly begged him to flee before the dragon awoke, but he didn't want to; he took his mace instead, and he gave it a good swing and struck the dragon in the head, but the dragon waved his hand in his sleep and pointed to the place where he had struck him, and said to the girl: "Something bit me right here." When he said this the emperor's son struck him once more on the head, and the dragon again said to the girl: "Something bit me here again." When he wound up a third time to strike the dragon, his sister indicated with her hand that he should strike him in the stomach, and he struck

га кћи стури с крила, па притрчи брату своме, те се с њиме пољуби, па онда узевши га за руку стане га водити кроз све собе. Најприје га уведе у једну собу у којој је био један вран коњ за јаслима привезан с цијелијем такумом од чистога сребра. По том га одведе у другу собу, у којој је за јаслима стајао бијел коњ с такумом од сухога злата. Најпослије га одведе и у трећу собу ђе је за јаслима био кулатаст коњ и на њему такум драгијем камењем искићен. Кад прође те собе, онда га сестра одведе у једну собу у којој је ђевојка једна сједила за златнијем ђерђефом и златном жицом везла. Из те собе одведе га у другу у којој је друга ђевојка златне жице испредала. А најпослије уведе га у једну собу у којој је трећа ђевојка бисер низала, и пред њом на златној тепсији од злата квочка с пилићима бисер кљуцала. Све ово обишавши и виђевши врати се натраг у ону собу ђе је змај мртав лежао, па га извуче на поље и баци на земљу, а браћа кад га виде, умало их грозница не ухвати. По том најмлађи брат спусти најприје сестру своју браћи, па онда све три ђевојке, сваку с њезинијем радом, једну за другом; спуштајући ђевојке браћи, сваку је намјењивао чија ће која бити, а кад спусти трећу, и то ону с квочком и пилићима, он њу за себе намијени. Браћа његова завидећи му што је он био јунак те је сестру нашао и избавио, пресијеку опуту да он не би могао сићи, па онда нађу у пољу једно чобанче код оваца, и преобуку га и мјесто брата свога оцу поведу, а сестри својој и ђевојкама оштро запријете да никоме не казују шта су они учинили. Послије некога времена дозна најмлађи брат на чардаку да се браћа његова и оно чобанче онијем ђевојкама жене. Онај исти дан у који се најстарији брат вјенчавао, он узјаше на вранца, па баш кад су сватови из цркве излазили долети међу њих, те свога брата, младожењу, удари мало буздованом у леђа да се одмах с коња преметнуо, па онда одлети опет натраг у чардак. Кад дозна да му се средњи брат жени, а он у оно исто вријеме кад су сватови из цркве ишли, долети на ђогату, те и средњега брата онако удари да се одмах с коња преметнуо, па између сватова опет одлети. На пошљетку дознавши да се чобанче његовом ђевојком жени, узјаше на кулаша, и долети у сватове баш кад су из цркве излазили, те младожењу буздованом удари у главу да је на мјесто мртав пао, а сватови онда ђипе да га ухвате, али он не шћедне

him there, and as soon as he had struck him the dragon died on the spot, and the emperor's daughter pushed him from her lap and ran to her brother, and they kissed one another, and then taking him by the hand she began to lead him through all the rooms. First she took him into a room in which there was a black horse tied to a stall, and all its tackle was of pure silver. Next she led him into a second room in which a white horse stood in his stall, and his tackle was of pure gold. Finally she took him into a third room where a dun horse was in his stall, and his tackle was decorated with precious stones. When he had gone through those rooms his sister led him into a room in which a maiden was seated at a golden embroidery frame and was embroidering with gold thread. From that room she took him into a second room in which a second maiden was spinning gold thread. And finally she took him into a room in which a third maiden was stringing pearls, and in front of her was a gold tray on which a mother hen with her chicks was pecking at pearls. Having walked around and seen all this he returned to that room where the dragon lay dead, and he dragged him outside and tossed him down to the ground, but his brothers, when they saw him, almost broke out in a fever. After that the youngest brother first of all lowered his sister to the brothers, and then all three maidens, each with her work, one after the other; as he lowered the girls to his brothers he indicated which girl was to be whose, and when he lowered the third maiden, the one with the mother hen and the chicks, he chose her for himself. His brothers, envying him because he had been a hero and had found their sister and saved her, cut the strap so he wouldn't be able to come down, and then they found a young shepherd in a field with his sheep, and they dressed him up and brought him home to their father in place of their brother, and they sharply warned their sister and the maidens to tell no one what they had done. After some time the youngest brother, who was in that house, found out that his brothers and the young shepherd were marrying the maidens. The very same day on which the eldest brother was to be married he mounted the black horse, and just when the wedding party was coming out of the church he swooped down among them and he gave his brother, the groom, a little blow on the back with his mace, so that he immediately tumbled off the horse, and then he flew back again to the house. When he learned that his middle brother was getting married, at the very same time that the wedding party was leaving the church he swooped down on the white horse and he gave the middle brother such a blow that he immediately tumbled off his horse, and again he flew off through the wedding party. Finally, learning that the young shepherd was about to marry his maiden, he mounted the dun horse and swooped down among the wedding guests just as they were coming out of the church, and he struck the bridegroom a blow on the head with his mace, so that he fell dead on the spot, and the wedding guests then leaped to seize him,

ни бјежати, него остане међу њима, па се покаже да је он најмлађи царев син а не оно чобанче, и да су га браћа из зависти оставила на ономе чардаку у коме је он сестру нашао и змаја убио, а то све засвједочи и сестра и оне ђевојке. Кад цар то чује, он се наљути на своја два старија сина и оћера их одмах од себе, а њега ожени ђевојком коју је себи изабрао и остави га наком себе да царује.

but he had no intention of running; instead he remained among them, and it was shown that he was the youngest of the emperor's sons, and not the young shepherd, and that his brothers, out of envy, had left him in that house in which he had found his sister and killed the dragon; and his sister and those maidens all testified to this. When the emperor heard that he became infuriated at his two older sons and banished them at once, and he married him to that maiden whom he had chosen for himself, and he left him the kingdom to rule after him.

These exorcisms against vampires, pests, and various illnesses, reflect a combination of Roman Catholic and Bogomil influences, the latter betraying a pre-Christian, pagan belief that illnesses were the personifications of various evil spirits that found their way into the body. The glagoljaši *or local village priests of the Northern Croatian Coast accepted these primitive folk ideas about illness, while applying Roman Catholic exorcistic rituals to them, in an effort to drive out the evil spirit that was making the person sick.*

These exorcisms are taken from seventeenth and early eighteenth century Croatian glagolitic manuscripts, as transcribed and published by Rudolf Strohal, in Zbornik za narodni život i običaje južnih slavena *(Vol. XV, Zagreb:JAZU, 1910, 120-160, and 306-315). The language is* čakavian-ikavian, *with a sprinkling of* ekavisms. *Because the authors or transcribers of these exorcisms were village priests, their language has a heavily local flavor, and individual words are not always easy to decipher.*

Unlike the exorcisms, there are no Christian elements in the three incantations reproduced here. They seem to contain remnants of pre-Christian folk belief.

Reci tri salmi i letenije: prvi salam 56.: „Da voskrsnet bog" drugi: „Prikloni, gospode, uho tvoje" 71., treti: „Blagoslovi duša moja gospodina i sva uternaja" 79., i salam: „Živi v pomoći visnjego"

Zakletve kruto korisne za odagnati napasti od ukodlakov, ma valja biti bez griha smrtnoga i priporučiti se bogu i divici Mariji

Jezus, u jime oca i sina i duha svetoga, amen. † Ovo sveti križ †, bižite (v) strane protivne, pridobi lav od kolina Judina, korin Davidov, aleluja! A sada zapovidan tebi ali vam svaki, prinečisti dusi, ukodlaci, ukodlačice, koji si nečisti duh u košću ovih slug božjih po ovomu svetomu križu † gospodinovu, koga činin svrhu vas ali svrhu tebe, da imi sinjal, ako si u tomu grobu †, zaklinam tebe čudnovatin upućeni(je)m Isukrsta u pričistu divicu Mariju po duhu svetomu onim pričistin mlikon divice Marije, s kojim dojaše Isukrsta, sina svoga, tebe zaklinam †, da mi jimaš dati sinjal, ako si u ovomu grobu †. U jime oca i sina i duha svetoga, amin . . . Učini tri † † †.

Na grobu, ako bude unutra, oće se pridati, kazati sinjal od konpišća. – „Izajdi iz ovoga groba, dijavle pakleni, koji mučiš ove kosti. . . . Zapovidam tebi, dijavle pakleni, od strane vičnjega gospodina boga, da me jimaš poslušati, ovoga službenika božjega, mene redovnika, prem ako bude grišnik nedostojan, oćeš se boga bojati, a njega sl(ugu) mene slišati †. Zapovidam tebi, dijavle pakleni, od strane vičnjega gospodina boga našega, da jimaš izajti iz ovoga groba, ma da nimaš nauditi ni meni ni ljudin ni puku kršćanskomu, ni živini, ni vinogradon ni njivan posijanim ni nijednoj stvari, ob čin žive čovik, ob čin živu kršćane, nego ti jimaš pojti u pusto misto, malo posli odlučeno †. Zaklinam tebe petim ranami Isukrstovimi †, zaklinan tebe onimi čavli u jistinu, ki uda gospodinova probodoše †, zaklinan tebe onon sulicon, koja rani našega spasitelja Isukrsta †, zaklinan onon krvljon i vodon, koja isteče iz boka našega spasitelja Isukrsta †, zaklinan tebe onon trudnon i prigorkon mukon našega spasitelja Isukrsta †, zaklinam te onim priteškim križem, na komu bi propet i mučen naš spasitelj Isukrst, da jimaš iziti iz groba ovoga iz kosti ovoga službenika božjega ili službenice. Izajdi dakle, nemili dijavle, daj misto duhu svetomu, utišitelju, u koga jime tebe tiram i zaklinam †, da jimaš izajti šubito i pojti šubito u pusto misto...

Say three psalms and litanies: first, psalm 56 "Let God Arise"; second, psalm 71 "Bow Down Thine Ear, O Lord"; third, psalm 79 "Bless The Lord, O My Soul, And All That Is Within Me"; and the psalm "Live In The Help Of The Most High."

An Exorcism against Vampires

Exorcisms are very useful in repelling attacks by vampires, but one should be without mortal sin and should commend oneself to God and to the Virgin Mary.

Jesus, in the name of the Father, and the Son, and the Holy Spirit, Amen. † This is the holy cross †, run away, the lion from the tribe of Juda, the root of David has won, allelulia! And now I command thee or you, all you most impure spirits, male vampires and female vampires, whatever unclean spirit may be in the bones of these servants of God, by this holy cross † of the Lord, which I make over you, or over thee, to give me a signal if you are in that grave †, I adjure you by the miraculous incarnation of Jesus Christ in the most pure Virgin Mary through the Holy Spirit, (and) by that most pure milk of the Virgin Mary by which she nursed Jesus Christ, her son, I adjure you to give me a signal if you are in this grave †. In the name of the Father and the Son and the Holy Spirit, Amen . . . Make three † † †.

At the grave, if he is inside, he will give himself away, he will give as a signal a horse's whinny.—"Come out of that grave, you infernal devil, who torments these bones. . . . I command you, infernal devil, on the part of the eternal Lord God, to obey me, this servant of God, me, a friar; even though I be an unworthy sinner you will fear God and hear me, his servant †. I command you, infernal devil, on the part of our eternal Lord God, to come out of this grave, but you mustn't harm either me or the people, either the Christian folk or the cattle, either the vineyards or the planted fields, or a single thing that a man lives from, that Christians live from, but you must go to a deserted place, to be decided a little later †. I adjure you by the five wounds of Christ, I adjure you in truth by those nails which pierced the limbs of the Lord †, I adjure you by that lance which wounded our Savior Jesus Christ †, I adjure you by that blood and water which flowed from the side of our Savior Jesus Christ †, I adjure you by that painful and most bitter torment of our Savior Jesus Christ †, I adjure you by that most heavy cross on which our Savior Jesus Christ was crucified and tortured, that you have to come out of this grave, out of the bones of this man or woman servant of God. Come out, therefore, unwelcome devil, make room for the Holy Spirit, the comforter, in whose name I am driving you out, and I adjure you that you have to leave at once and go at once to a deserted place. . . .

Zakljinjan vas, stvari na zlo učinjene, † † † Bogom živim i svetim i dvorom nebeskim i hori anjelskimi i 72 jimena gospodina Boga i divom Marijom i jimenom gospodina Boga i trojstva nebeskoga, da nimate toti stati ni naškoditi nijednim slugam ni službenicam božjim, a navlastito ovdi mir, da ne činite zla nijednoga, nego da jimate pojti u pustinju u misto kadi ni nijedne muke karšćanske. Vas zakljinam † † †, sve zviri, da se smaknete i da otajdete odovle, gadi, miši, husi, zavijače, rilji, čarvi i sve druge zviri zale, da otajdut i da iščeznut od obraza karšćanskoga i od trudov slug božjih i mir božji. Zakljinan vas, † zale zviri, da izajdete iz ovih vinogradov karšćanskih, kako pobigoše čarvi iz blaženoga Joba, † u jime oca † i sina † i duha svetoga, amen.

Molitva: Pomolimo se.

Vsemogi vični Bože i milosardni gospodine, molimo te, oče, vičnji Bože, koji meju sve potribe, ke po gospodinu našemu Isukarstu, sinu tvojemu, zapovidil jesi učiniti ovi vinogradi, u kih ova sveta molitva postavljena bude po zazivanju pričiste divice Marije i svih svetih tvojih od kraljestva nebeskoga, hotij hraniti i čuvati ovi vinogradi oda svakoga zla i da bude koristan i plodan i obilan i budi obran po velikon milosardju tvomu od svake suprotivšćine dijavaljske i od škodnoga daždja i od škodnoga vitra i od leda i od studeni i od mraza i od grada i od munje i od triska i od tata iliti lupeža zaloga po velikoj milosti tvojej.

TO JE RAZGOVOR OD VETRA I OD NIŽITA I OD SIČCA

Pop Anton Brzac

To je razgovor od vetra i od nižita i od sičca. Ma umij dobro štiti i niš ne pusti i umi sam sebe braniti. Križaj sve, kako najdeš, i kada oćeš se stavit za zaklinjat, čini reć tri mise, parvu od svete Trojice, drugu od svetoga duha, a tretu od gospoje. I ne daj slabomu jisti leće ni nijedne šorte glave ni riba, ka se zove čifal, ni od arbuna, zač to su nezdrave ribe. I ovdi oćeš najti mnogo moćnih riči i vridnih. – Ja pop Anton Brzac: ovo je knjiga moja.

I adjure you, things made for evil, † † † by the living and holy God and by the heavenly court and the angelic choirs and by the seventy-two names of the Lord God and by the Virgin Mary and by the name of the Lord God and the Heavenly Trinity, not to stay here or bring harm to any of God's male or female servants, and especially not to the people here; do not do a single evil thing, but instead you must go into the wilderness, into a place where [you cannot do] a single torment to a Christian. I adjure you † † †, all wild animals, to take off and leave here, repulsive things, mice, weevils, caterpillars, moles, worms, and all other evil animals, that they [sic] leave and disappear from the sight of a Christian and from the works of God's servants and God's world. . . . I adjure you, † evil wild animals, to leave these Christian vineyards, just as the worms fled from blessed Job, † in the name of the Father † and the Son † and the Holy Spirit, Amen.

An Exorcism against Pests

Prayer: Let us pray.

All powerful, eternal God and merciful Lord, we pray you, Father, eternal God, who among all the requirements which [you made] through our Lord Jesus Christ, your son, you ordered that these vineyards be created, in which this holy prayer will be placed; through the intercession of the most pure Virgin Mary and all your saints in the heavenly kingdom, deign to preserve and keep these vineyards from every kind of evil and grant that they may be useful and fruitful and bountiful and that they may be protected by your great mercy from every kind of hostile action of the devil and from harmful rain and from harmful wind and from ice and from cold and from frost and from hail and from lightning and from breaking, and from the thief or any evil rascal, in your great mercy. . . .

A CONVERSATION ABOUT COLIC AND MORTAL ILLNESS AND TUBERCULOSIS

by Father Antun Brzac

This is a conversation about colic and mortal illness and tuberculosis. But be sure to read it well and omit nothing and know how to protect yourself. Make the sign of the cross over everyone, as you come to them, and when you want to do the exorcism, have them say three masses, the first to the Holy Trinity, the second to the Holy Spirit, and the third to Our Lady. And don't allow any feeble person to eat lentils or any sort of head, or the fish that is called *čifal,* or bream, because these are unhealthy fish. And herein you will find many powerful and valuable words.—I am the priest Anton Brzac; this is my book.

Va ime † oca † i sina † i duha † svetoga, † amen, † i svetih † božjih. † Svetih † listje † pade † va vodu † z ajera † i voda proteče v mori † i valjahu se vali po moru veliki. Ne mogući tarpiti more toga ljutoga nežita i sičca i ustriljenoga vetra i pride sveti Mihovil arhanjel i prigradi more na četire strane i pripelja tri devet divac i divic i reče sveti Mihovil arhanjel: „Kamo greste vi, duhi zali?“ I rekoše: „Mi gremo k nikim goram tri varhi zlomiti i goram korenja pod vratiti i cesara nevjitskoga slugam(i) njegovimi gremo utruditi!“ I reče njim sveti Mihovil arhanjel: † „Zaklinjam vas † zale duhi † bogom † živim, † bogom † svetim † ne mozite varhi goram žgati ni lomiti, ni goram korenja pod vratiti, ni cesara nevjitskoga slugami njegovimi utruditi, † nego pojdi van, nižite i sičce i ustriljeni vetre, z ovoga raba božjega!“ I izide. Zato sunce kralji, noseći dar nižita i sičca i ustriljenoga vetra, i zaklopiše ga v kladi od železa, da ne vrati se veće rabu božjemu (imenuj) nigdare, † amen †. Nižite i sičce, ki si (se) spal s nebesi, utaknute iž anjeli, iž svić noseći, i utaknu jih sveti Mihovil arhanjel i sveti Kuzma i Domijan i rekoše njim: „Kamo greš, nižite i sičce i ustriljeni vetre?“ A oni rekoše njimi: „Gremo va glavu človičasku i v život i kosti mu gremo iskusti i žile oslabiti i uši ogluhnuti i oči oslipiti i nos ognojiti i usta skriviti i zubi skrušiti i mozgi popiti i telo na smart predati!“ I reče njim † sveti Mihovil: „Ne more vas človik tarpiti, nego pojdi van, nižite i sičce i ti ustriljeni vetre, poj u pustu goru i najti oćete ondi jeleni pasući se v gorah pustih i pustu travu jadući i pustu vodu pijući. Va pustih strana jelen stojeć skruši se, toga tarpiti ne mogući, toga ljutoga nežita i sičca i ustriljenoga vetra. I preda njih sveti Mihovil tvardomu drivu, skruši se, ne mogući tarpiti toga ljutoga nežita i sičca i ustriljenoga vetra. I prida njih kamenju tvardomu, i kamenje raspukne se, zač ne mogaše tarpit toga ljutoga nežita i sičca i ustriljenoga vetra. I preda njih sveti Mihovil miru božjemu, † va ime † svetoga † Trojstva, † amen. Prireni te † sveto Trojstvo, † zač mučiš telo, amen. † Zaklinjam vas svetimi mučenici Kuzmom i Domijanom i svetim Andrejom, apoštolom, † va ime † oca † i sina † i duha † svetoga, † amen †. Petar i Paval, naučitelji naroda, o vi se molite za ovoga raba božjega (imenuj). Mir † viki † vikom † amen †. . . .

In the name † of the Father † and the Son † and the Holy † Spirit, Amen, † and God's † saints. The leaves † of the saints † fell † into the water † from the air † and the water flowed † into the sea † and great waves rolled over the sea. And the sea, not being able to endure this fierce mortal illness and tuberculosis and colic, Saint Michael the Archangel came and he blocked off the sea on four sides, and he met thirty-nine little male and female monsters, and Saint Michael the Archangel said: "Where are you going, evil spirits?" And they said: "We are going to some mountains, to break off three peaks, and to turn the mountains upside down, and we are going to work for the King of Nineveh as his servants!" And Saint Michael the Archangel said to them: † "I adjure you † evil spirits † by the living † God, † by the † holy God: may you not be able to burn or break the peaks off mountains, or turn the mountains upside down, or work for the King of Nineveh as his servants; instead, go outside, mortal illness, and tuberculosis, and colic; get away from this slave of God!" And they went outside. Then the sun king [came], bearing a gift of a mortal illness and tuberculosis and colic, and they locked him up in iron shackles, so he couldn't return to God's slave (here give the name) ever again, † Amen †. The mortal illness and the tuberculosis which had fallen from heaven were met by angels bearing candles, and Saint Michael the Archangel met them, and the Saints Cosmas and Damian, and they said to them: "Where are you going, mortal illness and tuberculosis and colic?" And they said to them: "We are going into a man's head and we are going into his stomach and bones, to eat at them, and to weaken his veins, and deafen his ears, and blind his eyes, and make his nose fester, and twist his mouth, and destroy his teeth, and drink his brains, and give his body over to death." And Saint Michael said to them: "A man can't bear you, so go outside, mortal illness and tuberculosis and colic, go to a deserted, wooded hill, and you will find there a deer grazing in the deserted hills [sic] and eating wild grass and drinking fresh water." In that deserted area the standing deer was destroyed, being unable to bear the fierce mortal illness and tuberculosis and colic. And Saint Michael the Archangel passed them on to a hard tree, and it was destroyed, being unable to bear the fierce mortal illness and tuberculosis and colic. And he passed them on to hard rocks, and the rocks burst, because they were unable to bear that fierce mortal illness and tuberculosis and colic. And Saint Michael passed them on to God's peace, † in the name † of the Holy † Trinity, † Amen. May the Holy Trinity drive you away, because you torment this body, Amen. I adjure you, by the holy martyrs Cosmas and Damian, and Saint Andrew the Apostle, † in the name † of the Father † and of the Son † and of the Holy † Spirit †, Amen. † Peter and Paul, teachers of the people, O pray ye for this slave of God (name him). Peace unto all ages. Amen. . . .

About Colic and Mortal Illness

Наша дода бога моли,
  ој додо, ој додо ле!
Да удари росна киша,
  ој додо, ој додо ле!
да покисну сви орачи,
  ој додо, ој додо ле!
сви орачи и копачи,
  ој додо, ој додо ле!
и по кучи пословачи,
  ој додо, ој додо ле!

Iznad mjesta ujeda načini se križ i govori:

Oj alojko, alilojko
pušti svoj ijed
iz kosti u meso
iz mesa pod kožu
iz kože na dlaku
sa dlake u zelenu travu.

Poslije tih riječi nagne se nad blago i reče npr.:

Ljubava, ništa ti neće biti.

Izlazi vujo van,
na bijeli dan.
Tu ti nema mjesta,
ni na moru mosta,
ni u kamenu noga,
ni u gavranu bijela biljega.

A RAINMAKING CHANT

Our dodola asked God,
    Oj dodo, oj dodo le!
That a drizzly rain might fall,
    Oj dodo, oj dodo le!
So that all the plowmen might get wet.
    Oj dodo, oj dodo le!
All the plowmen and the diggers,
    Oj dodo, oj dodo le!
And those who are working at home,
    Oj dodo, oj dodo le!

AN INCANTATION AGAINST SNAKEBITE

One makes a cross above the
place of the bite, and says:
Oj alojko, alilojko
Let your poison go
From the bones to the flesh
From the flesh to beneath the skin
From the skin to the hair
From the hair into the green grass.
After these words, one bends over the person tenderly and says, for instance:
Love, nothing is going to happen to you.

AN INCANTATION AGAINST FLEAS

Go outside flea,
Into the light of day.
There's no room for you here.
Just as on the sea there's no bridge,
And on a rock no leg,
And on a raven no white marking.

The Adriatic Coast

NOTES

Proglas

p. 7

1. This translation of St. Constantine-Cyril's "Proglas" to the Gospels is dedicated to Nada Rajnvajn Toomey, born in Cetinje, Yugoslavia, November 24, 1925, died in Madison, Wisconsin, November 19, 1976. A member of the Njegoš family, Mrs. Toomey was a lady of high culture, who showed strong courage in the face of adversity and death itself.

2. The thirteenth-century manuscript from which this version is taken shows linguistic features typical of early Serbian Slavonic writing: for example, the reflexes *e* and *u* for the Common Slavic front and back nasals (ę and ǫ) and a single reflex, indicated by the symbol ь, for the front and back jers.

Croatian Missal Fragment

p. 19

3. While the morphology of this early Croatian missal fragment is close to Old Church Slavonic, its phonology clearly reflects the Croatian writing of its time.

Miroslav Gospels

p. 23

4. The Miroslav Gospel gives evidence of the standard Serbo-Croatian development of the late Common Slavic vowels, one similar to that shown in the twelfth-century Croatian Missal Fragment and in the thirteenth-century manuscript of the "Proglas."

The Homily by St. John Chrysostom

p. 27

5. John Chrysostom writes so pointedly of the responsibilities of the righteous ruler, perhaps because as a high church dignitary he had the opportunity to observe the behavior of the Byzantine rulers. Because of his forthright approach to public morality, and his criticisms of the Byzantine Court, he became the enemy of the Empress Eudoxia (in 399 A.D.) and of corrupt special interest groups. When Chrysostom writes of John the Baptist: "For John was not afraid of death, but he was afraid not to speak the truth," we are reminded of his own banishment from Constantinople by Eudoxia and his eventual death (407 A.D.) after a forced march of some 400 miles.

Life of Stefan Nemanja

p. 39

6. "Our holy monastery" refers to the monastery of Studenica founded by Stefan Nemanja while he was still ruler of the Serbian lands.

7. Stefan Nemanja, founder of the medieval Nemanja dynasty, united the Serbian tribes in the state of Raška.

p. 39

8. Zeta was an ancient name for Montenegro.

9. "Pomoravlje" refers to the lands bordering the Morava River, a central waterway of Serbia.

p. 41

10. The Monastery of St. George at Ras, not far from today's Novi Pazar, became known as "Djurdjevi Stubovi" (St. George's Columns); famed for its beautiful frescoes, it was destroyed in 1912, during a war with the Turks. Milovan Djilas wrote a beautiful piece about the ruins of "Djurdjevi Stubovi" in his *The Leper and Other Stories.*

p. 43

11. The "thrice-cursed heresy" refers to the medieval religious heresy called "Bogomilism" in the Balkans, and known elsewhere in Southern Europe as Catharism, Patarenism, and Albigensianism. For more on this movement see the introduction to the "Apocalypse of St. John" in this book.

p. 44

12. Arius (265A.D.?-356A.D.) was an Eastern churchman who denied the divinity of Christ. According to Arius and his followers Christ, the "Logos" is an intermediary between God and the world. He existed before time but not eternally, and therefore he is inferior to God. The Council of Nicaea (325AD), presided over by Constantine the Great, condemned Arius's teachings, declaring that the Son was of the same substance as the Father ("homousios"). No direct connection has ever been shown between Arianism and Bogomilism, although both movements do share an unwillingness to accept the standard church doctrine concerning the Trinity.

p. 46

13. "He cut the tongue from the throat of their teacher . . ."–a clear indication that Stefan Nemanja showed no mercy toward the Bogomil sect. It is interesting that Prvovenčani, in keeping with his father's injunction, mentions neither the name of the sect, nor its leader.

14. Prvovenčani's comment that his father "burned the impious books" indicates that Bogomil tracts did once exist, although none have survived in Yugoslavia.

Life of Saint Sava

p. 55

15. There is an earlier Life of St. Sava, written by a monk named Domentijan. His work, more flowery than Teodosije's, and given to biblical citations, seems to have served as the foundation for Teodosije's *Life of St. Sava.* Some scholars believe that Teodosije was commissioned to rewrite the *Life of Sava* in order to "correct" the impression given by Domentijan that not only Prvovenčani, but Sava too was favorably inclined at one time toward the West and the Pope. (Stefan received his first crown from Pope Honorius III, and Domentijan tells us that it was Sava who sent the mission that sought the crown.) Teodosije makes no mention of this mission.

p. 59

16. Here the marriage motif, and Sava's flight, remind one of the *Žitije i žizn' čelověka božija Aleksija,* although Sava, unlike Aleksij, does not get married before he makes his escape.

Siluan's Song to St. Sava

p. 69

17. "There whence glory appeared to your people" is a reference to Sava's flight to Mount Athos, where he found glory, and built the monastery of Hilandar, a source of glory to his people.

Life of Stefan Dečanski

p. 73

18. "The great Simeon" is Stefan Nemanja, who took the monastic name of Simeon.

19. Flavius Valerius Constantinus, born at Naissus (today's Niš), of Illyrian stock. The first Christian Roman Emperor (ruled 306-337A.D.), Constantine founded "the second Rome" at Byzantium. This second Roman or Byzantine Empire lasted more than a thousand years, submitting finally to the Turks in 1453.

p. 75

20. "If a woman's deceit . ."–such a malicious,unfounded remark is characteristic of the misogyny of medieval writers, East and West.

Vinodol Law Code

p. 83

21. An indiction was a fifteen-year cycle, used as a supplementary chronological unit in ancient and medieval times. Originally used to designate a period between tax reassessments, it was fixed at fifteen years by Constantine in 312A.D. Dating by indiction became a law during the era of Justinian (483-565). According to R. Dean Ware ("Medieval Chronology: Theory and Practice," in *Medieval Studies:* An Introduction, James M. Powell, ed.) only the position of the year within the cycle is identified and only extraordinarily is the number of the cycle given, but this rarely creates a problem because other chronological data are given. Ware gives the following rule for computing an indiction: "Take a date, subtract 312 from it, and divide the result by 15. The remainder is the indiction. If there is no remainder the indiction is XV. Thus the year 1066 would be Indictio IV."

22. "King Ladislav the most glorious Hungarian king"–a reference to Ladislaus IV of Hungary (ruled 1272-1290). Croatia had been under Hungarian suzerainty since 1202, and it was natural and normal that the Lords of Vinodol,Krk and Modruša would acknowledge King Ladislaus.

23. It is impossible to give a precise English equivalent of the word *dvornik,* although chancellor might be an approximation. The *Dictionary* of the Yugoslav Academy states, concerning *dvornik*: "A man in some public service (what kind is unknown)." At times *dvornik* seems to be the Croatian equivalent of the Serbian *župan,* the highest official under a local ruler.

p. 85

24. (Article 1) A *soldin* was a copper coin (from the Italian *soldo*). *Vernezi* were also coins, originally minted in Verona, whence the name.

25. A *bolanča,* from the Latin *balantia,* was a monetary unit, the exact value of which is unknown.

26. Both the *Vinodol Law Code* and the *Law Code of Emperor Stefan Dušan* provide some insight into the relationship between Church and State in medieval Croatia and Serbia. The *Vinodol Code,* as Articles 1 and 2 illustrate, tried to limit the church hierarchy's powers by defining them, whereas the Serbian law code, patterned on the Byzantine, tended to regard the Church as the partner of the State, and saw Orthodoxy and Autocracy as mutually supporting institutions.

p. 85

27. Article 5 of the *Vinodol Code* defines the Prince's powers under the feudal right of "descensus."

28. (Article 6) A *libra* was a larger monetary unit, equivalent to 20 soldins. Like the Italian lira, it derives from the Latin *libra.*

Law Code of Emperor Stefan Dušan

p. 97

29. The year 6857 is equivalent to 1349 A.D. The former date derives from a system commonly used in the Byzantine Empire from the seventh century on; this system (annus mundi) assumes that Christ was born 5508 years after the creation of the earth.

p. 99

30. (Article 6) "The Latin heresy" refers to Roman Catholicism. Dušan's expanded Serbian Empire included Roman Catholic subjects, particularly on the Southern Dalmatian Coast and in Northern Albania.

31. "The Law of the Holy Fathers" was the Byzantine compilation of ecclesiastical law known as the *Sintagmat,* prepared by Blastares in 1335 A.D.

32. (Article 7) "The Great Church" refers to the Serbian Patriarchate, first established in Dušan's time.

33. "That everyone should return to Christianity" means that Dušan and his *Sabor* expect that all his Christian subjects will return to or convert to Orthodoxy.

p. 100

34. (Article 20) The wergeld ("man payment") was the indemnity a murderer or his family and clan paid the family of a victim; in the Serbian kingdom the indemnity varied from 300 to 1000 *perpera* (see footnote 36 for a definition of *perpera*). The wergeld fine could be levied not only for murder, but also for other serious crimes, as is the case here.

p. 101

35. Article 97 illustrates the overwhelming importance of the beard as a symbol of an Orthodox Christian male's psychic identity. "Good men" (Latin *boni homines*) were freemen who could serve as judges in local courts. This system is said to be the origin of the modern jury.

36. A *perpera* (article 98) was a small piece of money, the exact value of which is unknown. Vuk derives the word from the Greek hyperpiron, defining it as *mali novac.* The Yugoslav Academy *Dictionary* says that the *perpera* was worth more than a dinar and less than a ducat. Djuro Daničić devoted six pages of his *Rječnik iz književnih starina srpskih* to an attempt to define *perpera.* Burr, in his translation of this *Code,* values the *perpera* at six gold franks (by no means *mali novac*), while Radojčić in his edition gives it a value of twenty silver dinars.

37. Article 112 concerns the ancient right of sanctuary, inherited by medieval society from Graeco-Roman civilization. Under certain conditions, which varied according to the times and the locale, a fugitive criminal might seek sanctuary in a temple or church and remain immune from the law while within the confines of that building; this privilege was also extended to a ruler's castle. Such a right had its practical justification, in that it gave injured parties time "to cool off" and it also gave a fugitive and his family an opportunity to bargain for his release or exile.

Dubrovnik Treaties

p. 107

38. The wealthy house of Balša, descended perhaps from Vlah stock, ruled Zeta from 1360 to 1421. One of the Balšići married a daughter of Prince Lazar.

39. Drač was the Slavic name for the Albanian city of Durres (Greek Durrachium).

40. Danj was a medieval town in the vicinity of Scutari; it was a stopping place for caravans, and the Balšić family had a customs house there.

p. 108

41. Tuzi is a place in Montenegro, near Scutari.

42. *Protovistar* is a Serbian equivalent of the Greek *protovistiarios,* minister of finance or treasurer.

p. 109

43. Prince Lazar Hrebeljanović was a feudal lord who ruled part of Serbia after the end of the Nemanjić dynasty (1371-1389). He was a capable ruler, who maintained good relations with other Balkan heads of state, especially with Tvrtko Kotromanović of Bosnia. Lazar died at the battle of Kosovo, June 15, 1389, as the leader of an allied force opposing a Turkish army led by Sultan Murad.

44. "The Emperor Stefan" referred to here is Stefan Dušan, who had died some thirty years earlier.

p. 110

45. Saxons were active both as miners and traders in Novo Brdo, a thriving medieval Serbian city. The Saxon role in the economic development of the Serbian state has been described by Konstantin Jireček in his *Die Handelsstrassen und Bergwerke von Serbien und Bosnien während des Mittelalters* . . . (Prague, 1879), as well as (briefly) in his *Geschichte der Serben* (II, Gotha 1911-1918).

p. 112

46. The term *vlah* comes perhaps from an old Germanic name for the Romans *(Walh)*; it has been traditionally used by the Balkan Slavs to refer to the Rumanians (Wallachians), as well as to the Arumanian-speaking nomadic shepherds who trace their descent, at least in part, to the ancient Roman settlers in the Balkans. These *vlasi* were also called *mavrovlasi* or *karavlasi* (black Vlahs). The term *vlah* was also used by Serbs to refer to Roman Catholics, particularly those from the Dalmatian Coast, and by Turks to refer to all Christians.

p. 113

47. Kruševac was Prince Lazar's capital city.

48. A *logofet* (from Greek *logothetes*) was the chancellor or chief advisor of a ruler.

p. 114

49. A *kefalija* (from the Greek word for head, *kefali*) was the chief magistrate in a town. From the fourteenth century on, the *kefalije* were responsible for public security, not only in the towns but in the surrounding districts as well.

The Apocalypse

p. 115

50. Although the "Apocalypse" or "Revelation" of St. John is a canonical part of Holy Writ, there has been some question as to John's authorship of it. Some

critics have claimed that the language of the "Apocalypse" is "cruder" than the Greek of John's Gospel, while others have attributed the difference in language to the fact that John was in an altered state while experiencing and writing this revelation.

p. 119

51. John was banished to Patmos, an island in the Ionian Sea, not far from today's Turkey.

52. "I was in the power of the spirit"–evidently a reference to John's altered state as a result of fasting and prayer.

53. "Fall on us [and hide us] . . ."–throughout this book brackets will indicate portions of text omitted by an individual copyist, but restored here on the basis of other manuscripts.

Vladimir and Kosara

p. 123

54. The Emperor Samuel (Samuilo), ruler of the Macedonians and Bulgarians, had his capital at Ohrid. He died in 1014.

Barlaam and Josaphat

p. 149

55. The Slavic word *inorog* can signify either the mythical unicorn, or the rhinoceros.

Alexander of Macedonia

p. 155

56. Alexander the Great (365 BC-323 BC), son of Philip II of Macedonia and student of Aristotle, became King of Macedonia in 336 BC. His armies conquered most of the known civilized world, including Greece, Asia Minor, Syria, Egypt, Persia, Afghanistan, and part of India.

p. 157

57. The Persian Emperor Darius III ruled from 336 BC to 330 BC. He was killed by his own men, while fleeing from Alexander's armies.

58. (Jeremiah). The interpolation of Judaic and Christian elements in this story of a pagan conqueror is obviously the result of centuries of reworking of the Alexander saga, by a variety of adapters, of many nationalities and religious beliefs.

59. Antioch and Ptolemy were military commanders under Alexander. Ptolemy eventually established a ruling dynasty in Egypt.

60. Ar'sonor'skoj: this word seems to be a corruption of the word *Assirskaja* (Assyrian), which is used elsewhere in this mss. The "Assyrian River" is the Tigris, and the battle between Darius and Alexander was fought at Gaugamela, near the Tigris.

Judita

p. 229

61. Marko Marulić wrote in the čakavian-ikavian dialect common to his native city of Split. Archaic in many respects, and with a phonological development that does not always correspond to today's standard Serbo-Croatian literary language, Marulić's language is difficult to read without the aid of a glossary. Some of its characteristic features are the reflex *i* for Late Common Slavic ě (*niki* "some" where modern SC would have *neki*); the change of the Common Slavic *ję* to *ja* in initial

position *(jati/jazyk)*, contraction of the relative pronoun (*kâ* for *koja* and *kî* for *koji*), development of secondary *j* in pronominal-adjectival forms ending in a vowel (*tuj* for *tu*), and the retention of older nominal desinences such as the dative plural in *om* and the instrumental plural in *imi/ami.*

Dundo Maroje

p. 240

62. The opening synopsis of Maroje's previous adventures with his son probably repeats information from a previous Držić comedy, *Pomet,* which has been lost.

63. Saint Trifun was the patron saint of Kotor, Tripčeta's town.

Robinja

p. 247

64. A *ban* was the highest Croatian functionary under Hungarian rule. There were usually two bans appointed, and they served as regents of the Hungarian king in Croatia. Theirs was a non-hereditary position, of limited duration.

Kraljević Marko i brat mu Andrijaš

p. 257

65. Marko Kraljević ("King's Son"), son of Vukašin who lost his life fighting the Turks at the battle of the Marica River in 1371, was Lord of Prilep, in Macedonia, and vassal of the Sultan Bayazid. Marko lost his life fighting for the Turks in Wallachia (1394). He was the eldest son of Vukašin, while Andrija was the second eldest. After Marko was killed Andrija left Macedonia for Dubrovnik. He eventually settled in Hungary.

Osman

p. 267

66. "The wheel of fortune goes round and round"–the idea that capricious fortune holds sway over men's lives is a typical Renaissance conception of history.

67. "O pure and gentle maidens"–Gundulić here addresses the nine Muses, sister goddesses believed by the ancient Greeks to preside over learning and the arts.

68. Osman II (1618-1622) was elevated to the throne at the age of 14, with his uncle Mustafa as regent. Against the advice of his vezirs Osman went to war with Wladyslaw IV of Poland, and was defeated. The Janissary leaders rebelled against him, and the Grand Vezir, Da'ud Pasha (a Bosnian) had him strangled, May 20, 1622.

69. Wladyslaw IV ruled Poland 1632-1648; his forces defeated the Ottomans at the battle of Khotim (Chocim) in 1621.

Ballad about Janko Sibinjanin and John of Capistrano

p. 277

70. Janko Sibinjanin was the popular Serbian and Croatian name for János Hunyádi (1387-1456), a Hungarian military hero, who was also regent for the young Hungarian king Ladislaus V. Janko Sibinjanin appears more than once in Serbo-Croatian folklore; he is mentioned, for example, in the poem "Kraljević Marko i Mina od Kostura," which is given later in this book.

71. Saint John of Capistrano (1386-1456), an Italian Franciscan monk, preached a holy crusade against the Turks.

72. Sultan Mehmed (Mohammed) II ruled from 1451 to 1481; his armies captured Constantinople in 1453.

73. The Janissaries were an elite guard of Ottoman troops, originally recruited from Christian captives who converted to Islam. Later the Janissary corps was built from young recruits, taken as part of the "danak u krvi" (blood tribute) exacted by the Ottoman Empire from its Christian subjects approximately every six or seven years. The Janissary Corps was long noted for its ferocity in battle and for its unswerving loyalty to the Sultan, but gradually it became a political force and it helped to depose more than one sultan.

74. Adrianopolis (in Serbo-Croatian *Jedrena* or *Jedrene*), a city in Thrace, first Turkish capital in Europe (1402-1453).

The Life and Adventures of Dositej Obradović

p. 308

75. "Something good in Serbian" . . . Dositej is referring to the fact that by the late eighteenth century Serbs had not yet agreed on a modern literary language, but instead educated people wrote in a highly individual mish-mash of spoken Serbian and literary Russian, which they called "Slaveno-Serbski." At the time it was mistakenly believed that Russian Slavonic was the direct and pure descendant of Old Church Slavonic. Dositej Obradović wanted his countrymen to write in their spoken language, although he did condone the use of Russian vocabulary for specialized terms that had no Serbian equivalents.

76. "Devotees and admirers . . . of Sardanapalus"–according to Greek fable, Sardanapalus was the last king of Assyria. This name seems to be a corruption of Assurbanipal, a successful but decadent ruler, who committed suicide at Nineveh in 880 BC, as his city was being besieged.

77. "This knot can't be cut like the Gordian knot." Gordium was a Phrygian city in Asia Minor. According to legend the Phrygian king Gordius had a wagon tied to a pole, with thongs, in a complex knot. It was said that whoever would untie the knot would become Lord of Asia. When Alexander the Greek reached Gordium he slashed the knot through with his sword, saying: "What difference does it make how I untie it?"

The Serbian Governing Council

p. 322

78. Prota Matija Nenadović (1778-1854), a village priest from the Šumadija region of Serbia. An active participant in the First Serbian Insurrection (1804-1813) the Prota served both as an emissary to Russia and as a cannoneer. His *Memoari (Memoirs)*, written in a lively and entertaining style, have been translated into English by Lovett Edwards. (Oxford: Clarendon Press, 1969.)

79. Karadjordje or Black George Petrović (1760-1817), leader of the First Serbian Insurrection.

80. Trivalija was one name used for the medieval Serbian kingdom. The name is derived from that of an ancient Thracian tribe, the Triballi, who lived in the area between the Morava and the Iskur Rivers.

81. Bishop Leontije was a pro-Turkish Greek, who was bishop of Belgrade during the time of the First Serbian Insurrection.

82. The *dahije* (from the Turkish word *dayi,* originally meaning a military hero) were the Janissary leaders who seized power from the legally-appointed Ottoman authorities in various parts of the Ottoman Empire.

83. In the eighteenth and nineteenth centuries the word *krdžalije* (from Turkish Kirça Ali, a city in Eastern Rumelia) referred to irregular soldiers and mercenaries who served as attack units for the renegade *dayi.*

84. Jeremija Gagić (1781-1859) later became the Russian vice-consul in Dubrovnik, serving as the main link, at times, between the Russian government and Petar Petrović Njegoš II (1813-1851), poet and ruler of Montenegro. (An excerpt from Njegoš's *Mountain Wreath* is given in this book.)

85. Karabogdanska is the Rumanian province known today as Moldavia.

86. Jaşi is a major city in Rumania.

87. Karavlaška (literally "Black Vlah Country") is the Rumanian province of Wallachia.

88. A *tantula* was a broad-brimmed cap.

89. Kučuk Alija was one of the dayis, who ruled Serbia after assassinating the legitimate Turkish representative in Belgrade, Hadži Mustafa Pasha, who was well liked by the Serbs.

Hajduk Veljko Petrović

p. 332

90. A *hajduk* was a Balkan bandit or highwayman; occasionally he may have assumed the role of protector of local Christians, or even acted as their avenger against the Turks. In the eighteenth and nineteenth centuries the *hajduci* played an active role in the liberation struggle against the Ottoman Empire.

91. *Buljubaša* is a SC derivative from a Turkish word for captain; the *-ica* suffix makes the word a diminutive.

92. Crni Djordje is the pure Serbian equivalent for Karadjordje.

93. Mladen Milovanović, a participant in the Serbian uprising, known for his dishonesty and plotting.

94. *Bimbaša/binbaša:* a Serbo-Croatian derivative from the Turkish *binbaşi,* a major in the army. *Barjaktar/bajraktar:* a SC derivative from Turkish *bayraktar,* a standard bearer.

95. *Gospodar* ("lord"): Vuk Karadžić in his *Srpski rječnik* (1818) states that prior to 1804 only high-level Moslems were called "gospodar." Then Karadjordje and other Serbian leaders of the insurrection began to be called by this title.

96. *Vlah* here would seem to indicate "Christian," i.e. Vuk is using the word in the Turkish way.

97. A *thaler* was an Austrian silver coin.

The Death of Smail-aga Čengić

p. 346

98. A *vila* was a mythological being in South Slavic folklore. Similar to our fairies or spirits, vilas were said to be the spirits of unbaptized maidens, who lived in the woods, on mountains, and near bodies of water.

99. Cuce, Bjelice, and Ćeklići are the names of Montenegrin tribes.

100. Cetinje is the former capital of Montenegro.

The Mountain Wreath

p. 358

101. "The father of Serbia" refers to Karadjordje.

102. Bellona was the Roman goddess of war.

103. Karl Hapsburg, Blücher, Wellington, Suvorov, Schwarzenberg, and Kutuzov were military commanders of the allied forces in the Napoleonic wars (1796-1815).

104. Ares was the Greek god of war.

105. Pharaoh here means the Sultan.

106. Stefan Dušan, Emperor of Serbia (1308-1355); excerpts from his *Law Code* are given in this book.

107. Miloš Obilić (or Kobilić), hero-martyr at Kosovo, offered to surrender to Sultan Murad, and after stabbing Murad he was himself slaughtered by Murad's bodyguard.

108. Dmitrij Mikhailovič Pozharskij (1579-1642), a leader in the Russian struggle against the Poles, in 1612. He led the Russian forces that helped free Moscow.

109. The "Devil with seven mantles" is the Sultan.

110. "France's dike" is an allusion to France's role in stemming the Islamic "flood" into Europe via Spain. Noteworthy were the victories of Charles Martel (Charles the Hammer) against Arab armies at Tours, in 732 A.D., and at Narbonne, in 737 A.D.

111. Sultan Osman I (1288?-1326), founder of the Osmanli or Ottoman Dynasty. Osman was said to have won the daughter of a wealthy sheik as the result of a dream in which both his future bride and the future Osmanli Empire were symbolized by a moon. One is impressed, here and elsewhere, by Njegoš's knowledge of Turkish history and lore.

112. Sultan Orkhan (1326-1359) established a Turkish foothold in Europe, in Thrace; his armies served as mercenaries for both the Greeks and the Serbs.

113. Teodora, daughter of John VI Cantacuzene, was given to Orkhan in marriage (1346). The Turks later based their claim to Constantinople on this marriage.

114. John V. Paleologus (1341-1391), involved in a struggle for power with Cantacuzene, called on Sultan Murad to help him put down a Serbian threat to his state, thus contributing to the eventual "burial" of the Greeks and the Serbs.

115. Vuk Branković, who was in command of the reserve troops at Kosovo, was traditionally believed to have betrayed his allies during the battle. He later served as a vassal to Sultan Bayazid. Gerluka (Kir Lukas) was a Greek admiral whom folk tradition mistakenly held to have betrayed Constantinople to the Turks in 1453. Njegoš here compliments Mohammed II for having killed the traitor as a reward for his betrayal of the Greeks.

116. "Janko defends the dead Ladislav"–a reference to János Hunyádi, regent of King Ladislaus of Hungary. Hunyádi died in 1456 and Ladislaus was executed by the Turks.

117. Skenderbeg or Iskandar Beg (Lord Alexander), the popular name for George Castriota (1403-1468), the valiant leader of the Albanian struggle against the Ottoman Empire.

118. "And now I shall struggle with the worst one"–Bishop Danilo here refers to the conversion of Christian Montenegrins to Mohammedanism. The Bishop sees such conversions as an internal threat to national survival.

119. "One putting out the eyes of the other"–an allusion perhaps to King Milutin's blinding of his son Stefan Dečanski.

120. "O cursed Kosovo supper' "–a reference to the bickering and accusations of treason at the "last supper" of the Christian military leaders, on the eve of the battle of Kosovo.

121. Leonidas, King of Sparta, who heroically defended the pass at Thermopylae against the Persians (480 BC). C. Mucius Scaevola, a Roman hero who defied his Etruscan captors by holding his hand in a fire until it burned off (508 BC). As a result of this he gained the nickname "Scaevola" or "lefty."

122. Miloš Obilić–see note 107 above.

123. "Slave of the prophet's slave"–slave of the Sultan, who is the slave of the Prophet Mohammed.

124. *Raya* is the Turkish word for any non-Moslem subject of the Ottoman Empire. The word could be used individually or collectively.

125. *Serdar* is a Turkish word meaning a leader or military commander. In Montenegro a *serdar* was a tribal chieftain.

126. "Leopold's brave duke" refers to Charles IV, Duke of Lorraine, military commander of a relief army at the second battle of Vienna (1683). This battle was a great defeat for the Turkish Empire and led to its gradual withdrawal from Europe.

127. Jan Sobieski (1624-1696), a Polish king whose armies also arrived as a relief force at the second battle of Vienna.

128. "The two brothers with the same name"–Njegoš is using the word "brother" figuratively here, as he refers to Mohammed II who took Constantinople in 1453 and Mohammed IV who was defeated at Vienna in 1683.

129. *Burak* is the name of the legendary winged horse that took the prophet Mohammed to heaven.

130. "There are many tracks to the lion's den"–is an allusion to the fable about the aging lion who invites a fox to visit his cave; the fox notices that there are many tracks leading to the cave but none leading out, and so he politely declines the invitation.

131. "I once got myself into your clutches"–Bishop Danilo here refers to a visit he once made to a Turkish-held town, under a pledge of safe conduct, in order to consecrate a church. The Turks seized him and held him, until the Montenegrins paid a heavy ransom.

Marko Kraljević and Mina from Kostur

p. 400

132. *Kum* here means "godfather," but it can also designate other relationships as well, such as "wedding witness" *(venčani kum)* or the man who first cuts a boy's hair *(šišani kum)*.

133. *Kostur* is the Slavic name for the town of Kastoria in Northern Greece.

134. *Bakšiš* (from Turkish *bahşiş*) is a tip or gratuity.

135. "The glorious holy mountain" is Mount Athos, site of the Serbian monastery of Hilandar, as well as of other Orthodox monasteries.

Hasan Aga's Wife

p. 418

136. "For the sake of our mother"–the full expression in SC is *"tako te ne želila majka,"* literally: "May your mother never wish for you (lack you)."

137. "That when you assemble the wedding party"–Vuk Karadžić, in his first publication of this poem in the Pjesmarica of 1814, added a line here of his own: *"I kad podješ njenom b'jelu dvoru"* ("And when you set out for her white manor.")

The Building of Scutari

p. 430

138. The Mrljavčević or Mrnjavčević family were feudal lords in Macedonia, related by marriage to the Nemanjići.

139. The Boyana River is an offshoot of Lake Scutari, forming part of the boundary between Montenegro and Albania.

140. "Six loads of treasure"–the SC word is *tovar,* which today means "load," but once had a more precise value, equal to about 280 pounds.

The Building of the Bridge at Višegrad

p. 442

141. Mehmed Pasha Sokolović (1505?-1579), born a Christian in the village of Sokolovići, Bosnia, taken as part of the *danak u krvi* (blood tribute) by the Ottomans, when he was about eighteen. Bajo (his original name) was converted to Islam, educated at Jedrena (Adrianopolis), and eventually rose to be Grand Vizir. He left many *zadužbine* (memorials), and did not forget his own region; he provided the funds for the building of the bridge and its maintenance, as well as for the building of a *han* (inn) nearby. This same bridge at Višegrad is the subject of a novel by Ivo Andrić *(Na Drini Ćuprija).*

Exorcisms and Incantations

142. (First exorcism). The first three psalms mentioned here are psalms 68, 86, and 103 in the King James translation of the *Old Testament.*

143. (Third exorcism, by Father Brzac). Concerning the three diseases mentioned here, the *Dictionary* of the Yugoslav Academy suggests that *vjetar* or *ustrijeljani vjetar,* may be a folk term for colic. The folk belief (perhaps stemming from Bogomil times and earlier) was that the stomach pains which suddenly gripped a person with colic were shot into him by witches and vilas; of *nižit (nežit)* the Academy *Dictionary* states that it may be a folk term for any mortal illness (Matthias Murko, on the other hand, regards *nežit* as a Bogomil term for *any* illness, and he cites the Dalmatian word *nežitak* for the evil spirit that supposedly entered a person and caused illness); the word *sičce* did not appear in any dictionary available to this writer. There is a word *sičije* (tuberculosis), which is close enough to suggest a similar meaning. *Sičce* may also be related to *sič,* a folk term for vertigo.

144. (Rainmaking chant). *Dodola* is believed to be the Slavic name for a pre-Christian rain goddess. Until relatively recent times, during a period of drought, a young village girl (the *dodola*), dressed only in her shift and covered with green branches, would go about the village with a group of maidens who would sing this or similar *dodolske pesme.* At every house at which they stopped the girls would be sprinkled with water and given presents.

BIBLIOGRAPHY

Aitzetmüller, R. *Mihanović Homiliar: Editiones monumentorum slavicorum veteris dialecti* (Graz, 1957).

Banašević, Nikola. "Le cycle de Kosovo et les chansons de geste," *Revue des études slaves, VI* (Paris, 1926), 224-244.

________. *Letopis popa dukljanina i narodna predanja* (Beograd, 1971), 301p.

Barac, Antun. *Hrvatska književnost od preporoda do stvaranja Jugoslavije* (Zagreb, 1954), 315p.

________. *Jugoslavenska književnost* (Zagreb, 1959), 331p. [Translated by Petar Mijušković and published as *A History of Yugoslav Literature* by *Michigan Slavic Publications*, Ann Arbor, 1974].

Berčić, Ivan. *Dvie službe rimskoga obreda za svetkovinu svetih Ćirila i Metuda.* Introd. by Vatroslav Jagić (Zagreb, 1870), 79p.

Birnbaum, Henrik. "Byzantine Tradition Transformed: The Old Serbian Vita," in *Aspects of the Balkans: Continuity and Change.* Eds. H. Birnbaum and S. Vryonis (The Hague/Paris, 1972), 243-284.

Bogišić, Rafo, ed. *Zbornik stihova xv i xvi stoljeća. Pet stoljeća hrvatske književnosti, 5* (Zagreb, 1968), 493p.

Bošković-Stulli, Maja. *Narodne pripovijetke* (Zagreb, 1963), 430p.

Burr, Malcolm. *The Code of Stephan Dušan: Translation and Notes by Malcolm Burr, D.Sc.* London: *Slavonic and East European Review*, 1950 (an offprint).

Ćorović, Vladimir, ed. *Spisi Sv. Save, Zbornik za istoriju, jezik i književnost srpskog naroda* (Beograd, 1928).

________. *Sveti Sava u narodnom predanju* (Beograd, 1927), 267p.

________. *Svetosavski zbornik, II. Žitije Simeona Nemanje od Stevana Prvovenčanoga* (Beograd, 1939).

Daničić, Djura, ed. "Apokalipsa iz hvalova rukopisa," *Starine, IV* (Zagreb, 1872), 86-109.

________. *Život Svetoga Save napisao Domentijan* [Teodosije] (Beograd, 1960). [A photographic reproduction of this book was published privately, in 1973, by Djordje Trifunović, Beograd, ul. Geršićeva, 18].

Držić, Marin. *Novela od stanca, Tirena, Skup, Dundo Maroje.* Ed. Ivan Dončević. *Pet stoljeća hrvatske književnosti,* 6 (Zagreb, 1962).

Entwistle, William J. *European Balladry* (Oxford, 1951), 404p.

Fine, John. *The Bosnian Church: A New Interpretation* (Boulder, 1975), 447p.

Fortis, Alberto. *Viaggio in Dalmazia* (Venice, 1774).

Gesemann, Gerhard. *Erlangenski rukopis starih srpskohrvatskih narodnih pesama* (Sremski Karlovci, 1925), 344p.

Grabar, B., Nazor, A., Pantelić, M., Štefanić, V. eds. *Missale Hervoiae ducis spalatensis croatico-glagoliticum: transcriptio et commentarium* (Zagreb/Ljubljana/Graz, 1973).

Grekov, B. D. *Vinodol'skij statut ob obščestvennom i političeskom stroe Vinodola* (Moskva, 1948).

Gundulić, Ivan. *Osman.* Ed. Milan Ratković. *Pet stoljeća hrvatske književnosti, XIII: 2* (Zagreb, 1964).

Hektorović, Petar. *Ribanje i ribarsko prigovaranje.* Ed. Ramiro Bujas (Zagreb, 1951), 91p.

Hörmann, Kosta. *Narodne pjesme muslimana u Bosni i Hercegovini* (Sarajevo, 1933).

Ivšić, Stjepan. "Iz hrvatske književnosti: 'legenda o Ivanu Zlatoustom '," *Prilozi za književnost, jezik, istoriju i folklor, XI* (Beograd, 1931), 59-82.

————. "Tundalovo vidjenje u Lulićevu zborniku," *Starine, XLI* (Zagreb, 1948) 119-157.

Jagić, Vatroslav. "Glagolitica: Würdigung neuentdeckter Fragmente," *Kaiserliches Akademie der Wissenschaften, Denkschriften der phil.-hist. Cl. XXXVIII. Bd. II. Abhandlung* (Vienna, 1890), 1-62.

————. *Historija književnosti naroda hrvatskoga i srbskoga. I* (Zagreb, 1867) 204p.

————. *Zakon vinodol'skij: podlinnyj tekst s russkim perevodom, kritičeskimi zamečanijami i ob''jasnenijami* (Sankt-Peterburg, 1880).

Jireček, Konstantin. *Geschichte der Serben* (Gotha, 1911-1918), 2 vols.

————. *Die Handelsstrassen und Bergwerke von Serbien und Bosnien während des Mittelalters: Hist.-geog. studien* (Prag, 1879), 92p.

Karadžić, Vuk Stefanović. *Pravitelstvujuščii sovět serbskii za vremena karadjordjijeva ili otimanje ondašnjijeh velikaša oko vlasti* (Vienna, 1860). [Reprinted in *Sabrana dela, XVI,* 2 (Beograd, 1969), 49-186].

————. *Srpske narodne pjesme* (Beograd, 1932), 4 vols.

————. *Srpske narodne pripovijetke: skupio ih i na svijet izdao Vuk Stef. Karadžić* (Vienna, 1853), 263p.

————. "Žitije Ajduk-Veljka Petrovića," in *Sabrana dela* (Beograd, 1969), 70-94.

Kiselkov, V. Sl. *Prezviter* Kozma *i negovata beseda protiv bogomilite* (Karnobat, 1921), 96p.

Kombol, Mihovil. *Povijest hrvatske književnosti do narodnog preporoda* (Zagreb, 1961), 481p.

Kostrenčić, Marko, ed. and transl. "Vinodolski zakon," *Rad Jugoslavenske akademije znanosti i umjetnosti,* 227 (Zagreb, 1923), 110-230.

Kul'bakin, St. M. "Paleografska i jezička ispitivanja o miroslavljevom jevandjelju," *Posebna izdanja LII* (Sremski Karlovci, 1925), 1-120.

Latković, Vido. *Narodna književnost* (Belgrade, 1967), 288p.

Lord, Albert B. "The Effect of the Turkish Conquest on Balkan Epic Tradition," in *Aspects of the Balkans: Continuity and Change.* H. Birnbaum and S. Vryonis, eds. (The Hague/Paris, 1972), 298-318.

————. *The Singer of Tales* (New York, 1968), 304p.

Lucić, Hanibal. *Skladanja izvarsnih pisan razlicih.* [Napisao] Hanibal Lucić. *Ribanje i ribarsko prigovaranje i razlike stvari ine* [napisao] Petar Hektorović. Ed. Marin Franičević. *Pet stoljeća hrvatske književnosti* (Zagreb, 1968), 360p.

Magoun, Frank P. *The Gests of King Alexander of Macedon* (Cambridge, 1929), 261p.

Maretić, Tomo. *Kosovski junaci i dogadjaji u narodnoj epici* (Zagreb, 1889).

————. *Naša narodna epika* (Beograd, 1966), 350p.

Marinković, Radmila. *Srpska alexandrida: istorija osnovnog teksta* (Beograd, 1969), 348p.

Marulić, Marko. *Judita, Suzana, Pjesme.* Ed. Ivan Slamnig. *Pet stoljeća hrvatske književnosti,* 4 (Zagreb, 1970).

Matić, Svetozar. *Naš narodni ep i naš stih: ogledi i studije* (Novi Sad, 1964), 357p.

Mažuranić, Ivan. *Smrt Smail-age Čengića, stihovi, proza.* Ed. Ivo Frangeš. *Pet stoljeća hrvatske književnosti, 32* (Zagreb, 1965).

Miklosich, Franz, ed. *Monumenta serbica spectantia historiam Serbiae, Bosnae, Ragusii* (Vienna, 1858), 580p.

Mirković, Lazar, trans. *Spisi Svetoga Save i Stevana Prvovenčanoga* (Beograd, 1939), 234p.

Mladenović, Aleksandar. *Jezik Petra Hektorovića* (Novi Sad, 1969), 205p.

Mošin, Vladimir, ed., Mencinger S. and Štefanić, V., trans. *Ljetopis popa dukljanina: latinski tekst sa hrvatskim prijevodom i "hrvatska kronika"* (Zagreb, 1950), 105p.

________. "O periodizaciji russko-južnoslavjanskix literaturnyx svjazej x-xv vv.," in *Russkaja literatura xi-xvii vv. sredi slavjanskix literatur: Trudy otdela drevnerusskoj literatury, XIX* (Moskva-Leningrad, 1963), 28-106.

Nahtigal, Rajko. "Rekonstrukcija treh starocerkvenoslovanskih izvirnih pesnitev," *Razprave, I* (Ljubljana, 1943), 43-155.

Njegoš, Petar II Petrović. *Gorski vijenac, Luča mikrokozma.* Eds. Radosav Bošković, Vido Latković. Notes by Vido Latković (Beograd/Cetinje, 1974).

Novaković, Stojan. "Barlaam i Joasaf: prilog k poznavanju uporedne literarne istorije u Srba, Bugara i Rusa," *Glasnik srpskog učenog društva, L* (Beograd, 1881), 1-121.

________. *Primeri književnosti i jezika staroga i srpsko-slovenskoga* (Beograd, 1904), 673p.

________. "Pripovetka o Aleksandru Velikom u staroj srpskoj književnosti," *Glasnik srpskog učenog društva, IX* (Beograd, 1878).

Obolensky, Dimitri. *The Bogomils: A Study in Balkan Neo-Manichaeism* (Oxford, 1948), 317p.

Obradović, Dositej. *Dela.* (Beograd, 1911), 601p.

Pantić, Miroslav, ed. *Pesništvo renesanse i baroka: Dubrovnik, Dalmacija, Boka Kotorska* (Beograd, 1977), 359p.

Pavlović, Dragoljub, ed. *Dubrovačka poezija: zbornik* (Beograd, 1963), 305p.

Pavlović, Dragoljub and Marinković, Radmila. *Iz naše književnosti feudalnog doba* (Sarajevo, 1954), 377p.

________. *Stara srpska književnost.* Introd. by Dragoljub Pavlović (Novi Sad, 1970), 3 vols.

Pavlović, Miodrag. *Istorija srpske književnosti, I* (Beograd, 1968).

Popović, Pavle. *Pregled srpske književnosti* (Beograd, 1927), 255p.

Rački, Franjo. *Bogomili i patareni. Posebna izdanja, LXXXVII* (Beograd, 1931), 337-599.

________. "Dva nova priloga za povijest bosanskih patarena," in *Starine, XIV* (Zagreb, 1882), 1-30.

Radojčić, Nikola, ed. and transl. *Zakonik cara Stefana Dušana 1349 i 1354* (Beograd, 1960), 176p.

Reljković, Matija. *Djela.* Ed. T. Matić. *Stari pisci hrvatski, XXIII* (Zagreb, 1916), 679p.

Rešetar, Milan, ed. *Libro od mnozijeh razloga (1520) Zbornik za istoriju, jezik i književnost srpskog naroda, XV* (Sremski Karlovci, 1926), 221p.

________, ed. *Pjesme Šiška Menčetića i Džore Držića i ostale pjesme ranjinina zbornika. Stari pisci hrvatski, II* (Zagreb, 1937), 567p.

Ringheim, Allan. *Eine altserbische Trojasage* (Prague, 1951), 382p.

Rožin, Nikola Bonifačić, ed. *Narodne drame, poslovice i zagonetke. Pet stoljeća hrvatske književnosti, XXVII* (Zagreb, 1963), 370p.

Šafařik, Pavel, ed. "Žitije Stefana Uroša III sъpisano Grigorijemъ Mnixomъ " *Glasnik društva srbske slovesnosti,* XI (Beograd, 1859), 35-94.

Samardžić, Radovan. *Mehmed Sokolović. Srpska književna zadruga, LXIV, knj. 428* (Beograd, 1971), 572p.

Šišić, Ferdo, ed. *Ljetopis popa dukljanina, Posebna izdanja, LXVII* (Beograd, 1928), 480p.

________. *Pregled povijesti hrvatskoga naroda od najstarijih dana do godine 1873* (Zagreb, 1916), 361p.

Štefanić, V., Grabar, B., Nazor, A., Pantelić, M., eds. *Hrvatska književnost srednjeg vijeka. Pet stoljeća hrvatske književnosti, I* (Zagreb, 1969), 1-547.

Stojanović, Ljubomir, ed. *Evandjelie velikoslavnoga kneza Miroslava syna Zavidin* (Vienna, 1897).

Strohal, Rudolf. "Folkloristički prilozi iz starije hrvatske knjige," *Zbornik za narodn život i običaje južnih slavena,*XV (Zagreb, 1910).

Torbarina, Josip. *Italian Influence on the Poets of the Ragusan Republic* (London 1931), 236p.

Trifunović, Djordje, ed. *Stara srpska književnost* (Beograd, 1967).

________, with Bogdanović, Dimitrije (transl.). *Srbljak: službe, kanoni, akatis* (Beograd, 1970), 3 vols.

Van den Berk, C. A. *Der "Serbische" Alexanderroman* (Munich, 1970), 573p.

Vrana, Josip. *L'Évangeliaire de Miroslav* (The Hague, 1961), 206p.

Ware, R. Dean. "Medieval Chronology: Theory and Practice," *Medieval Studie* (Syracuse, 1976), 213-237.

Woodward, G. R. and Mattingly, H., eds. *St. John Damascene: Barlaam and Iosaph* (Cambridge, Mass., 1953).

Dalmatia

Antun Barac

A HISTORY OF YUGOSLAV LITERATURE

Reprinted from original English language edition, Belgrad 1955.

"Barac's *History of Yugoslav Literature* . . . has served very well more than a generation of students in this country and remains the best short history of the Yugoslav literatures available in English."

Albert B. Lord, Harvard University

"Wo need books of this quality for all the East European countries. Barac was a distinguished scholar, he clearly enunciated the basic issues and themes in South Slavic literature. . . ."

Charles Jelavich, Indiana University

"The main purpose of this book is to be an informative handbook, and it serves its purpose well. It is objective and convenient."

Thomas Eekman, U.C.L.A.

"The availability of this outstanding survey in English, at such a modest price, is a boon to students who wish to appreciate the growth and development of Yugoslav literature but who are unable to do so in the original language.

Eugene Hammel, University of California